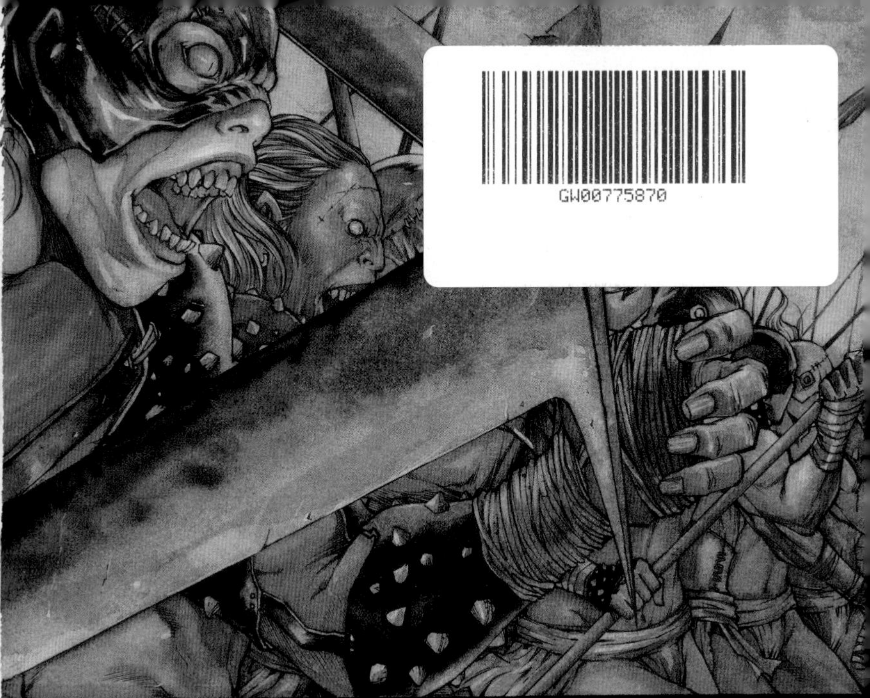

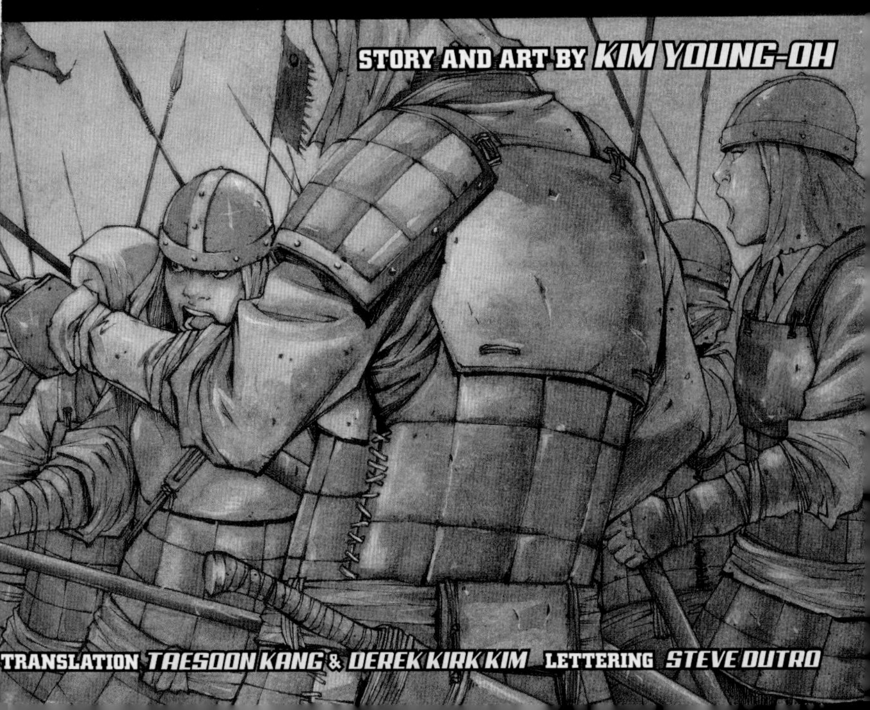

STORY AND ART BY KIM YOUNG-OH

TRANSLATION TAESOON KANG & DEREK KIRK KIM LETTERING STEVE DUTRO

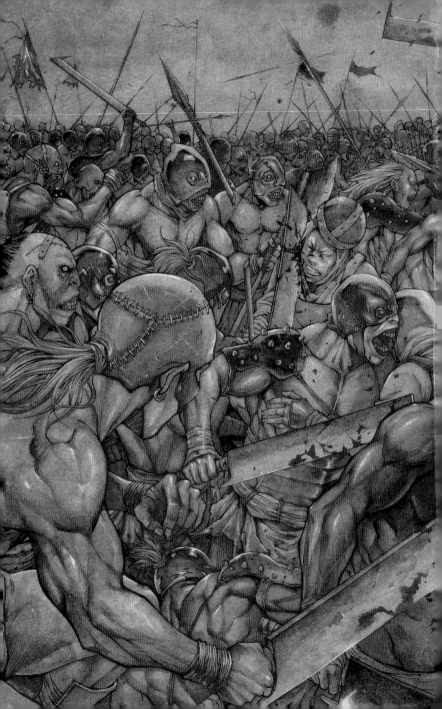

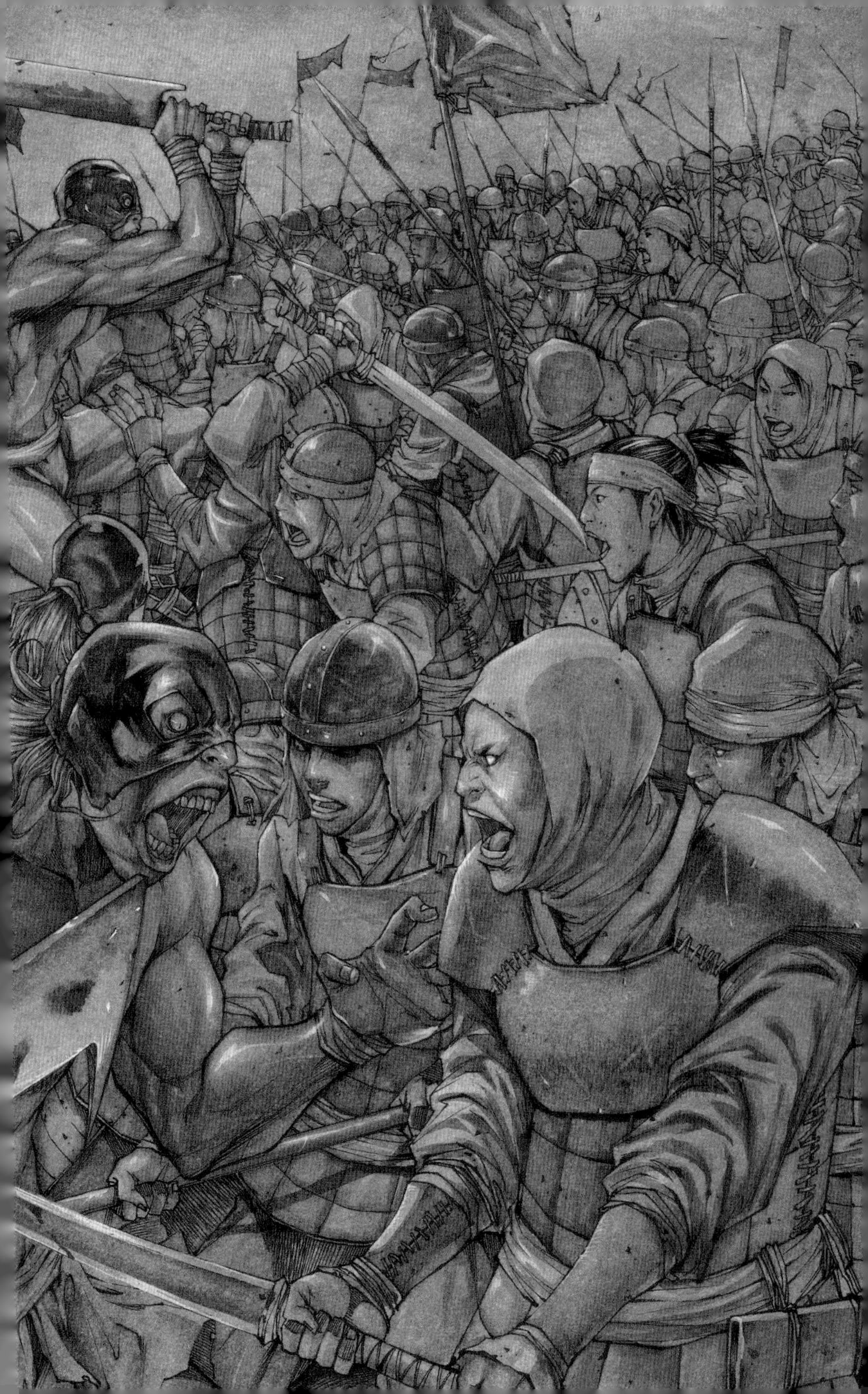

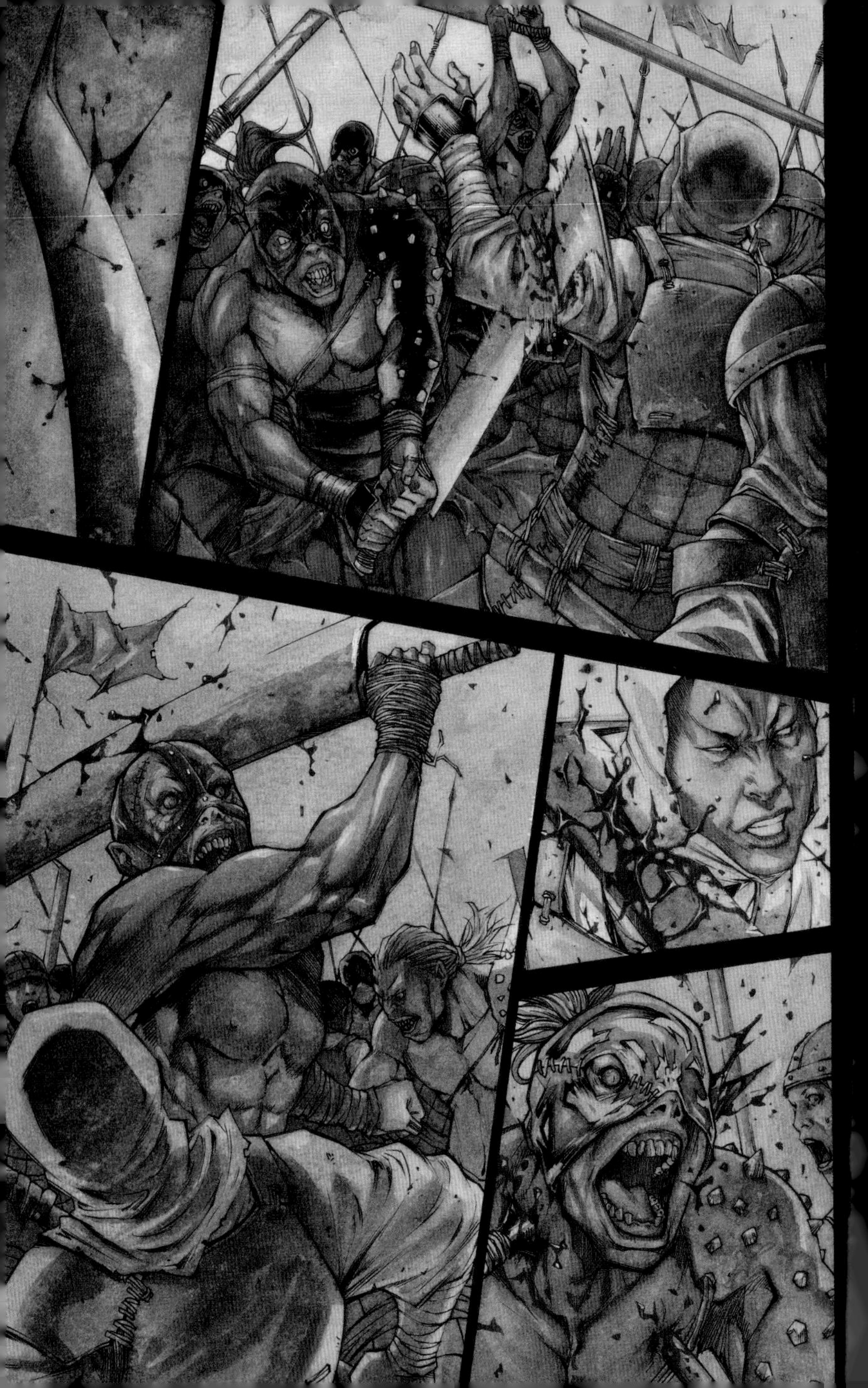

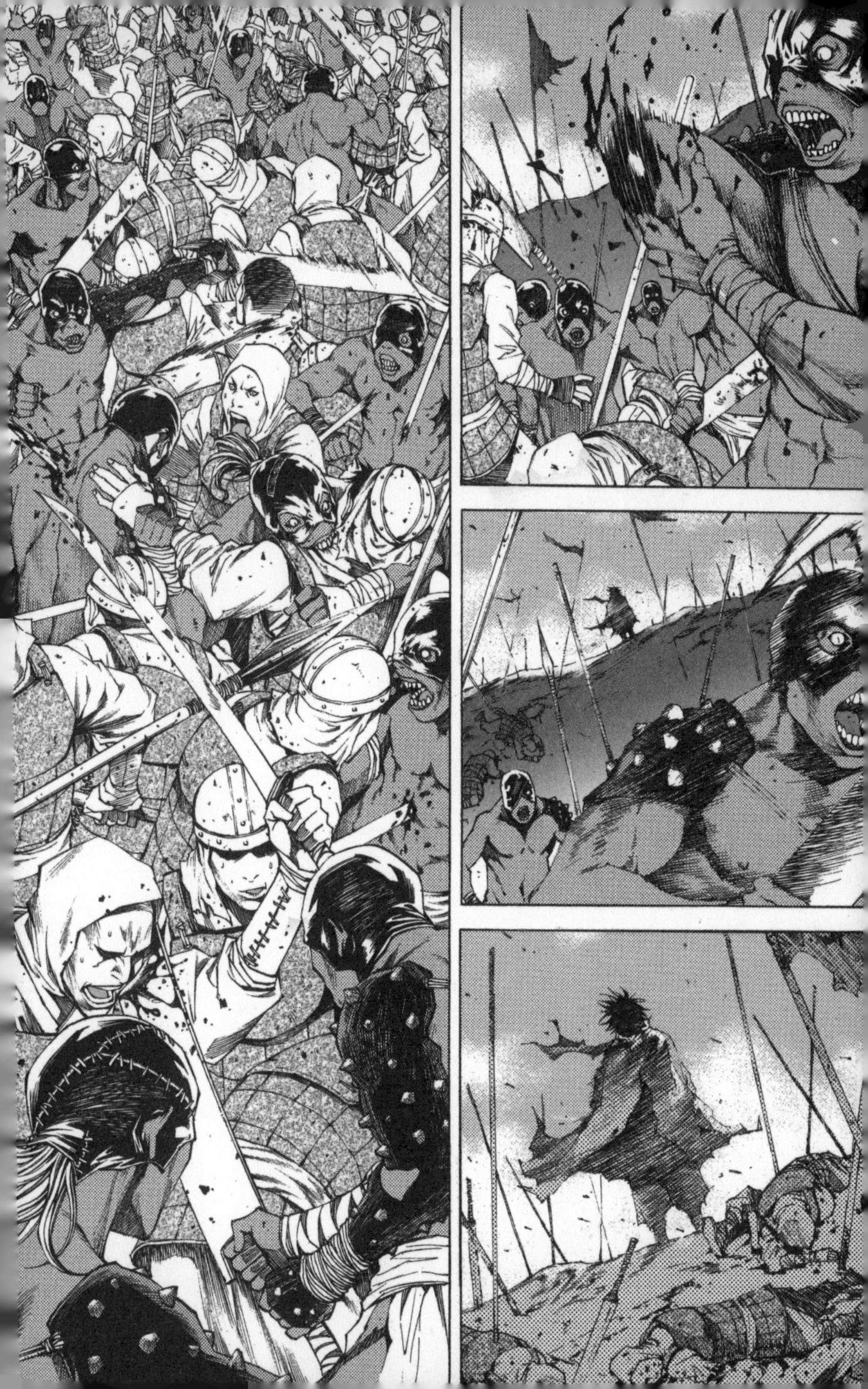

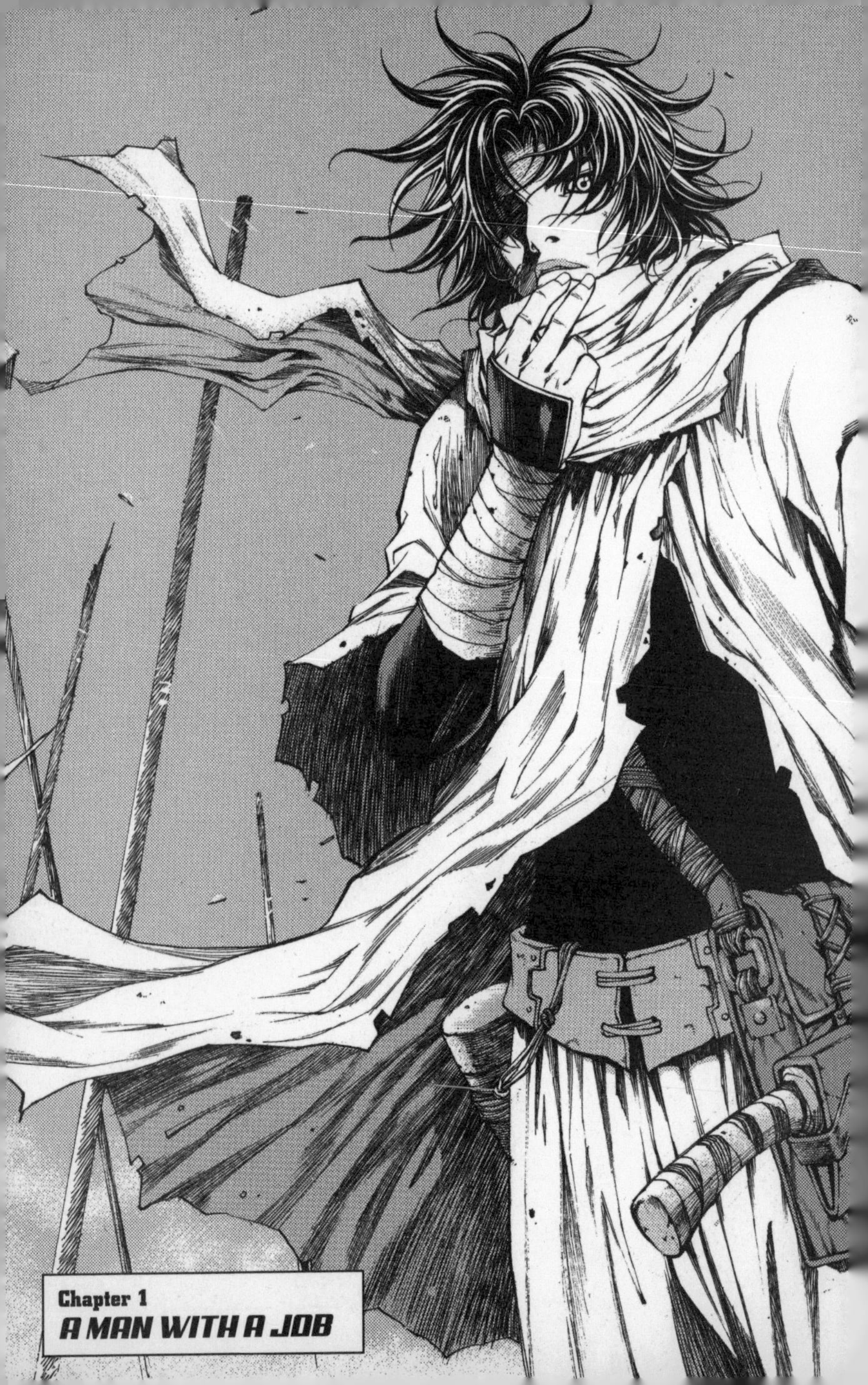
Chapter 1
A MAN WITH A JOB

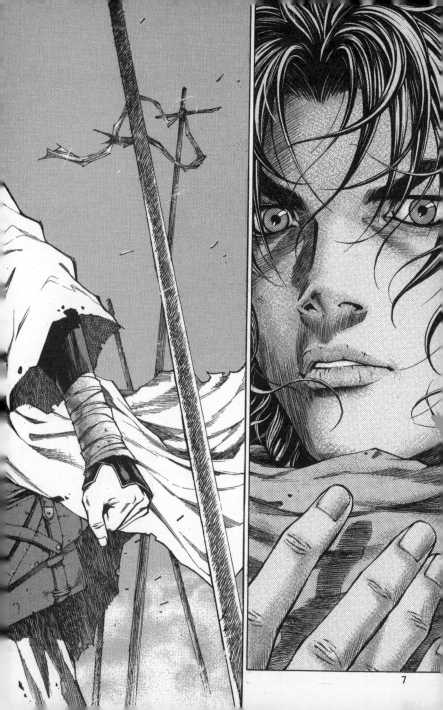

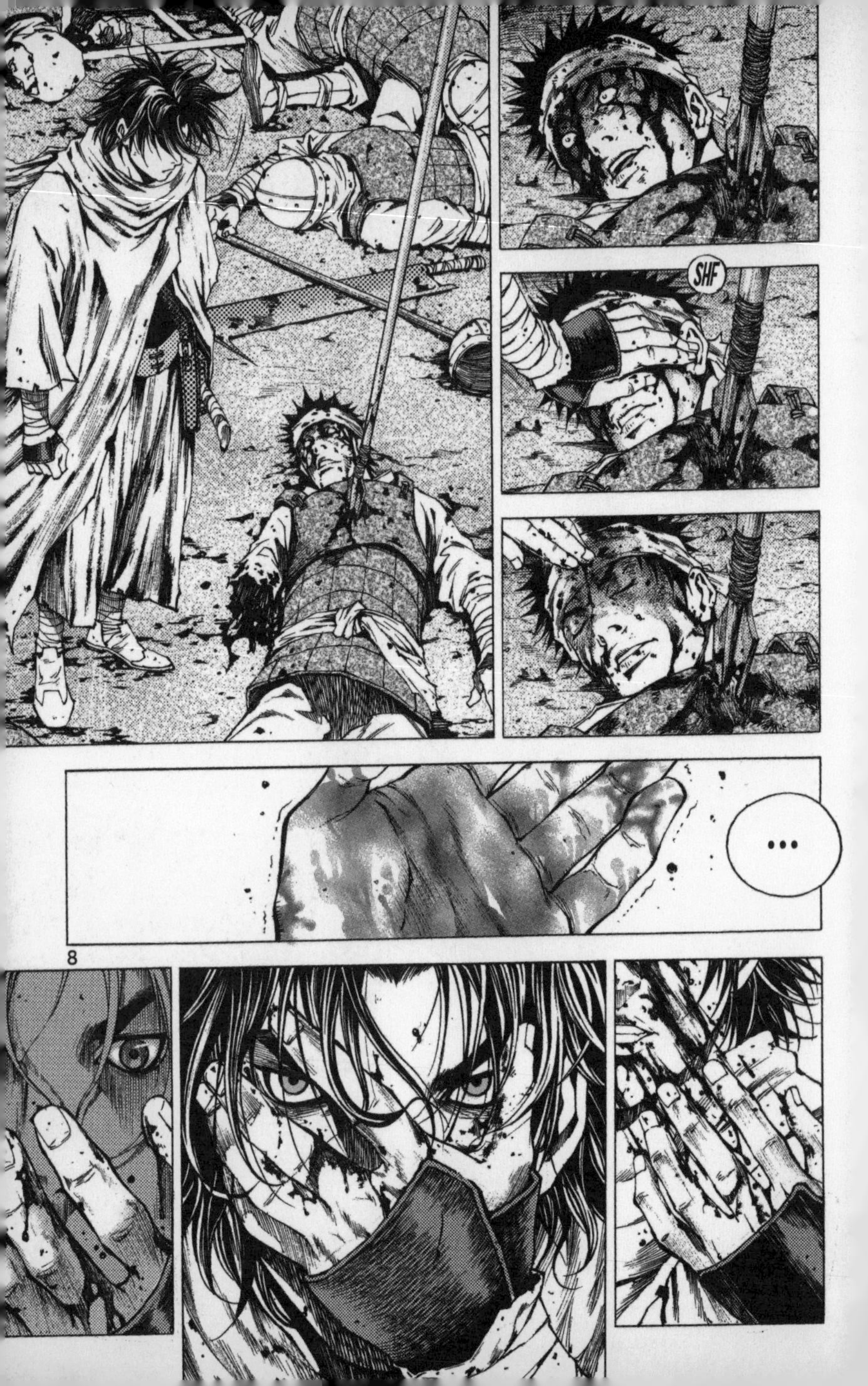
SHF
...

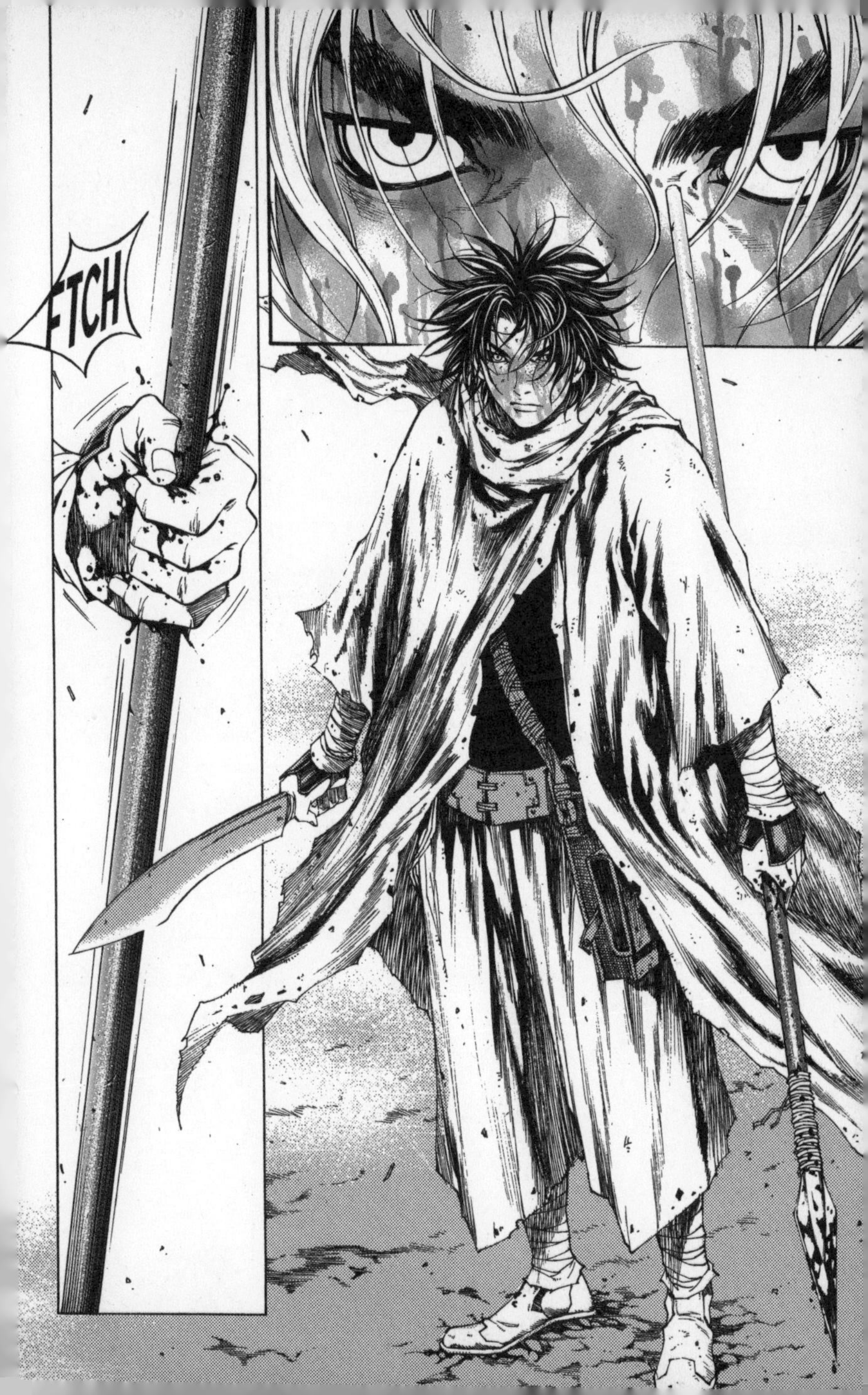
FTCH

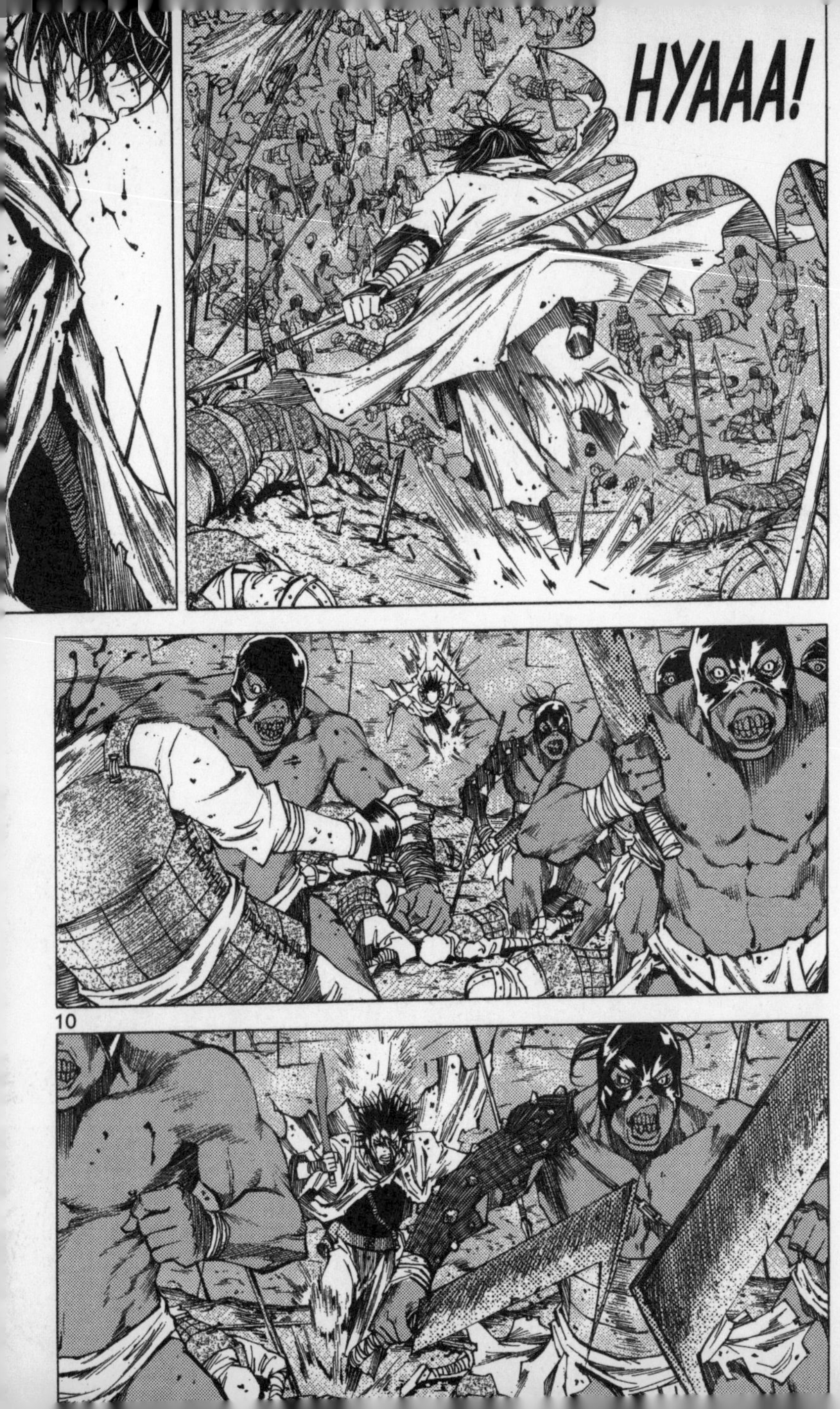
HYAAA!

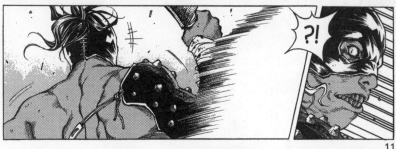

?!

?

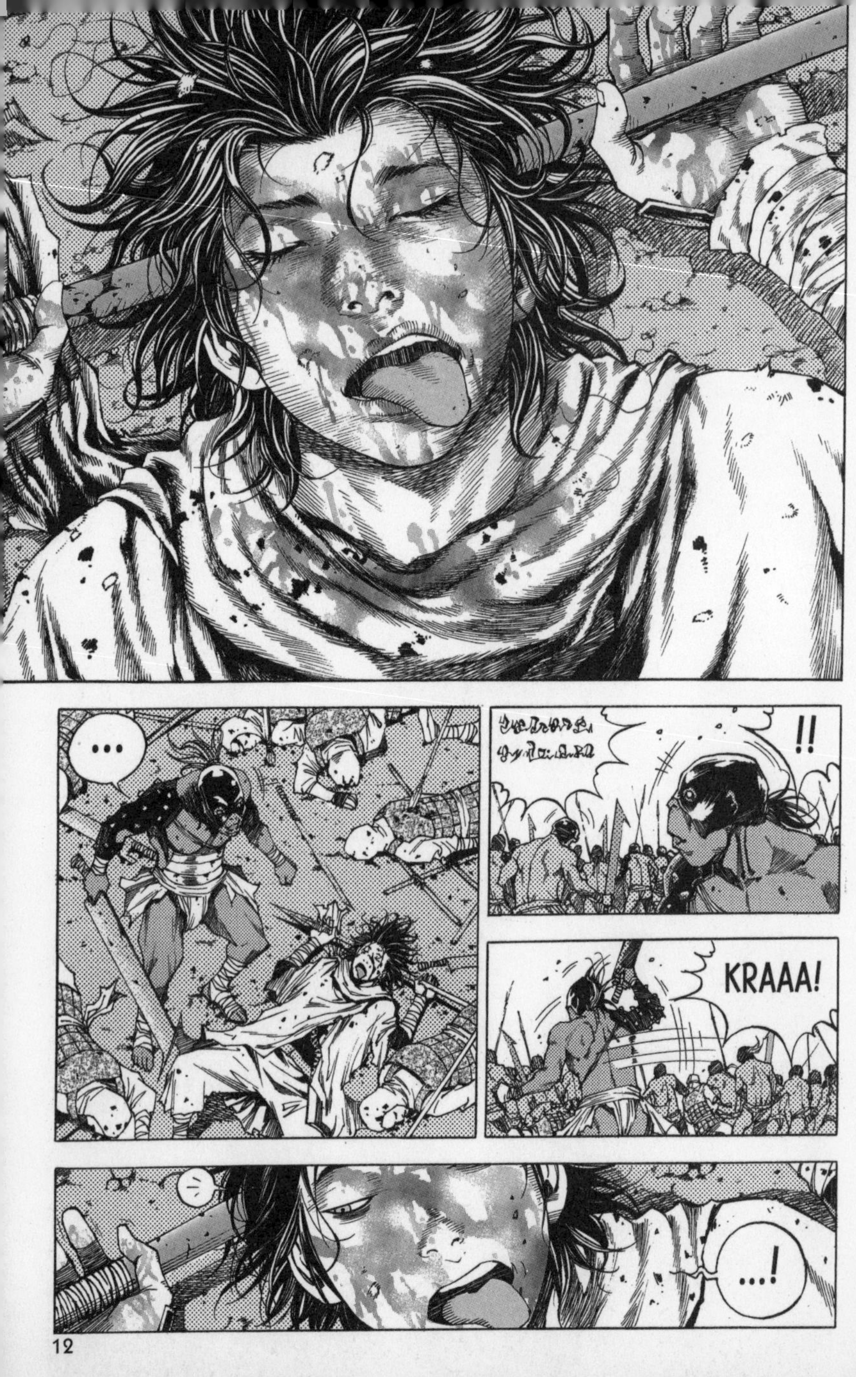
...
!!
KRAAA!
...!

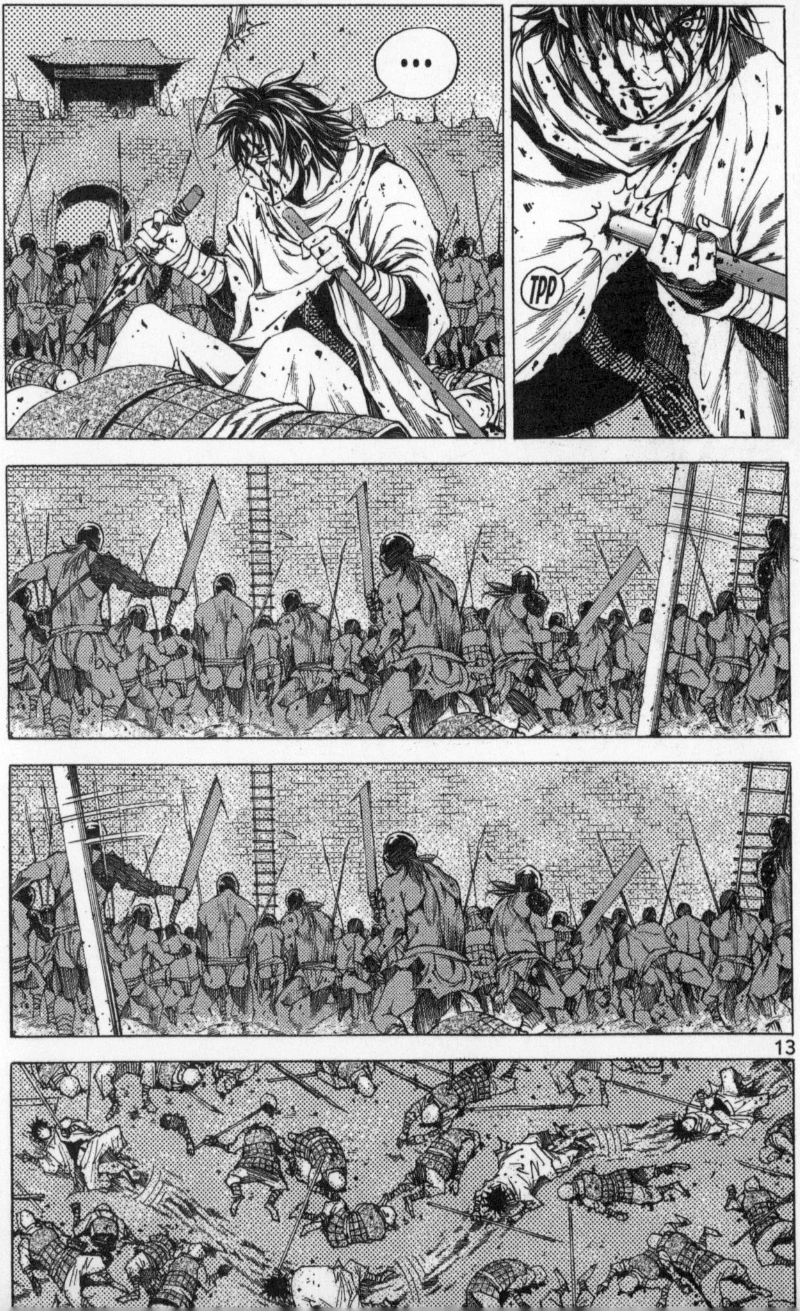
...
TPP

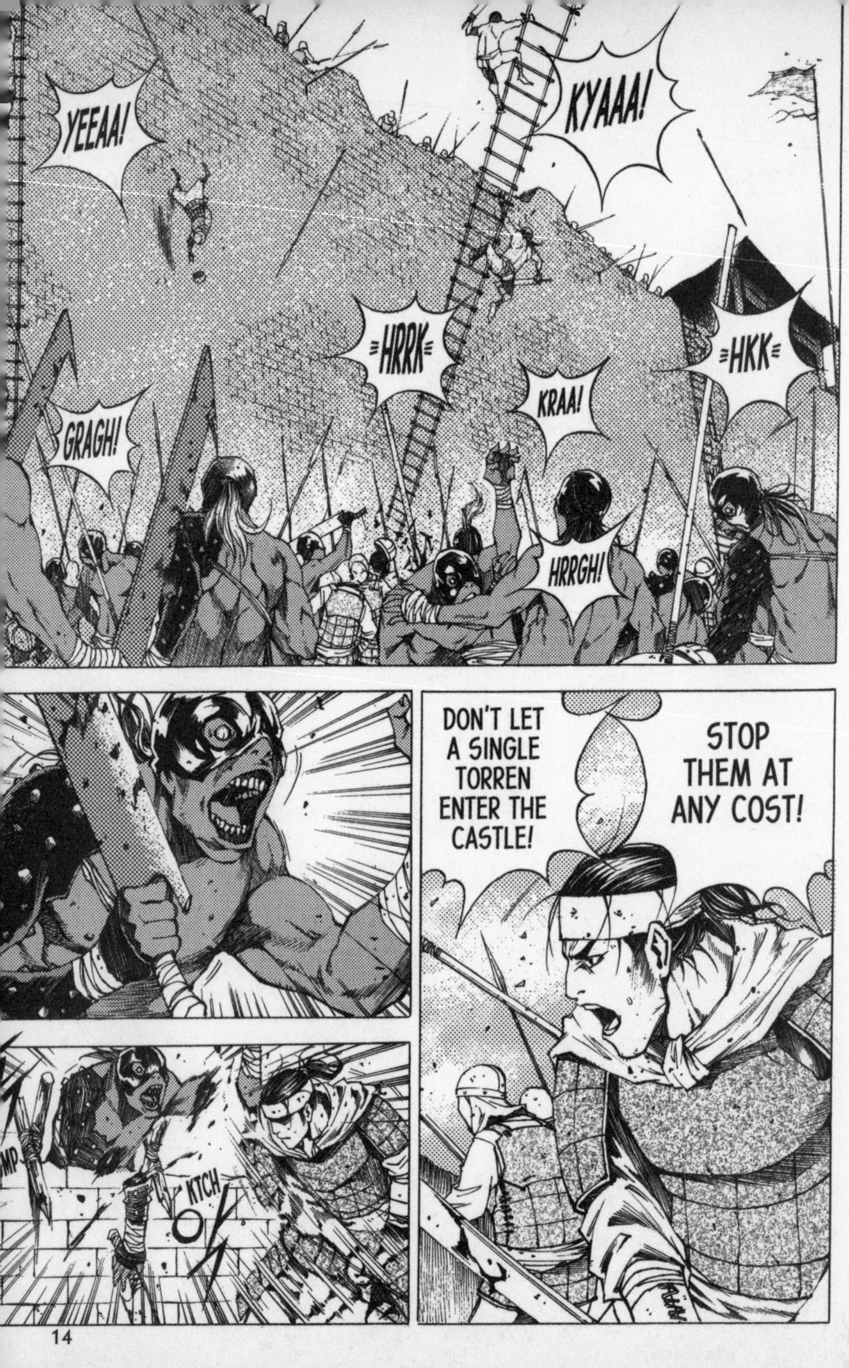
YEEAA!
KYAAA!
GRAGH!
HRRK
KRAA!
HKK
HRRGH!
MP
KTCH
DON'T LET A SINGLE TORREN ENTER THE CASTLE!
STOP THEM AT ANY COST!

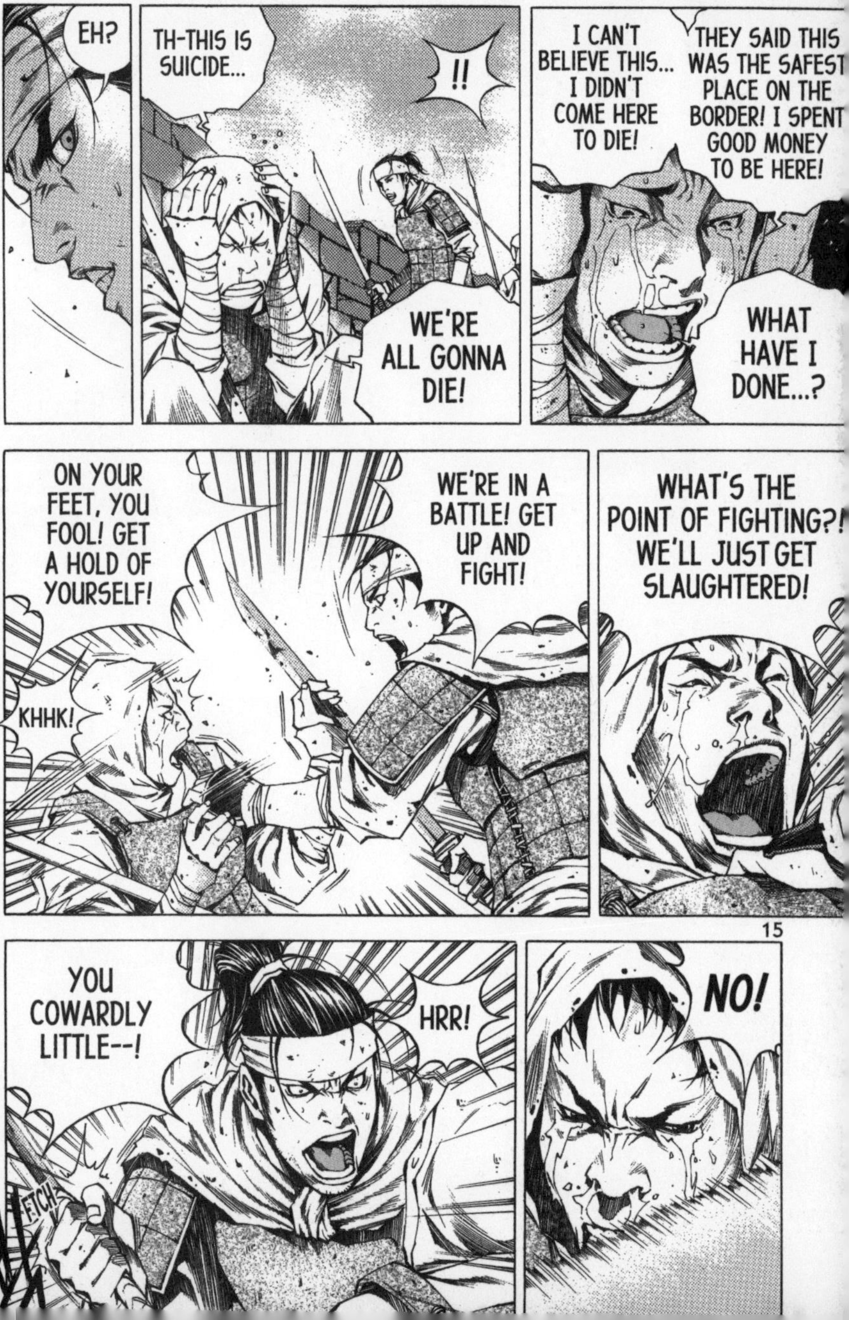
EH?
TH-THIS IS SUICIDE...
!!
WE'RE ALL GONNA DIE!
I CAN'T BELIEVE THIS... I DIDN'T COME HERE TO DIE!
THEY SAID THIS WAS THE SAFEST PLACE ON THE BORDER! I SPENT GOOD MONEY TO BE HERE!
WHAT HAVE I DONE...?
ON YOUR FEET, YOU FOOL! GET A HOLD OF YOURSELF!
WE'RE IN A BATTLE! GET UP AND FIGHT!
KHHK!
WHAT'S THE POINT OF FIGHTING?! WE'LL JUST GET SLAUGHTERED!
YOU COWARDLY LITTLE--!
HRR!
FTCH
NO!

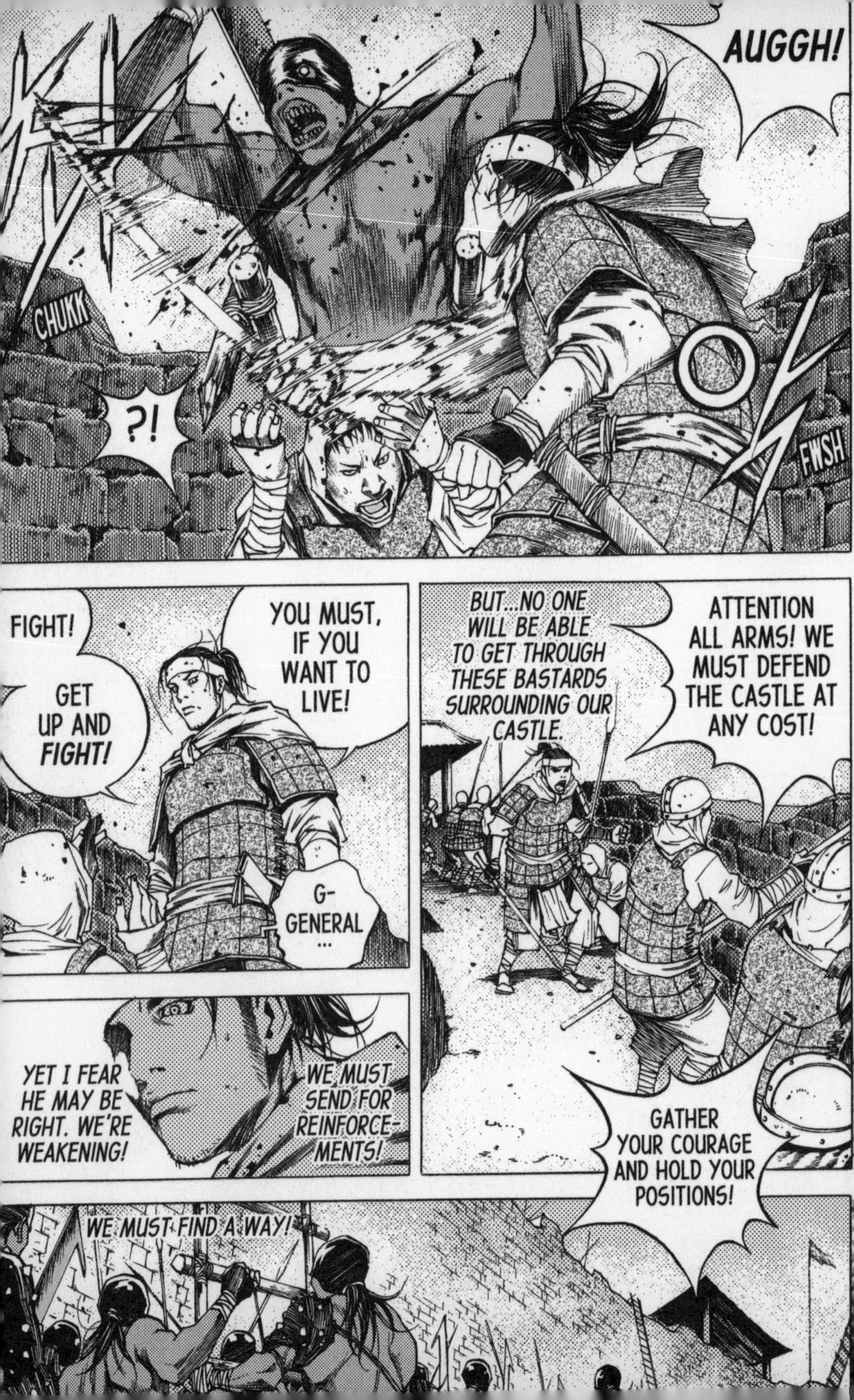
AUGGH!
CHUKK
?!
FWSH
FIGHT!
GET UP AND FIGHT!
YOU MUST, IF YOU WANT TO LIVE!
G-GENERAL...
YET I FEAR HE MAY BE RIGHT. WE'RE WEAKENING!
WE MUST SEND FOR REINFORCE-MENTS!
BUT...NO ONE WILL BE ABLE TO GET THROUGH THESE BASTARDS SURROUNDING OUR CASTLE.
ATTENTION ALL ARMS! WE MUST DEFEND THE CASTLE AT ANY COST!
GATHER YOUR COURAGE AND HOLD YOUR POSITIONS!
WE MUST FIND A WAY!

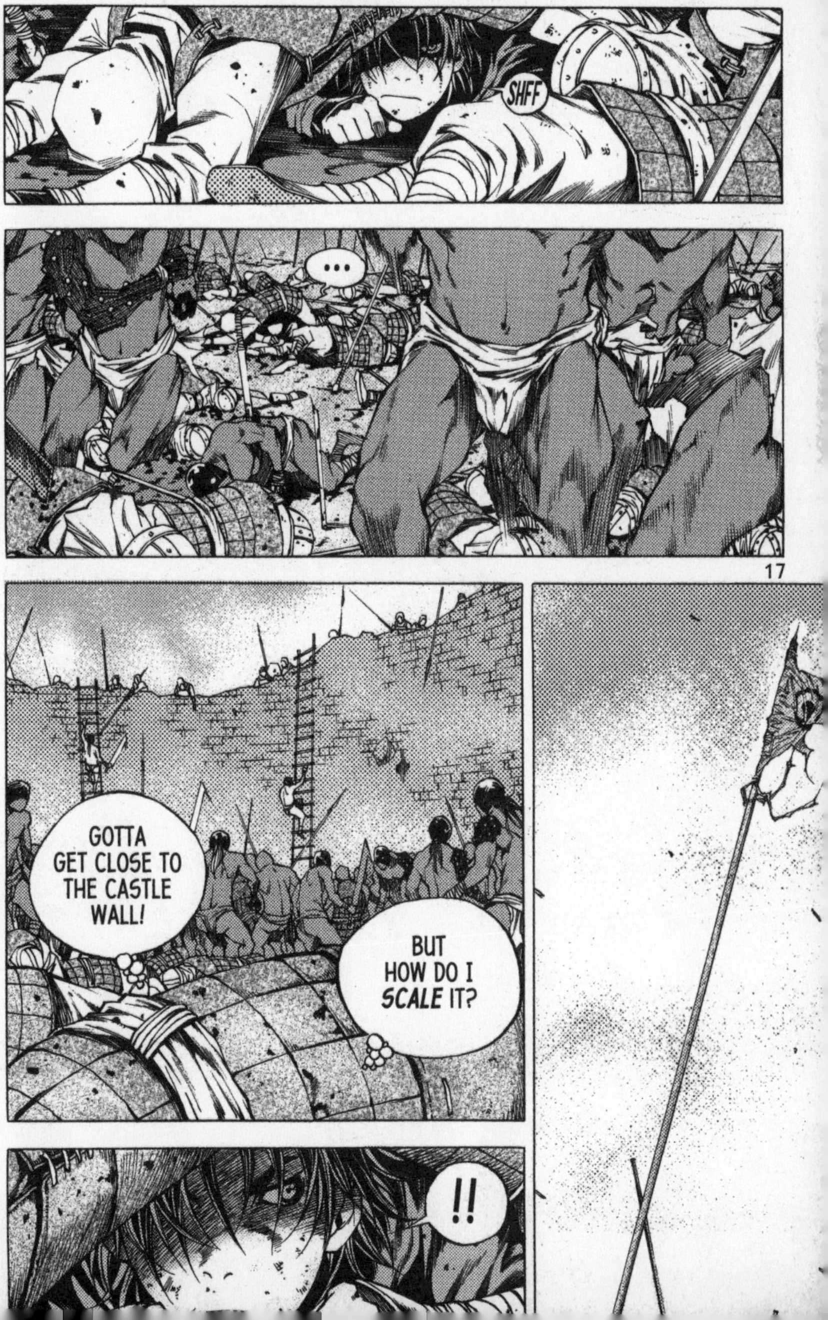
SHFF
...
GOTTA GET CLOSE TO THE CASTLE WALL!
BUT HOW DO I *SCALE* IT?
!!

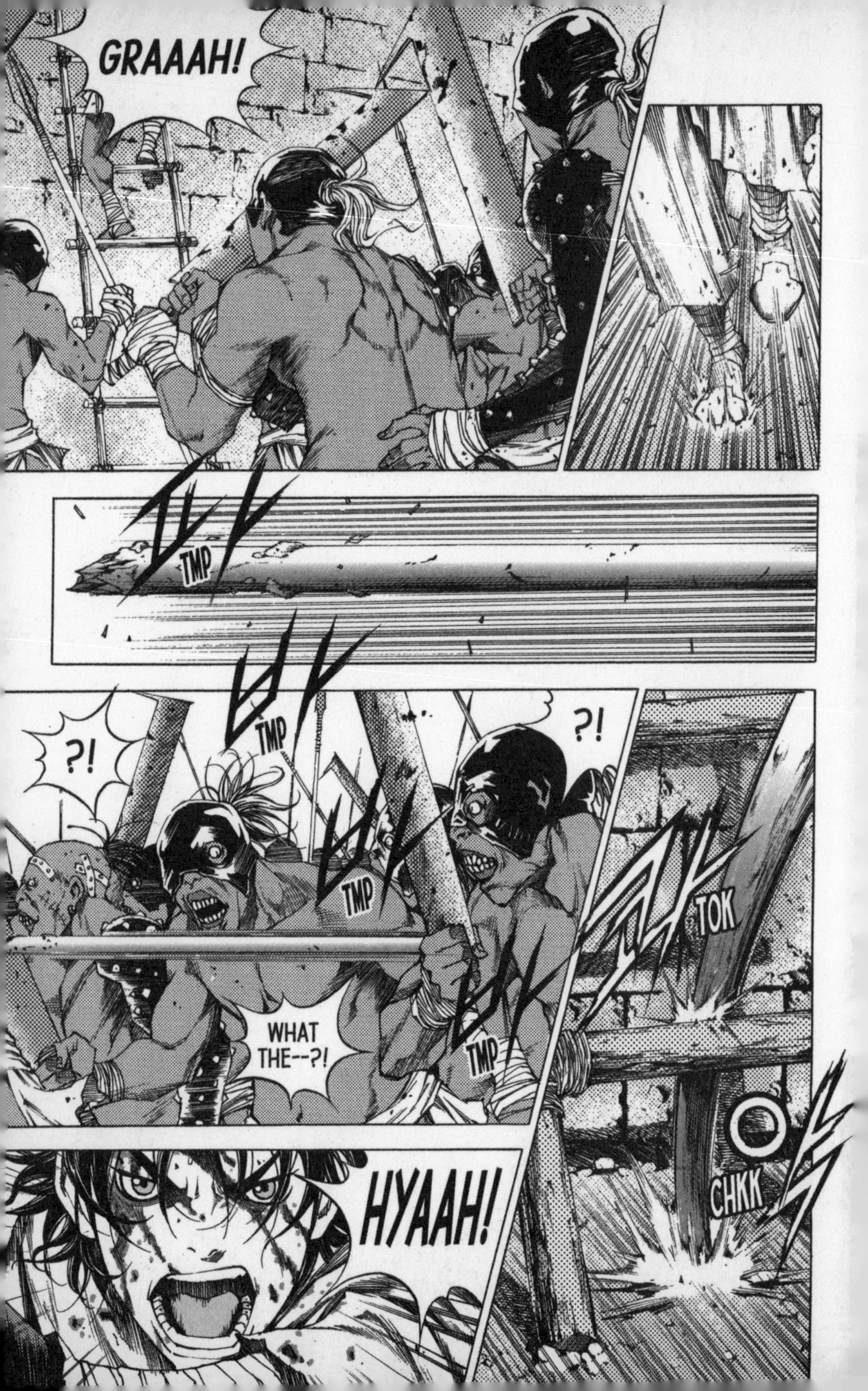
GRAAAH!
TMP
TMP
?!
?!
TMP
WHAT THE--?!
TMP
TOK
HYAAH!
CHKK

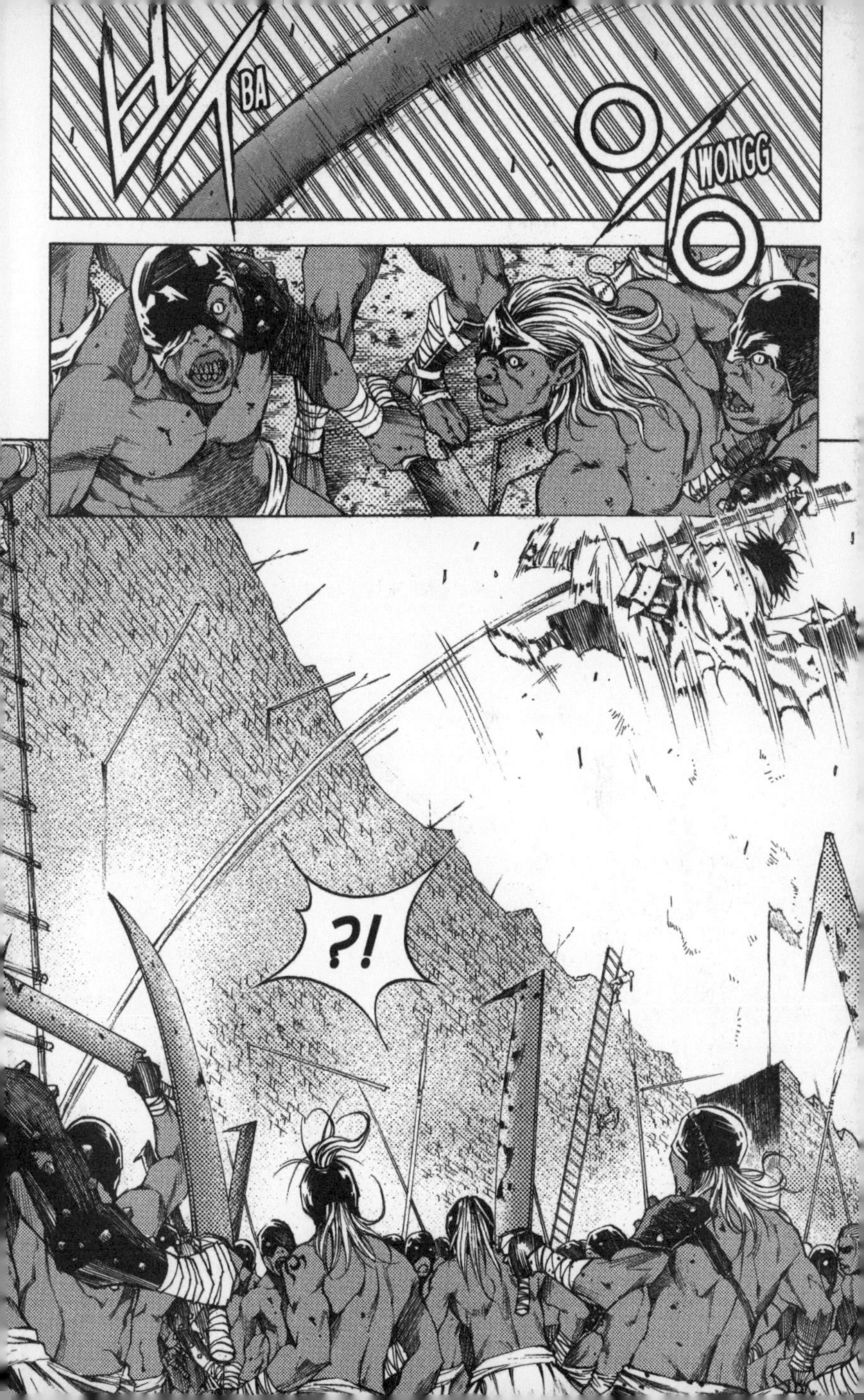
BA
WONGG
?!

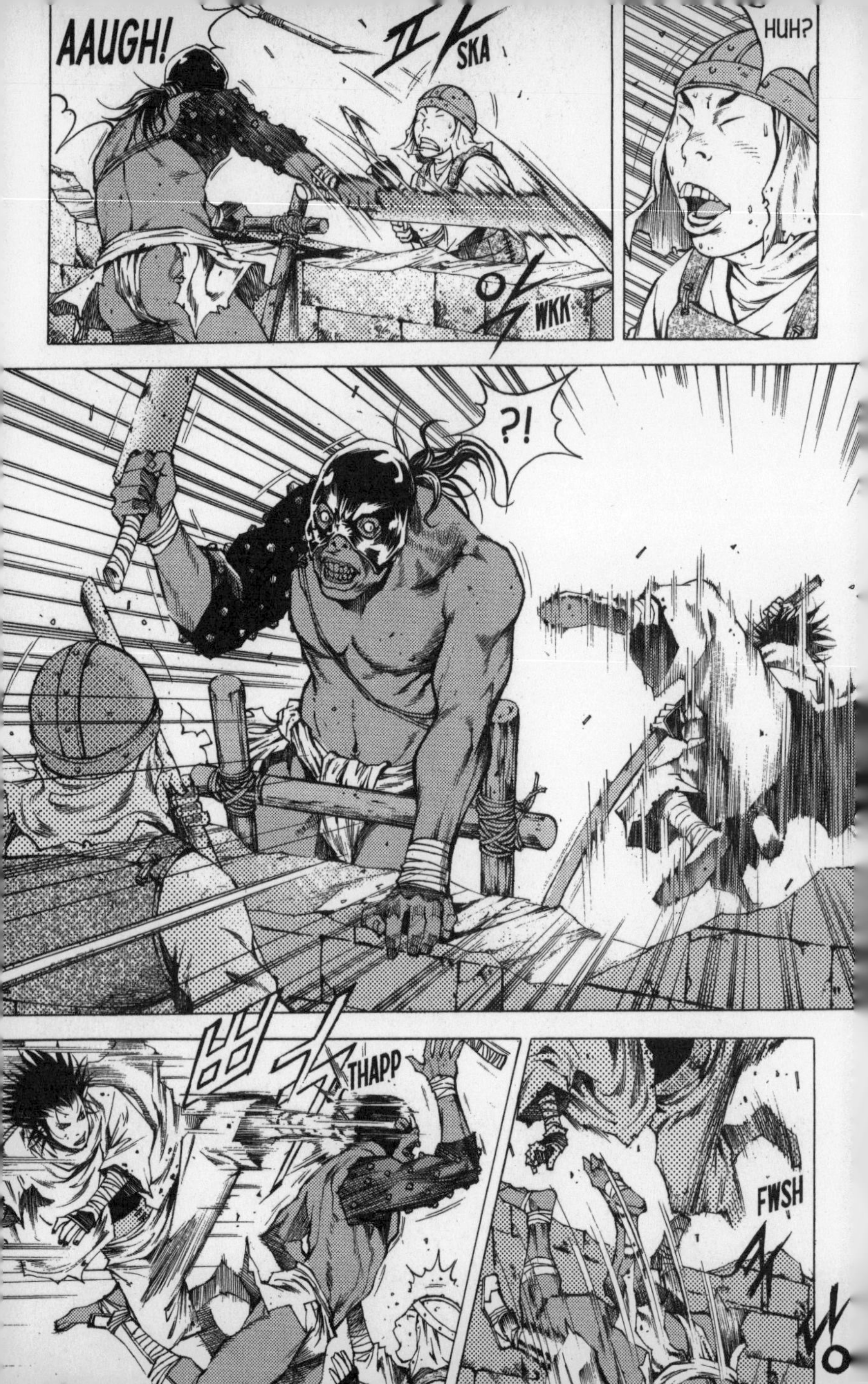
AAUGH!
SKA
WKK
HUH?
?!
THAPP
FWSH

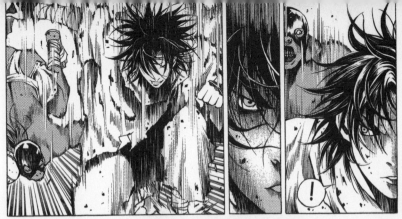

HRRK!

SLITCH

WH-WHO ARE YOU?!

HOW THE HELL'D YOU GET IN HERE?!

FWSH

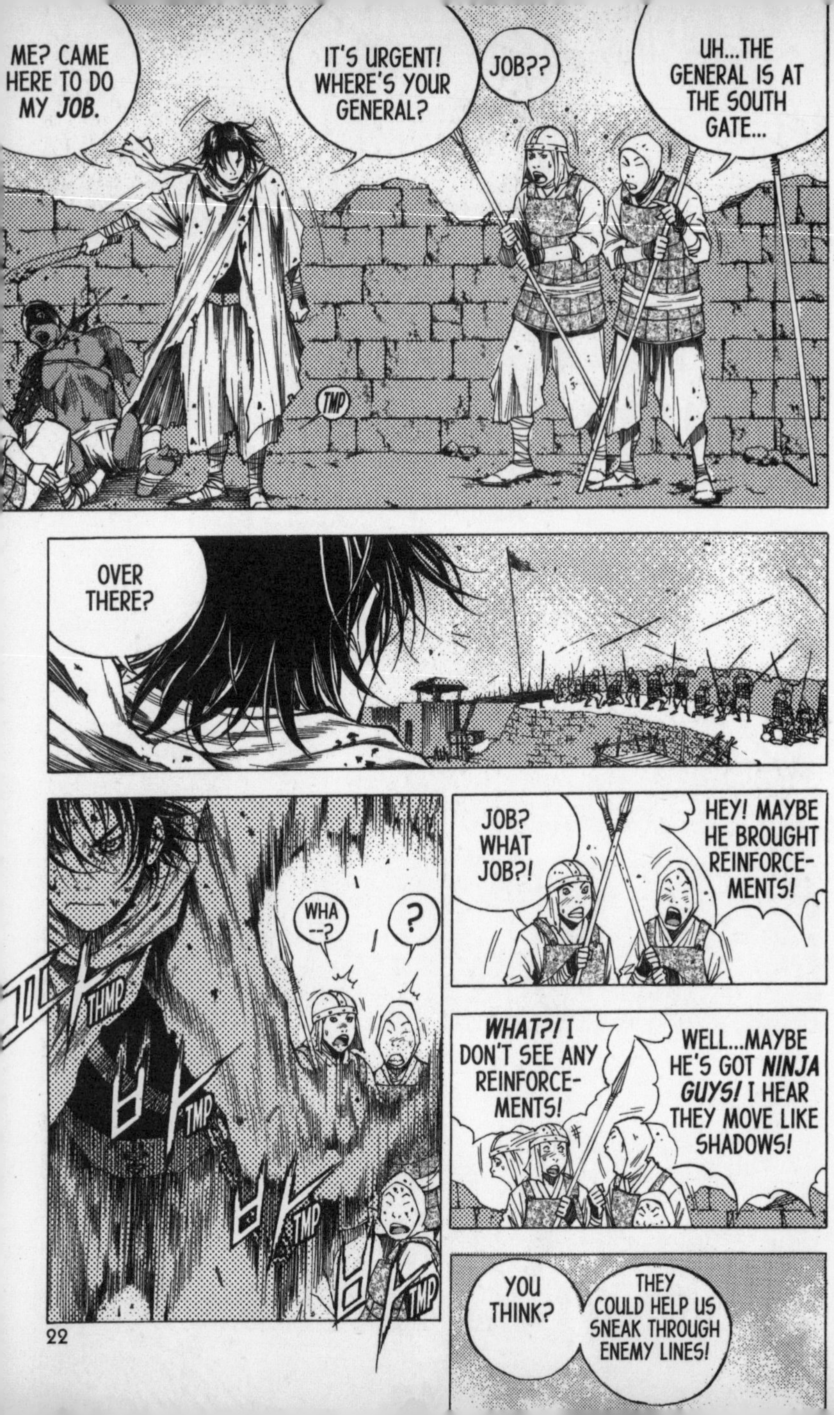
ME? CAME HERE TO DO MY *JOB.*
IT'S URGENT! WHERE'S YOUR GENERAL?
JOB??
UH...THE GENERAL IS AT THE SOUTH GATE...
TMP
OVER THERE?
THMP
WHA --?
?
TMP
TMP
TMP
JOB? WHAT JOB?!
HEY! MAYBE HE BROUGHT REINFORCE-MENTS!
WHAT?! I DON'T SEE ANY REINFORCE-MENTS!
WELL...MAYBE HE'S GOT *NINJA GUYS!* I HEAR THEY MOVE LIKE SHADOWS!
YOU THINK?
THEY COULD HELP US SNEAK THROUGH ENEMY LINES!

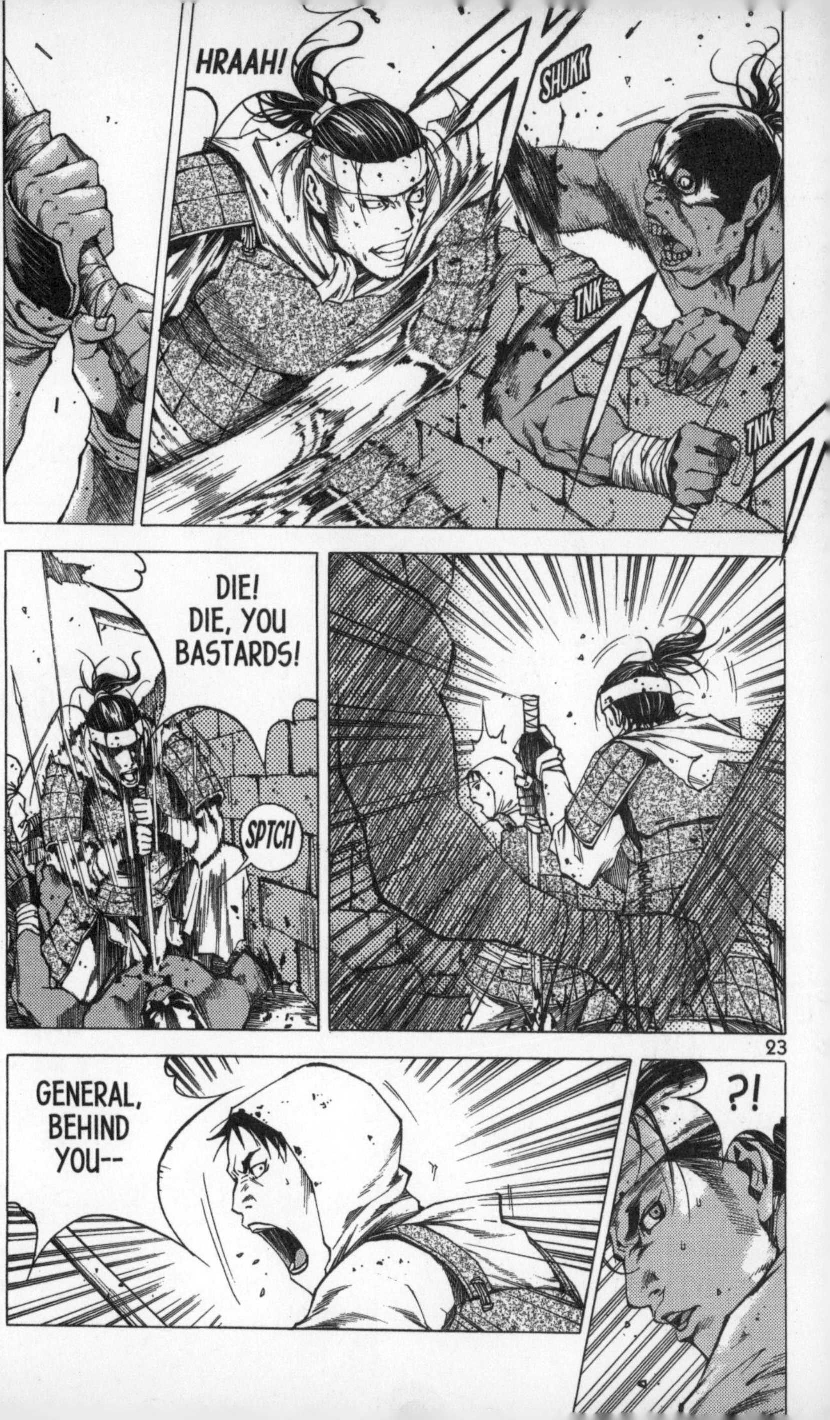
HRAAH!
SHUKK
TNK
TNK
DIE! DIE, YOU BASTARDS!
SPTCH
GENERAL, BEHIND YOU--
?!

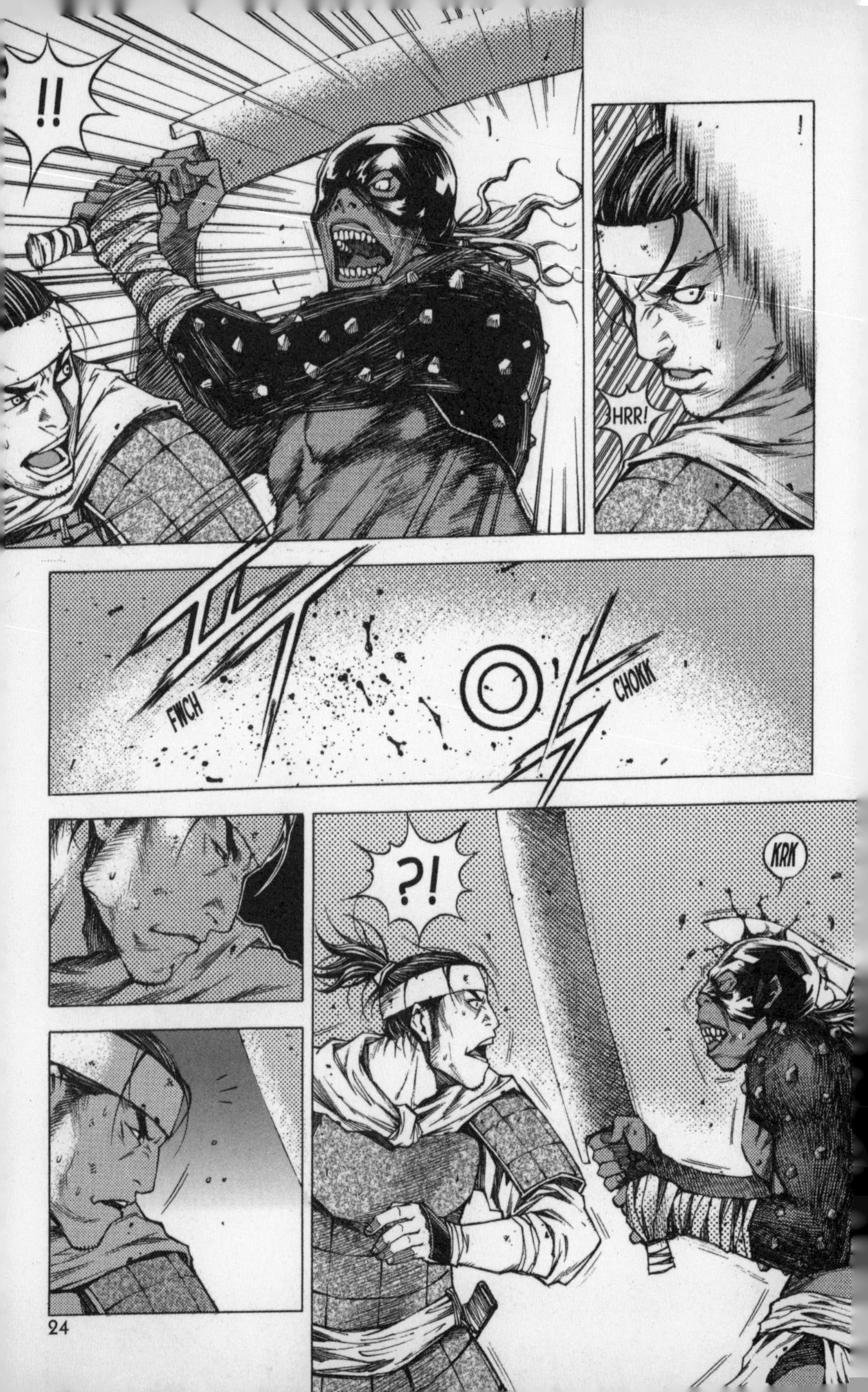
!!
HRR!
FWCH
CHOKK
?!
KRK

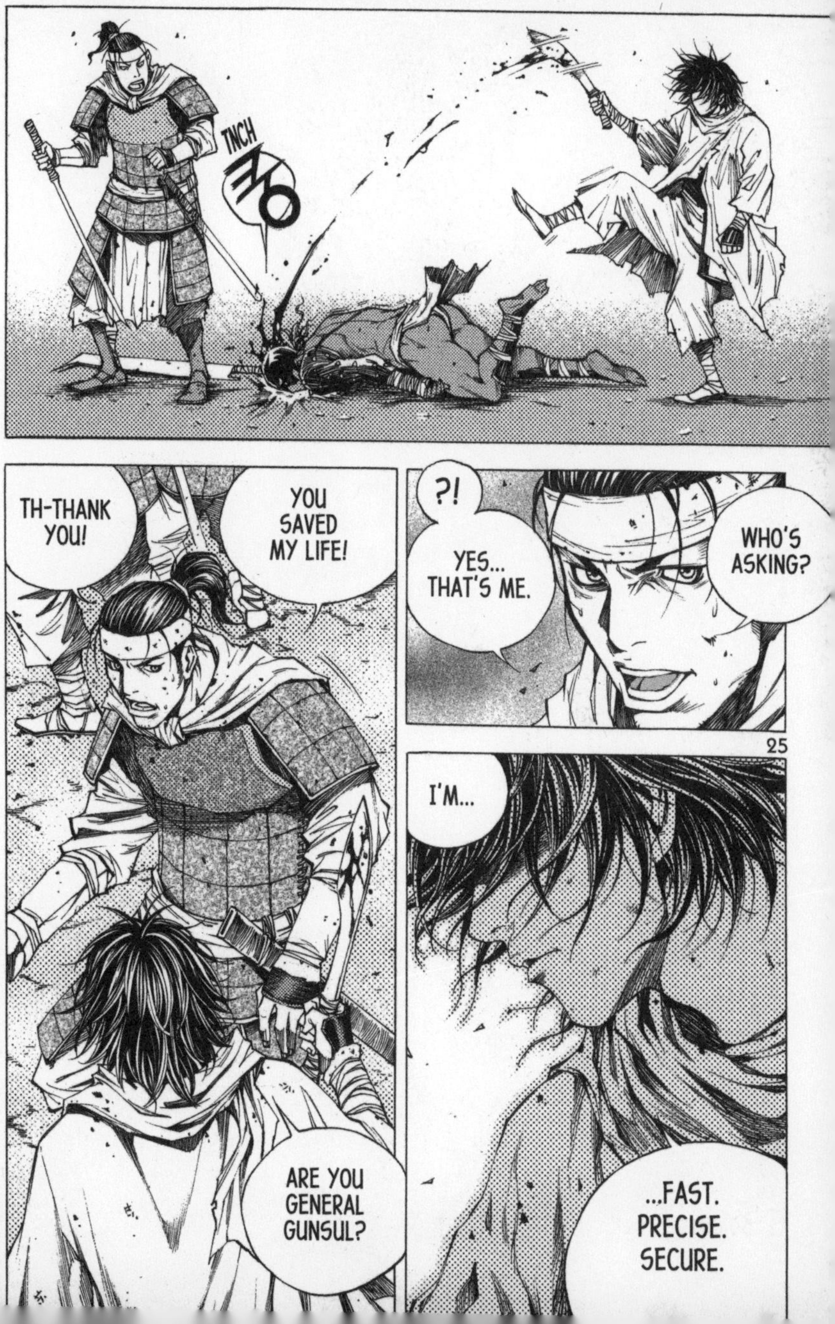
TNCH
TH-THANK YOU!
YOU SAVED MY LIFE!
ARE YOU GENERAL GUNSUL?
?!
YES... THAT'S ME.
WHO'S ASKING?
I'M...
...FAST. PRECISE. SECURE.

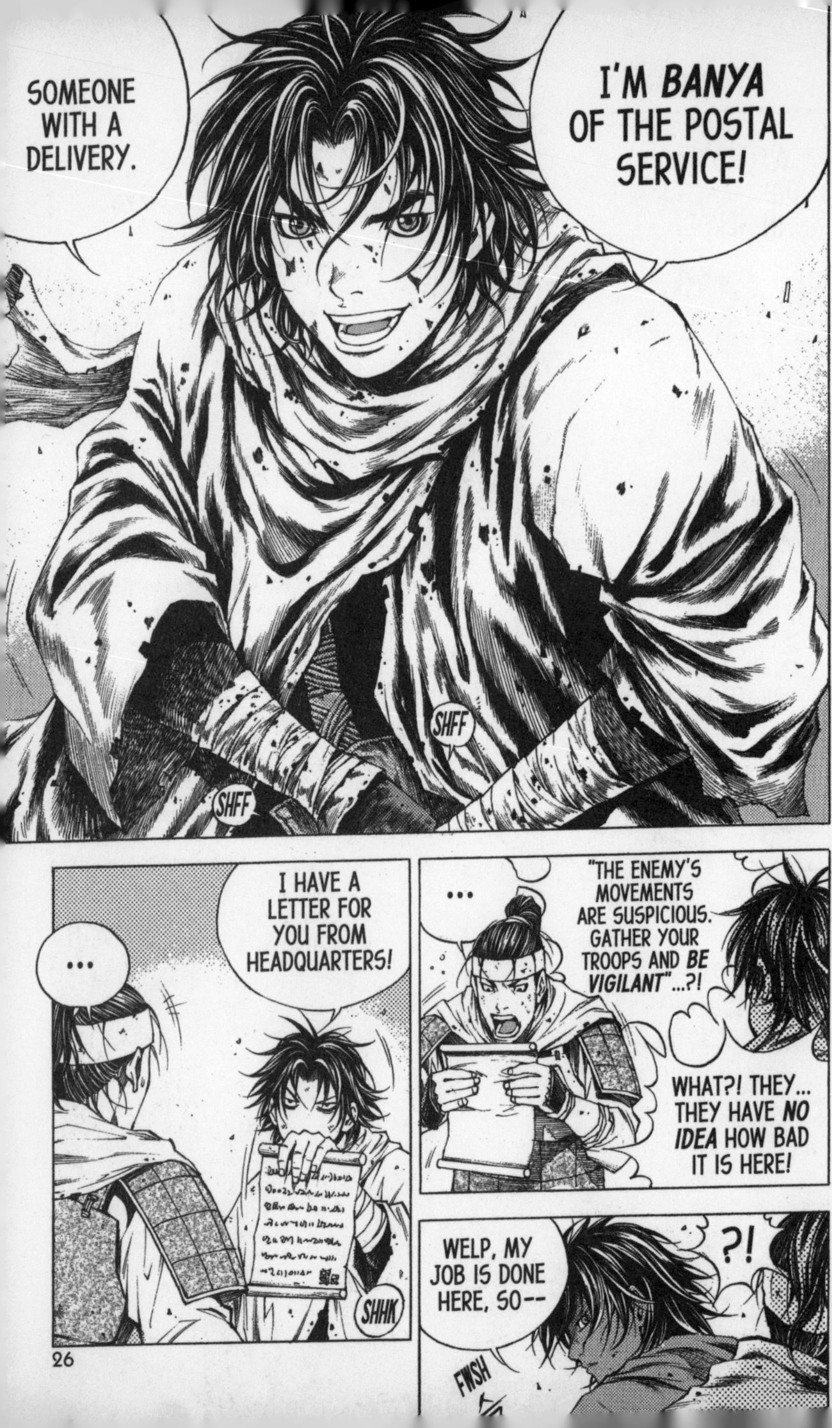
SOMEONE WITH A DELIVERY.
I'M BANYA OF THE POSTAL SERVICE!
SHFF
SHFF
I HAVE A LETTER FOR YOU FROM HEADQUARTERS!
...
SHHK
...
"THE ENEMY'S MOVEMENTS ARE SUSPICIOUS. GATHER YOUR TROOPS AND BE VIGILANT"...?!
WHAT?! THEY... THEY HAVE NO IDEA HOW BAD IT IS HERE!
WELP, MY JOB IS DONE HERE, SO--
?!
FWSH

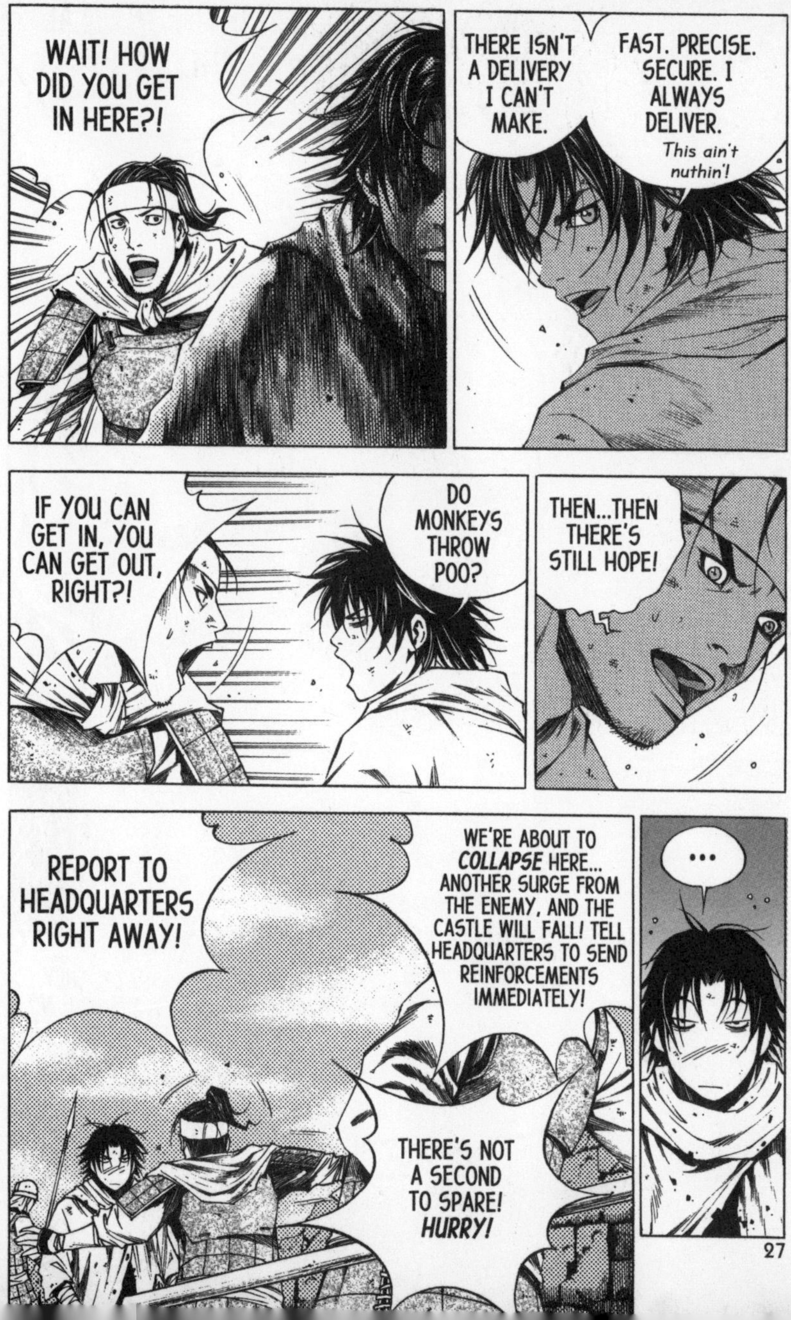
WAIT! HOW DID YOU GET IN HERE?!
THERE ISN'T A DELIVERY I CAN'T MAKE.
FAST. PRECISE. SECURE. I ALWAYS DELIVER.
This ain't nuthin'!
IF YOU CAN GET IN, YOU CAN GET OUT, RIGHT?!
DO MONKEYS THROW POO?
THEN...THEN THERE'S STILL HOPE!
REPORT TO HEADQUARTERS RIGHT AWAY!
WE'RE ABOUT TO *COLLAPSE* HERE... ANOTHER SURGE FROM THE ENEMY, AND THE CASTLE WILL FALL! TELL HEADQUARTERS TO SEND REINFORCEMENTS IMMEDIATELY!
THERE'S NOT A SECOND TO SPARE! *HURRY!*
...

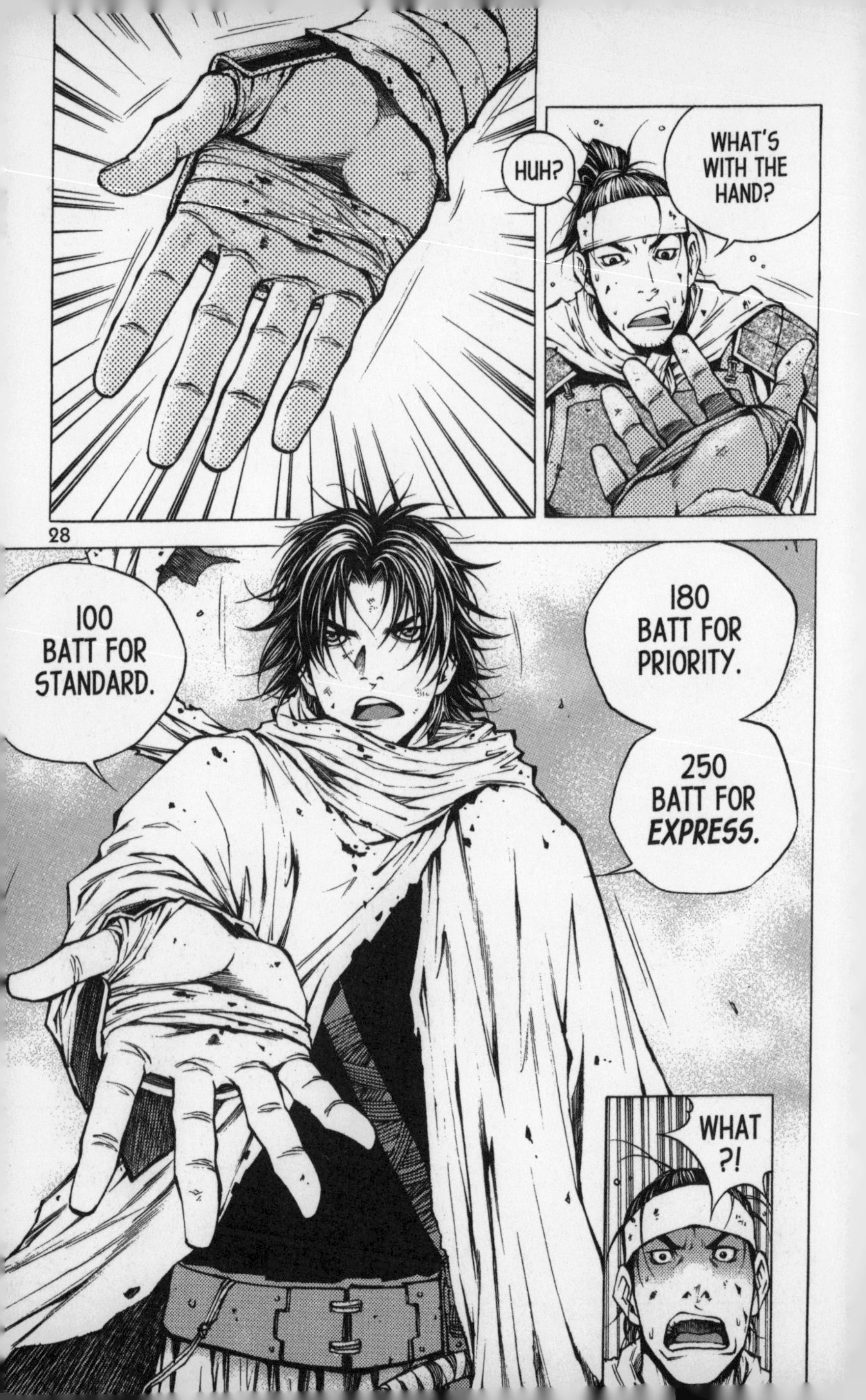
HUH?
WHAT'S WITH THE HAND?
100 BATT FOR STANDARD.
180 BATT FOR PRIORITY.
250 BATT FOR *EXPRESS.*
WHAT ?!

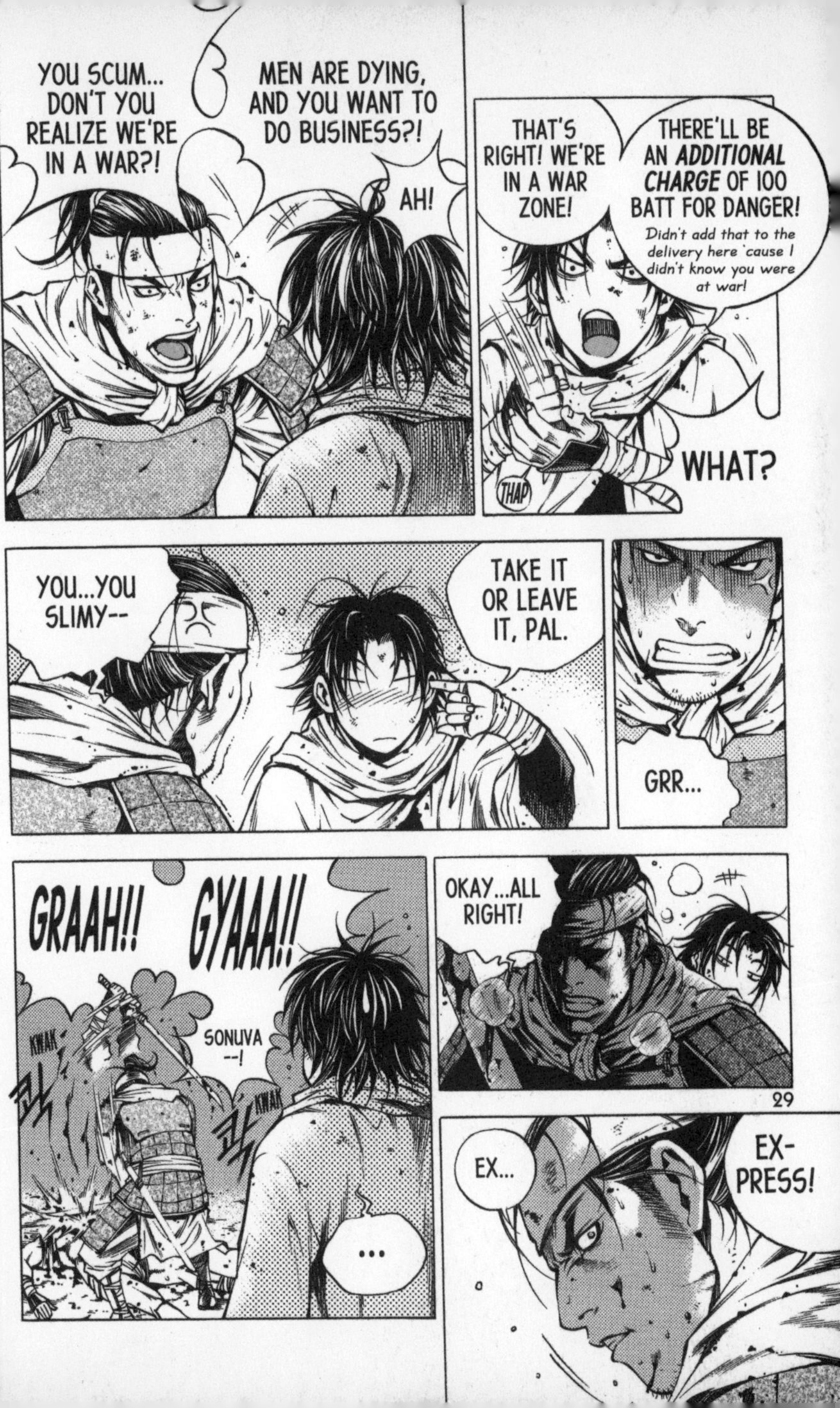
YOU SCUM... DON'T YOU REALIZE WE'RE IN A WAR?!
MEN ARE DYING, AND YOU WANT TO DO BUSINESS?!
AH!
THAT'S RIGHT! WE'RE IN A WAR ZONE!
THERE'LL BE AN ADDITIONAL CHARGE OF 100 BATT FOR DANGER!
Didn't add that to the delivery here 'cause I didn't know you were at war!
THAP
WHAT?
YOU...YOU SLIMY--
TAKE IT OR LEAVE IT, PAL.
GRR...
GRAAH!!
GYAAA!!
KWAK
SONUVA --!
KWAK
...
OKAY...ALL RIGHT!
EX...
EX-PRESS!

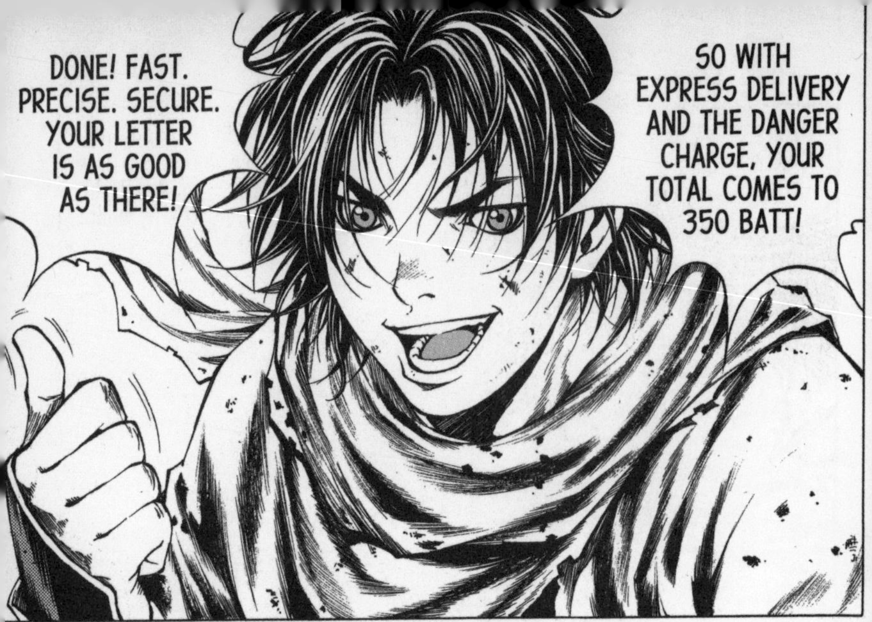
DONE! FAST. PRECISE. SECURE. YOUR LETTER IS AS GOOD AS THERE!
SO WITH EXPRESS DELIVERY AND THE DANGER CHARGE, YOUR TOTAL COMES TO 350 BATT!

30

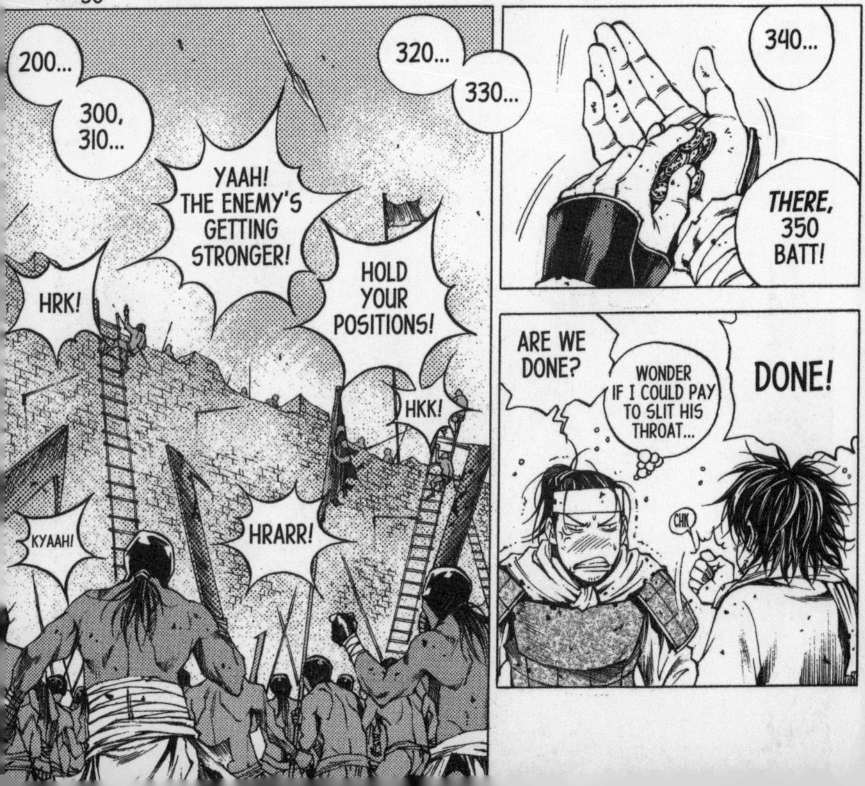
200...
300, 310...
320...
330...
YAAH! THE ENEMY'S GETTING STRONGER!
HRK!
HOLD YOUR POSITIONS!
HKK!
KYAAH!
HRARR!
340...
THERE, 350 BATT!
ARE WE DONE?
WONDER IF I COULD PAY TO SLIT HIS THROAT...
DONE!
CHK

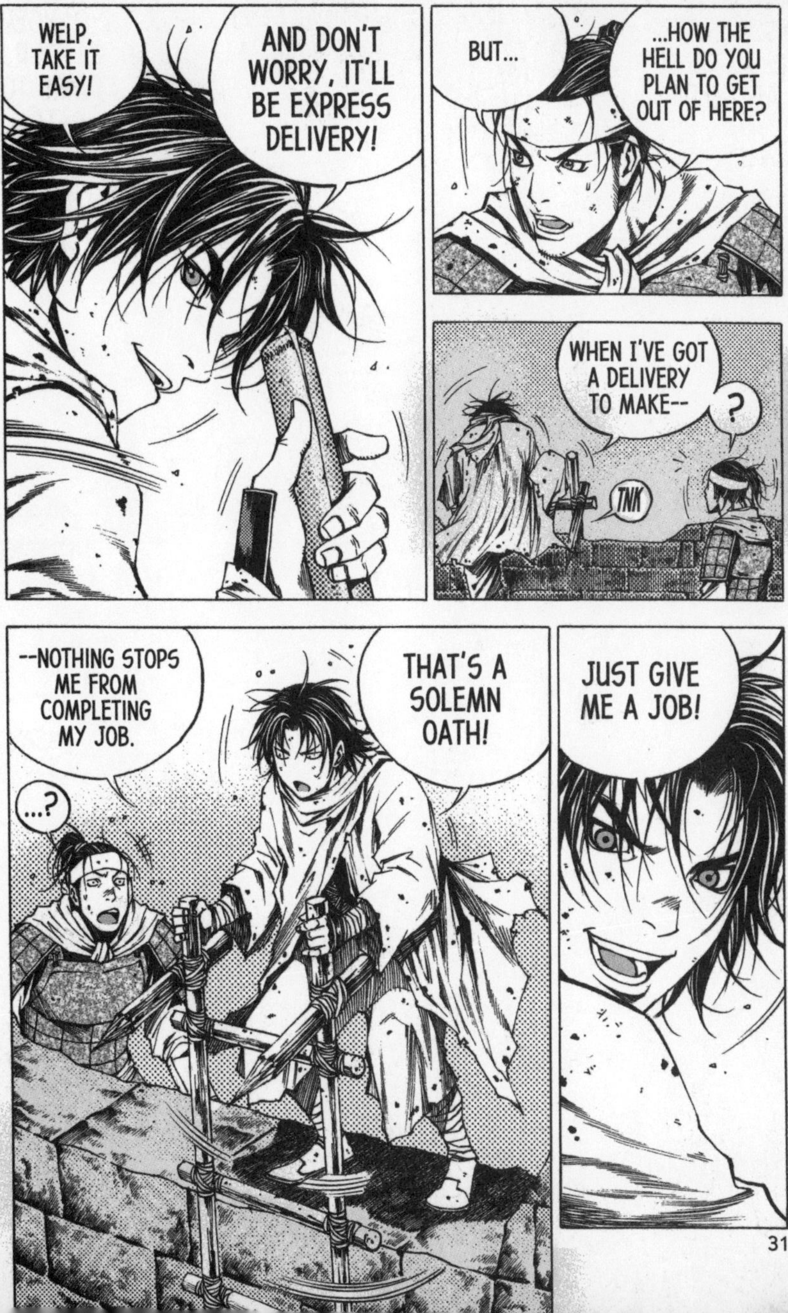
WELP, TAKE IT EASY!
AND DON'T WORRY, IT'LL BE EXPRESS DELIVERY!
BUT...
...HOW THE HELL DO YOU PLAN TO GET OUT OF HERE?
WHEN I'VE GOT A DELIVERY TO MAKE--
?
TNK
--NOTHING STOPS ME FROM COMPLETING MY JOB.
...?
THAT'S A SOLEMN OATH!
JUST GIVE ME A JOB!

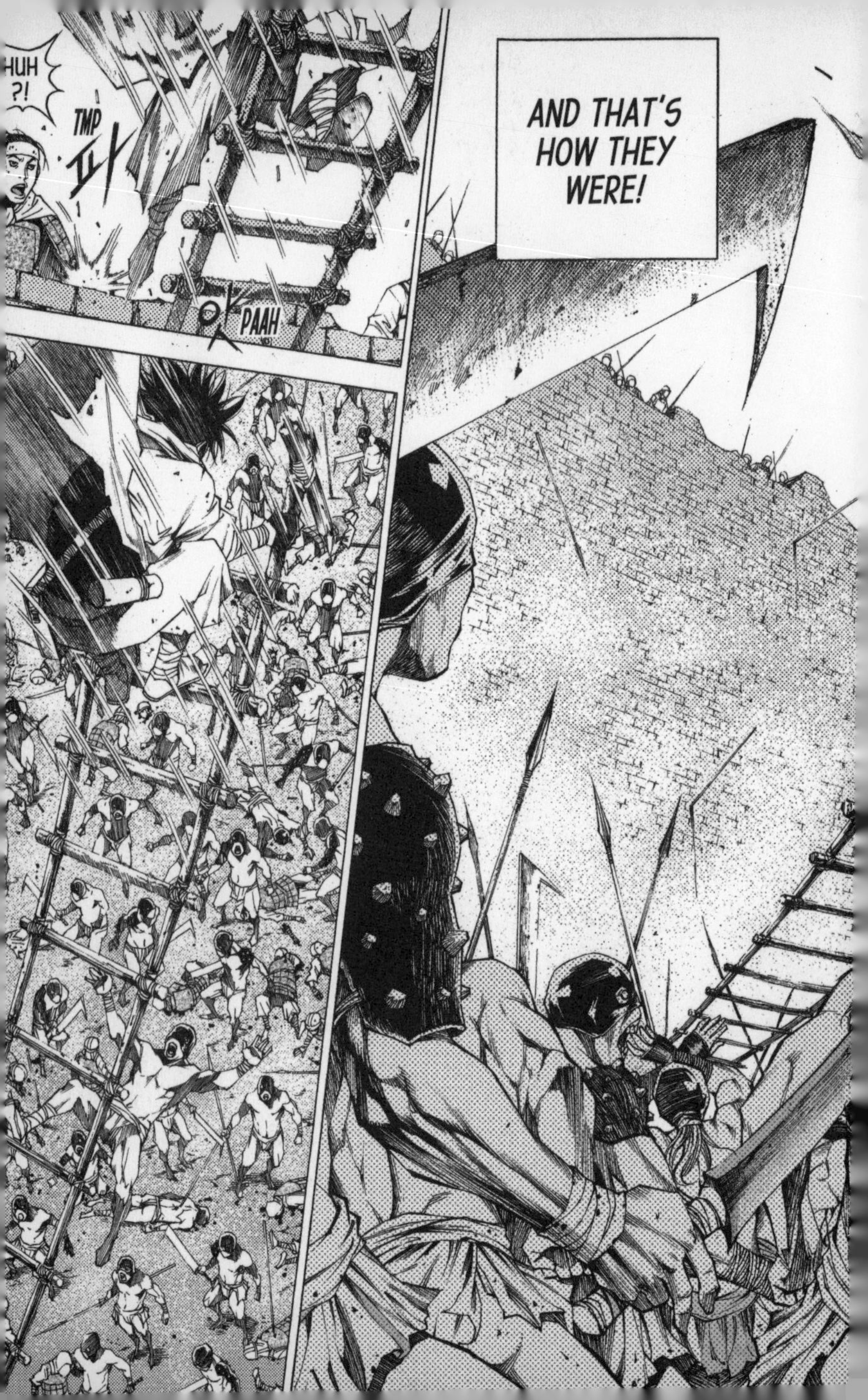

HUH ?!
TMP
PAAH
AND THAT'S HOW THEY WERE!

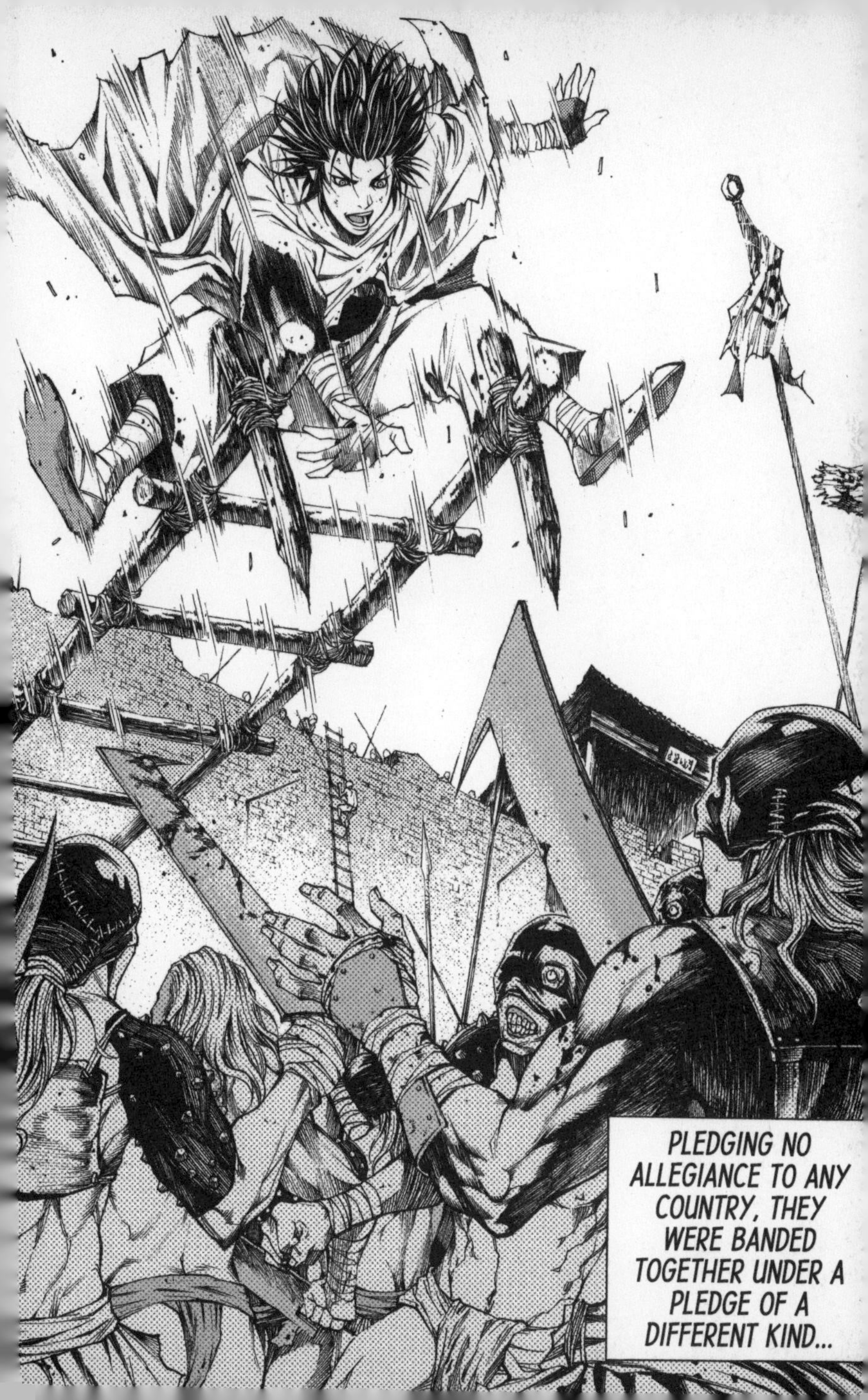
PLEDGING NO ALLEGIANCE TO ANY COUNTRY, THEY WERE BANDED TOGETHER UNDER A PLEDGE OF A DIFFERENT KIND...

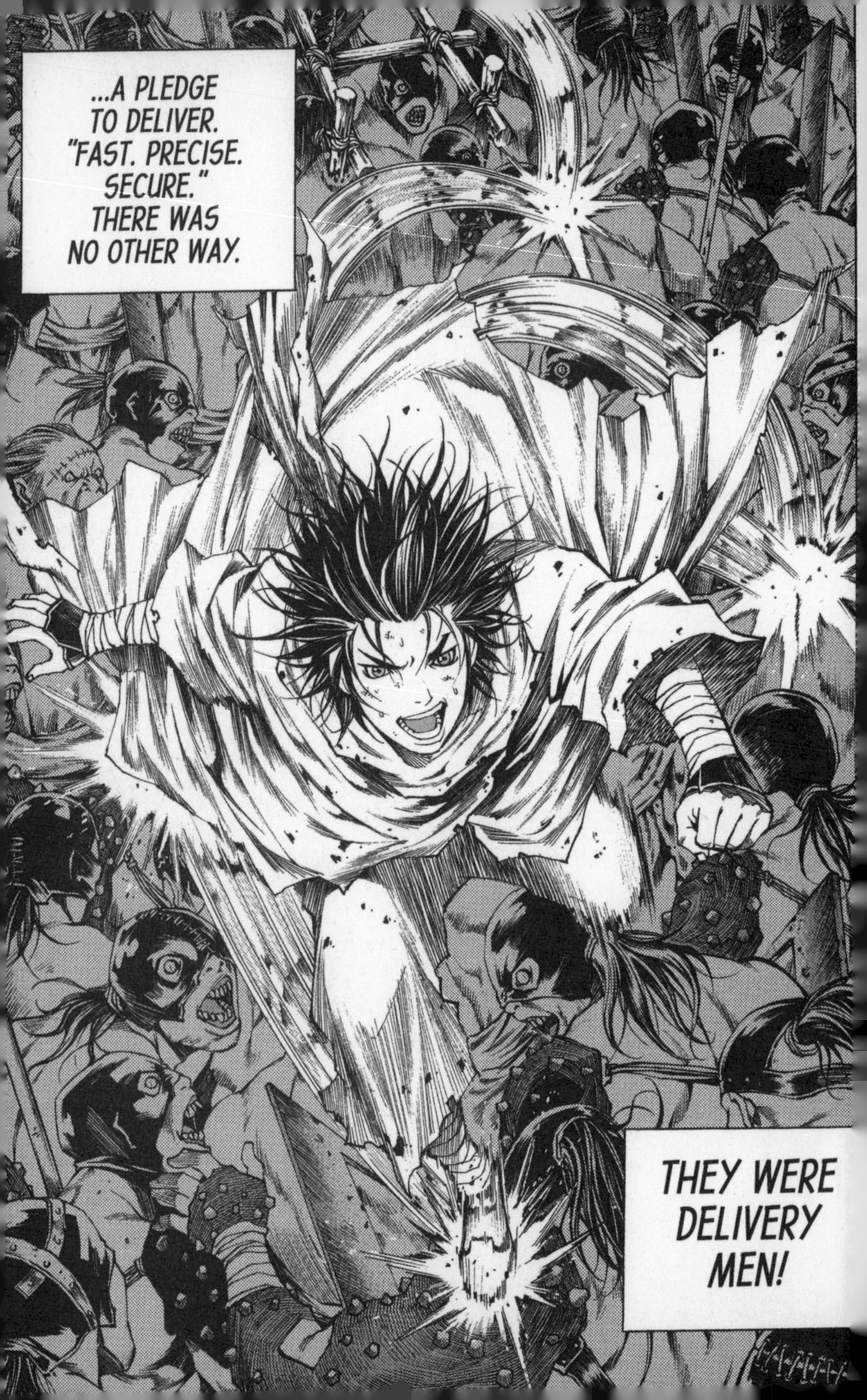
...A PLEDGE TO DELIVER. "FAST. PRECISE. SECURE." THERE WAS NO OTHER WAY.
THEY WERE DELIVERY MEN!

Banya

the explosive delivery man

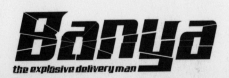

Chapter 2

BOY AND GIRL

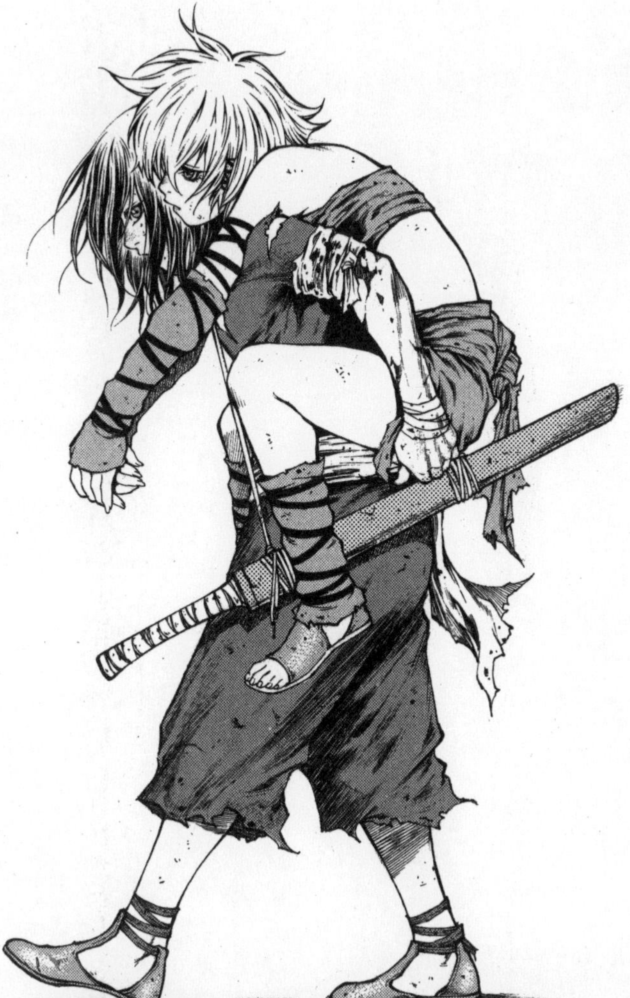

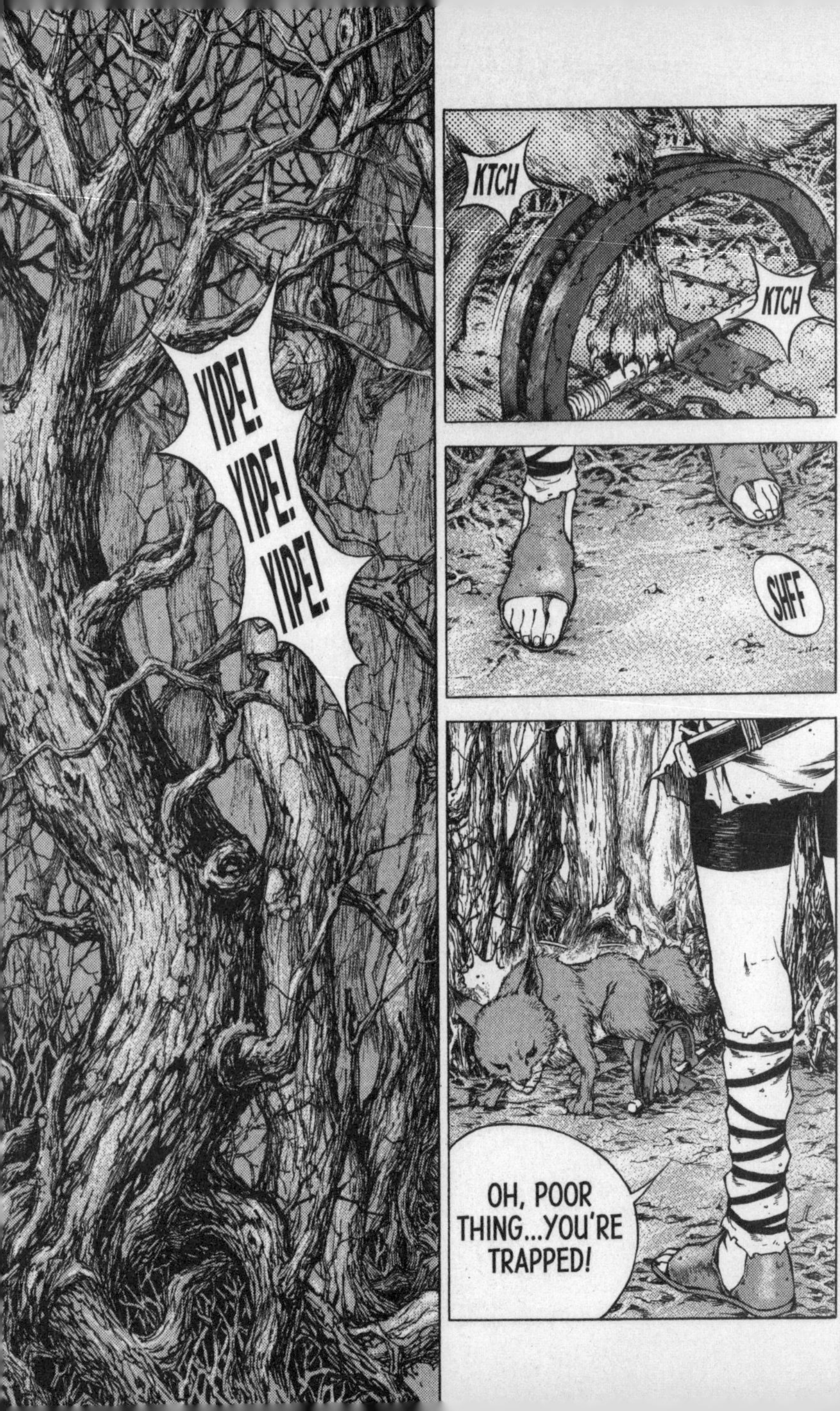
YIPE! YIPE! YIPE!
KTCH
KTCH
SHFF
OH, POOR THING...YOU'RE TRAPPED!

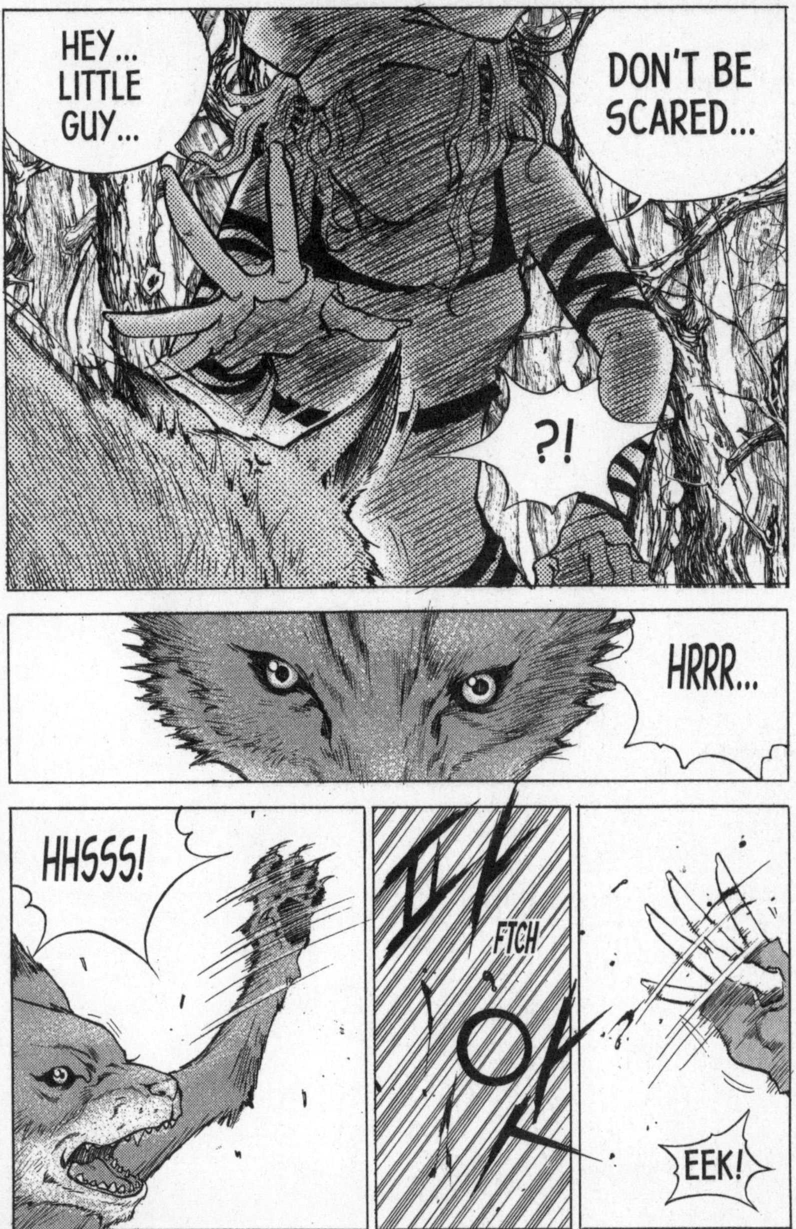
HEY... LITTLE GUY...
DON'T BE SCARED...
?!
HRRR...
HHSSS!
FTCH
EEK!

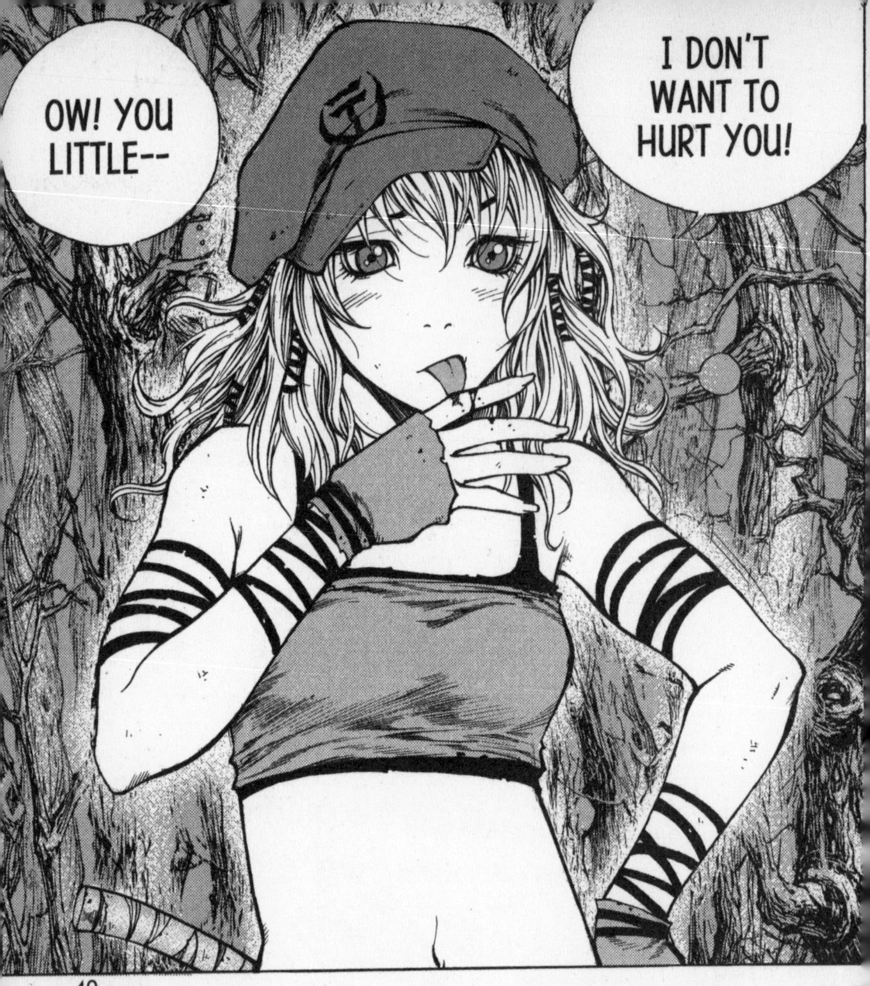
OW! YOU LITTLE--
I DON'T WANT TO HURT YOU!

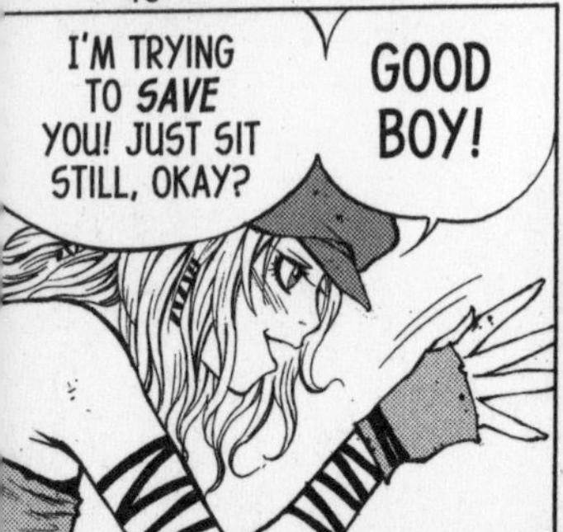
I'M TRYING TO *SAVE* YOU! JUST SIT STILL, OKAY?
GOOD BOY!

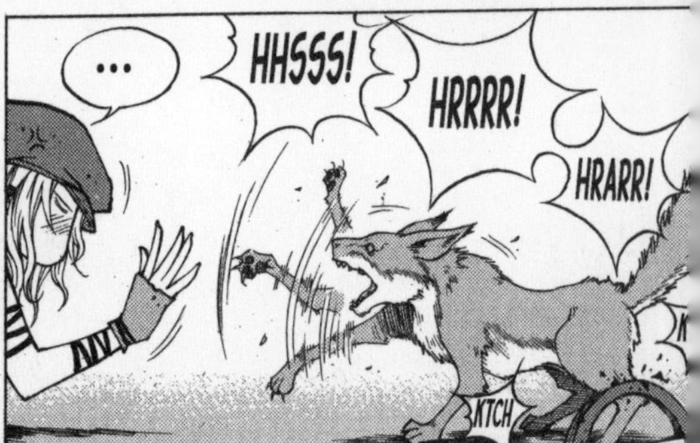
...
HHSSS!
HRRRR!
HRARR!
KTCH

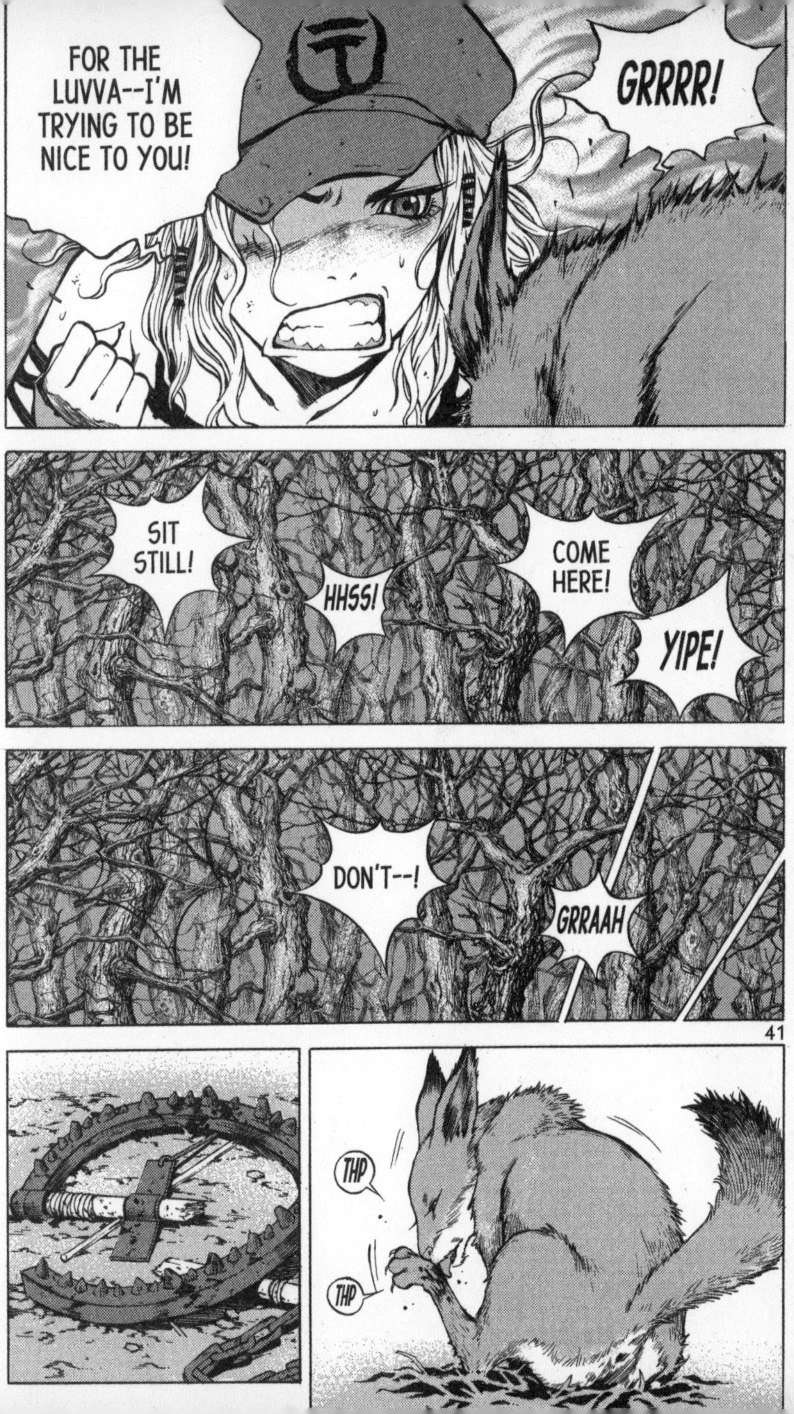

FOR THE LUVVA--I'M TRYING TO BE NICE TO YOU!
GRRRR!
SIT STILL!
HHSS!
COME HERE!
YIPE!
DON'T--!
GRRAAH
THP
THP

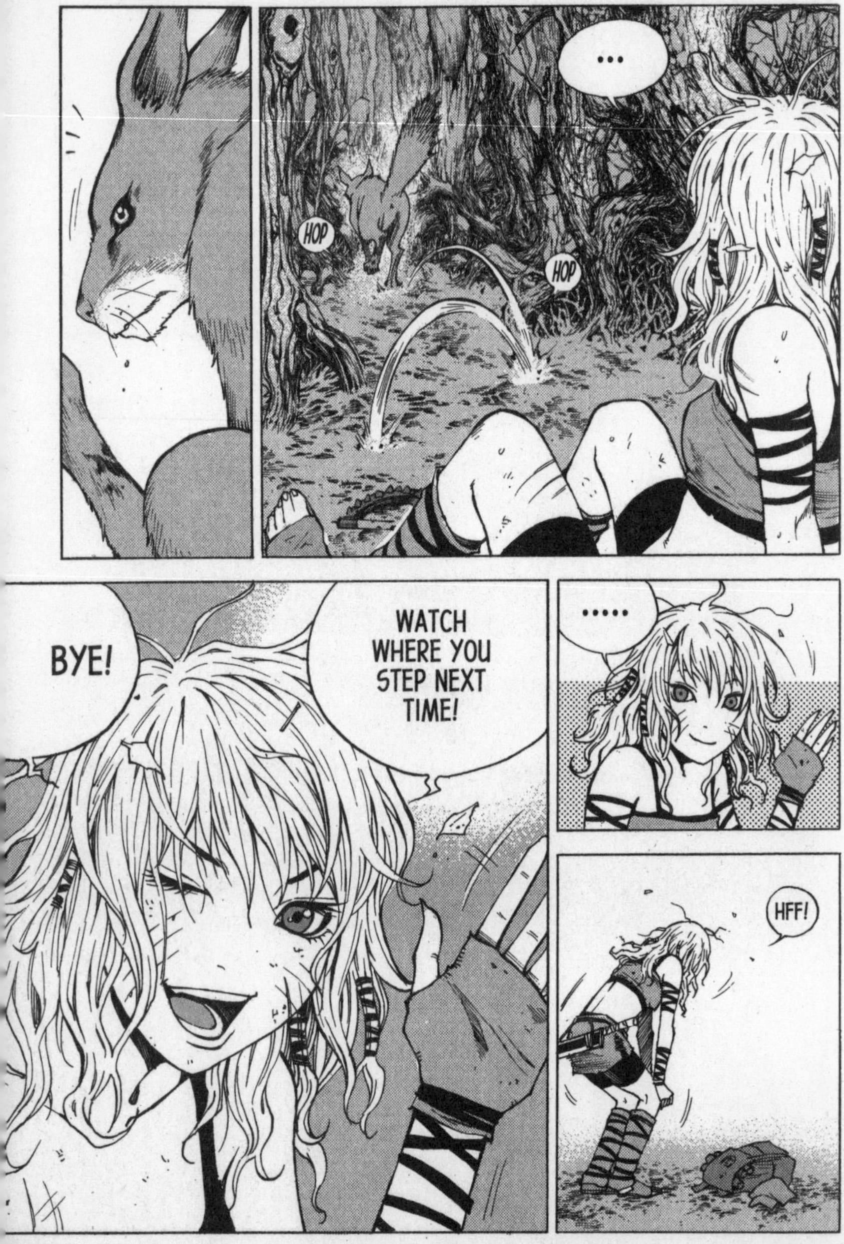
...
HOP
HOP
BYE!
WATCH WHERE YOU STEP NEXT TIME!
.....
HFF!

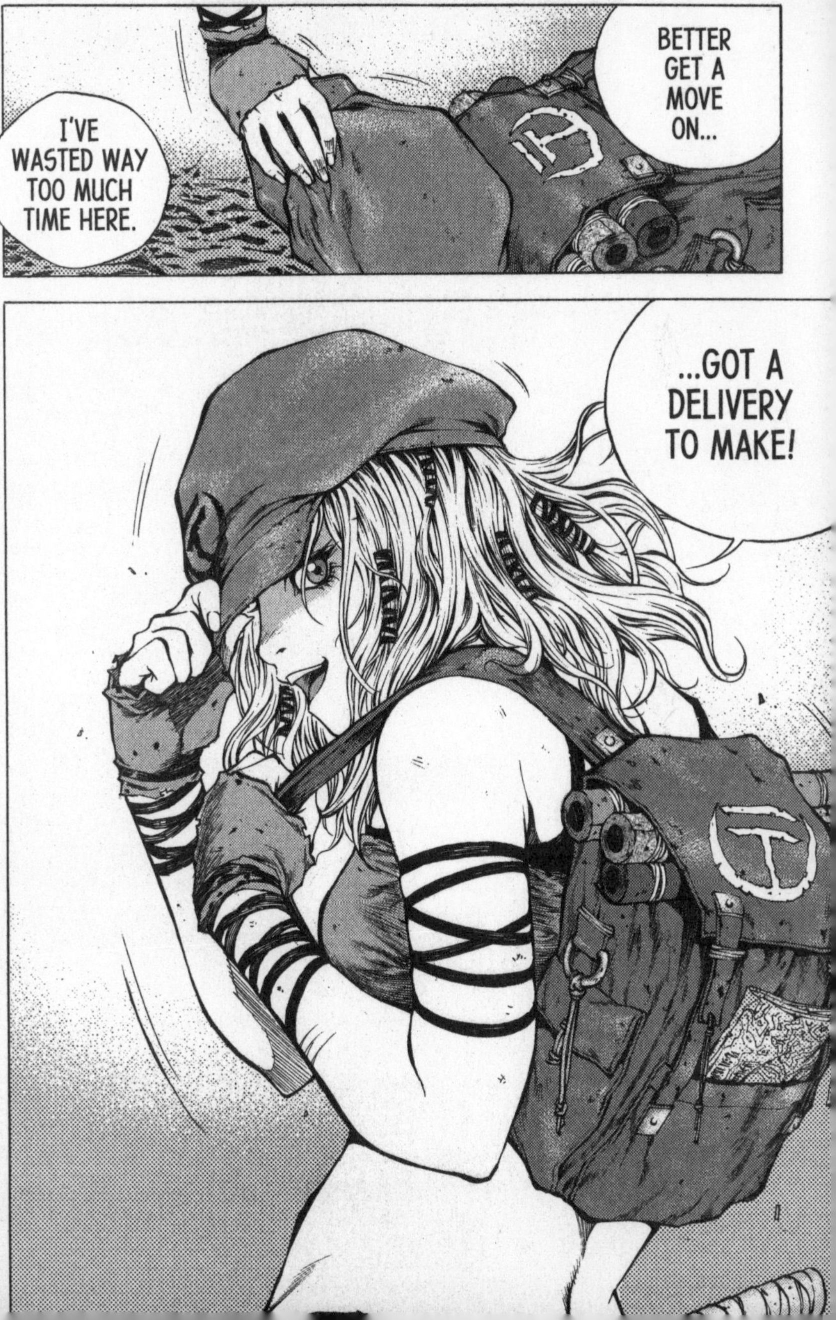
I'VE WASTED WAY TOO MUCH TIME HERE.
BETTER GET A MOVE ON...
...GOT A DELIVERY TO MAKE!

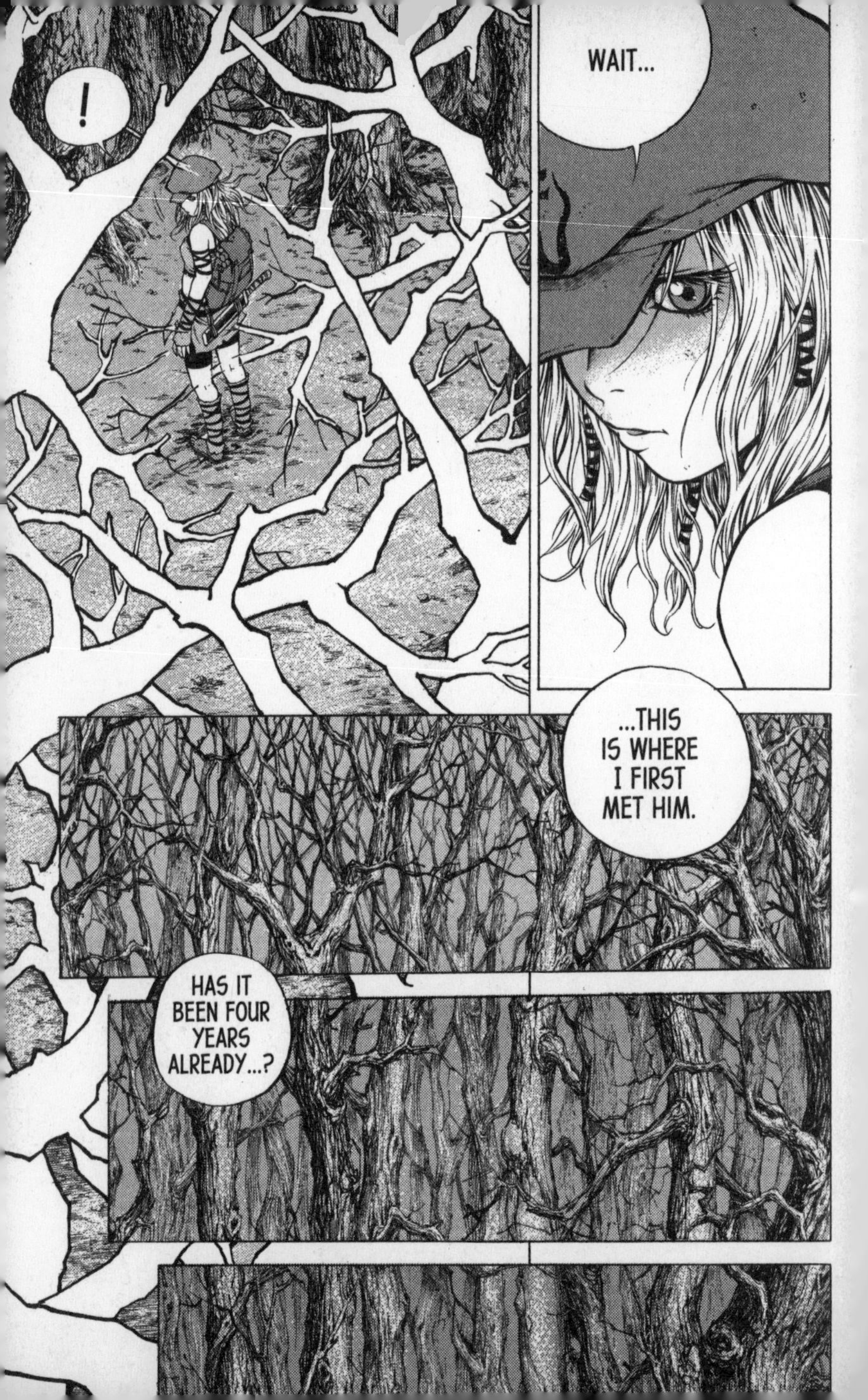
!
WAIT...
...THIS IS WHERE I FIRST MET HIM.
HAS IT BEEN FOUR YEARS ALREADY...?

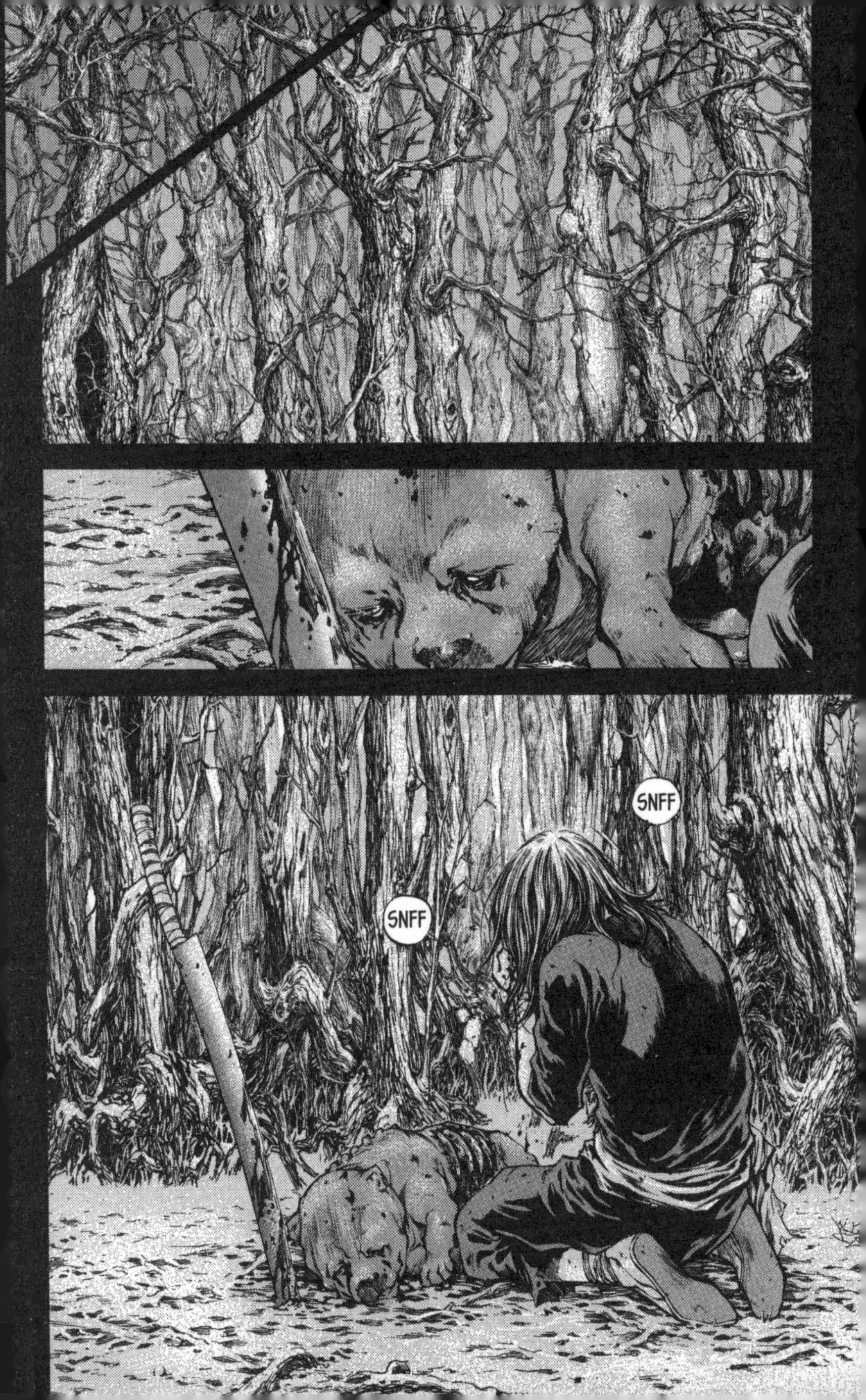
SNFF
SNFF

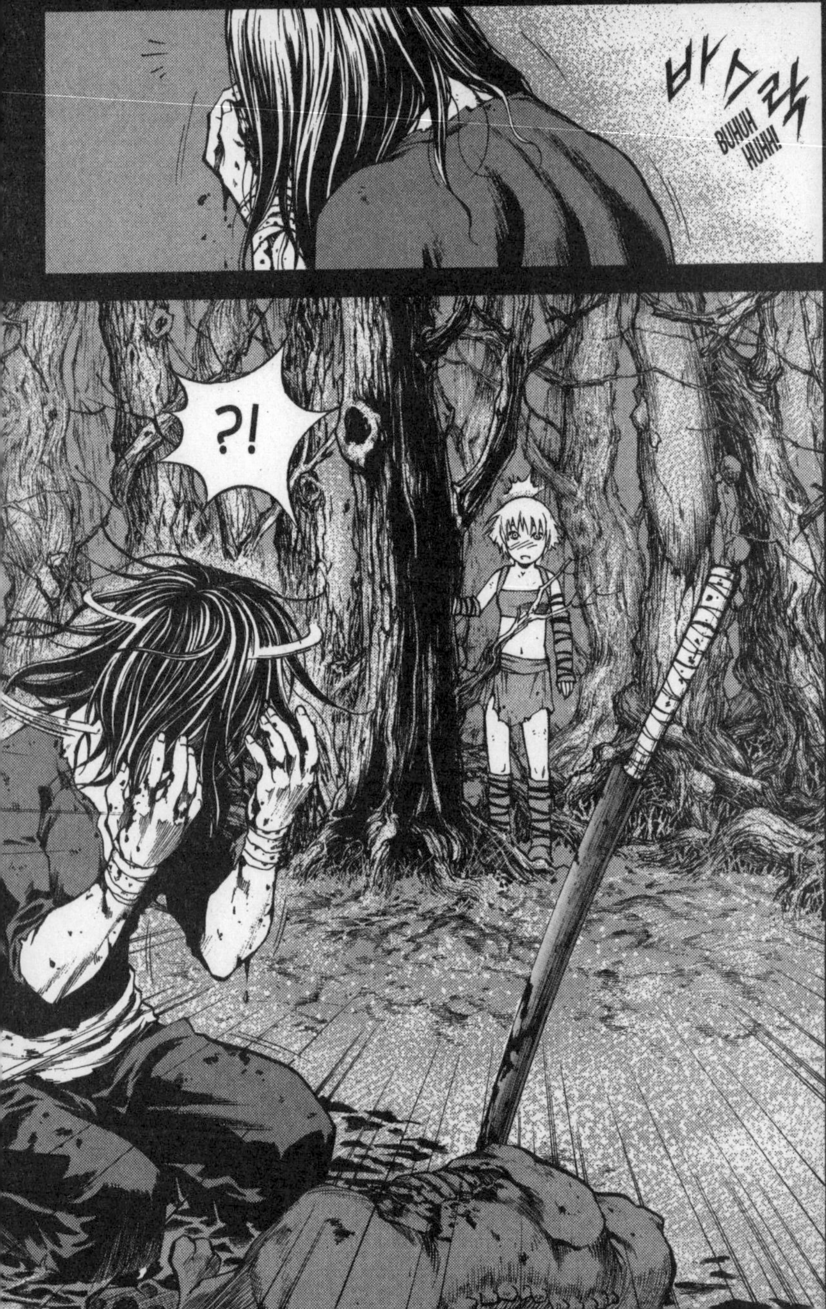
바스락
BUHUH HUHH!
?!

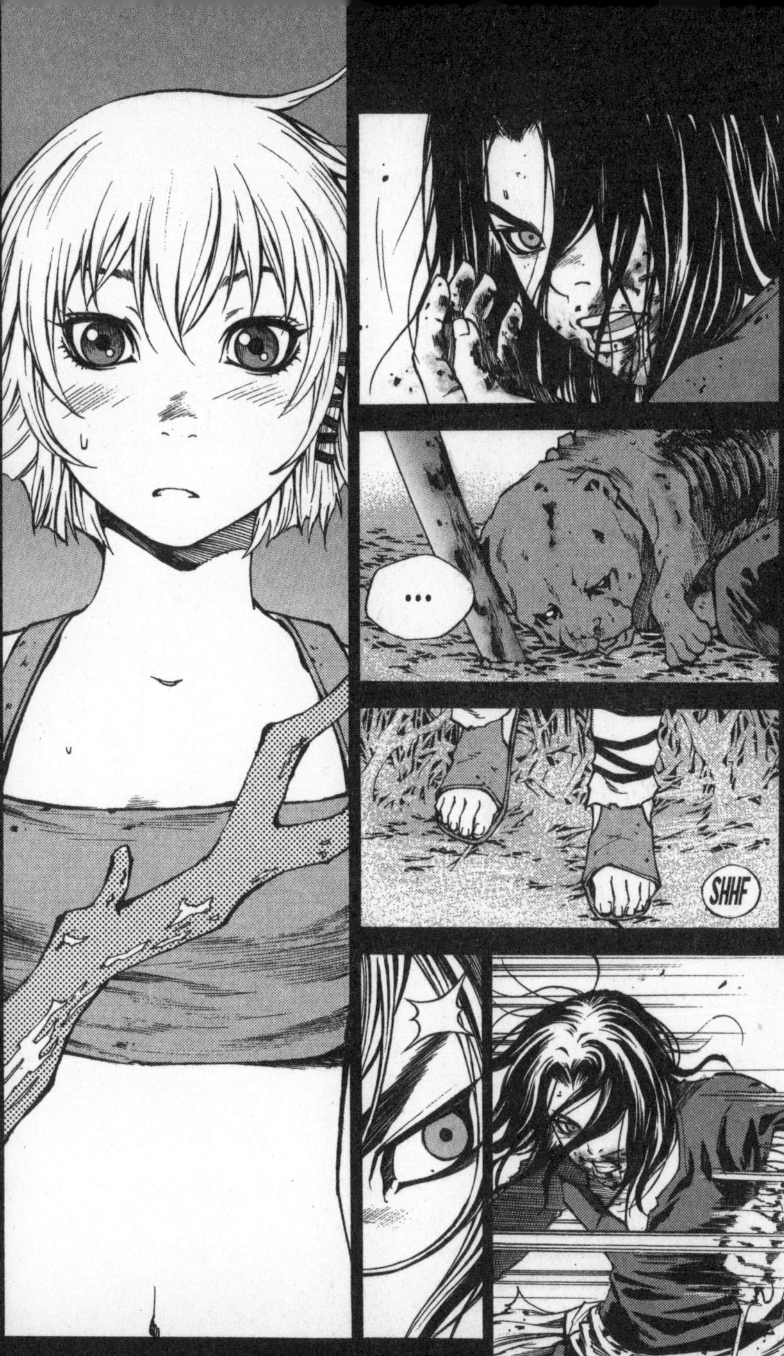
...
SHHF

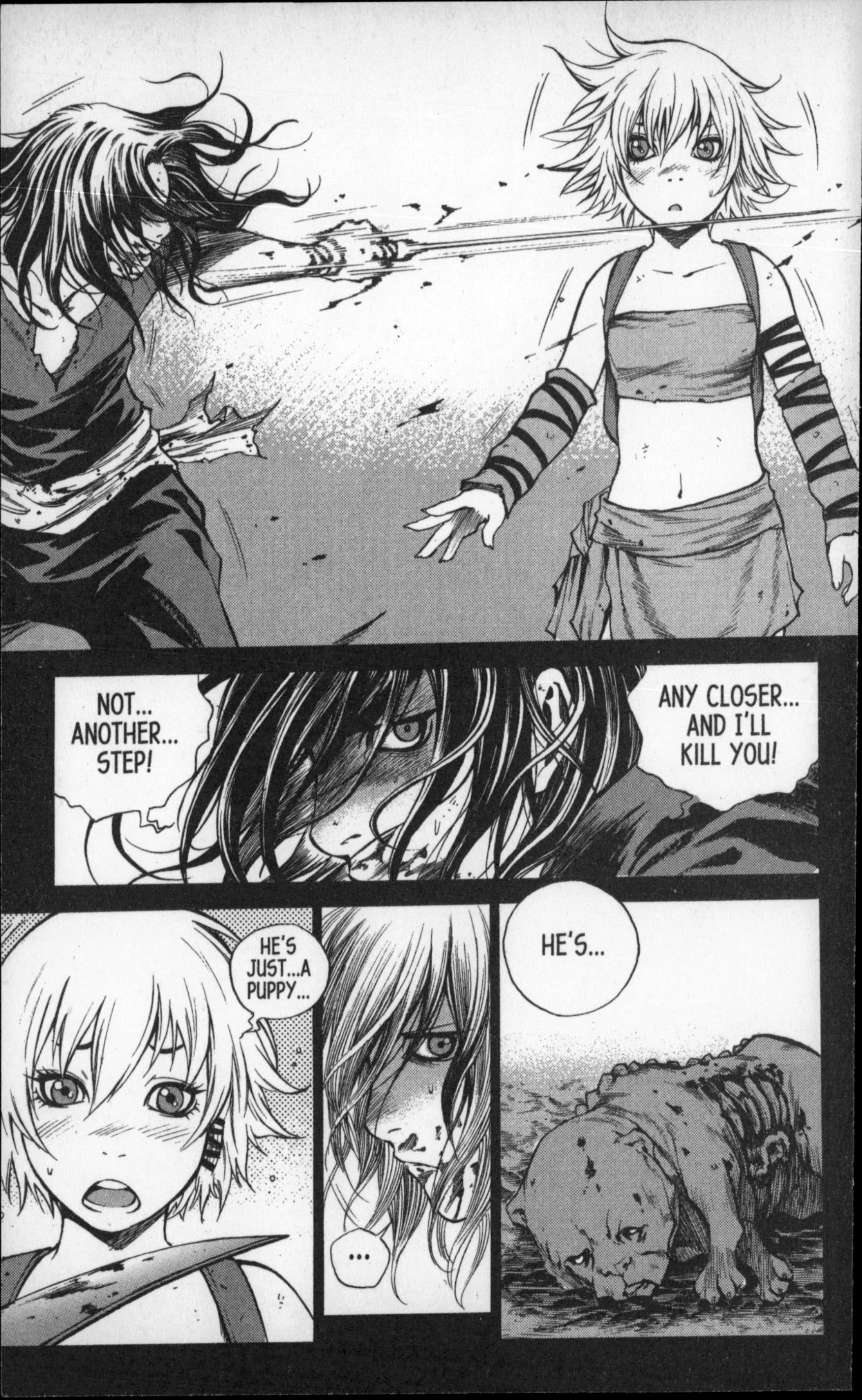
NOT... ANOTHER... STEP!
ANY CLOSER... AND I'LL KILL YOU!
HE'S JUST...A PUPPY...
...
HE'S...

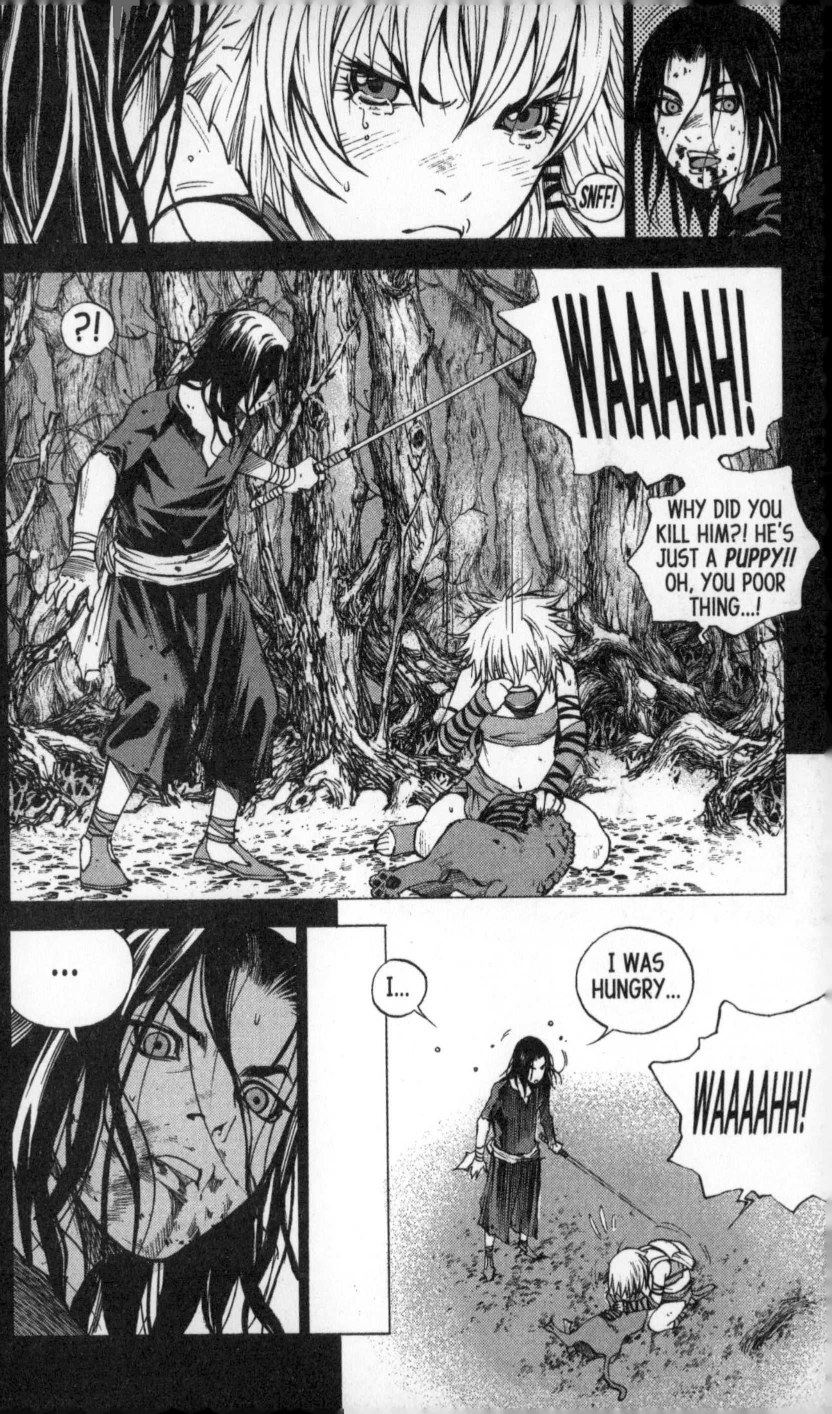
SNFF!
?!
WAAAAH!
WHY DID YOU KILL HIM?! HE'S JUST A *PUPPY!!* OH, YOU POOR THING...!
...
I...
I WAS HUNGRY...
WAAAHH!

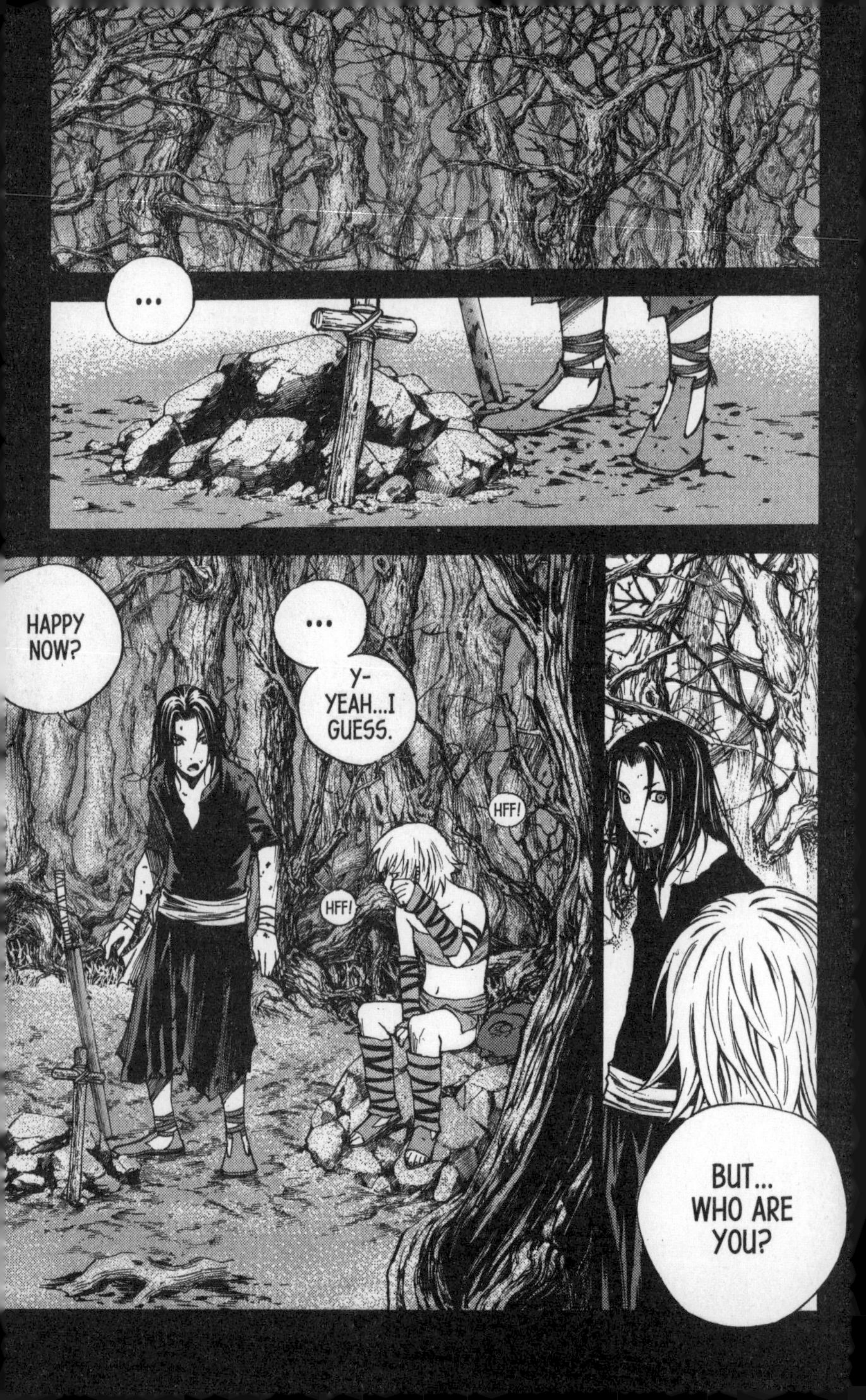
...
HAPPY NOW?
...
Y-YEAH...I GUESS.
HFF!
HFF!
BUT... WHO ARE YOU?

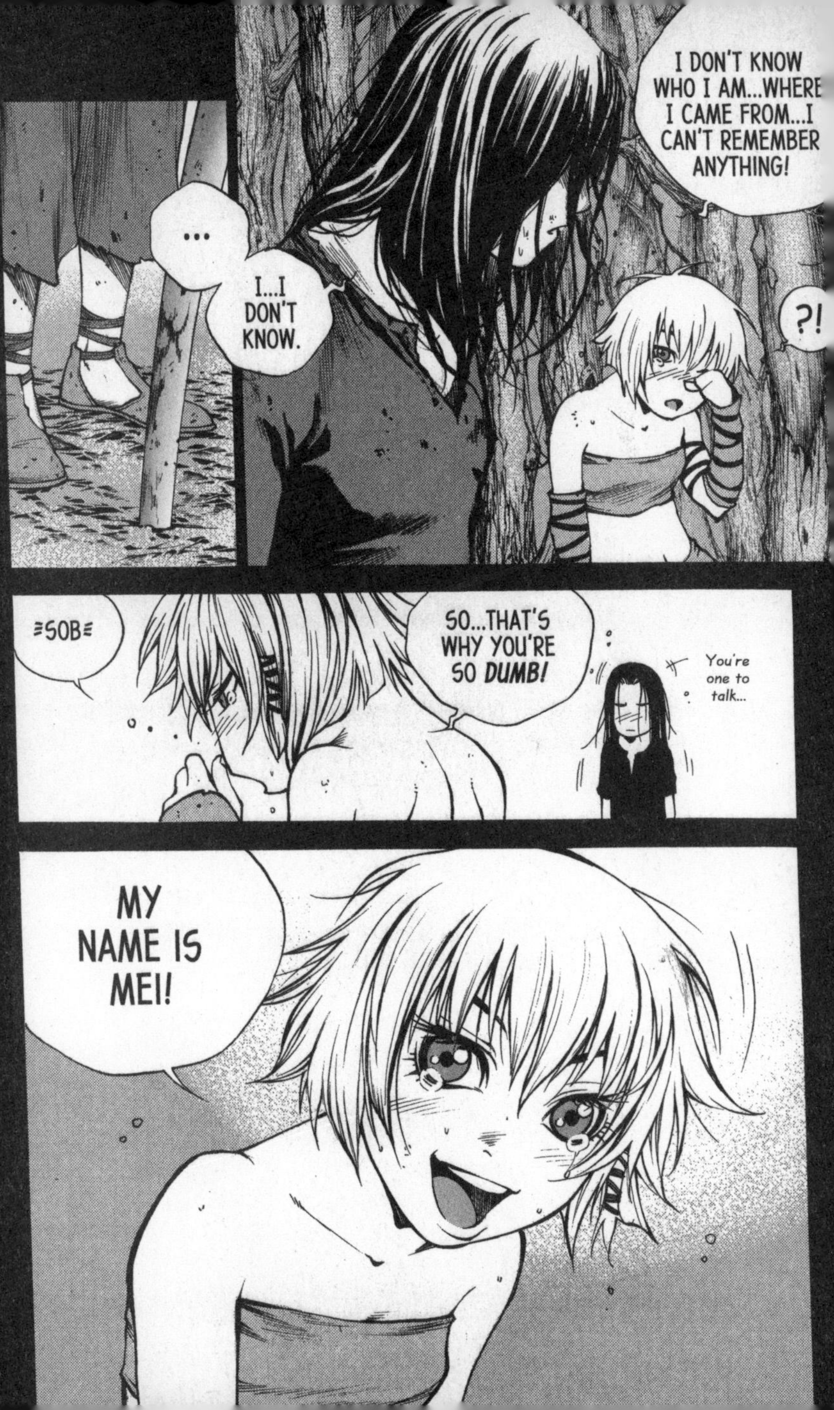
...
I...I DON'T KNOW.
I DON'T KNOW WHO I AM...WHERE I CAME FROM...I CAN'T REMEMBER ANYTHING!
?!
SOB
SO...THAT'S WHY YOU'RE SO DUMB!
You're one to talk...
MY NAME IS MEI!

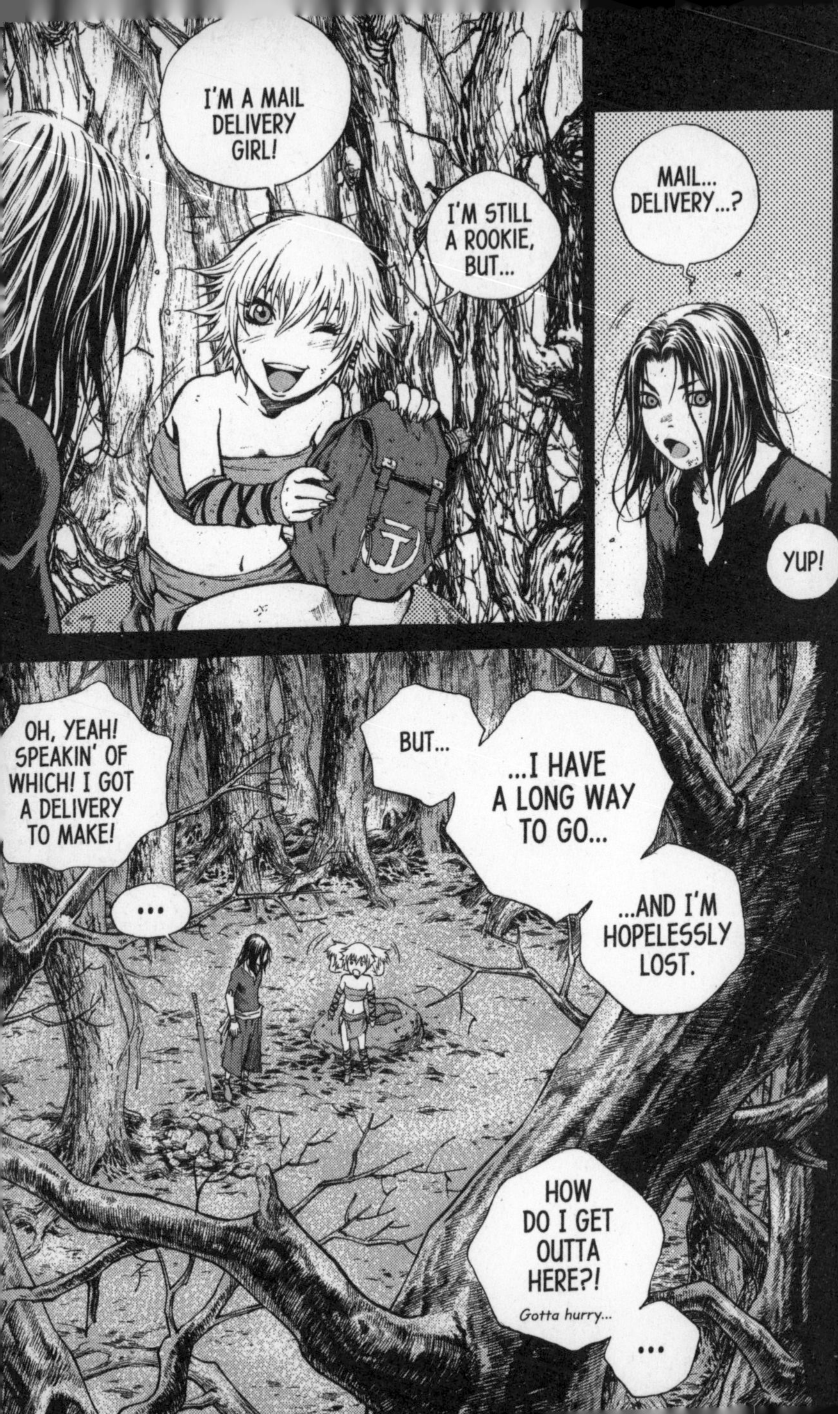
I'M A MAIL DELIVERY GIRL!
I'M STILL A ROOKIE, BUT...
MAIL... DELIVERY...?
YUP!
OH, YEAH! SPEAKIN' OF WHICH! I GOT A DELIVERY TO MAKE!
BUT...
...I HAVE A LONG WAY TO GO...
...AND I'M HOPELESSLY LOST.
...
HOW DO I GET OUTTA HERE?!
Gotta hurry...
...

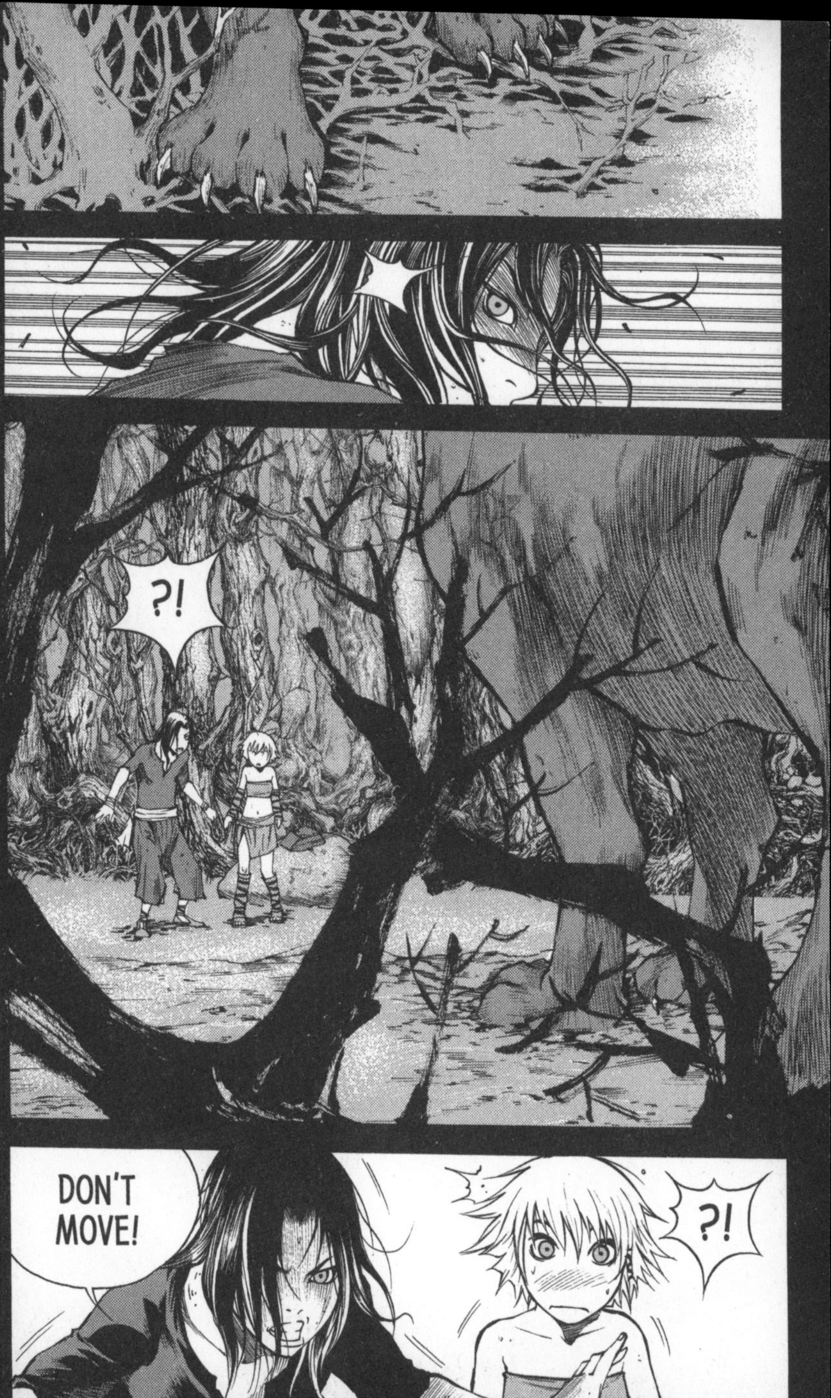
?!
DON'T MOVE!
?!

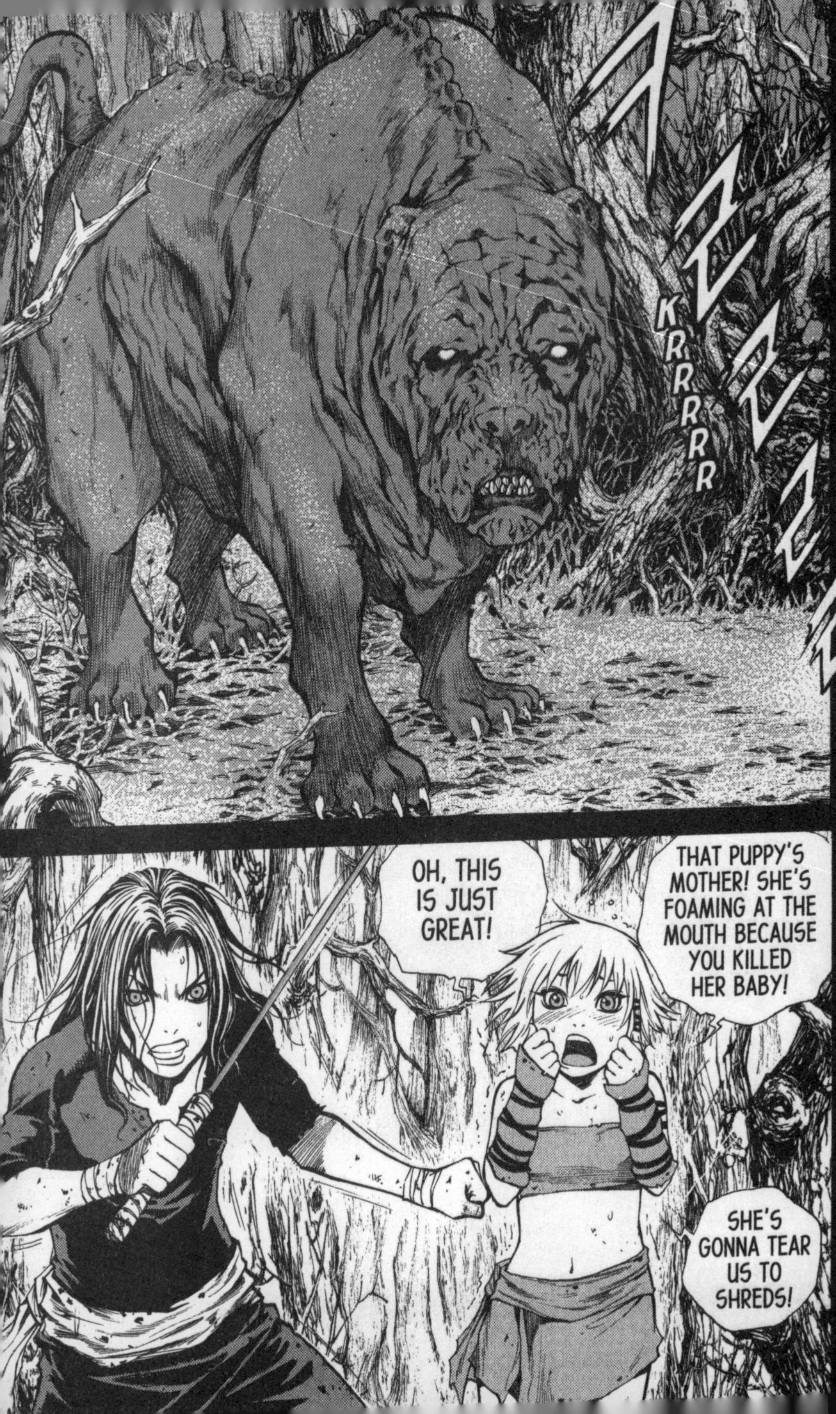
KRRRRRR
OH, THIS IS JUST GREAT!
THAT PUPPY'S MOTHER! SHE'S FOAMING AT THE MOUTH BECAUSE YOU KILLED HER BABY!
SHE'S GONNA TEAR US TO SHREDS!

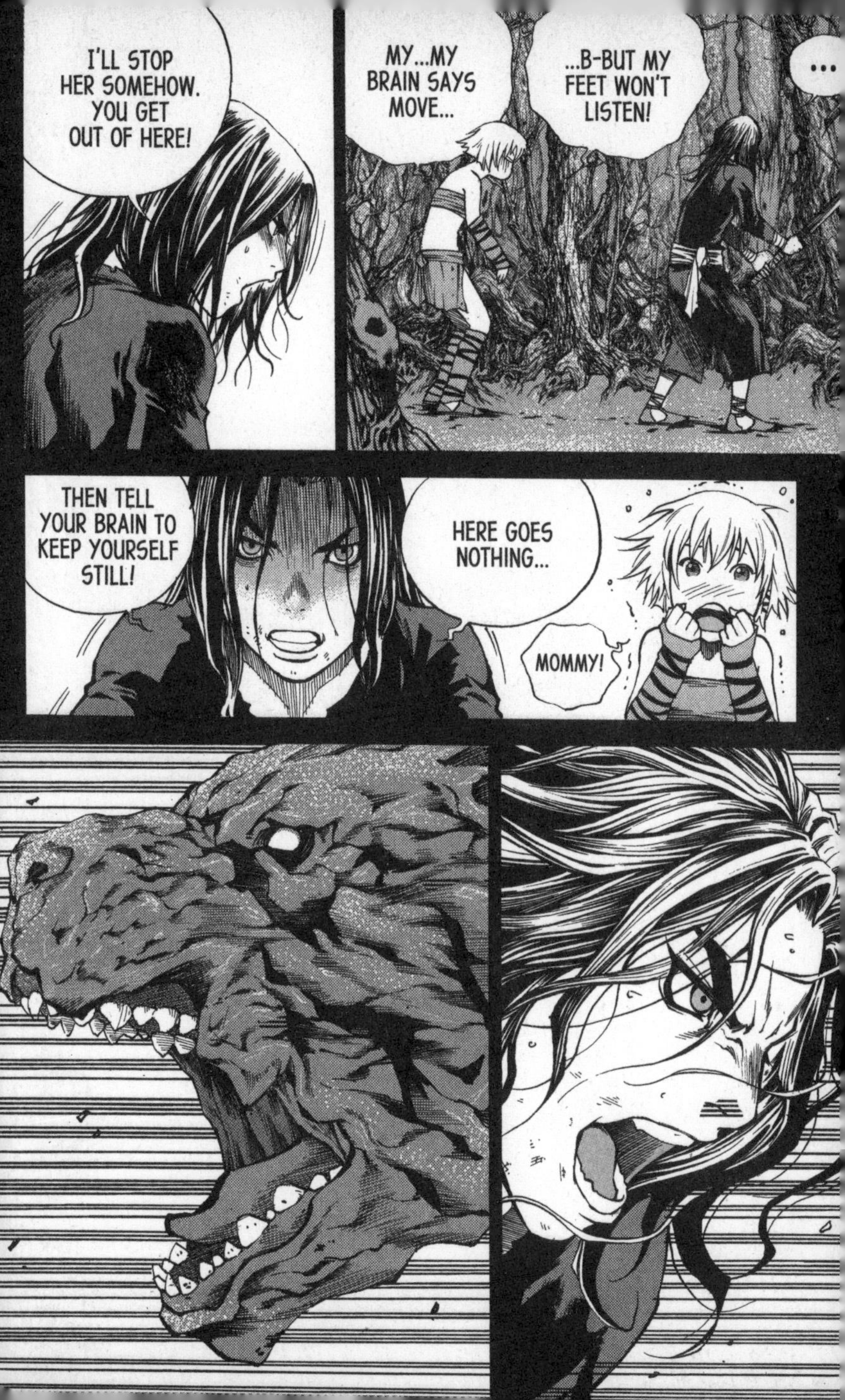
I'LL STOP HER SOMEHOW. YOU GET OUT OF HERE!
MY...MY BRAIN SAYS MOVE...
...B-BUT MY FEET WON'T LISTEN!
...
THEN TELL YOUR BRAIN TO KEEP YOURSELF STILL!
HERE GOES NOTHING...
MOMMY!

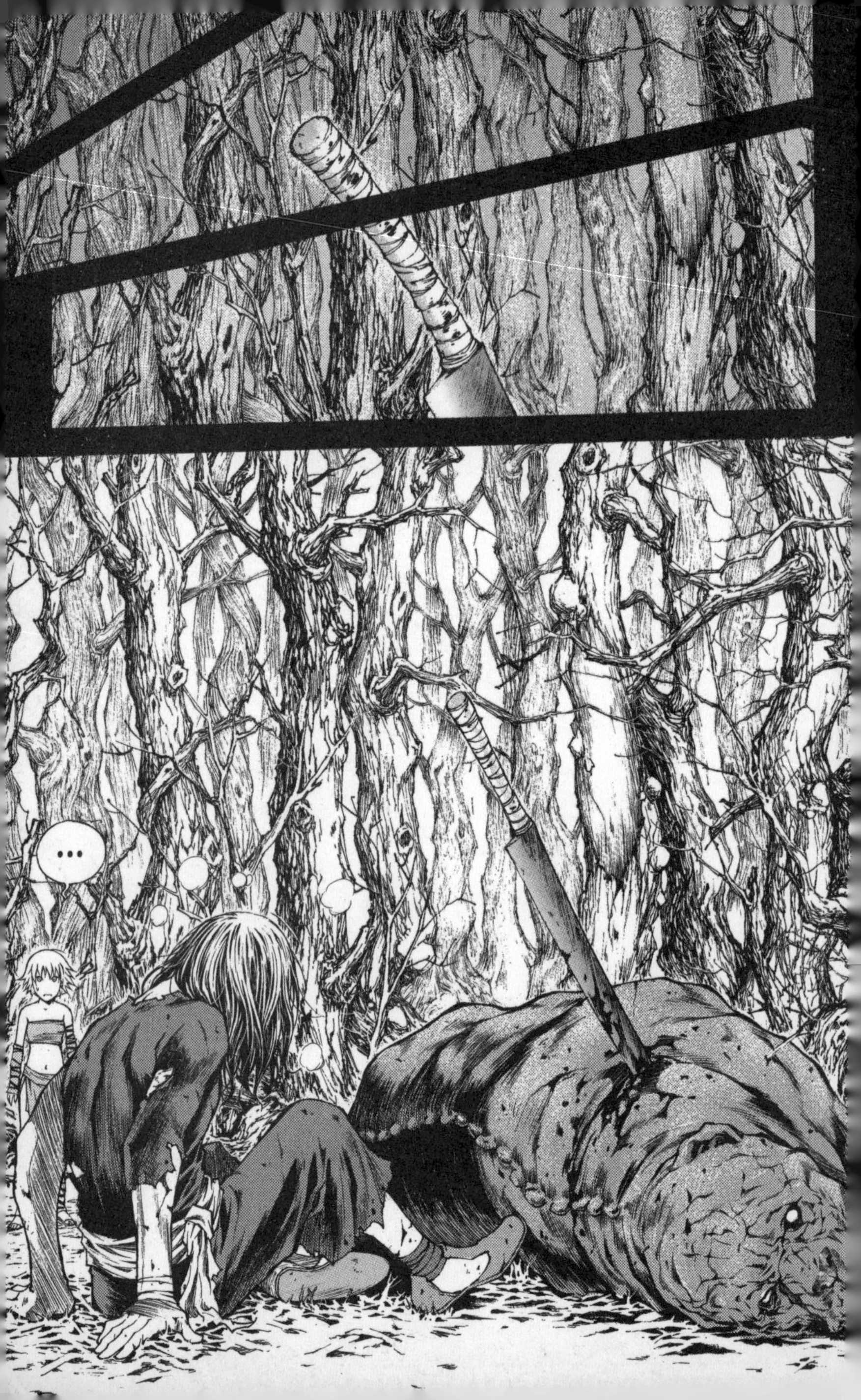
...

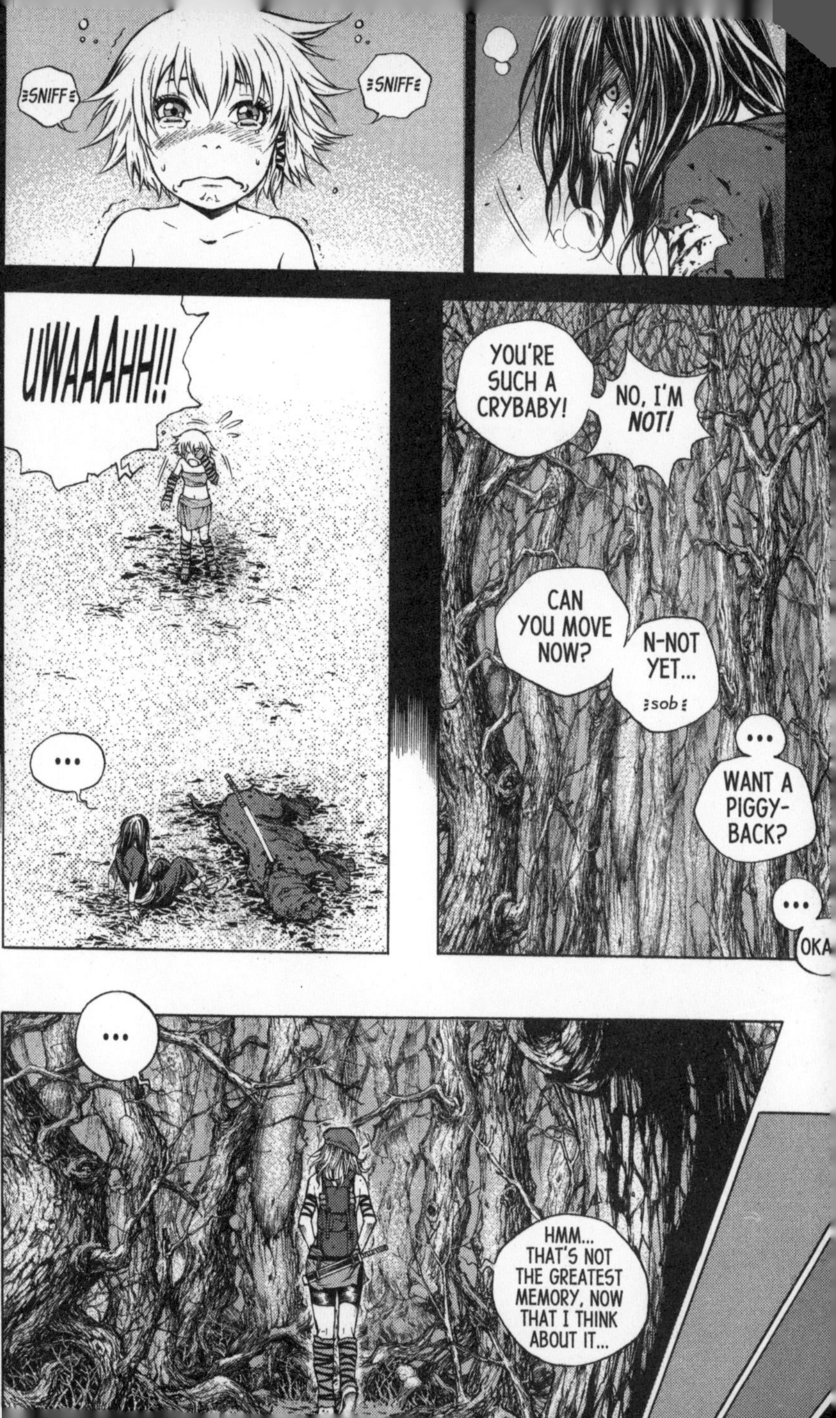
SNIFF
SNIFF
UWAAAHH!!
...
YOU'RE SUCH A CRYBABY!
NO, I'M *NOT!*
CAN YOU MOVE NOW?
N-NOT YET...
sob
...
WANT A PIGGY-BACK?
...
OKA
...
HMM... THAT'S NOT THE GREATEST MEMORY, NOW THAT I THINK ABOUT IT...

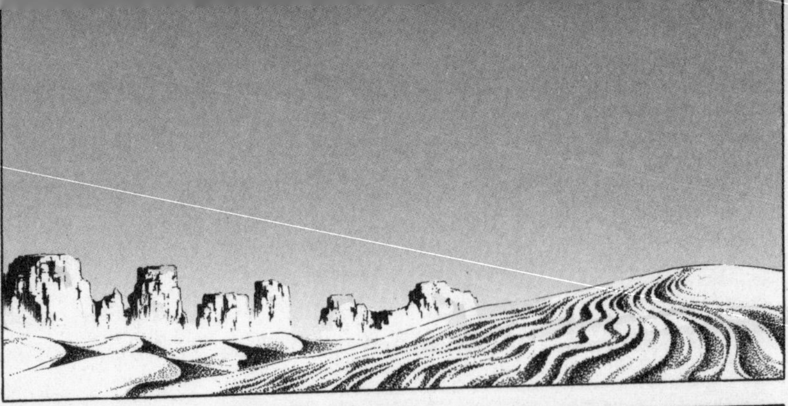

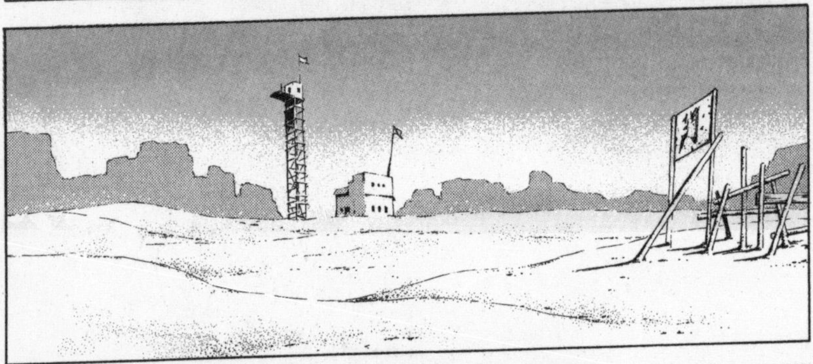

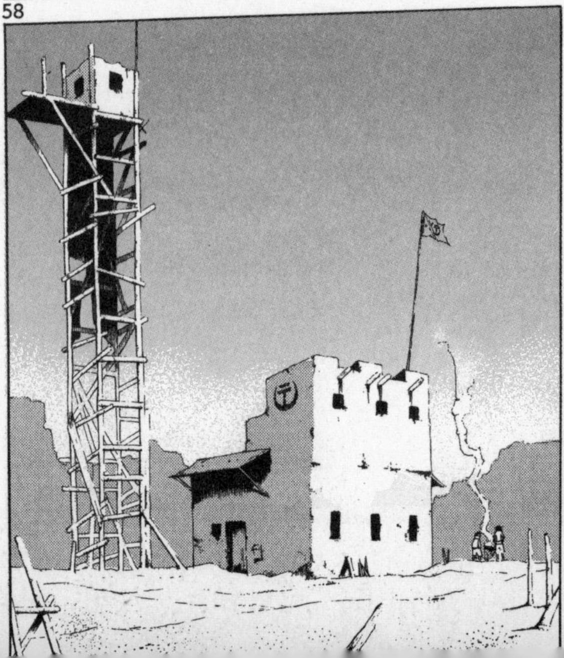

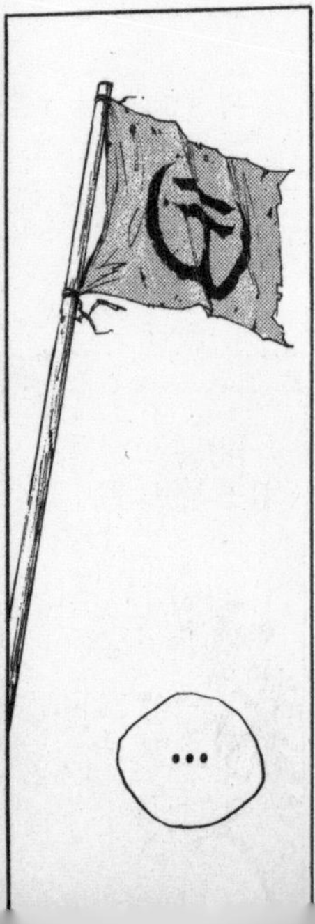
...

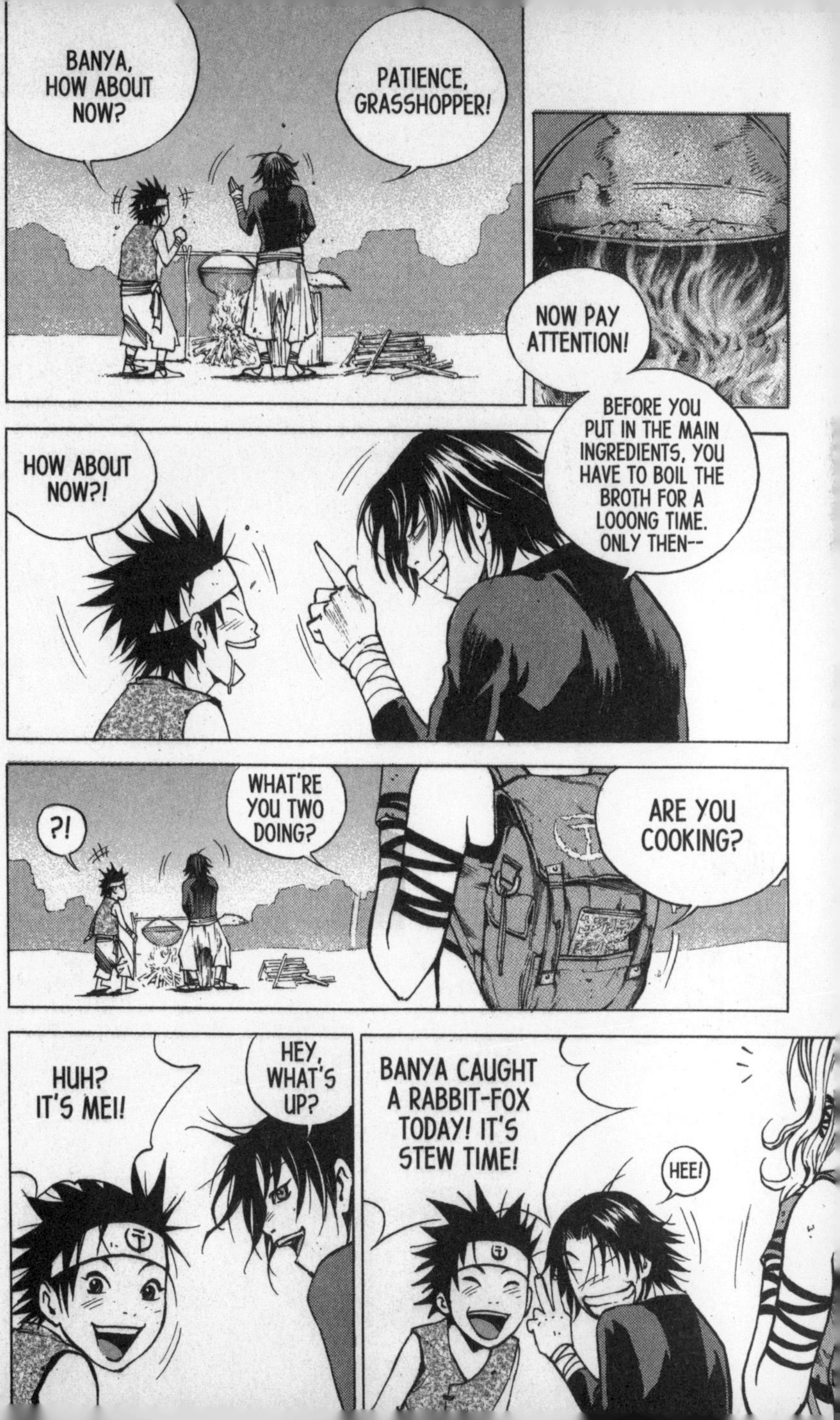
BANYA, HOW ABOUT NOW?
PATIENCE, GRASSHOPPER!
NOW PAY ATTENTION!
HOW ABOUT NOW?!
BEFORE YOU PUT IN THE MAIN INGREDIENTS, YOU HAVE TO BOIL THE BROTH FOR A LOOONG TIME. ONLY THEN--
?!
WHAT'RE YOU TWO DOING?
ARE YOU COOKING?
HUH? IT'S MEI!
HEY, WHAT'S UP?
BANYA CAUGHT A RABBIT-FOX TODAY! IT'S STEW TIME!
HEE!

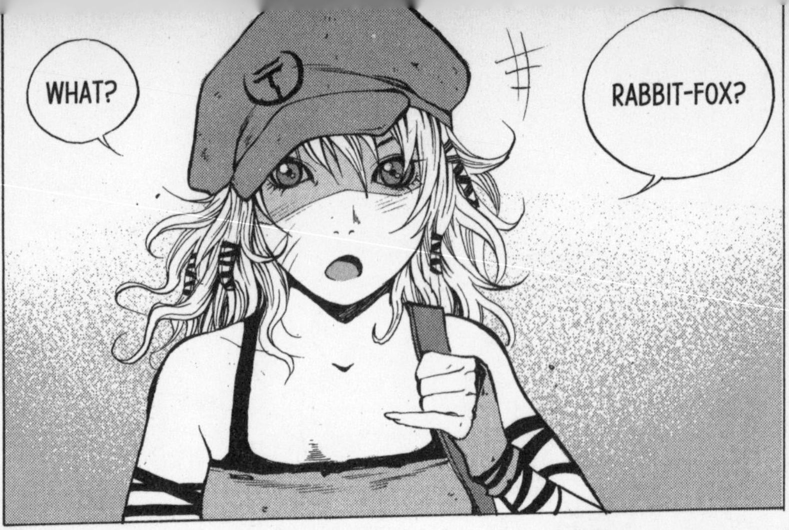
WHAT?
RABBIT-FOX?

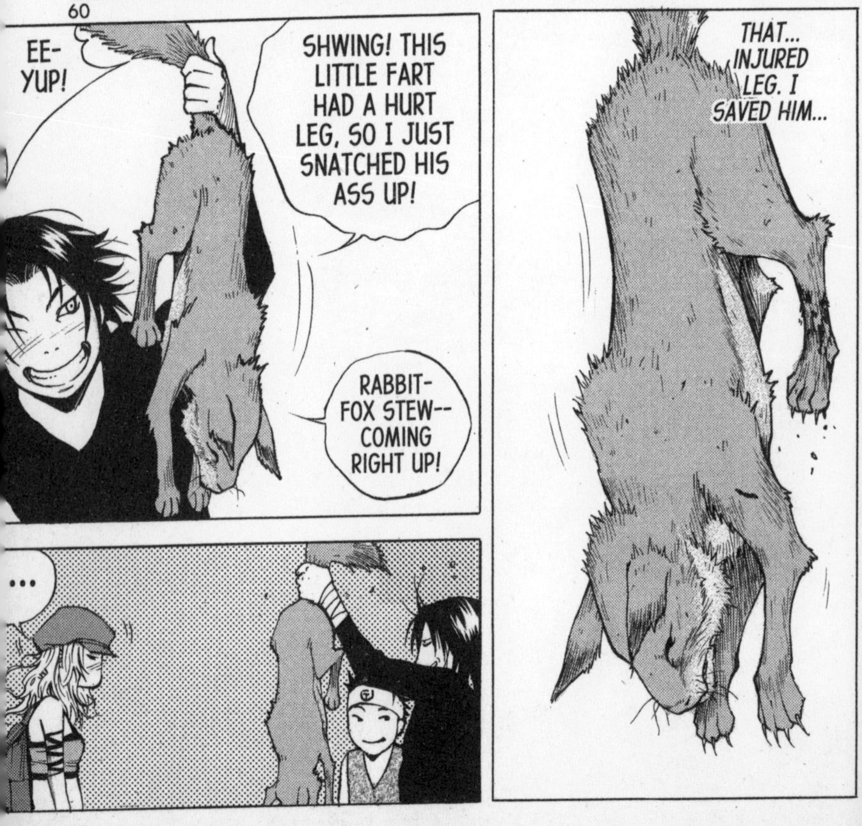
EE-YUP!
SHWING! THIS LITTLE FART HAD A HURT LEG, SO I JUST SNATCHED HIS ASS UP!
RABBIT-FOX STEW--COMING RIGHT UP!
...
THAT... INJURED LEG. I SAVED HIM...

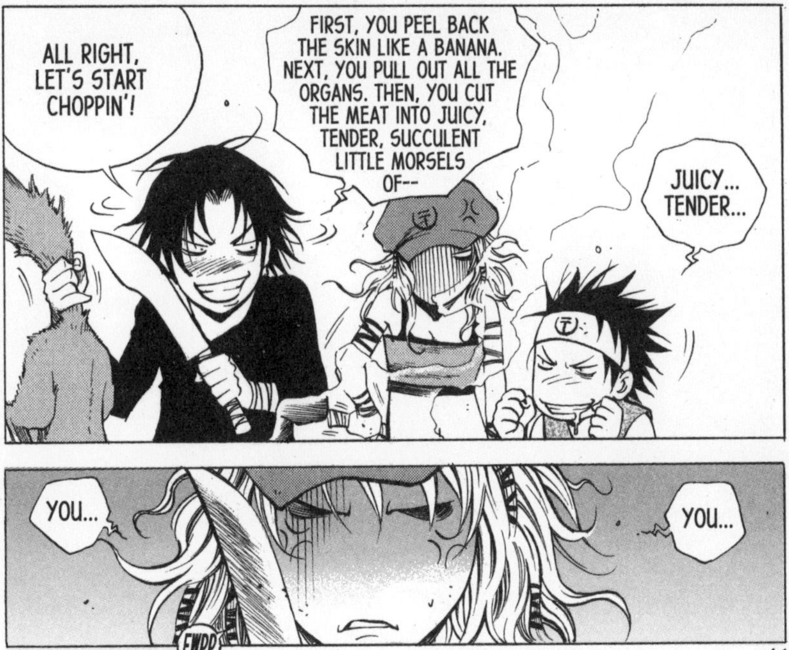
ALL RIGHT, LET'S START CHOPPIN'!
FIRST, YOU PEEL BACK THE SKIN LIKE A BANANA. NEXT, YOU PULL OUT ALL THE ORGANS. THEN, YOU CUT THE MEAT INTO JUICY, TENDER, SUCCULENT LITTLE MORSELS OF--
JUICY... TENDER...
YOU...
YOU...
FWPP

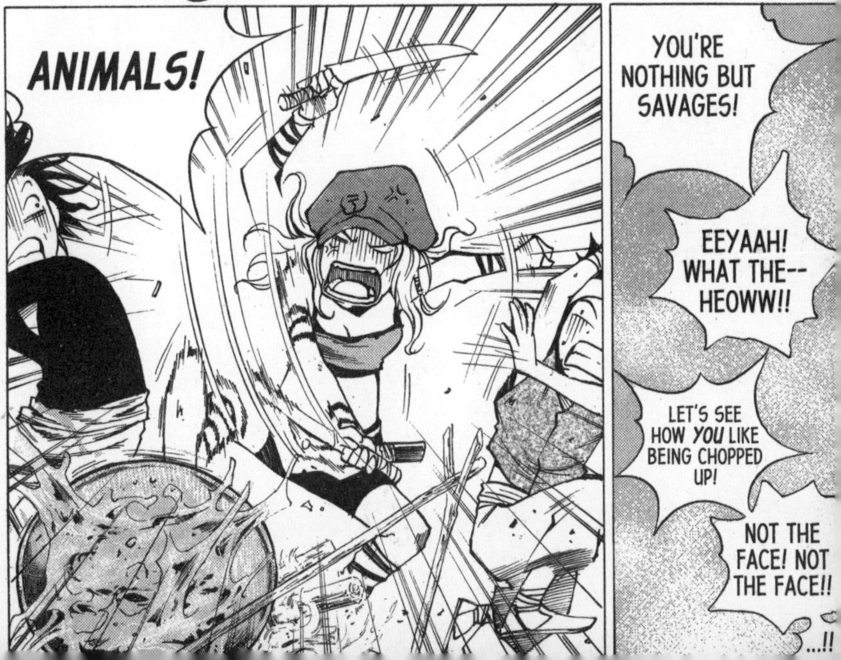
ANIMALS!
YOU'RE NOTHING BUT SAVAGES!
EEYAAH! WHAT THE-- HEOWW!!
LET'S SEE HOW *YOU* LIKE BEING CHOPPED UP!
NOT THE FACE! NOT THE FACE!!
...!!

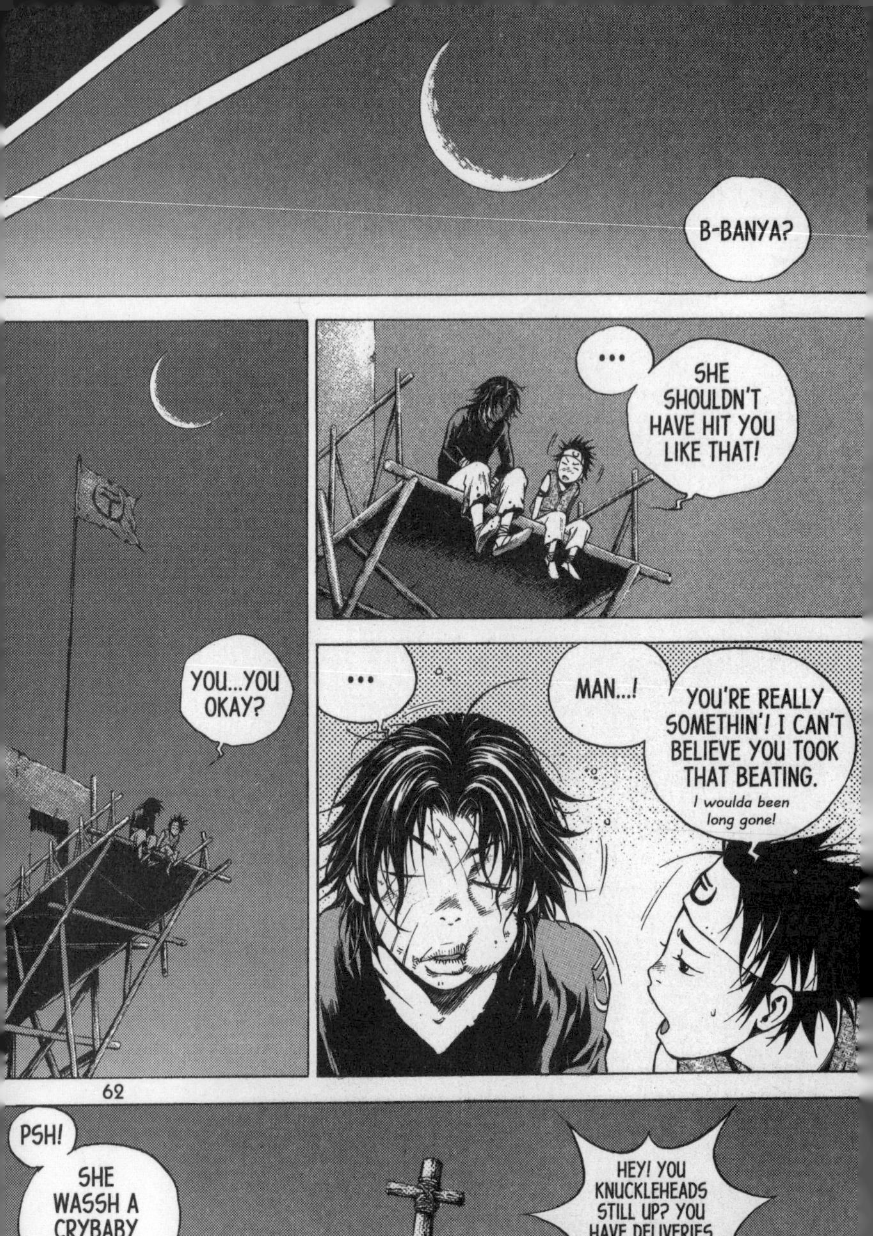
B-BANYA?
YOU...YOU OKAY?
...
SHE SHOULDN'T HAVE HIT YOU LIKE THAT!
...
MAN...!
YOU'RE REALLY SOMETHIN'! I CAN'T BELIEVE YOU TOOK THAT BEATING.
I woulda been long gone!

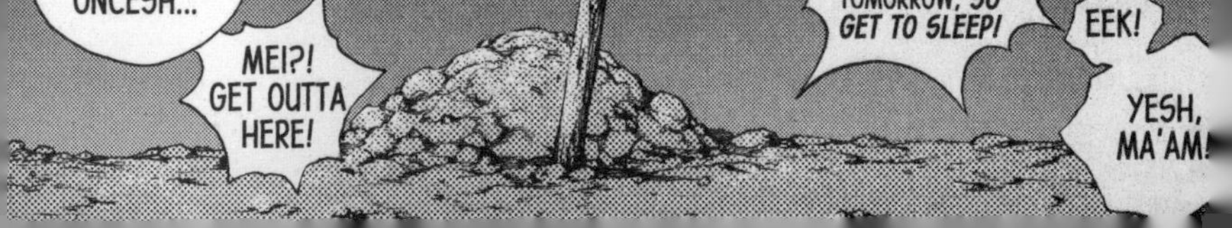
PSH!
SHE WASSH A CRYBABY ONCESH...
MEI?! GET OUTTA HERE!
HEY! YOU KNUCKLEHEADS STILL UP? YOU HAVE DELIVERIES TOMORROW, SO GET TO SLEEP!
EEK!
YESH, MA'AM!

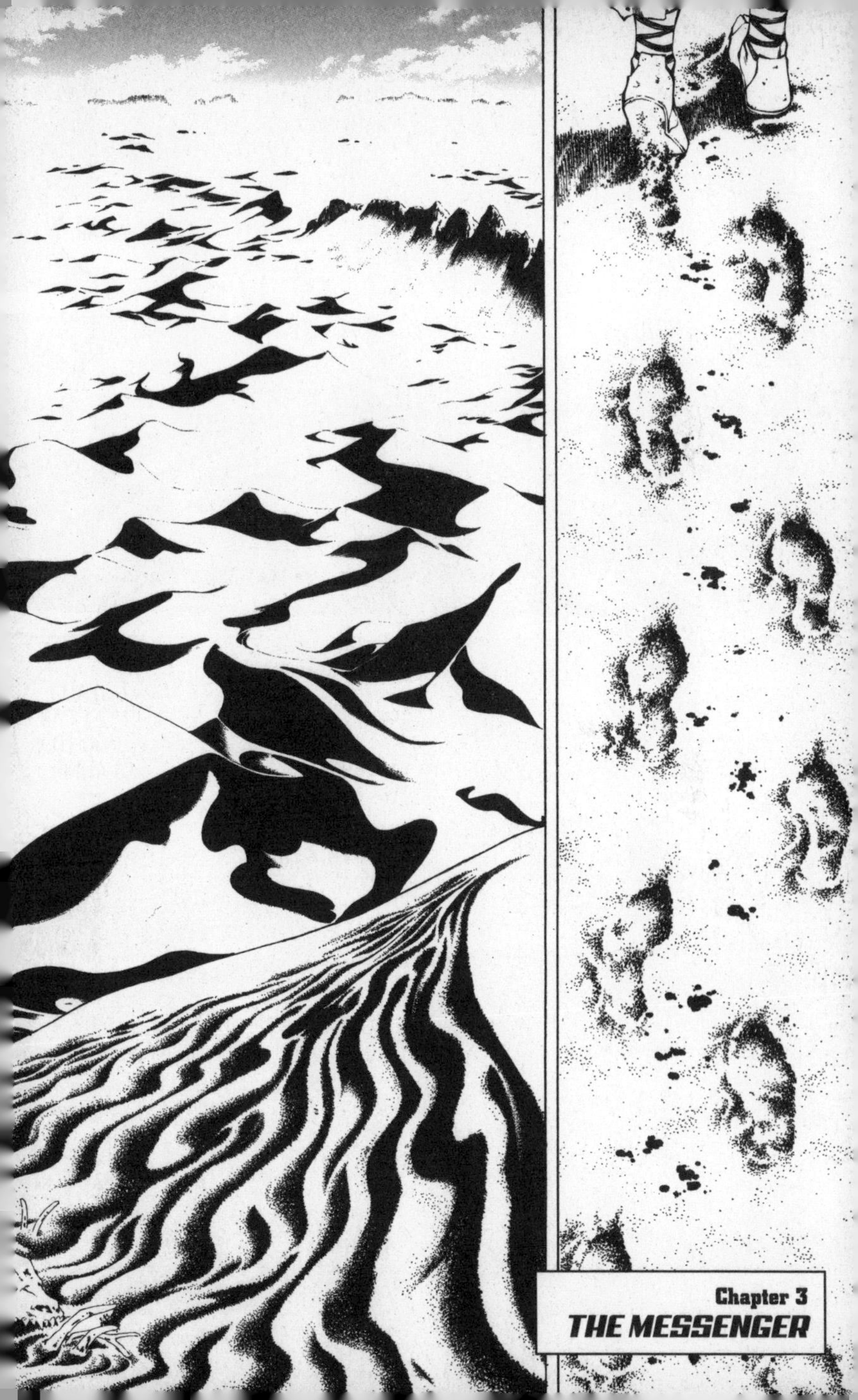
Chapter 3
THE MESSENGER

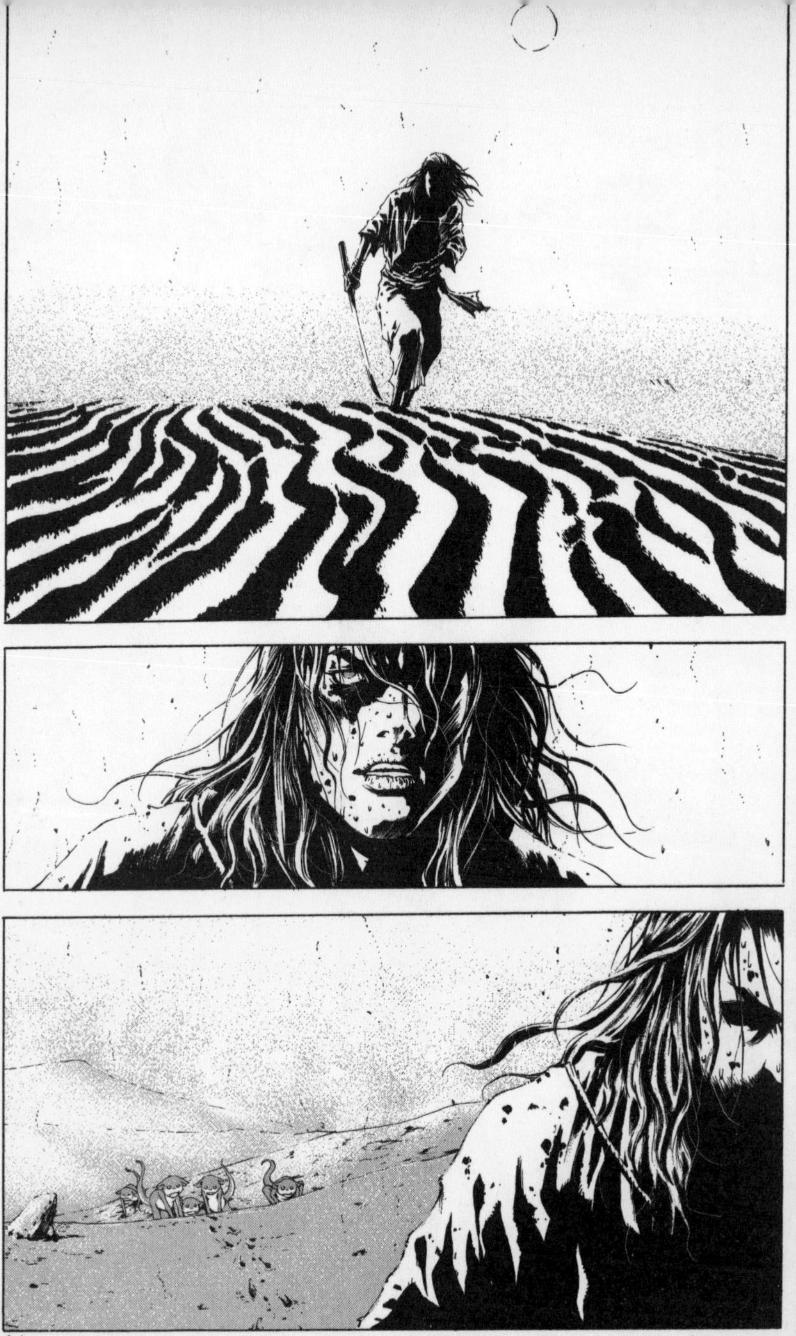

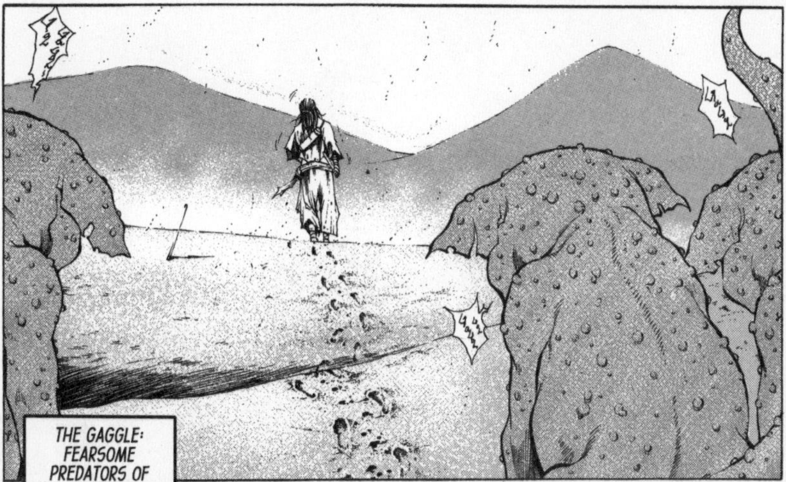

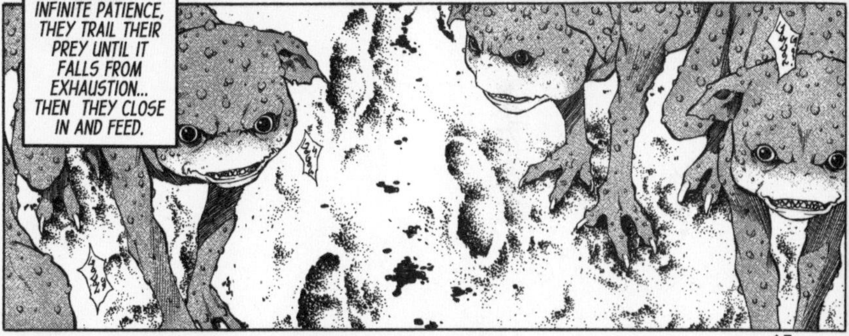
THE GAGGLE: FEARSOME PREDATORS OF THE DESERT. WITH INFINITE PATIENCE, THEY TRAIL THEIR PREY UNTIL IT FALLS FROM EXHAUSTION... THEN THEY CLOSE IN AND FEED.

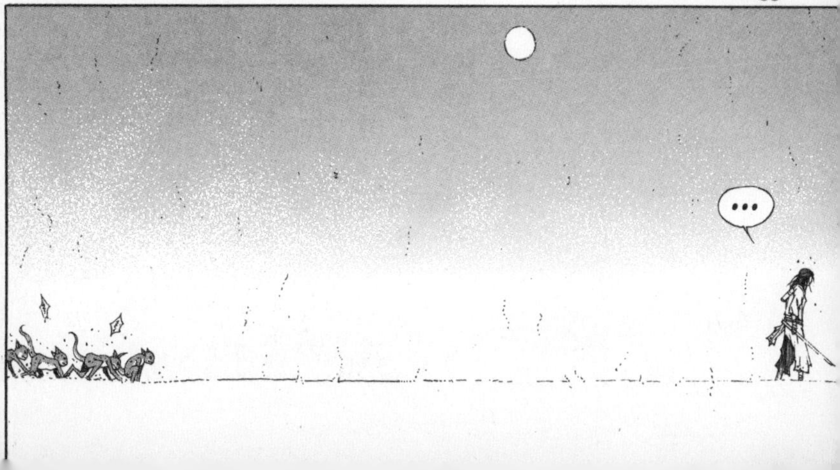
...

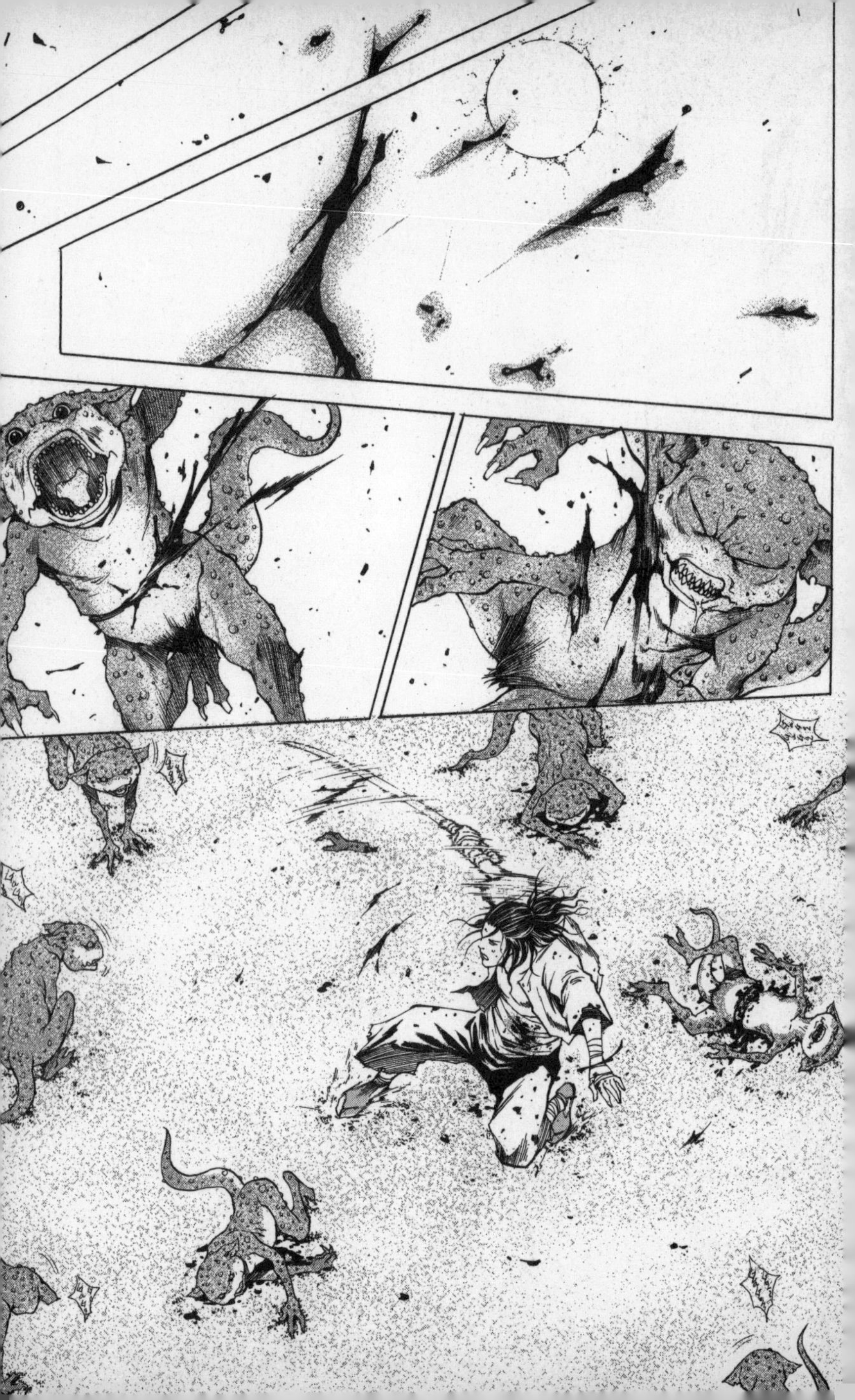

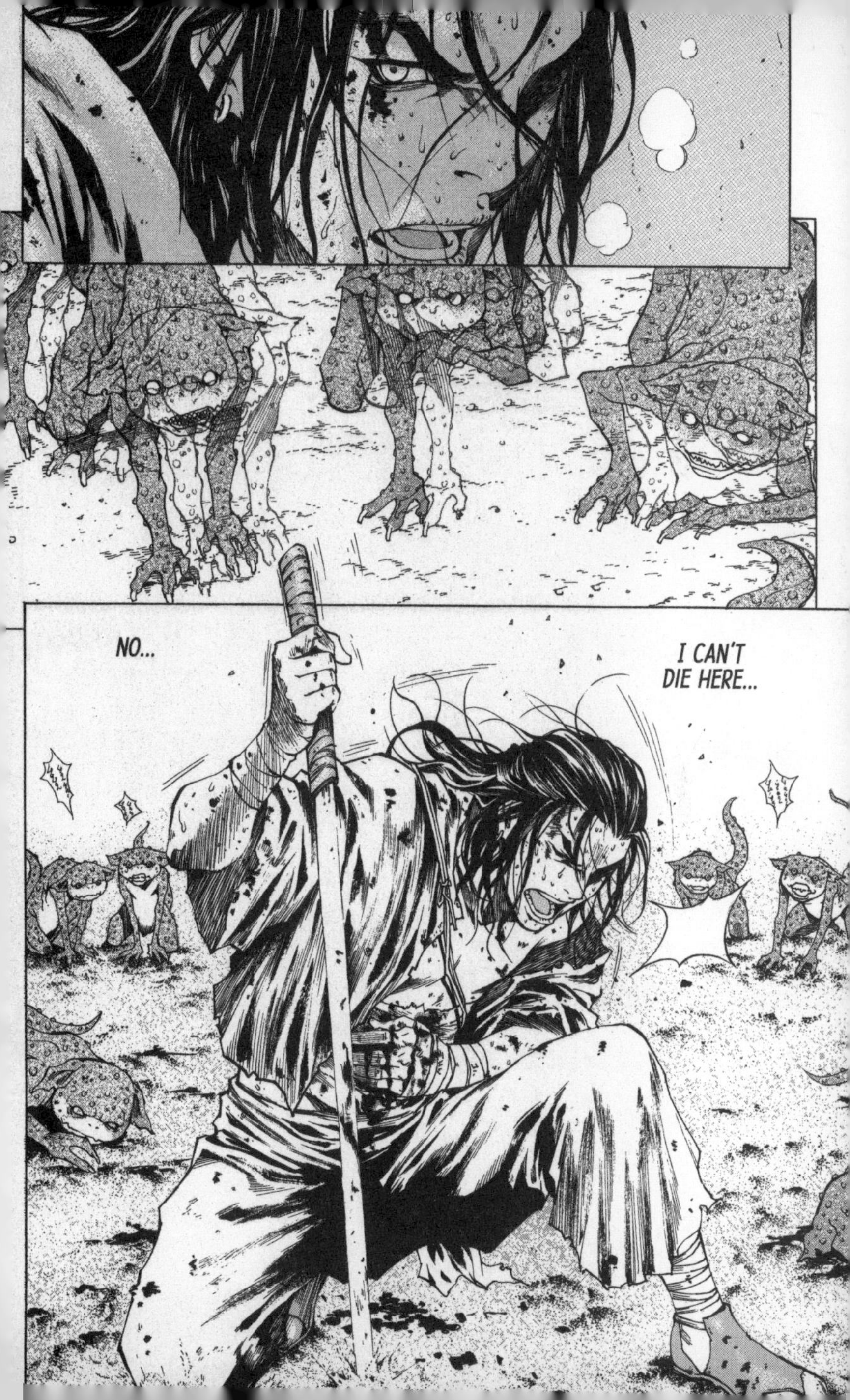
NO...
I CAN'T DIE HERE...

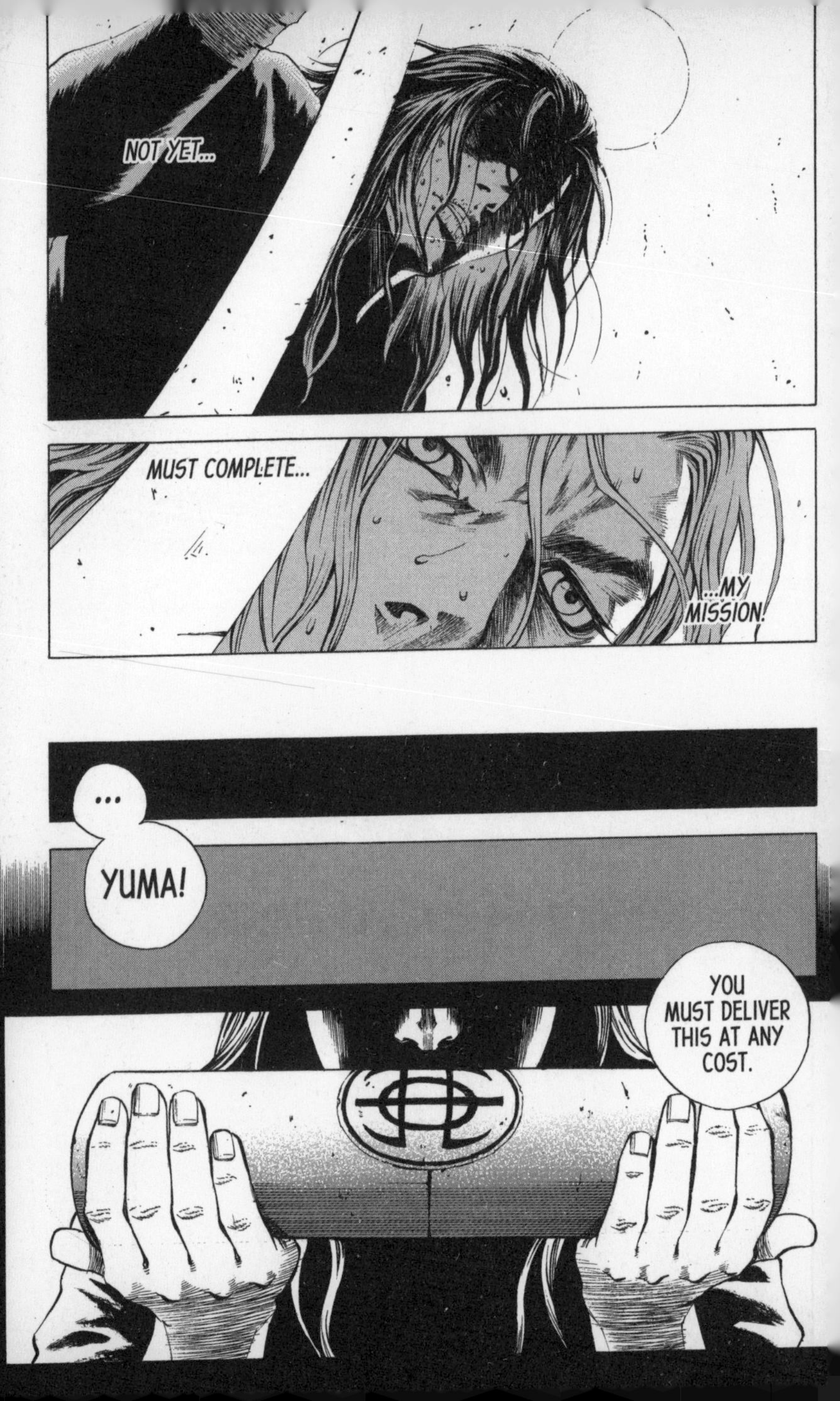
NOT YET...
MUST COMPLETE...
...MY MISSION!
...
YUMA!
YOU MUST DELIVER THIS AT ANY COST.

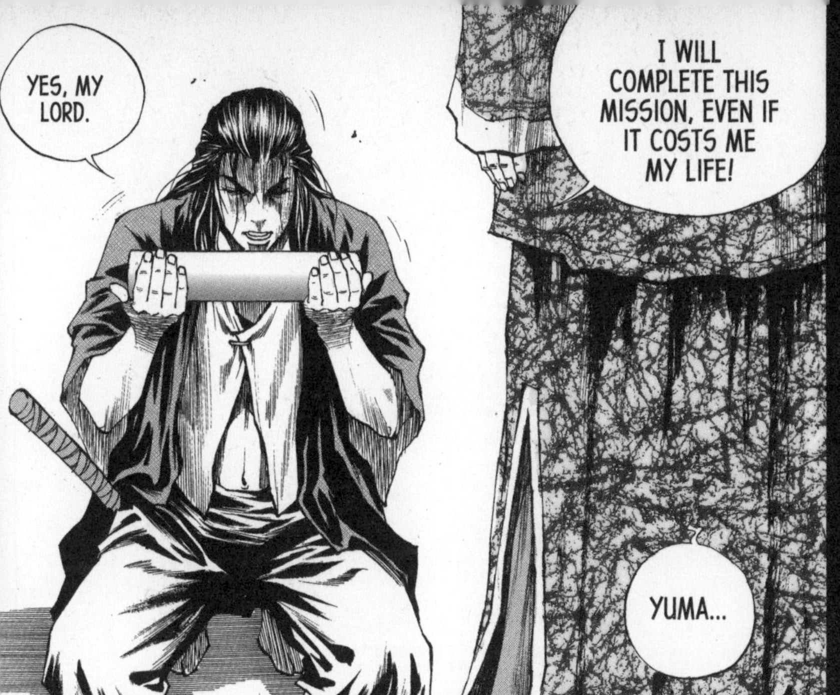
YES, MY LORD.
I WILL COMPLETE THIS MISSION, EVEN IF IT COSTS ME MY LIFE!
YUMA...
GAYA'S FUTURE DEPENDS ON YOU.

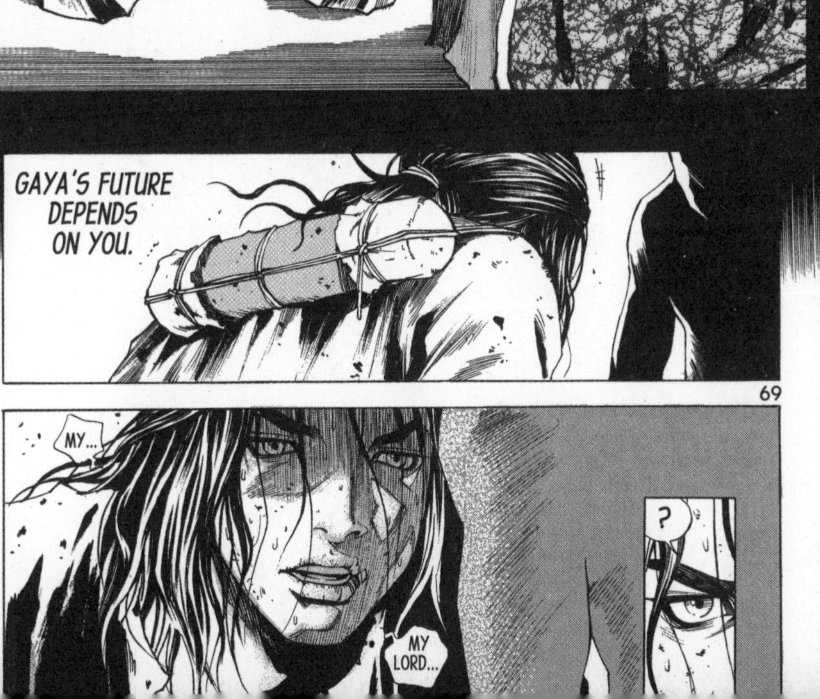
MY...
MY LORD...
?

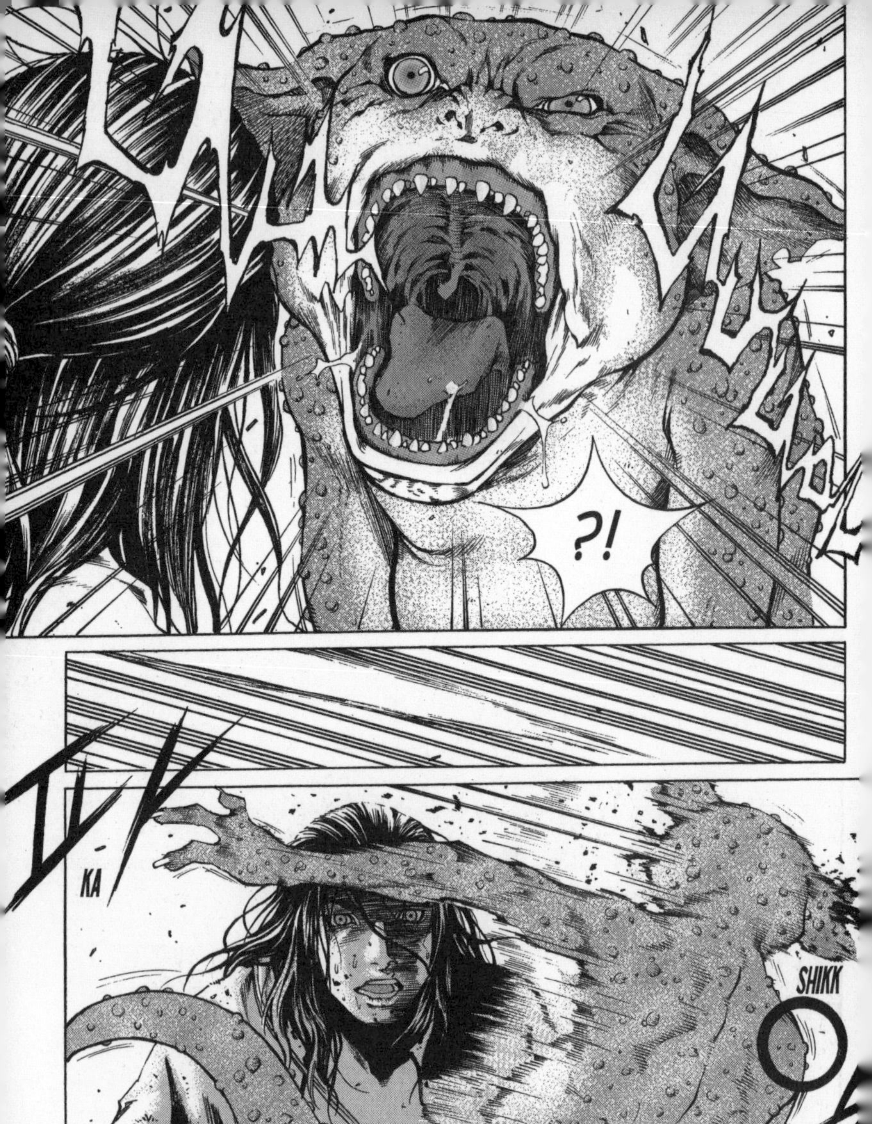
?!
KA
SHIKK

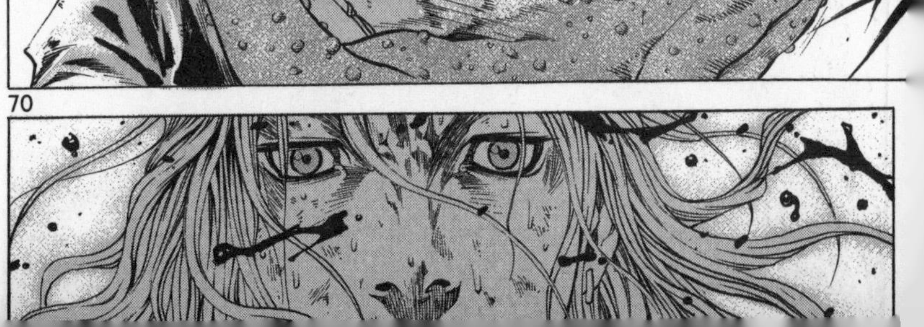

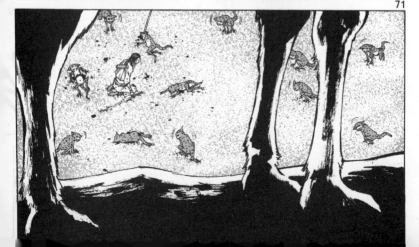

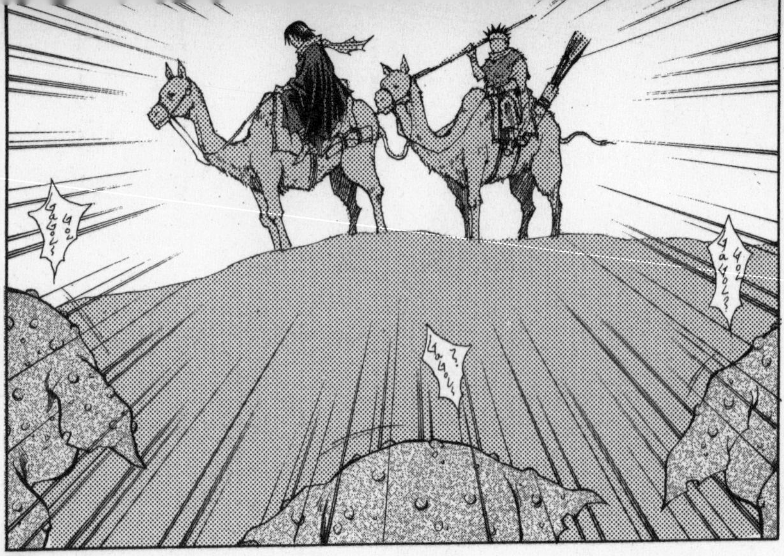

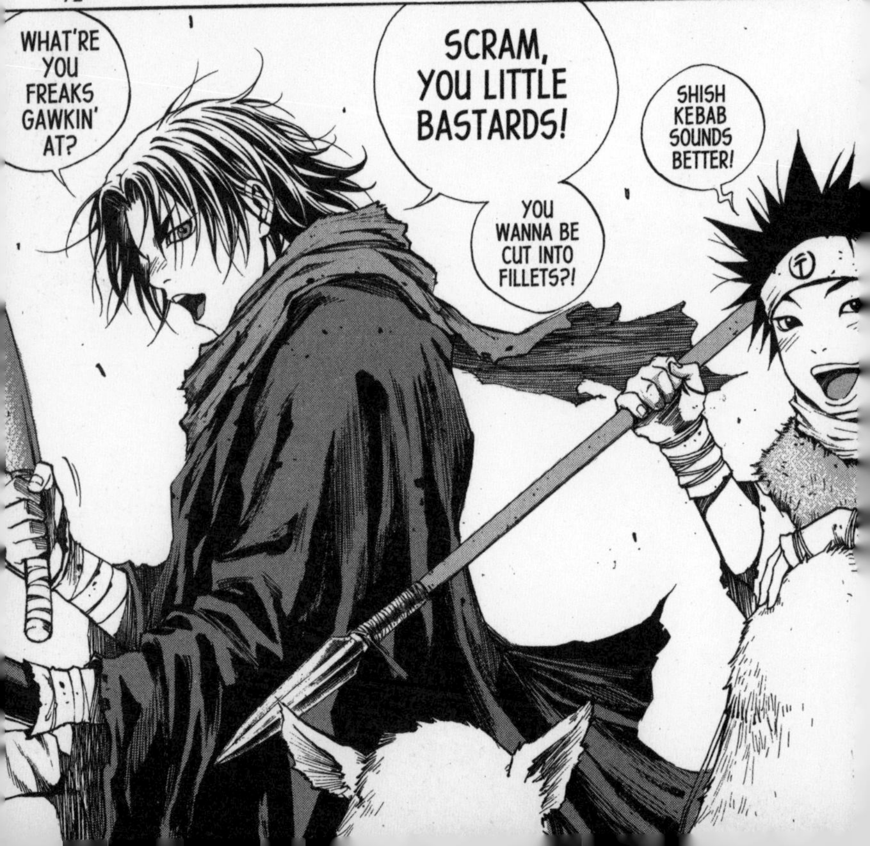
WHAT'RE YOU FREAKS GAWKIN' AT?
SCRAM, YOU LITTLE BASTARDS!
YOU WANNA BE CUT INTO FILLETS?!
SHISH KEBAB SOUNDS BETTER!

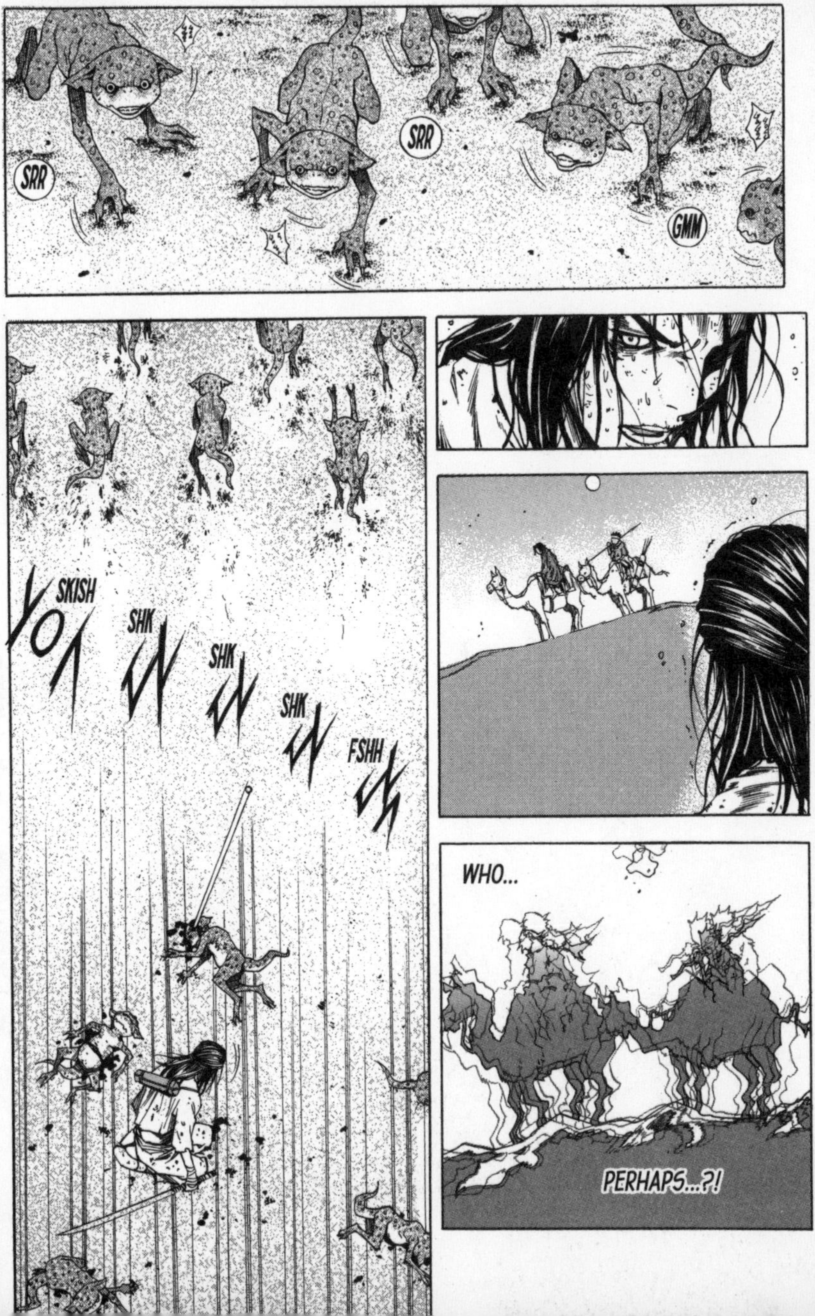
SRR
SRR
GMM
SKISH
SHK
SHK
SHK
FSHH
WHO...
PERHAPS...?!

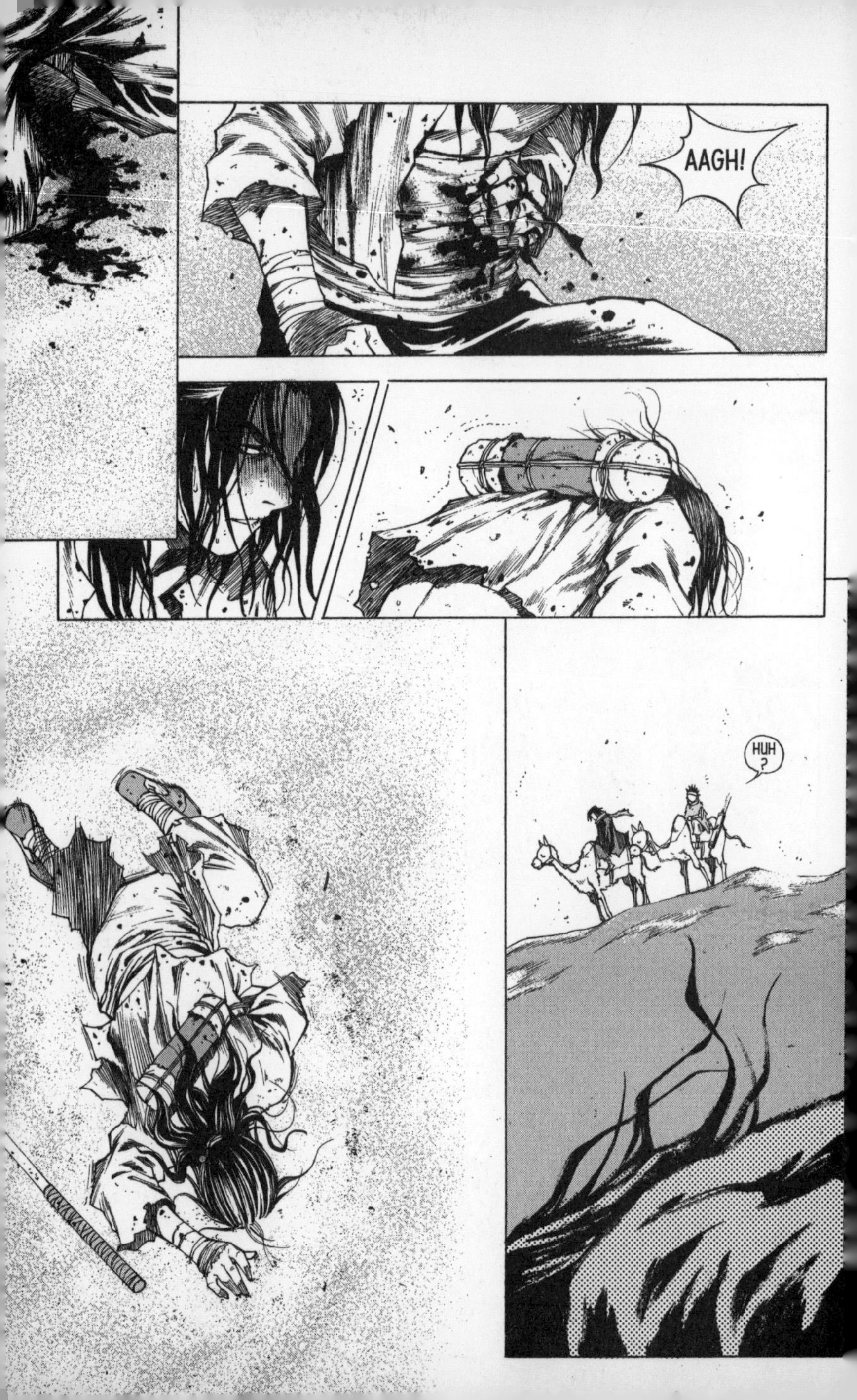
AAGH!
HUH?

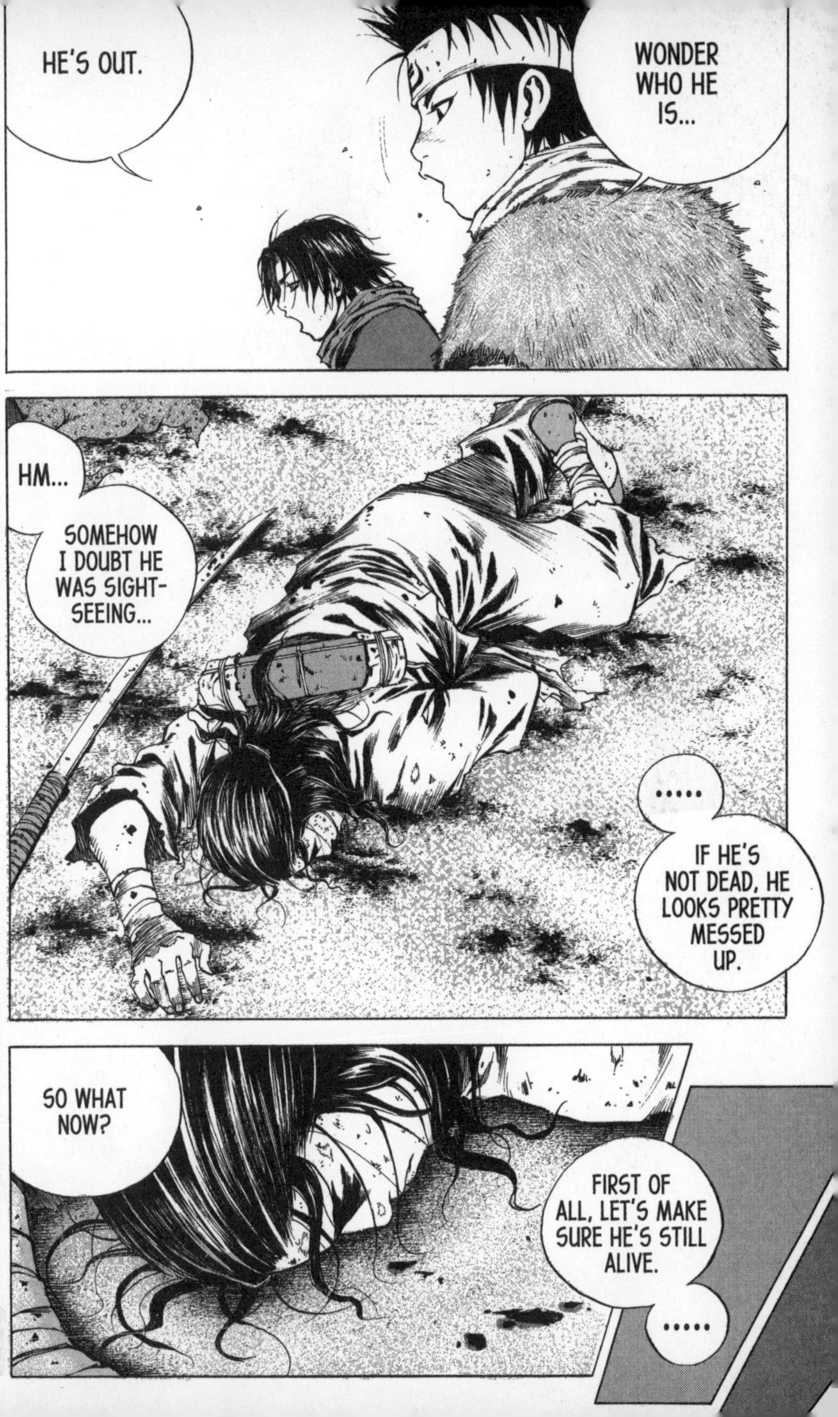
HE'S OUT.
WONDER WHO HE IS...
HM...
SOMEHOW I DOUBT HE WAS SIGHT-SEEING...
.....
IF HE'S NOT DEAD, HE LOOKS PRETTY MESSED UP.
SO WHAT NOW?
FIRST OF ALL, LET'S MAKE SURE HE'S STILL ALIVE.
.....

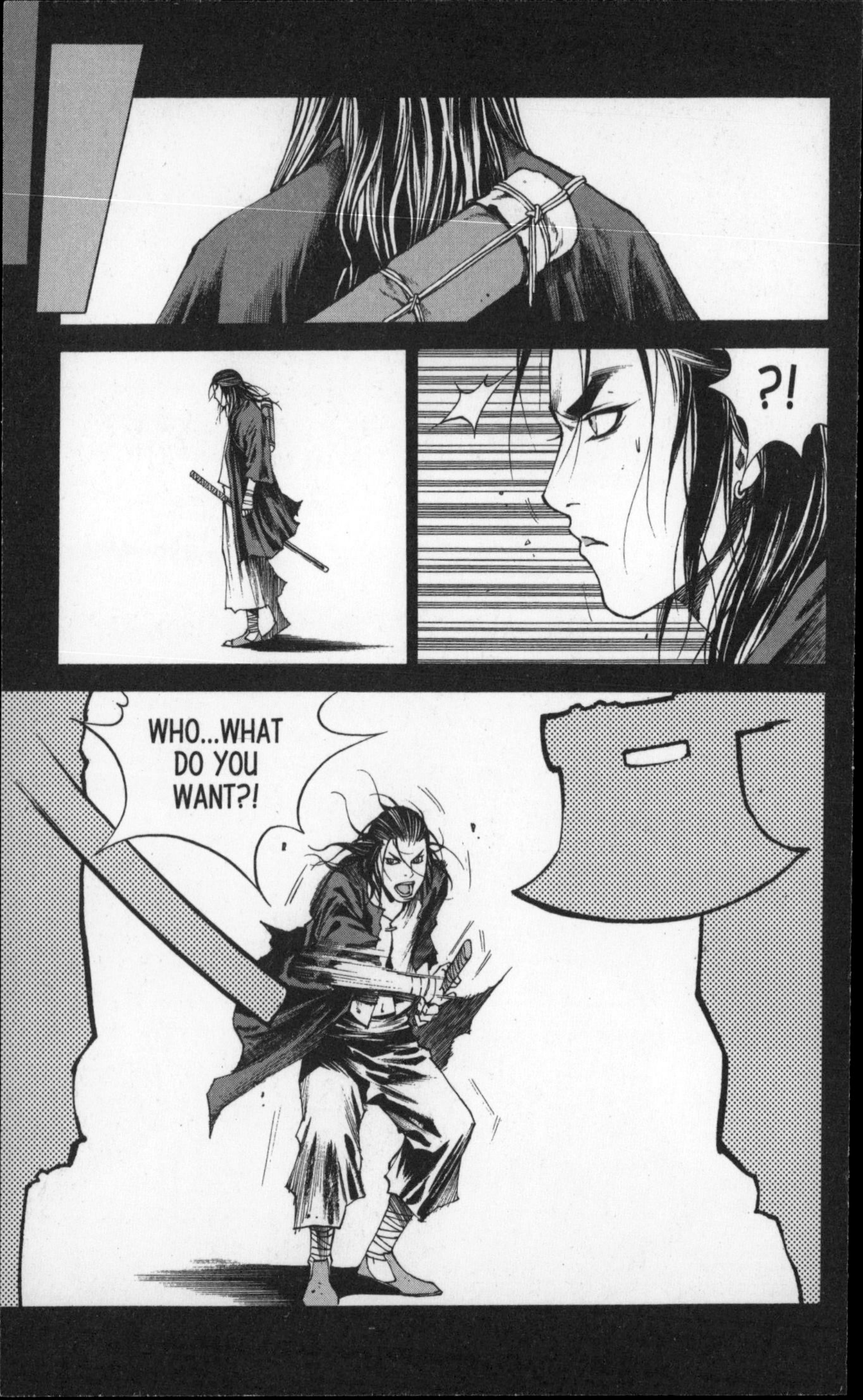
?!
WHO...WHAT DO YOU WANT?!

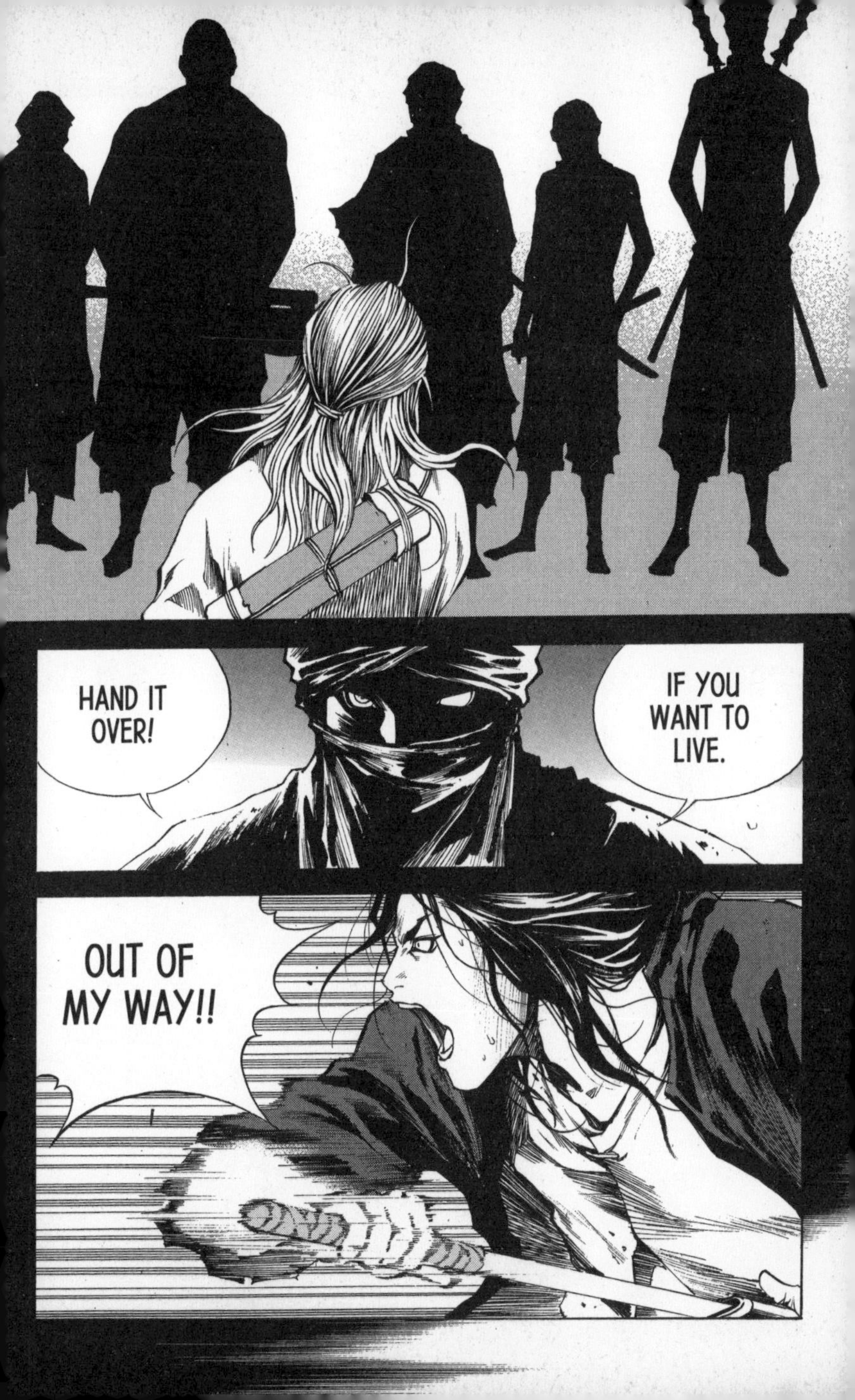
IF YOU WANT TO LIVE.
HAND IT OVER!
OUT OF MY WAY!!

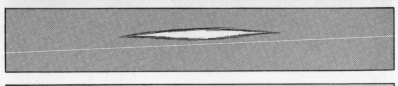

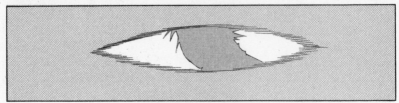

.....

HE'S
AWAKE!

?!

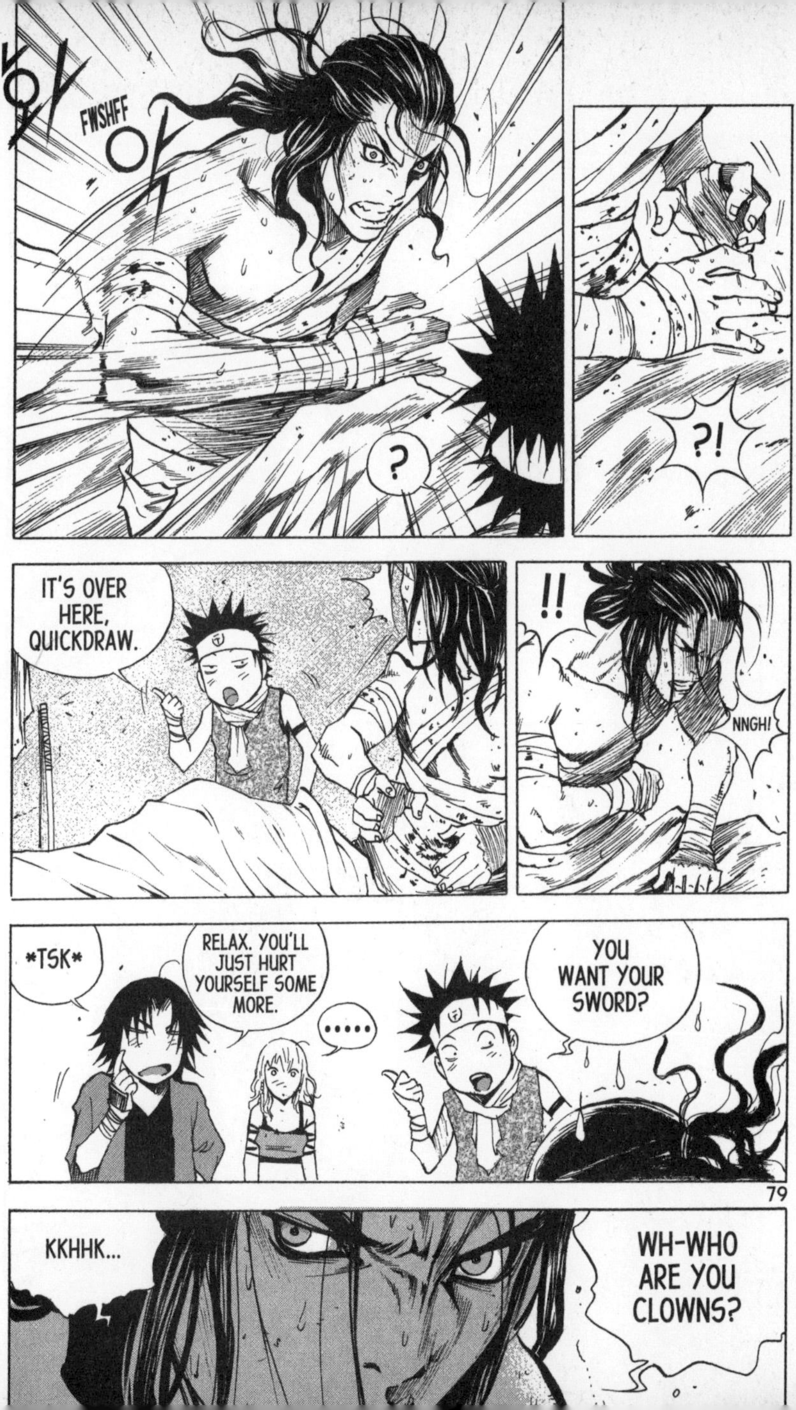
FWSHFF
?
?!
IT'S OVER HERE, QUICKDRAW.
!!
NNGH!
TSK
RELAX. YOU'LL JUST HURT YOURSELF SOME MORE.
.....
YOU WANT YOUR SWORD?
KKHHK...
WH-WHO ARE YOU CLOWNS?

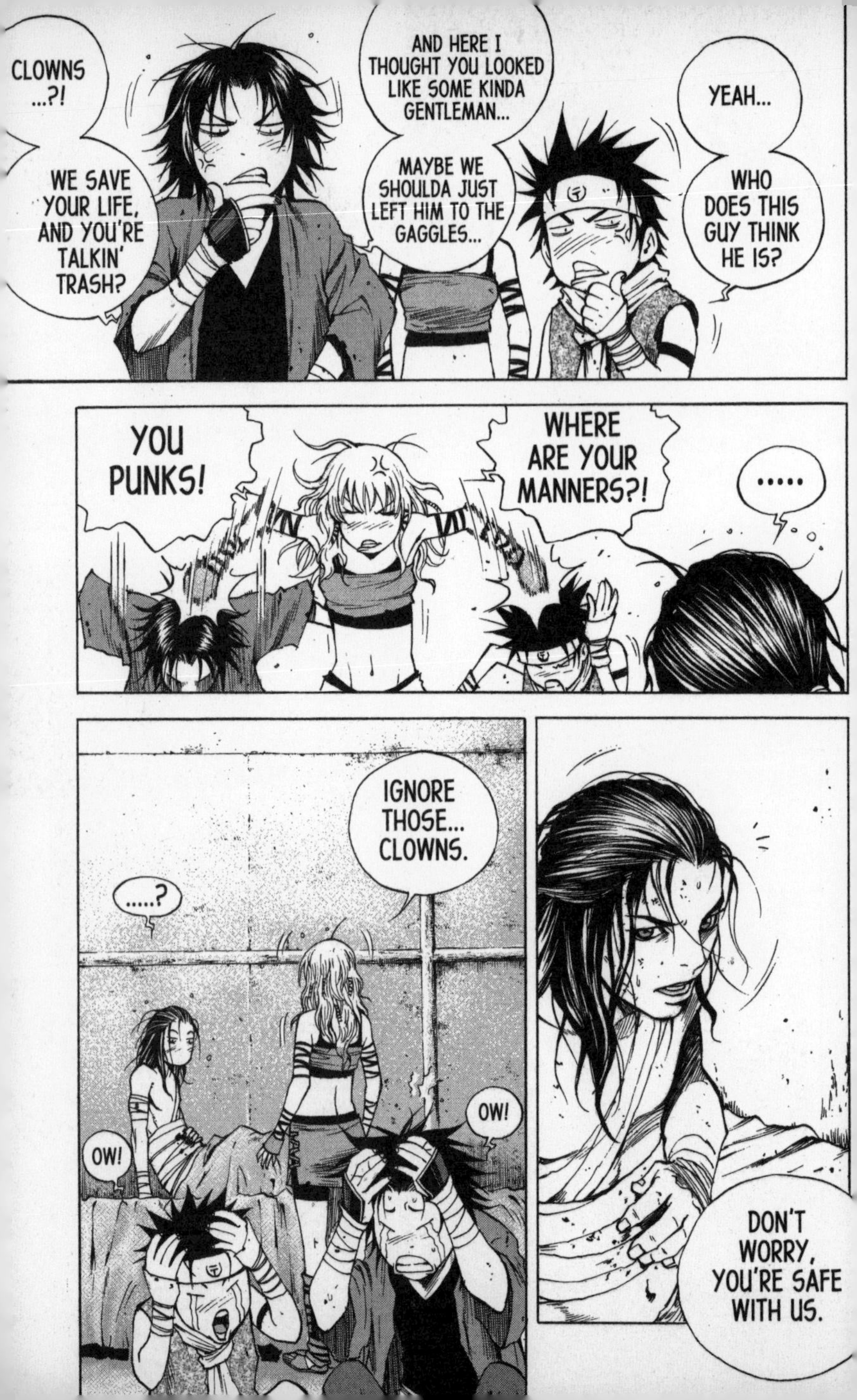
CLOWNS ...?!
WE SAVE YOUR LIFE, AND YOU'RE TALKIN' TRASH?
AND HERE I THOUGHT YOU LOOKED LIKE SOME KINDA GENTLEMAN...
MAYBE WE SHOULDA JUST LEFT HIM TO THE GAGGLES...
YEAH...
WHO DOES THIS GUY THINK HE IS?
YOU PUNKS!
WHERE ARE YOUR MANNERS?!
.....
.....?
IGNORE THOSE... CLOWNS.
OW!
OW!
DON'T WORRY, YOU'RE SAFE WITH US.

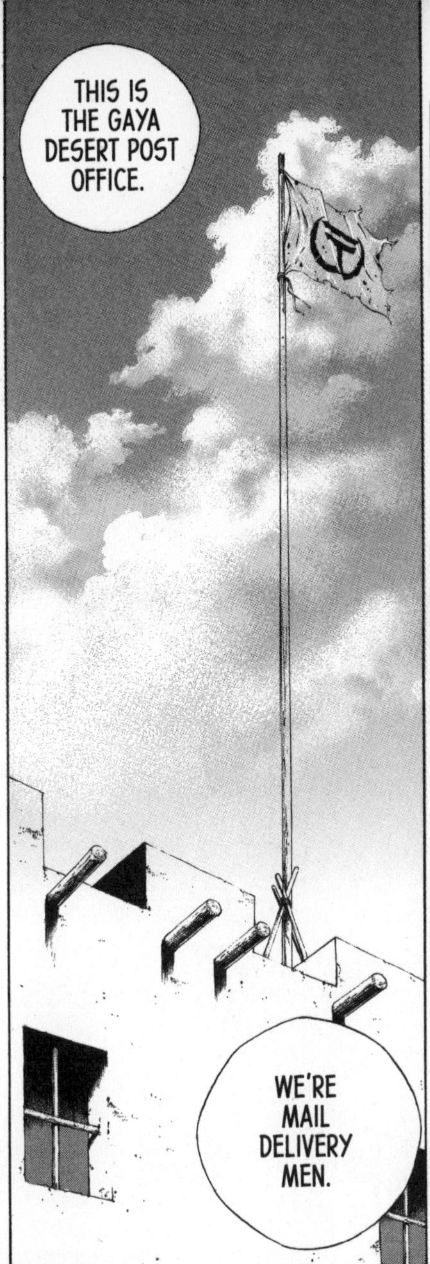
THIS IS THE GAYA DESERT POST OFFICE.
WE'RE MAIL DELIVERY MEN.

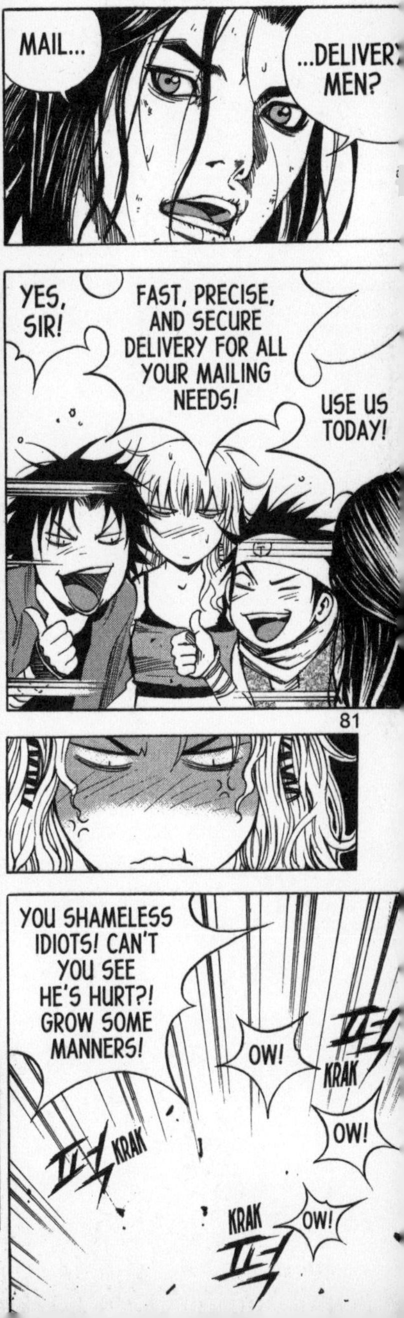
MAIL...
...DELIVERY MEN?
YES, SIR!
FAST, PRECISE, AND SECURE DELIVERY FOR ALL YOUR MAILING NEEDS!
USE US TODAY!
YOU SHAMELESS IDIOTS! CAN'T YOU SEE HE'S HURT?! GROW SOME MANNERS!
OW!
KRAK
OW!
KRAK
KRAK
OW!

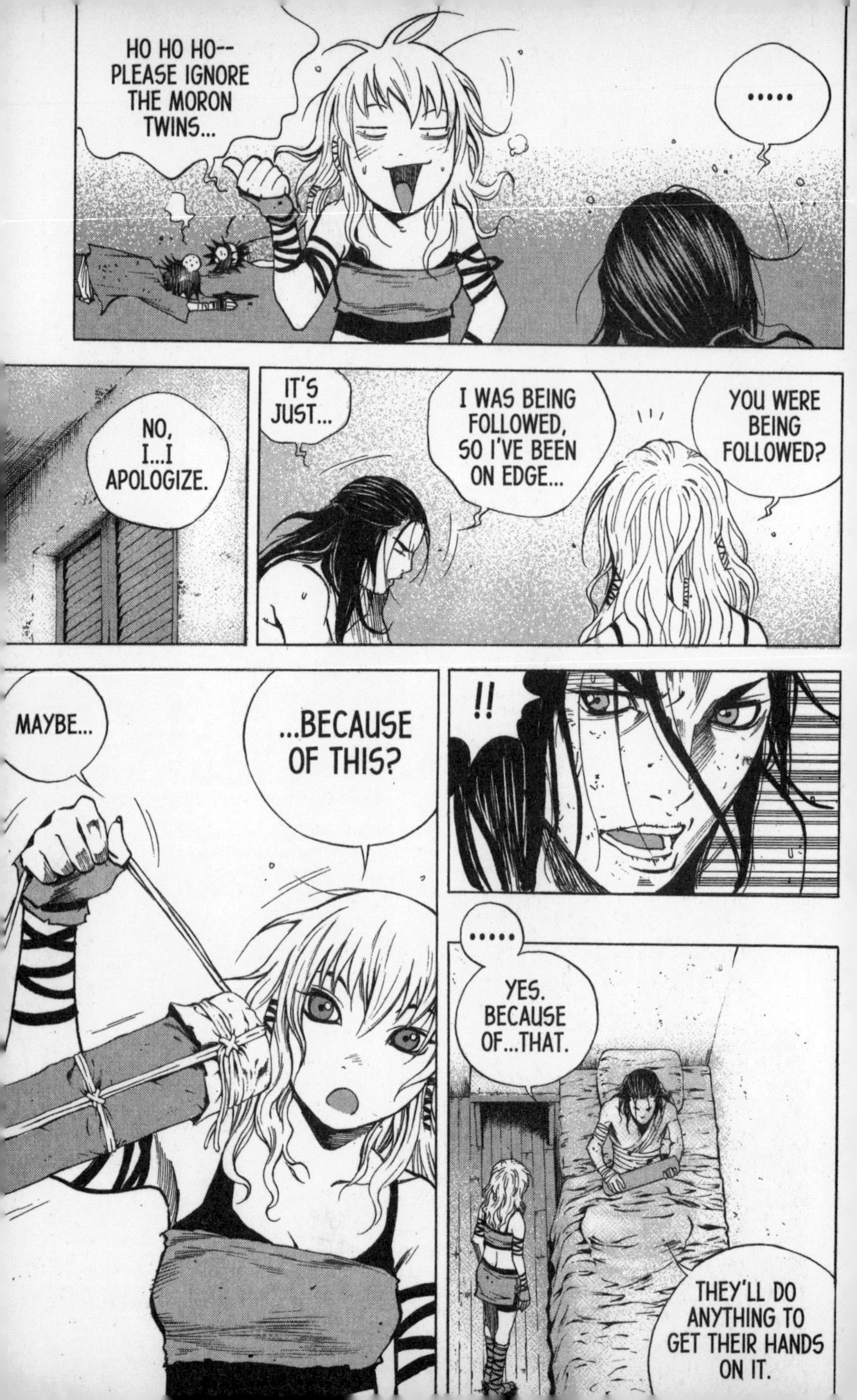
HO HO HO--
PLEASE IGNORE THE MORON TWINS...
.....
NO, I...I APOLOGIZE.
IT'S JUST...
I WAS BEING FOLLOWED, SO I'VE BEEN ON EDGE...
YOU WERE BEING FOLLOWED?
MAYBE...
...BECAUSE OF THIS?
!!
.....
YES. BECAUSE OF...THAT.
THEY'LL DO ANYTHING TO GET THEIR HANDS ON IT.

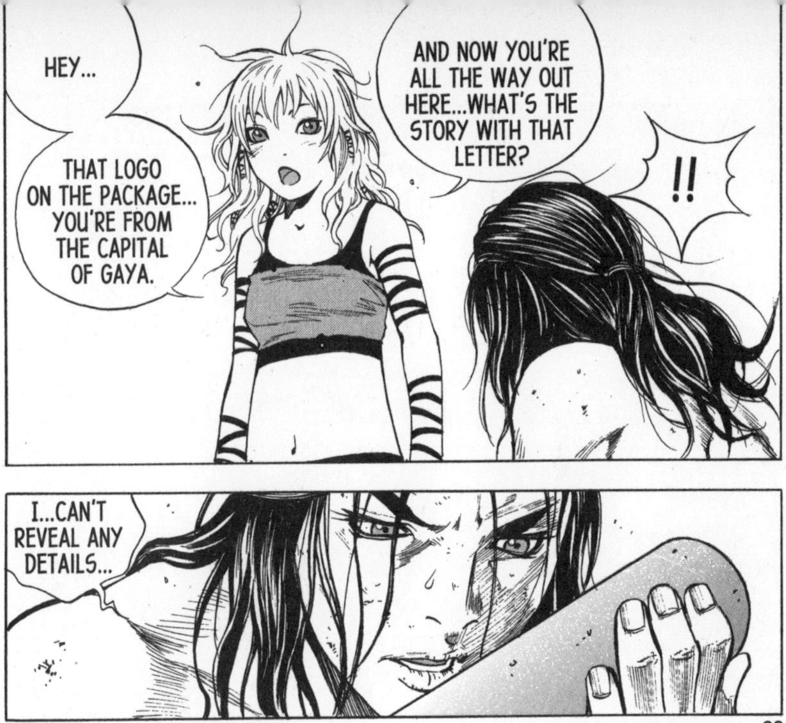
HEY...
THAT LOGO ON THE PACKAGE... YOU'RE FROM THE CAPITAL OF GAYA.
AND NOW YOU'RE ALL THE WAY OUT HERE...WHAT'S THE STORY WITH THAT LETTER?
!!
I...CAN'T REVEAL ANY DETAILS...

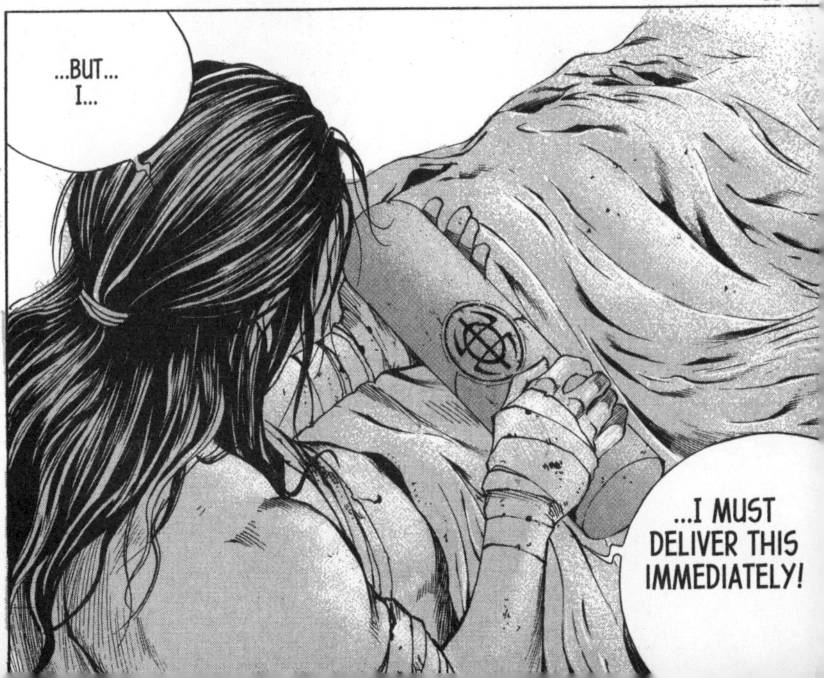
...BUT... I...
...I MUST DELIVER THIS IMMEDIATELY!

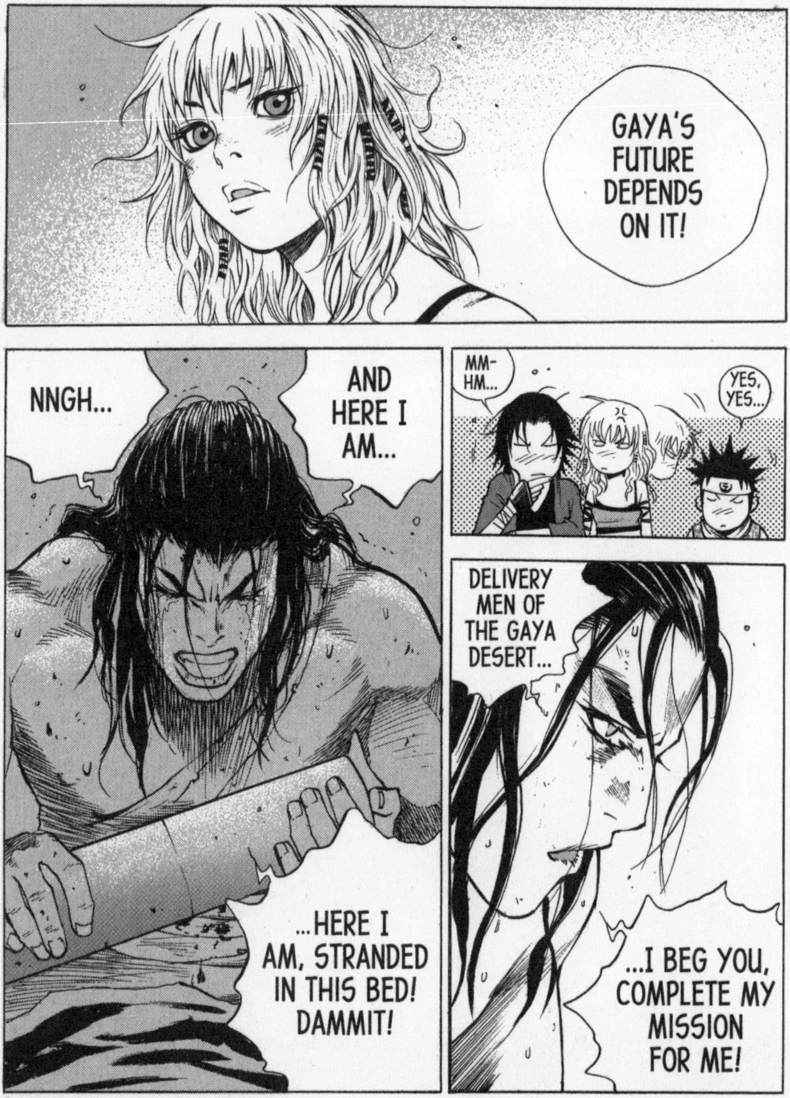
GAYA'S FUTURE DEPENDS ON IT!
NNGH...
AND HERE I AM...
...HERE I AM, STRANDED IN THIS BED! DAMMIT!
MM-HM...
YES, YES...
DELIVERY MEN OF THE GAYA DESERT...
...I BEG YOU, COMPLETE MY MISSION FOR ME!

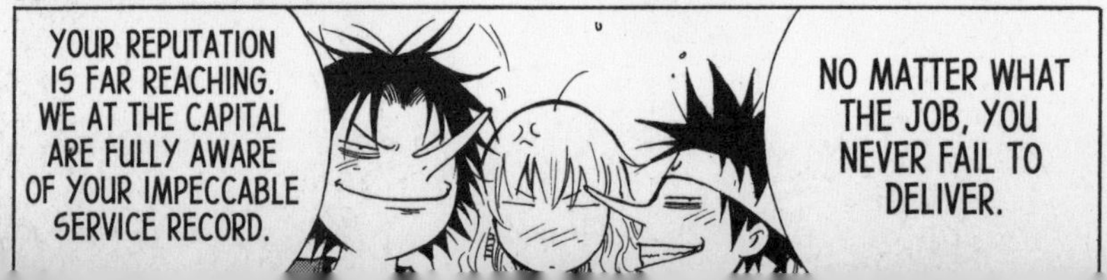
YOUR REPUTATION IS FAR REACHING. WE AT THE CAPITAL ARE FULLY AWARE OF YOUR IMPECCABLE SERVICE RECORD.
NO MATTER WHAT THE JOB, YOU NEVER FAIL TO DELIVER.

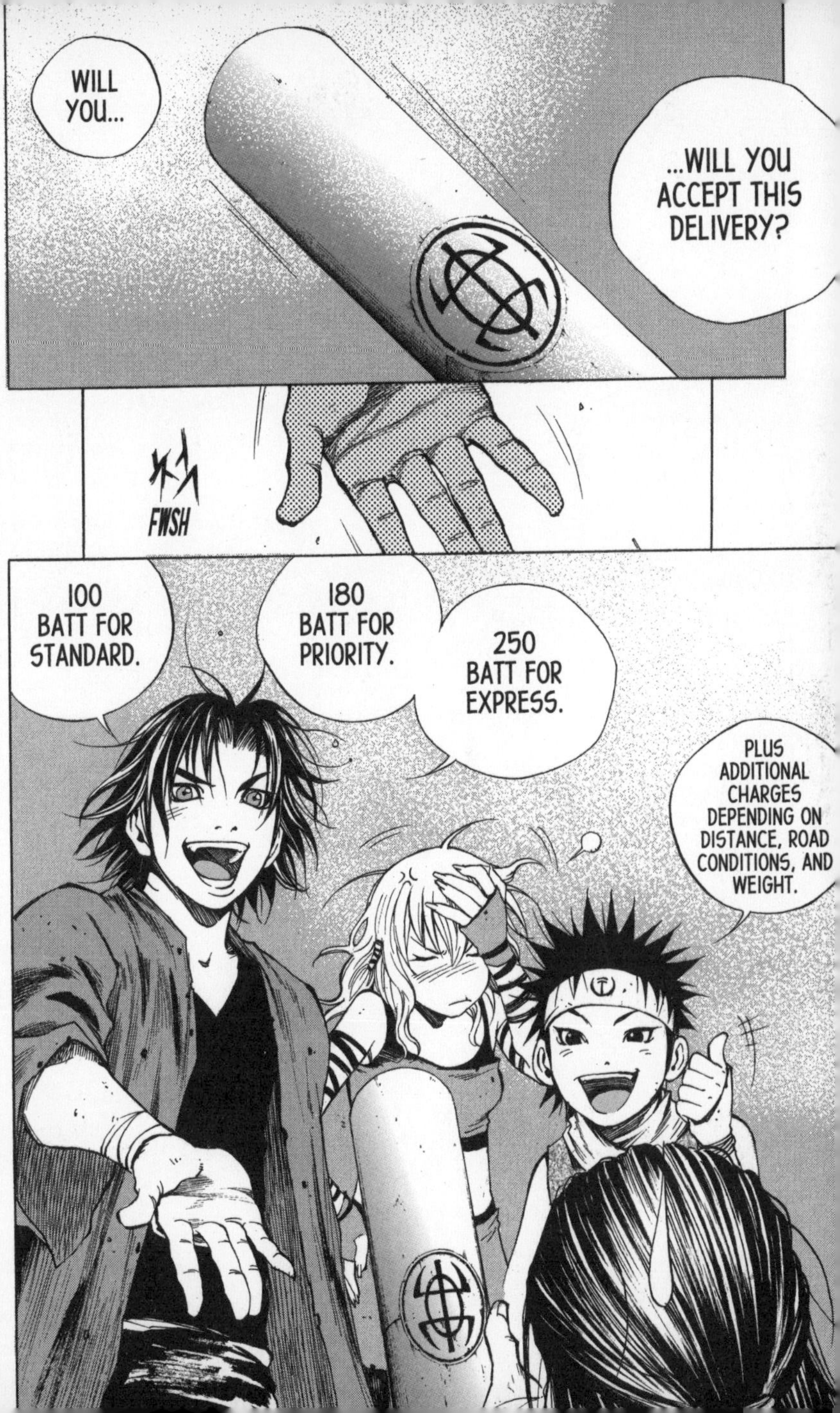
WILL YOU...
...WILL YOU ACCEPT THIS DELIVERY?
FWSH
100 BATT FOR STANDARD.
180 BATT FOR PRIORITY.
250 BATT FOR EXPRESS.
PLUS ADDITIONAL CHARGES DEPENDING ON DISTANCE, ROAD CONDITIONS, AND WEIGHT.

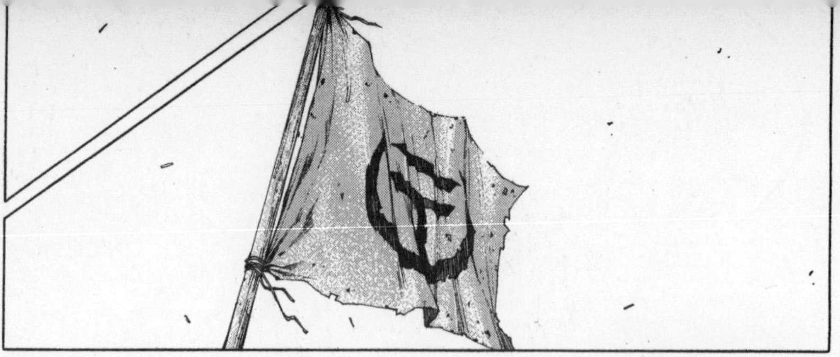

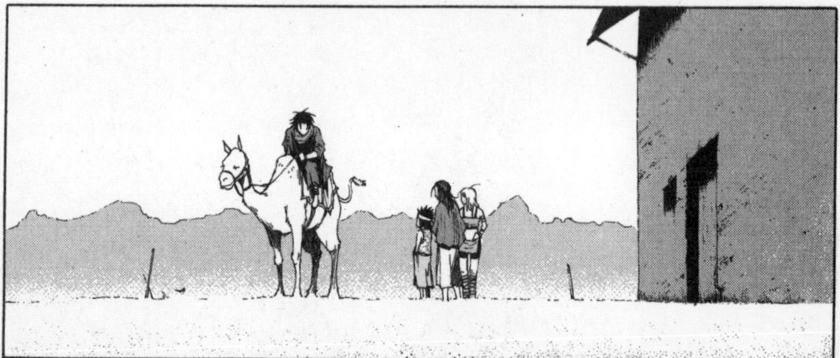

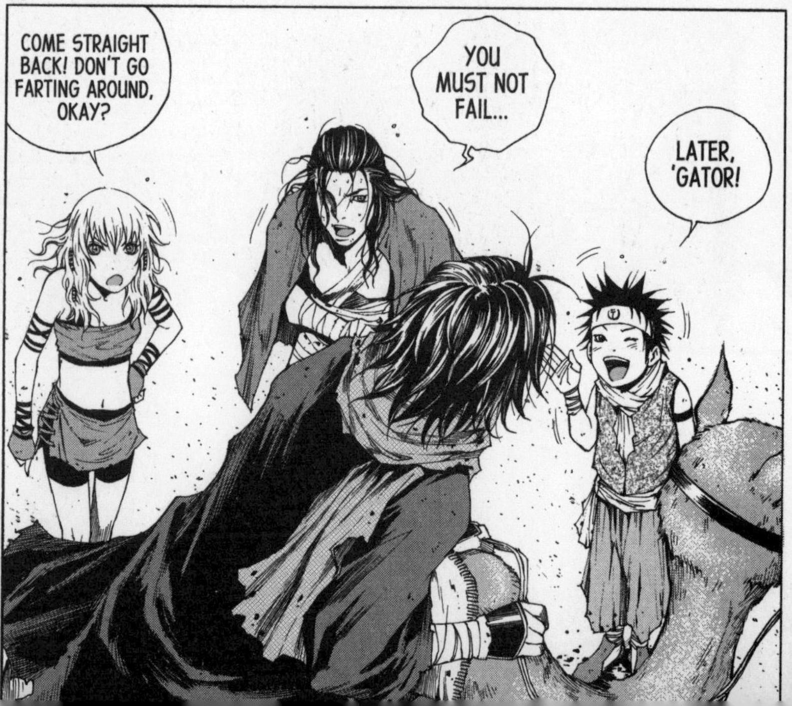
COME STRAIGHT BACK! DON'T GO FARTING AROUND, OKAY?
YOU MUST NOT FAIL...
LATER, 'GATOR!

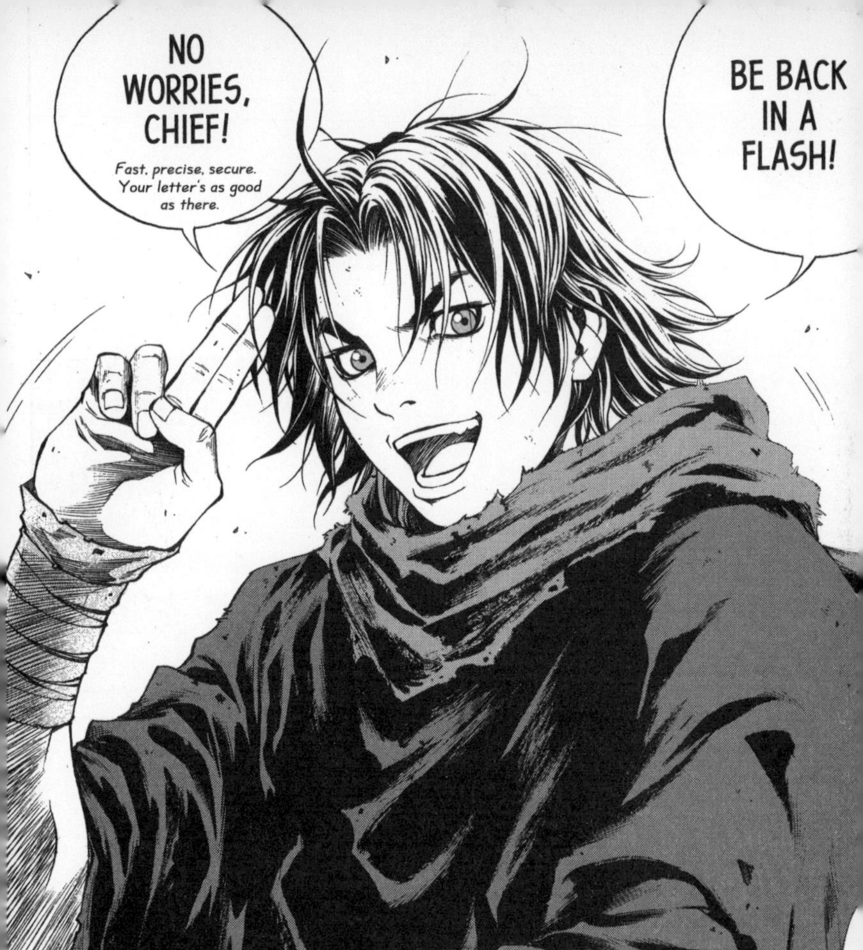
NO WORRIES, CHIEF!
Fast, precise, secure. Your letter's as good as there.
BE BACK IN A FLASH!
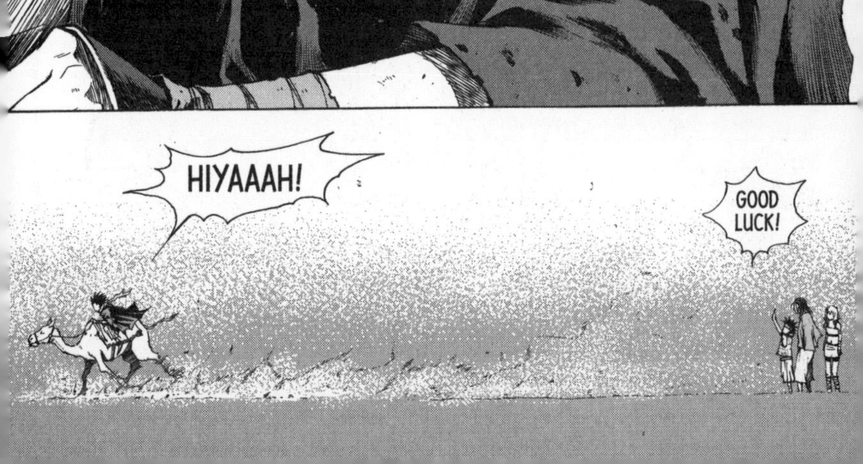
HIYAAAH!
GOOD LUCK!

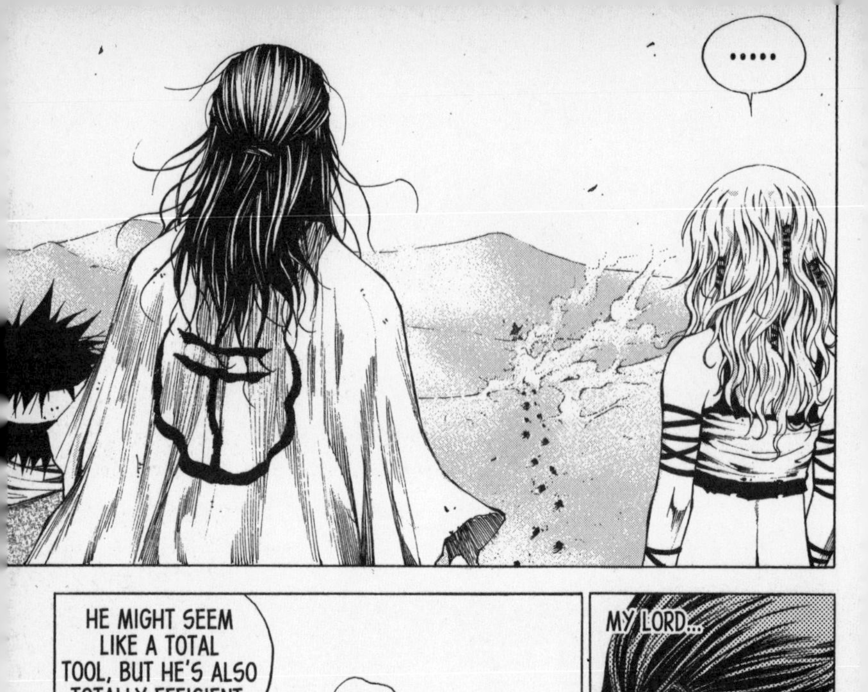
.....
HE MIGHT SEEM LIKE A TOTAL TOOL, BUT HE'S ALSO TOTALLY EFFICIENT. DON'T WORRY.
.....
BANYA RULES!
MY LORD...

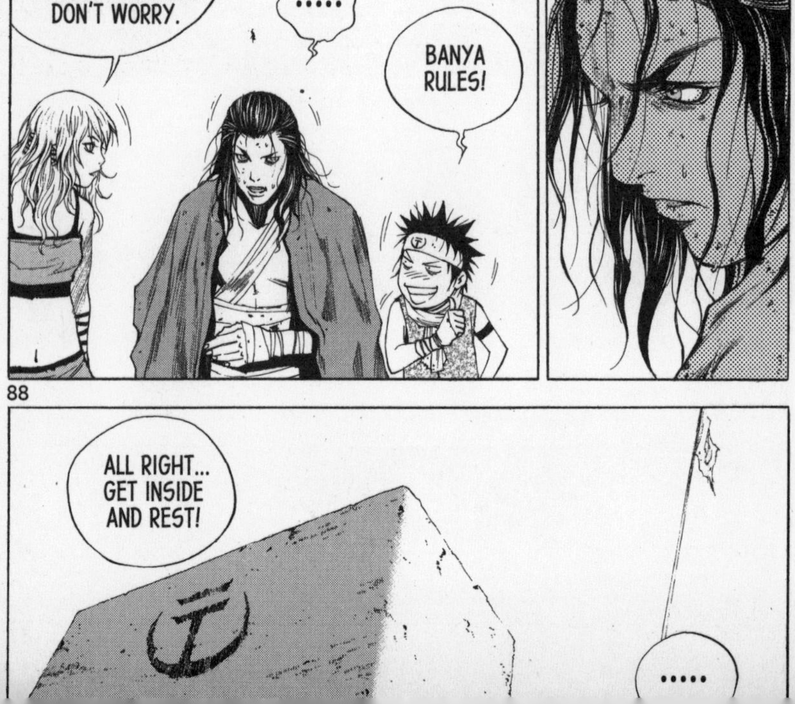
ALL RIGHT... GET INSIDE AND REST!
.....

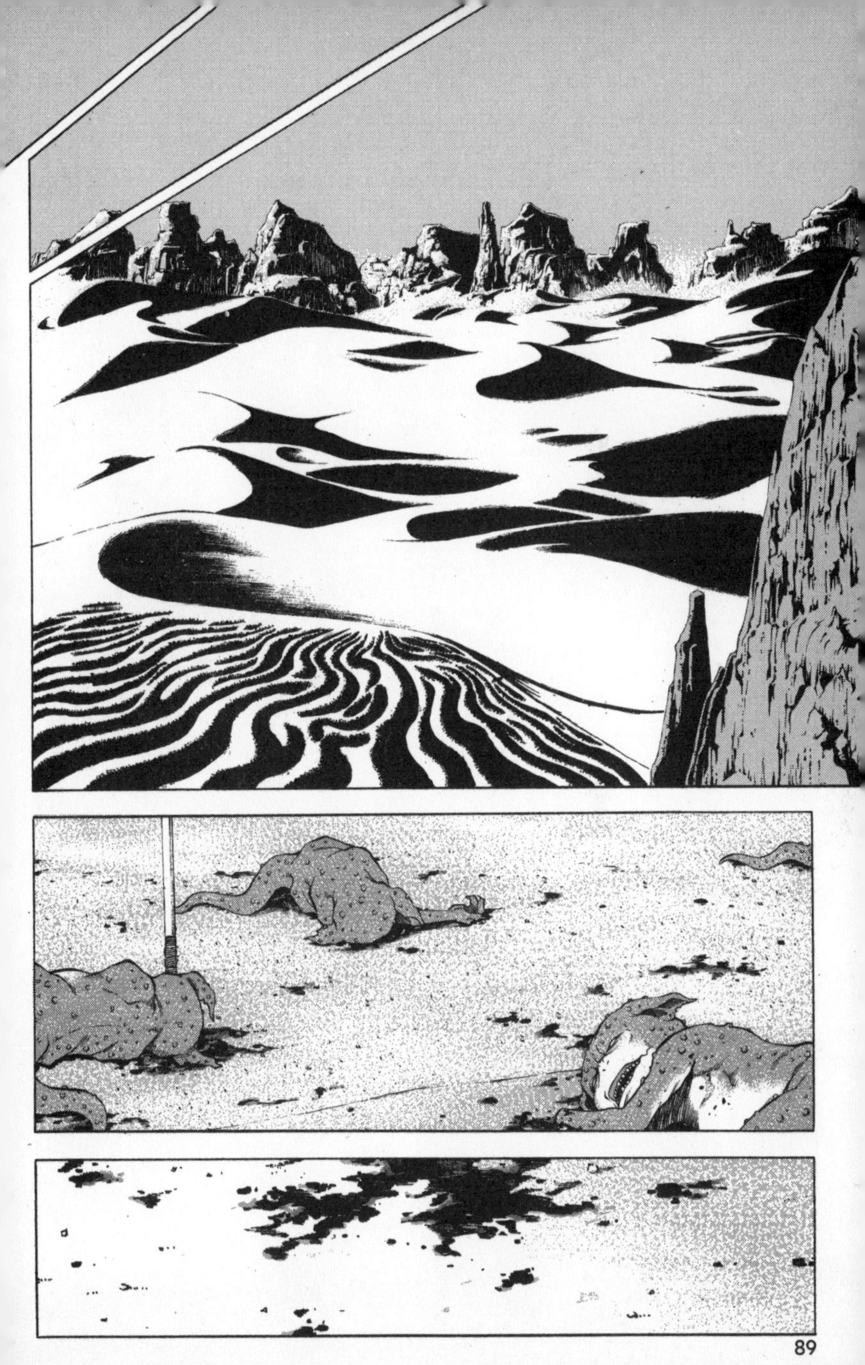

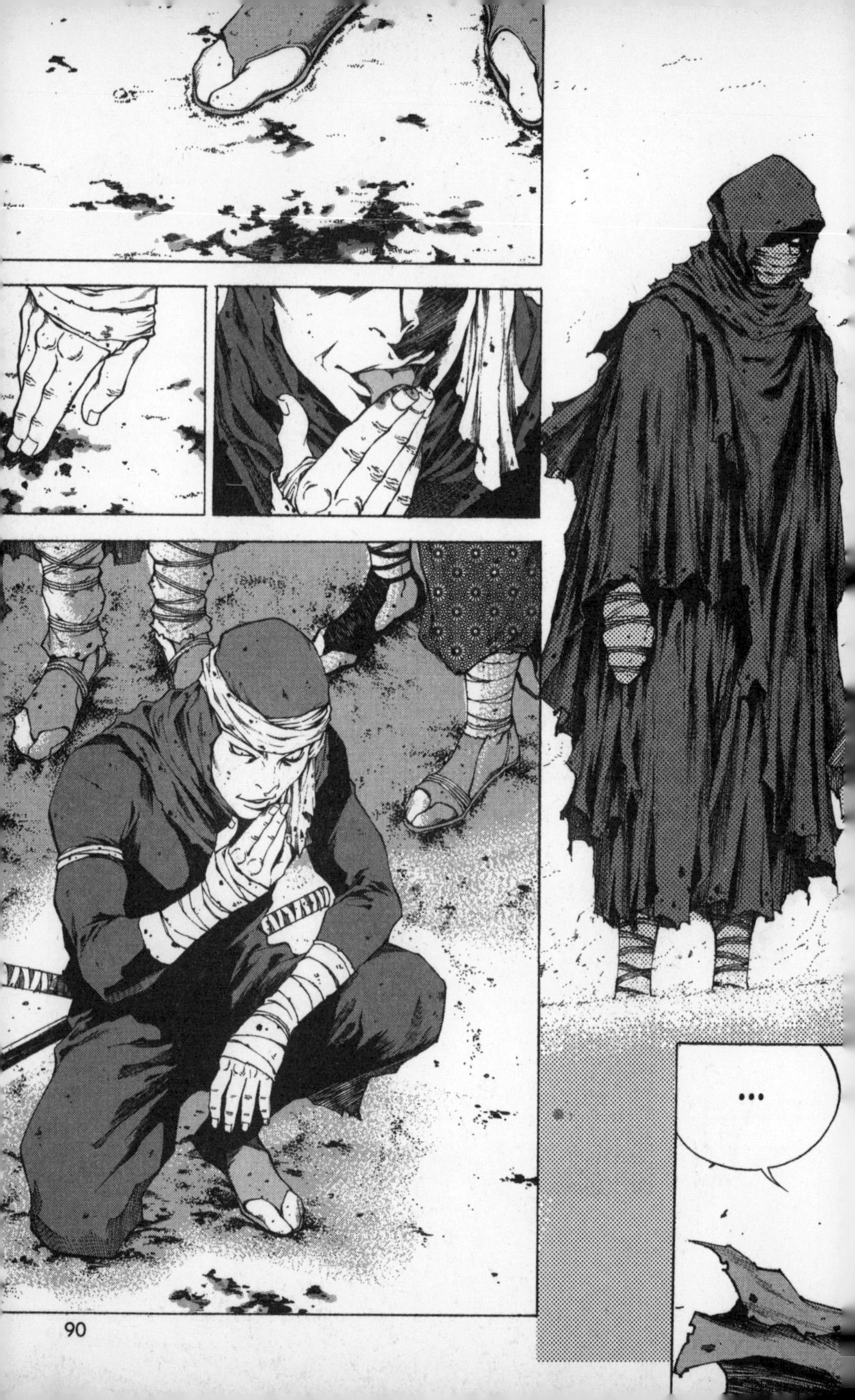
...

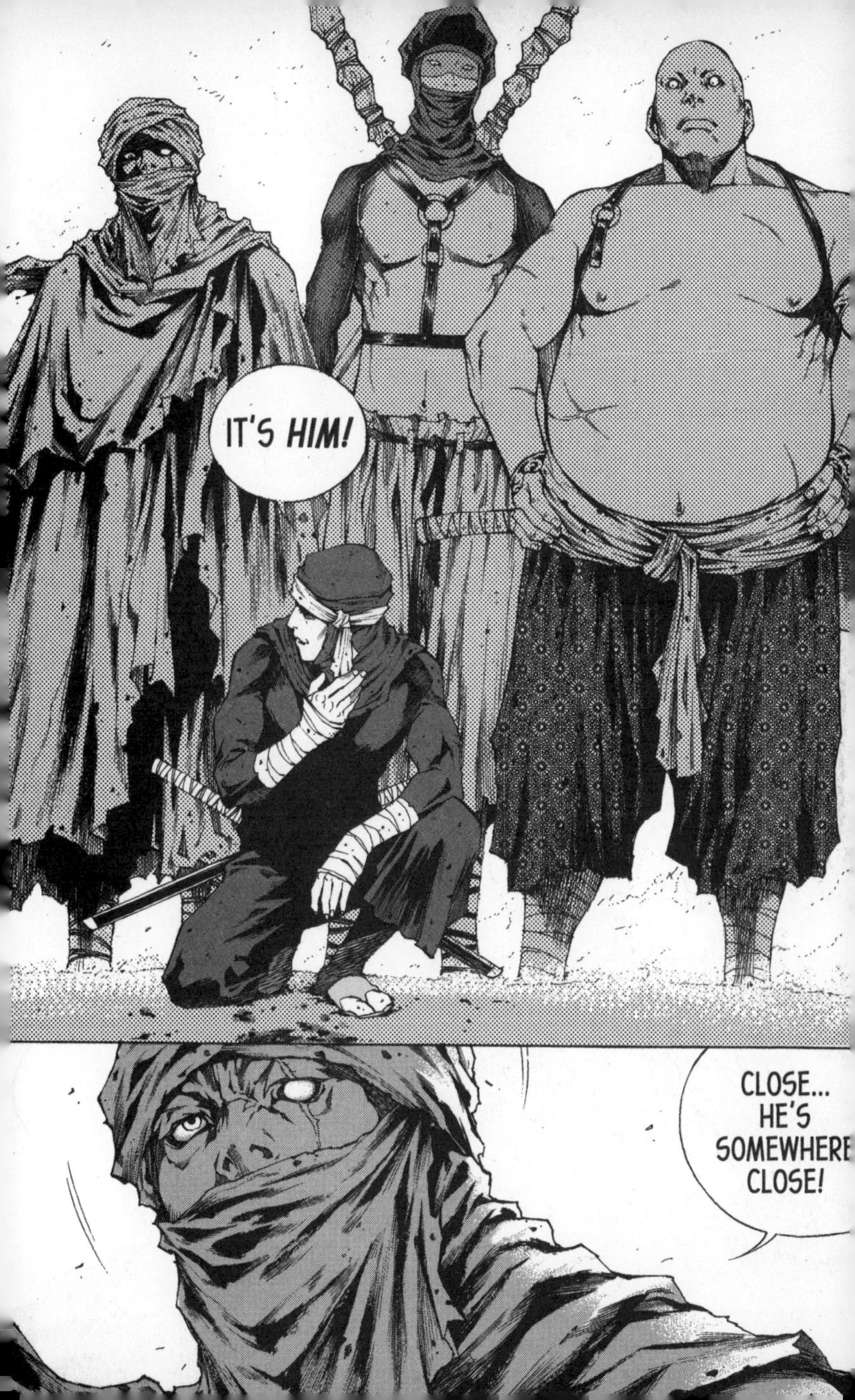
IT'S HIM!
CLOSE... HE'S SOMEWHERE CLOSE!

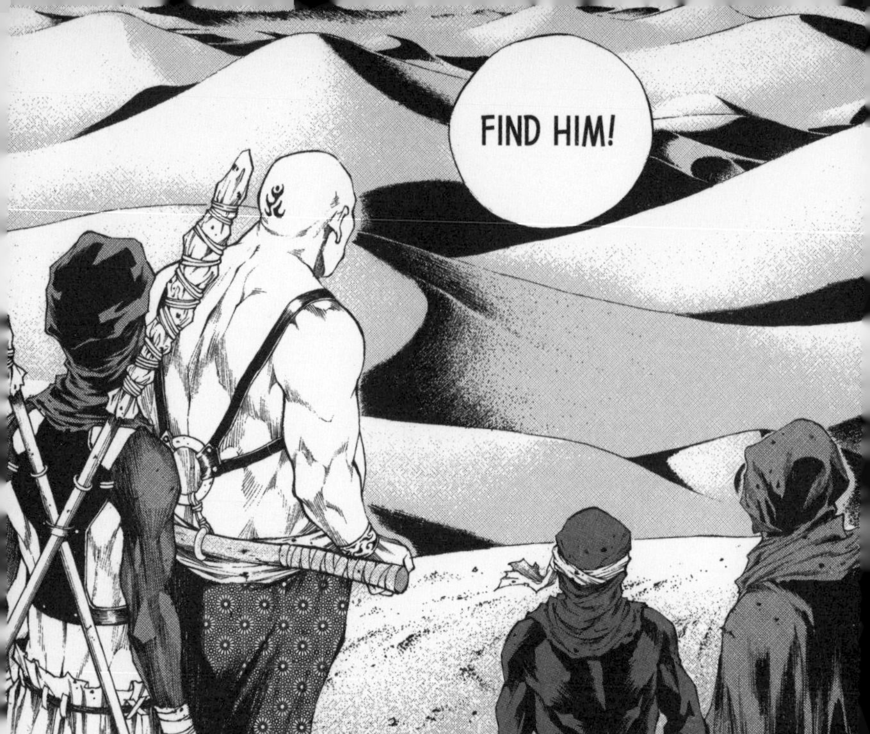
FIND HIM!

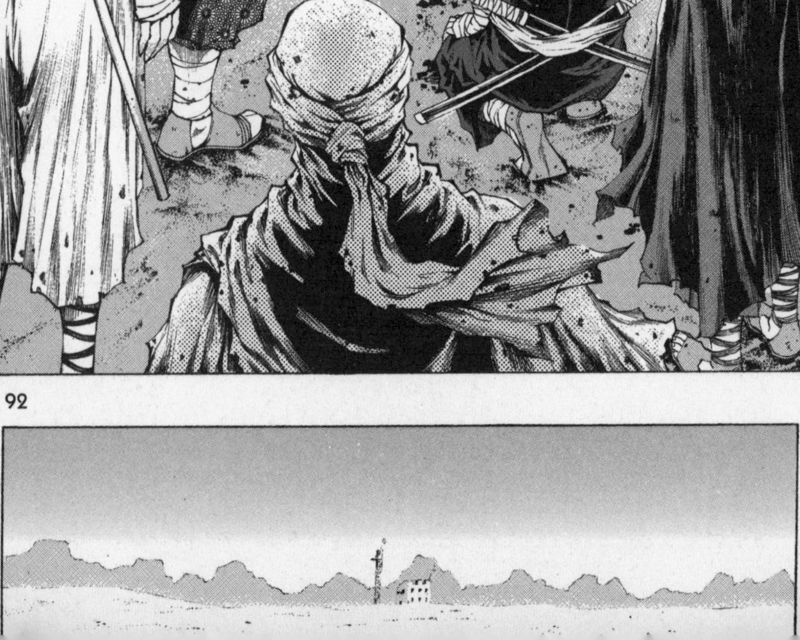

Banya
the explosive delivery man

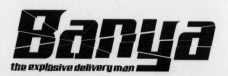

Chapter 4
TRACKERS

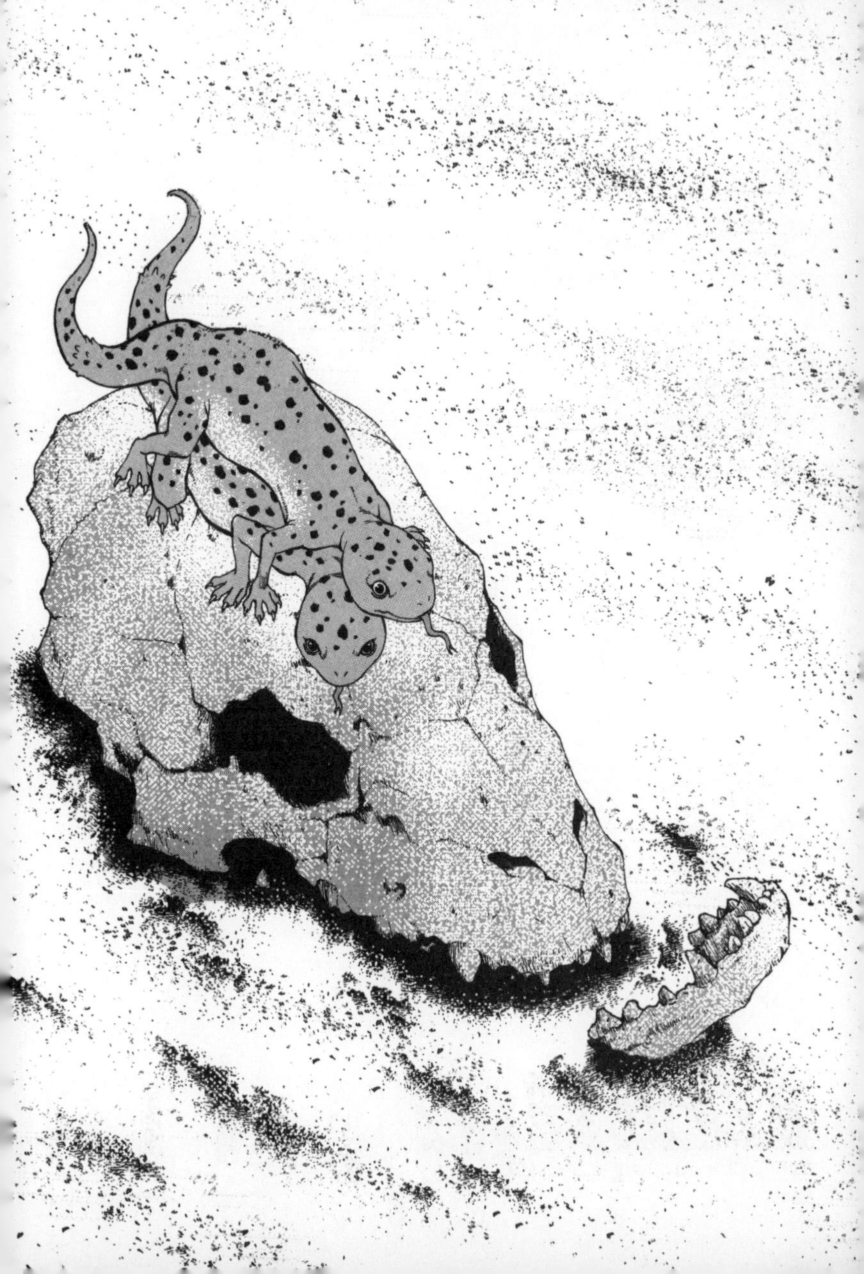

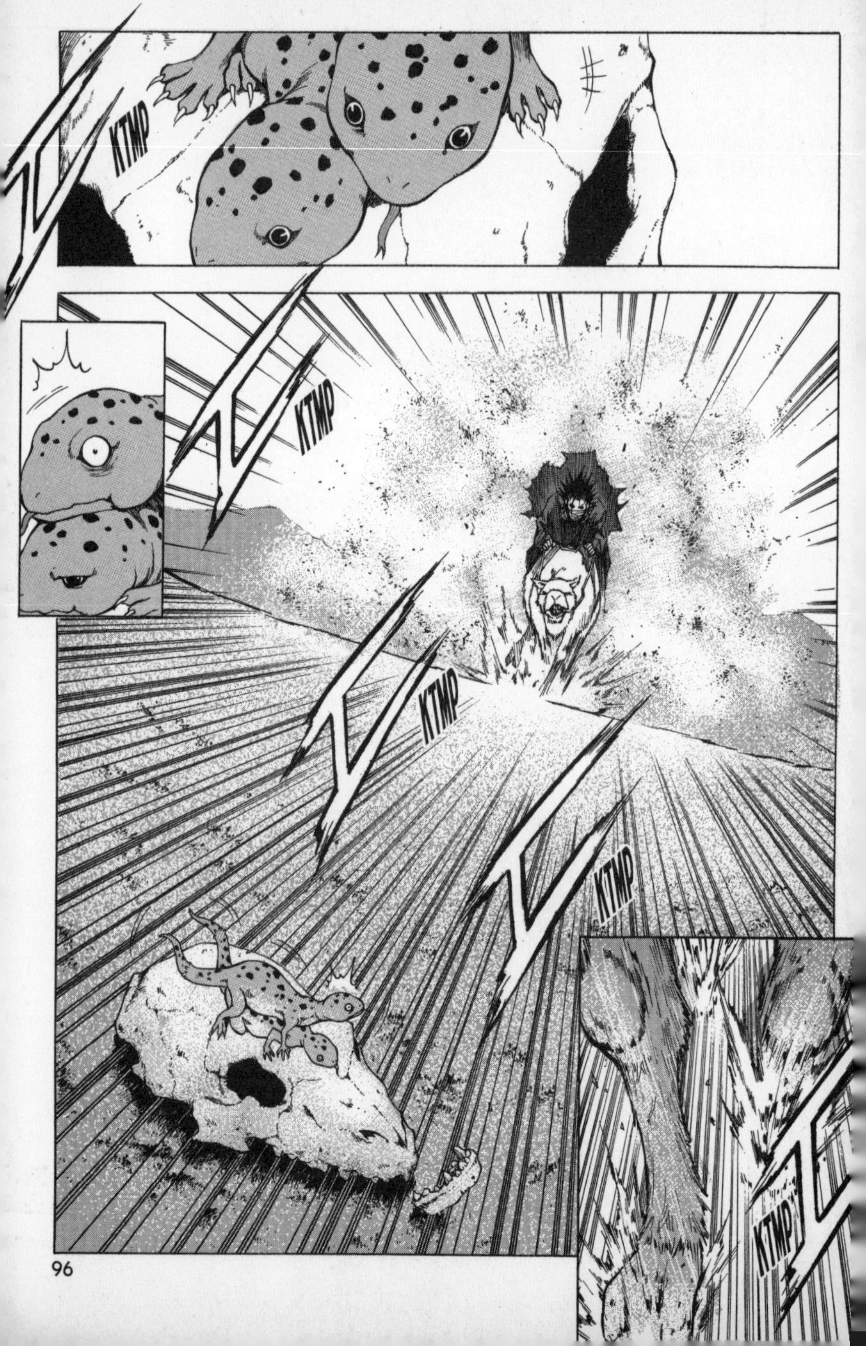
KTMP
KTMP
KTMP
KTMP
KTMP

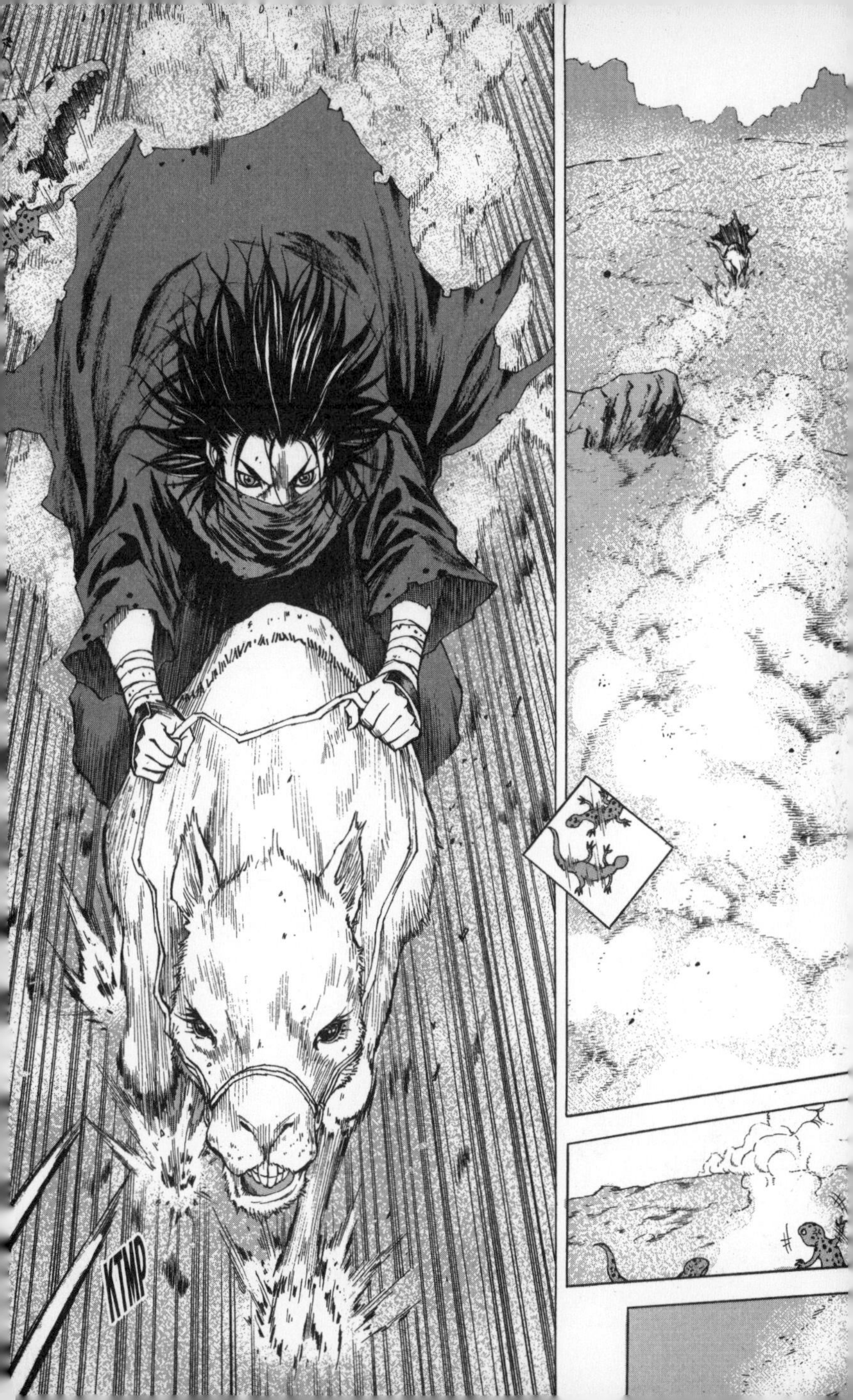
KTMP

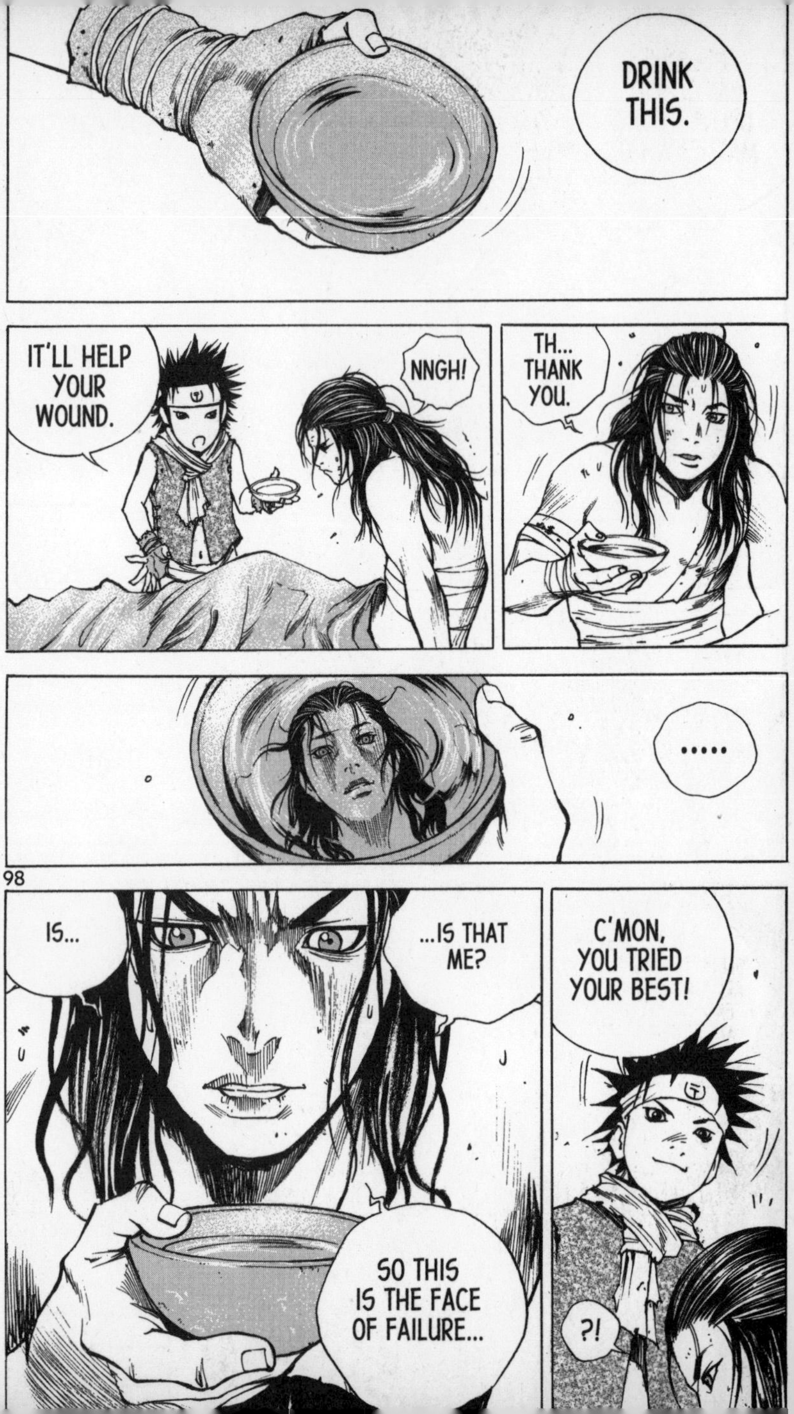
DRINK THIS.
IT'LL HELP YOUR WOUND.
NNGH!
TH... THANK YOU.
.....
IS...
...IS THAT ME?
SO THIS IS THE FACE OF FAILURE...
C'MON, YOU TRIED YOUR BEST!
?!

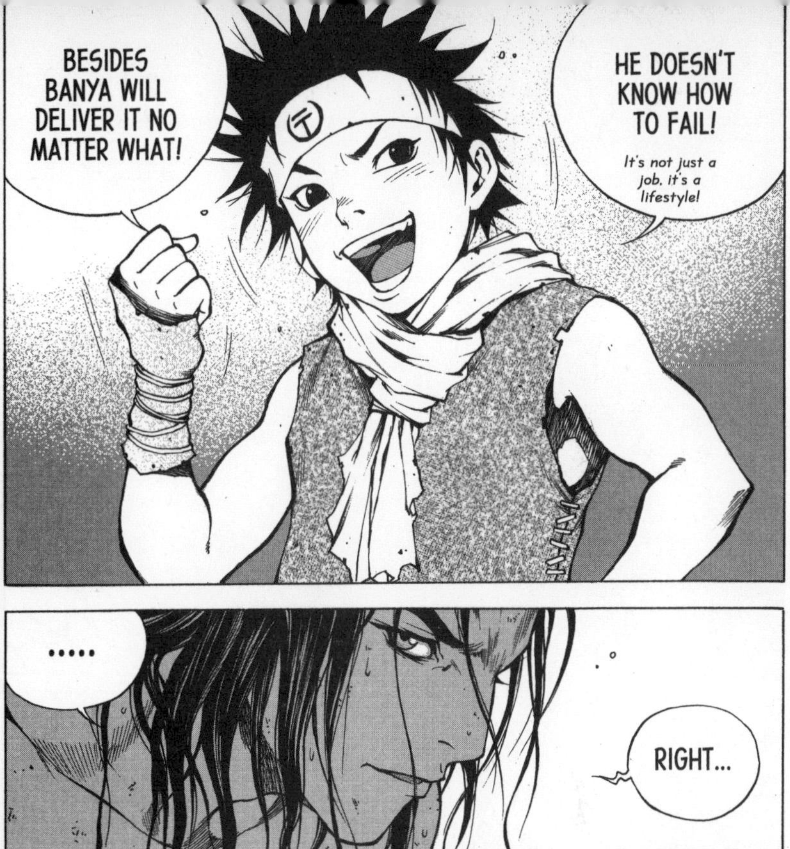

BESIDES BANYA WILL DELIVER IT NO MATTER WHAT!
HE DOESN'T KNOW HOW TO FAIL!
It's not just a job, it's a lifestyle!
.....
RIGHT...

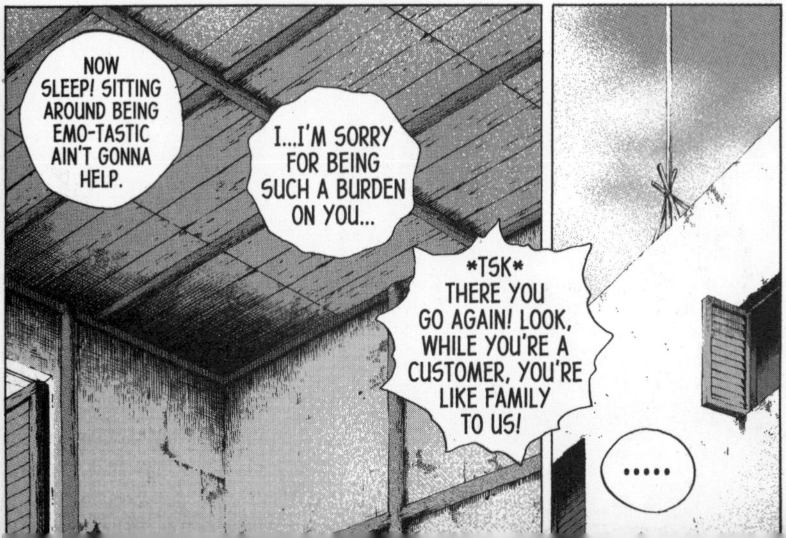

NOW SLEEP! SITTING AROUND BEING EMO-TASTIC AIN'T GONNA HELP.
I...I'M SORRY FOR BEING SUCH A BURDEN ON YOU...
TSK THERE YOU GO AGAIN! LOOK, WHILE YOU'RE A CUSTOMER, YOU'RE LIKE FAMILY TO US!
.....

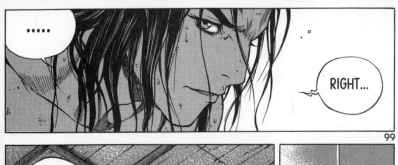

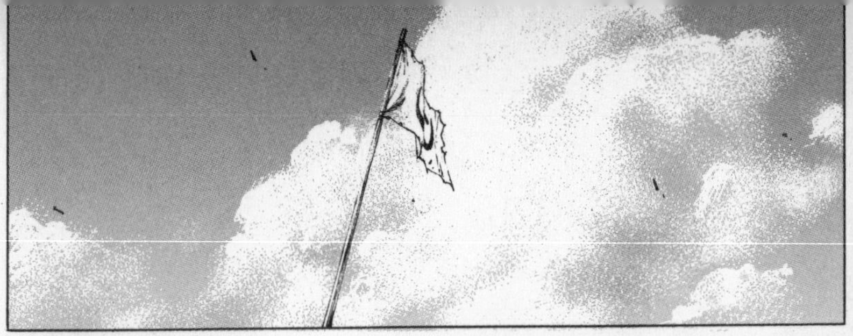
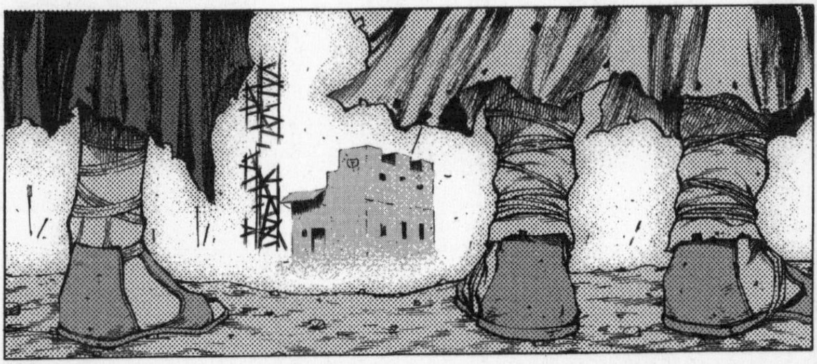

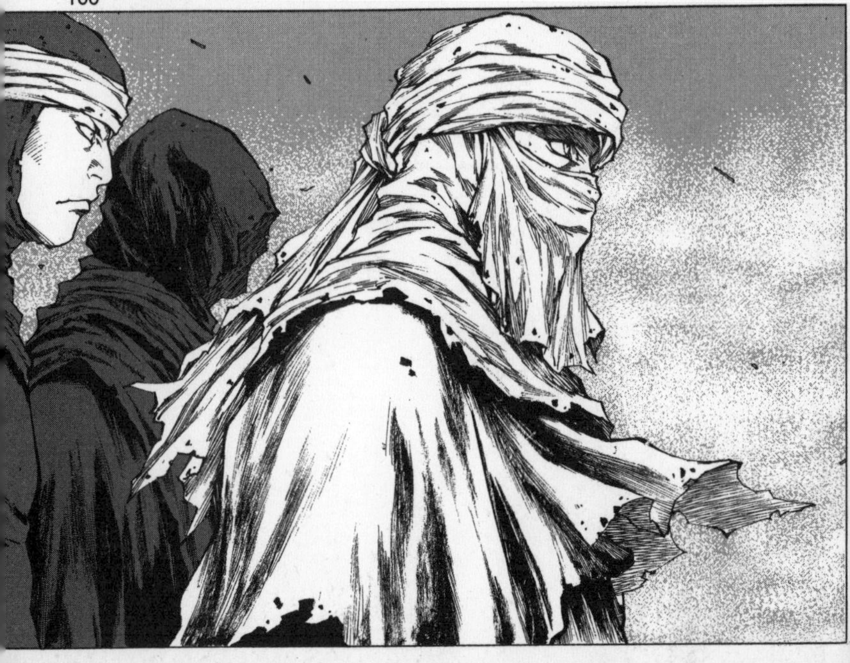

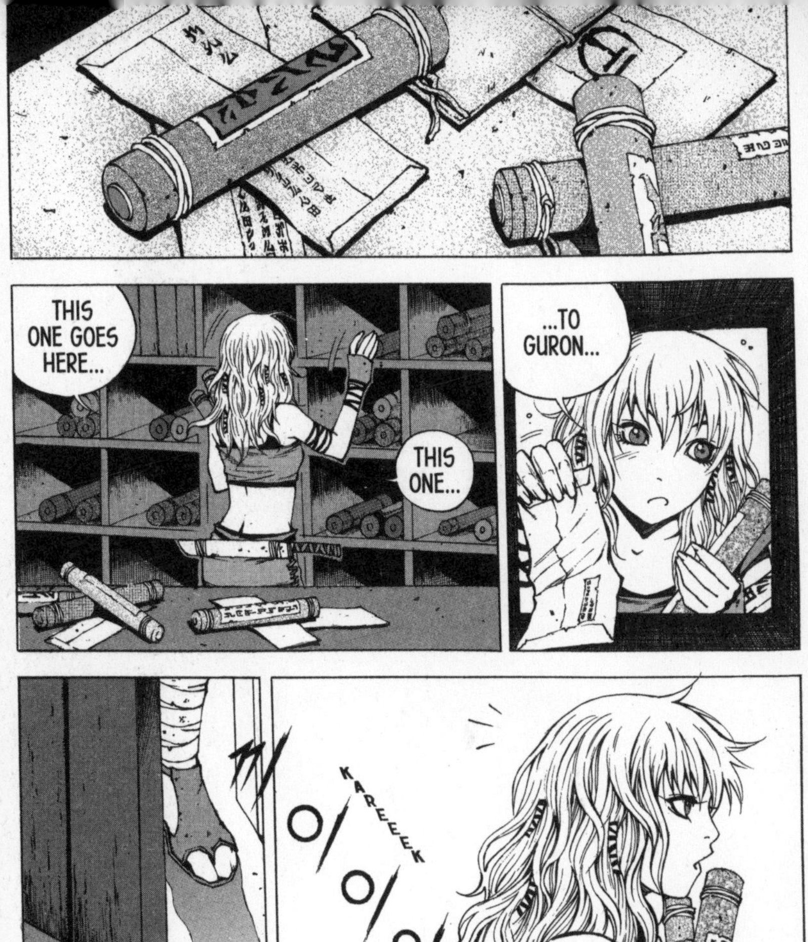
THIS ONE GOES HERE...
THIS ONE...
...TO GURON...
KAREEEK

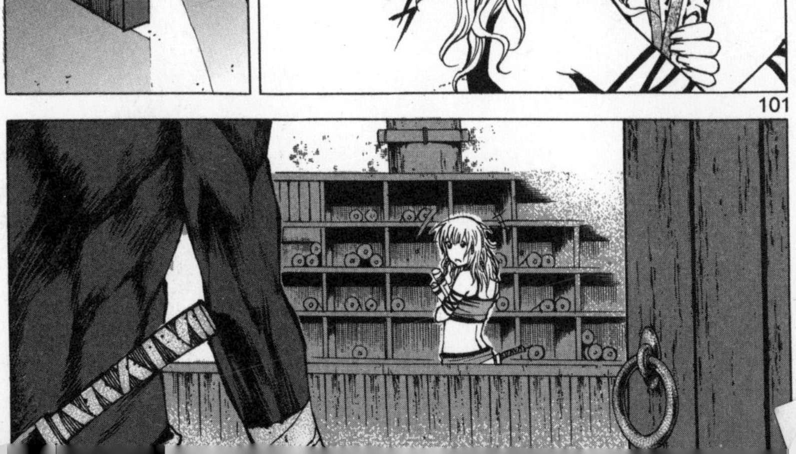

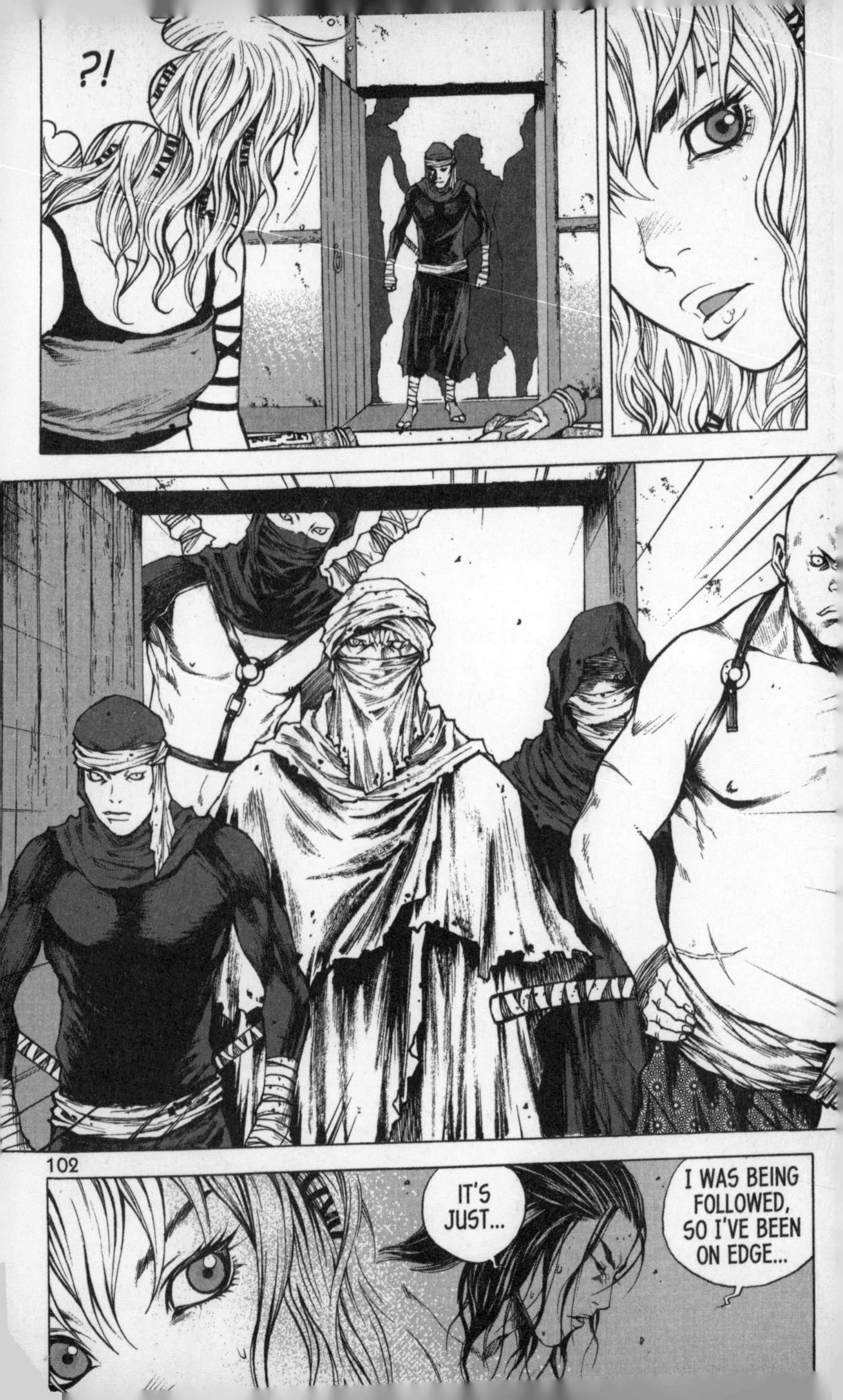
?!
IT'S JUST...
I WAS BEING FOLLOWED, SO I'VE BEEN ON EDGE...

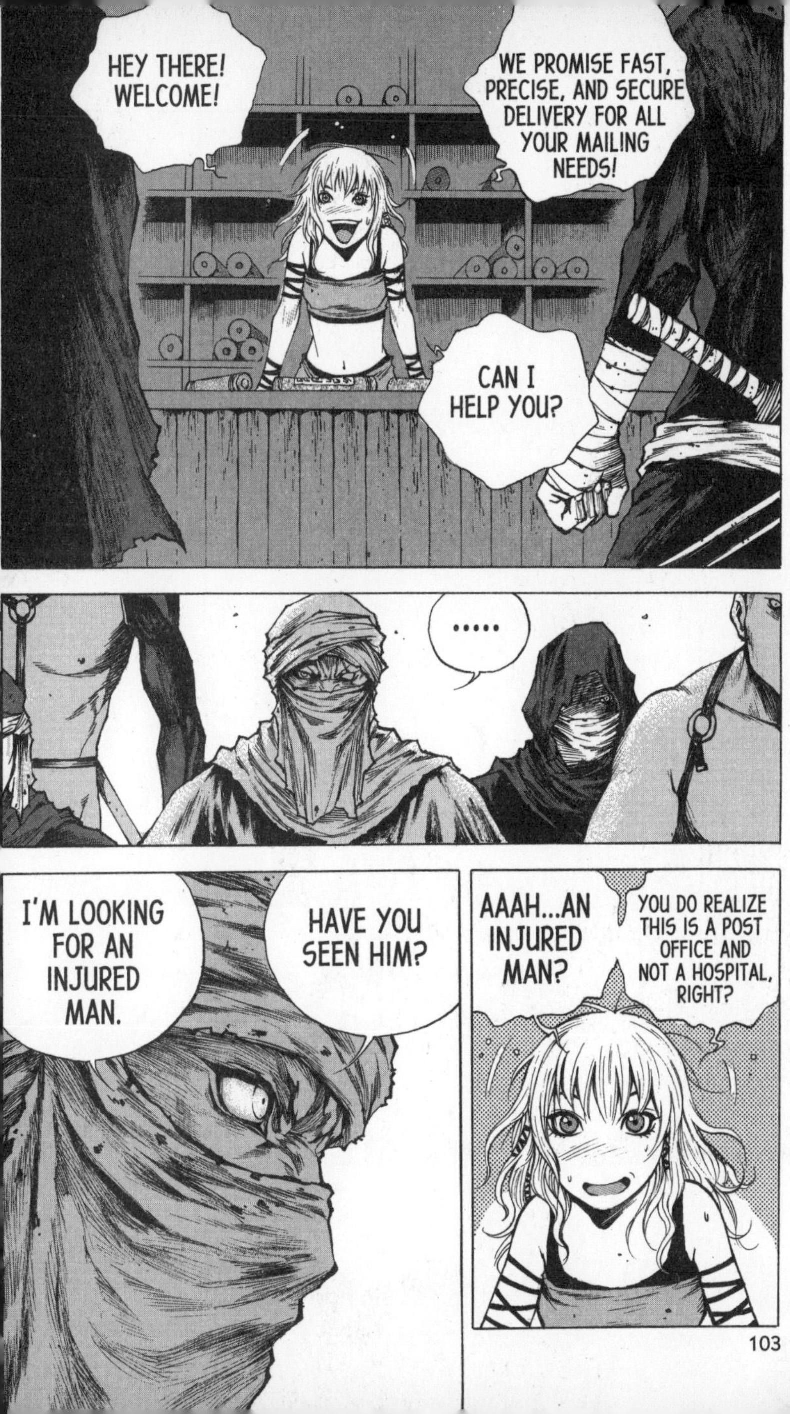
HEY THERE! WELCOME!
WE PROMISE FAST, PRECISE, AND SECURE DELIVERY FOR ALL YOUR MAILING NEEDS!
CAN I HELP YOU?
.....
I'M LOOKING FOR AN INJURED MAN.
HAVE YOU SEEN HIM?
AAAH...AN INJURED MAN?
YOU DO REALIZE THIS IS A POST OFFICE AND NOT A HOSPITAL, RIGHT?

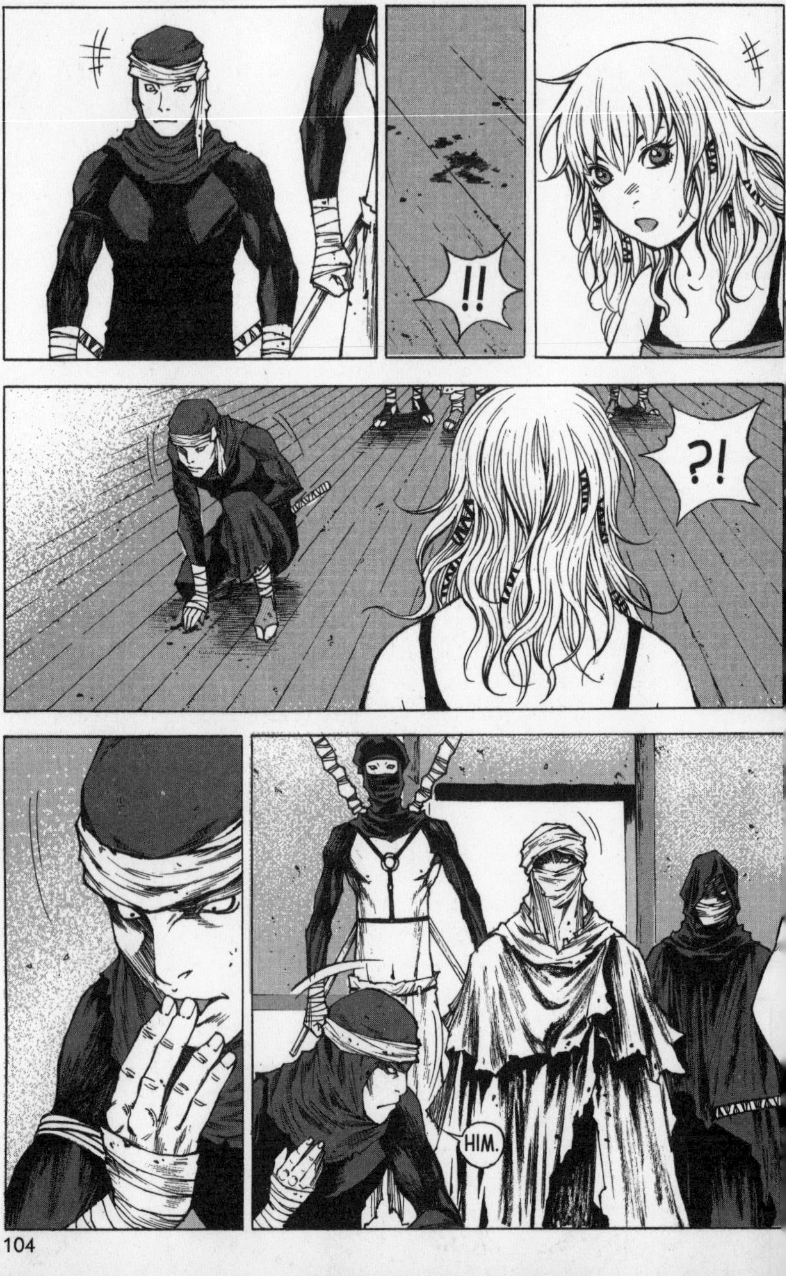
!!
?!
HIM.

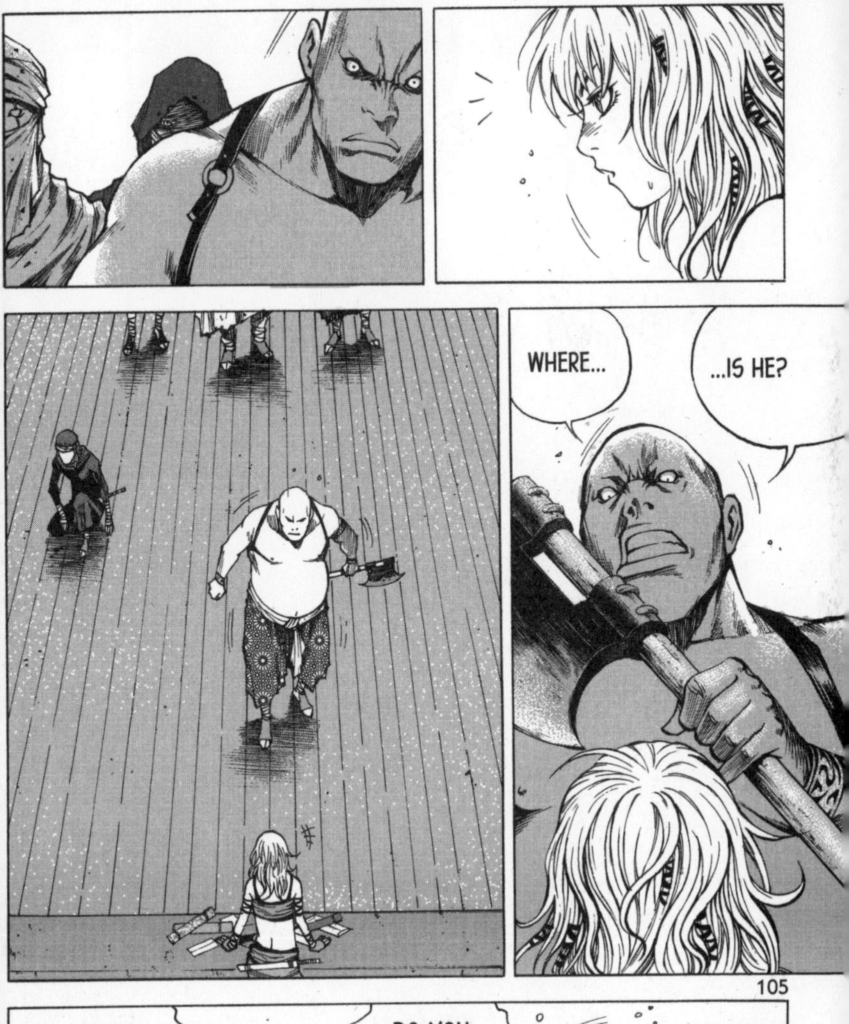
WHERE...
...IS HE?

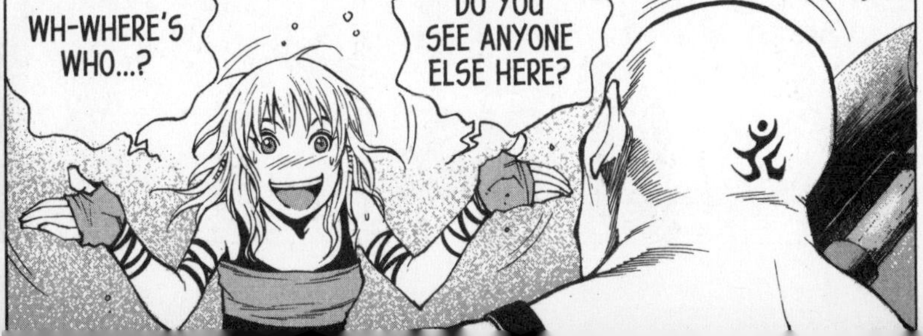
WH-WHERE'S WHO...?
DO YOU SEE ANYONE ELSE HERE?

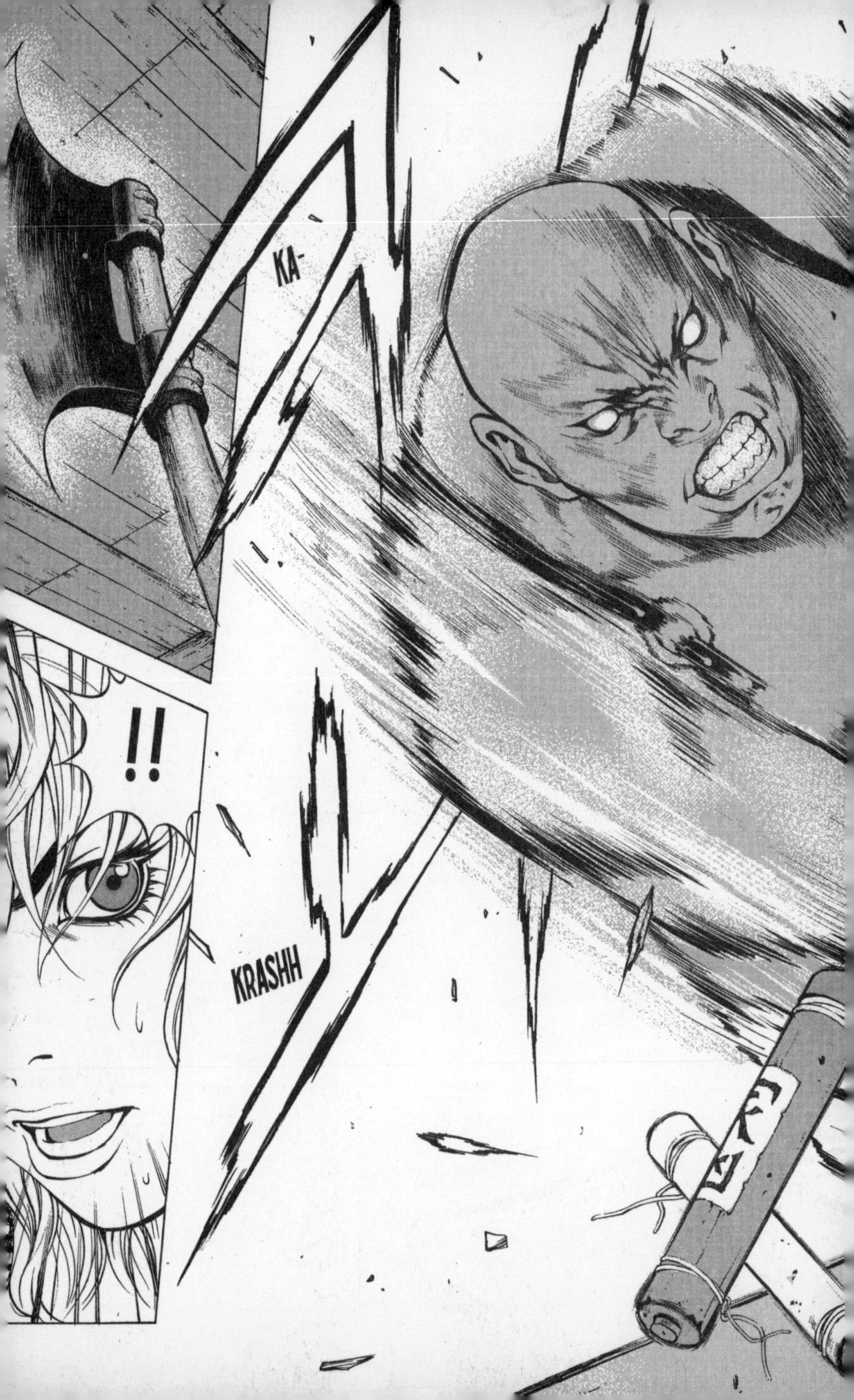
KA-
!!
KRASHH

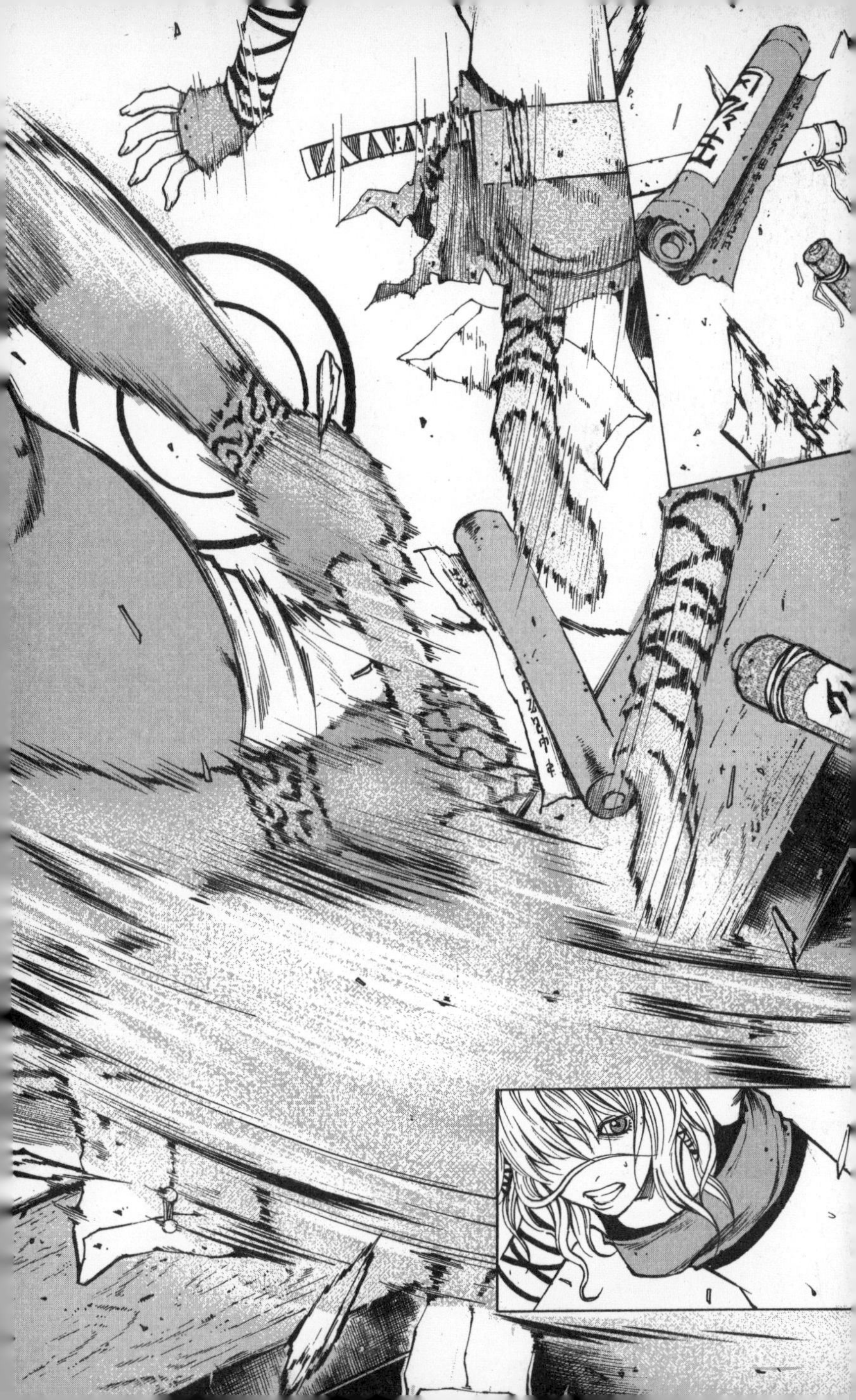

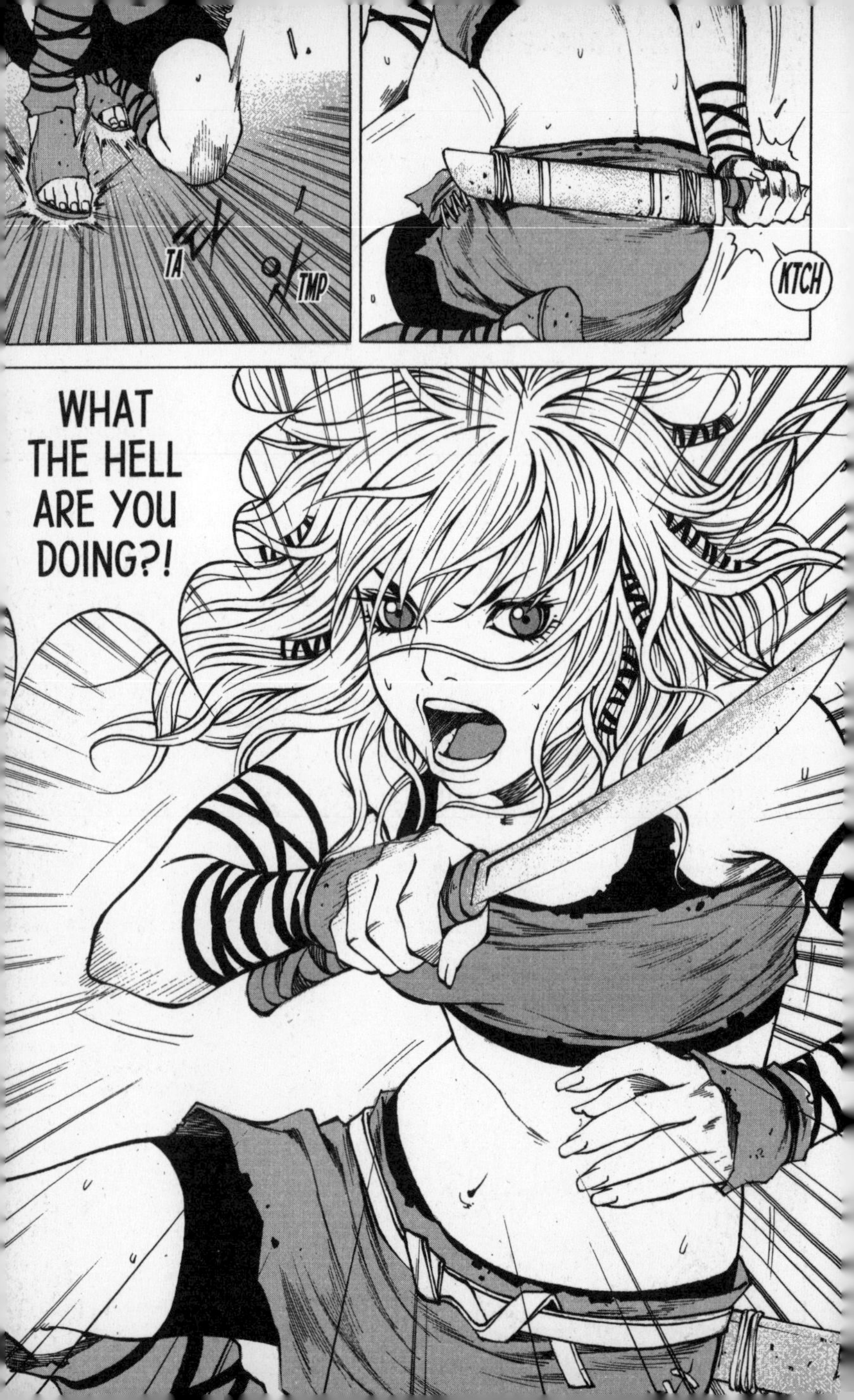
TA
TMP
KTCH
WHAT THE HELL ARE YOU DOING?!

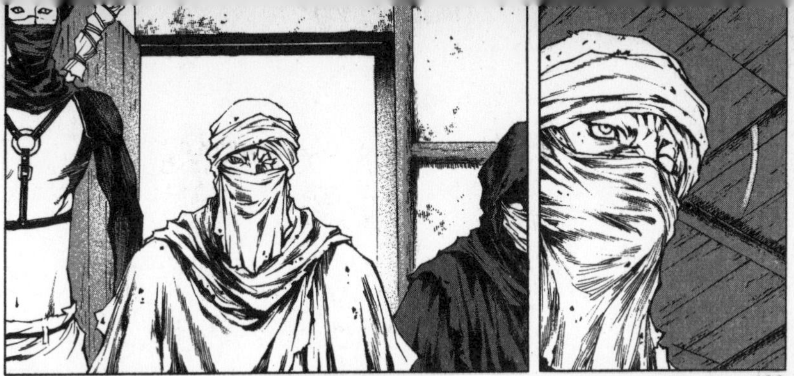

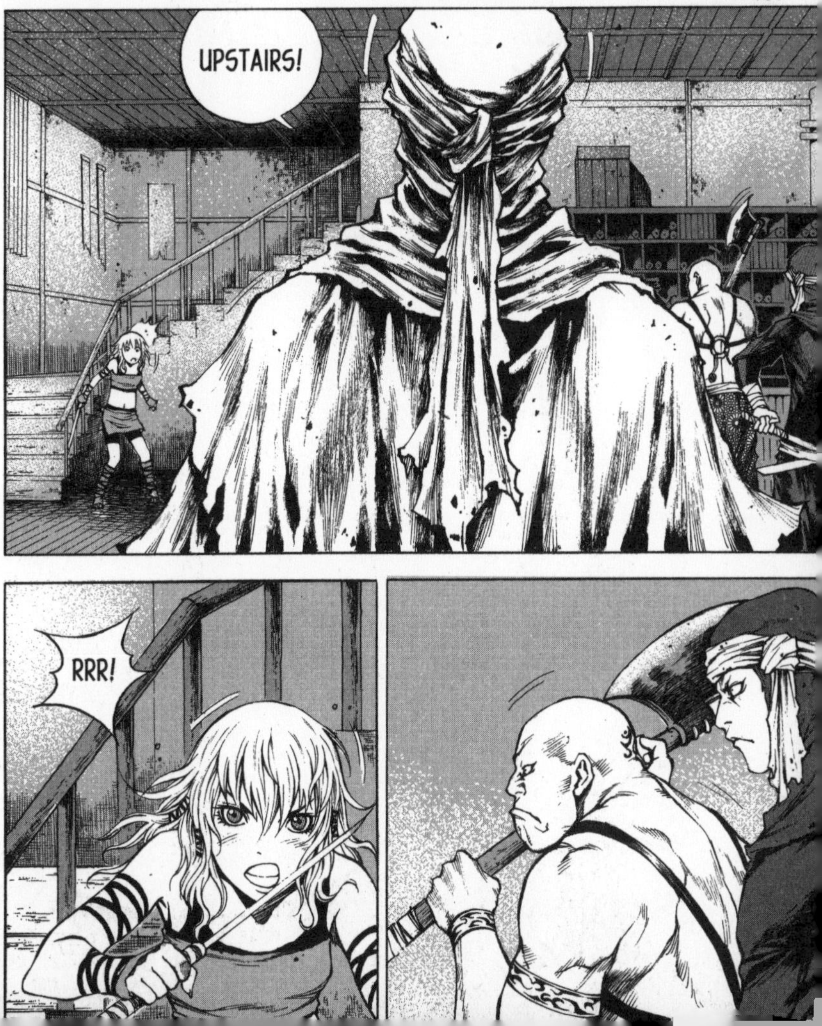
UPSTAIRS!
RRR!

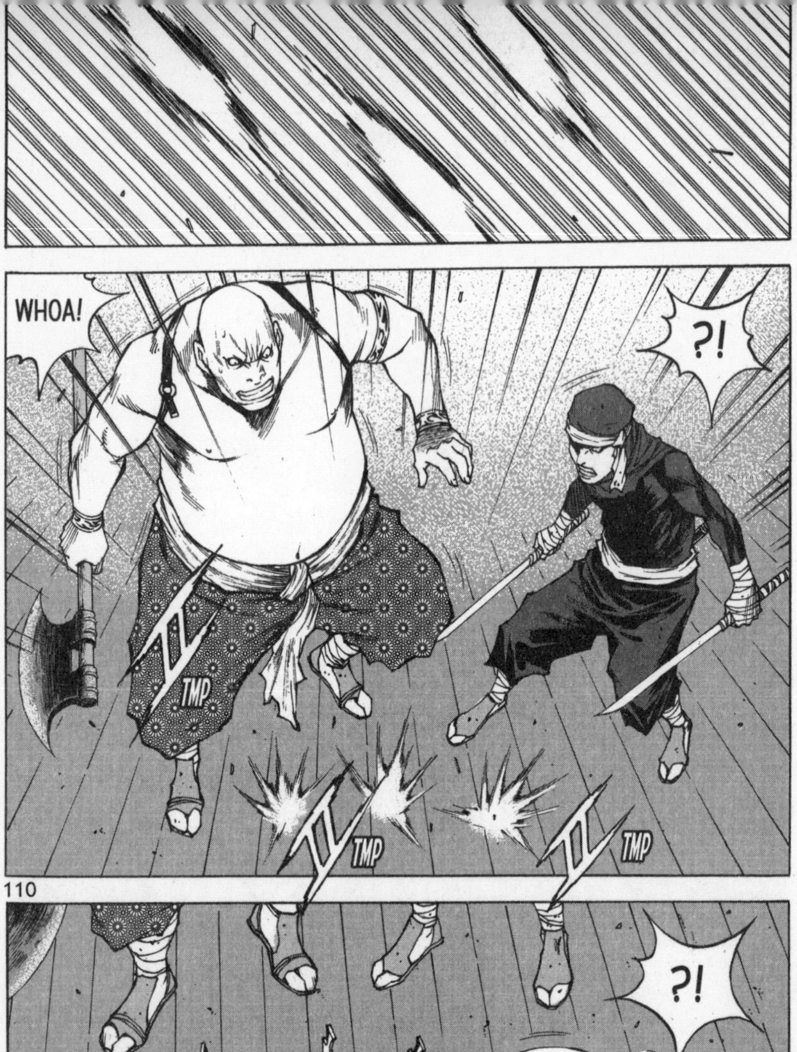
WHOA!
?!
TMP
TMP
TMP
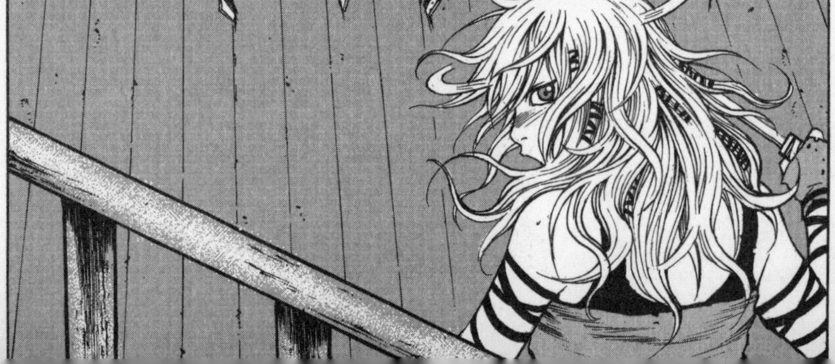
?!

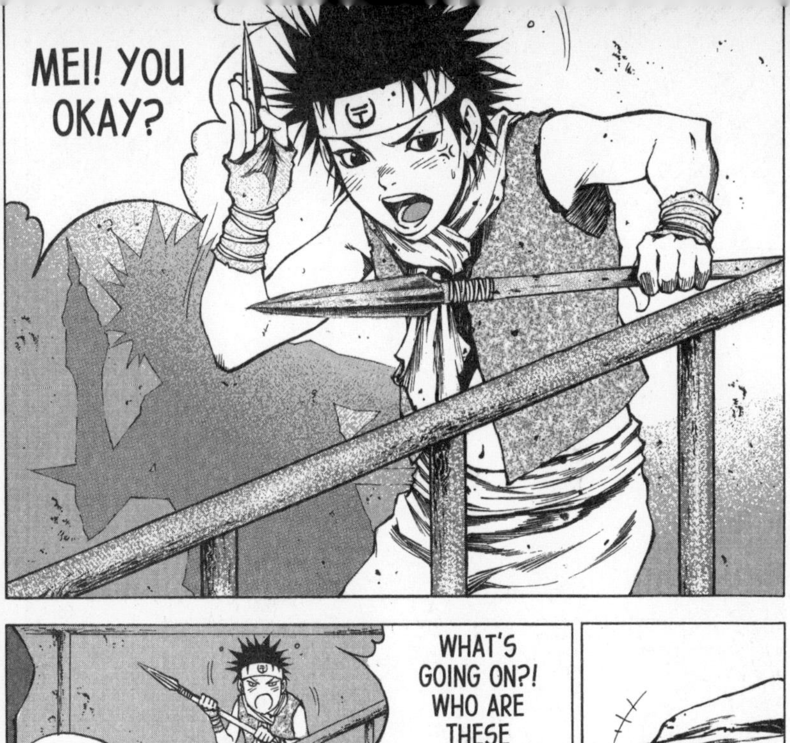
MEI! YOU OKAY?
YEAH... NEVER BEEN BETTER...
WHAT'S GOING ON?! WHO ARE THESE GOONS?!

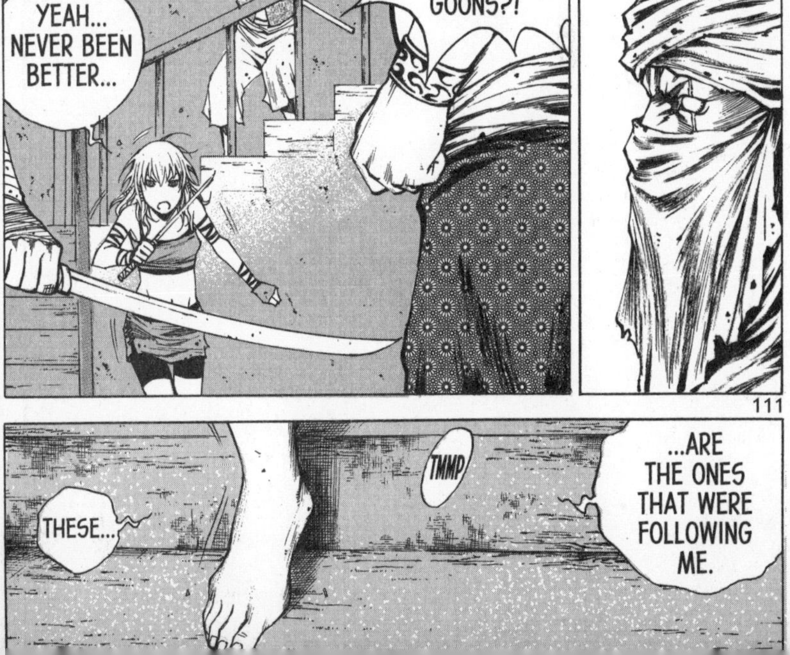
THESE...
TMMP
...ARE THE ONES THAT WERE FOLLOWING ME.

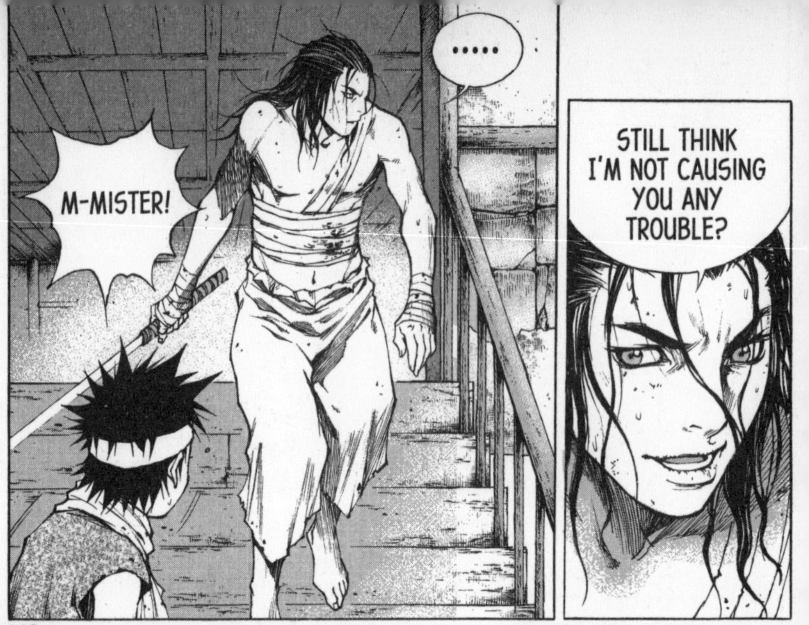
M-MISTER!
......
STILL THINK I'M NOT CAUSING YOU ANY TROUBLE?

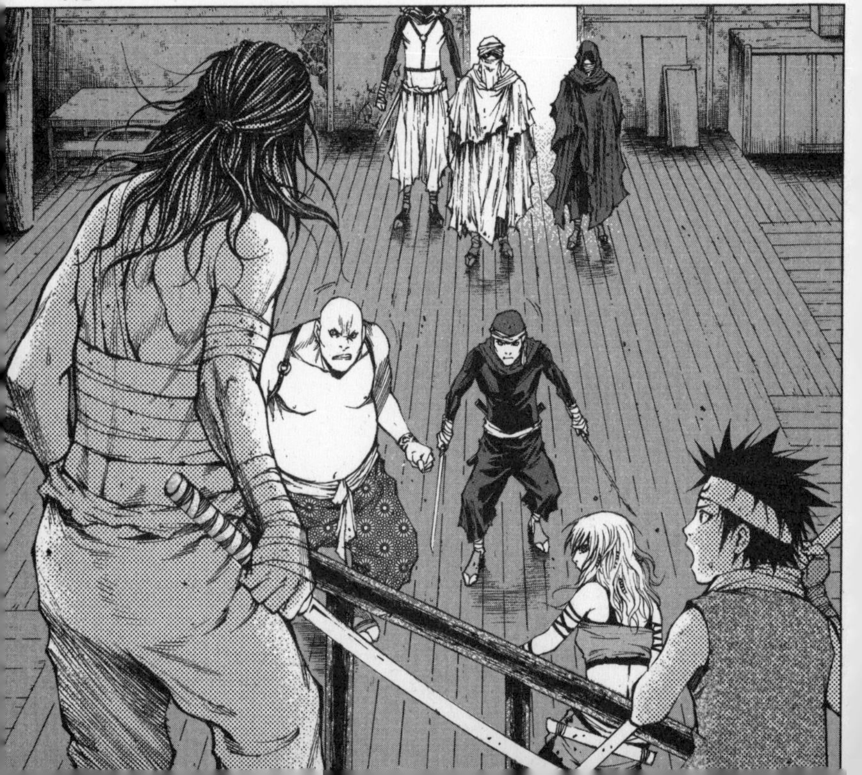

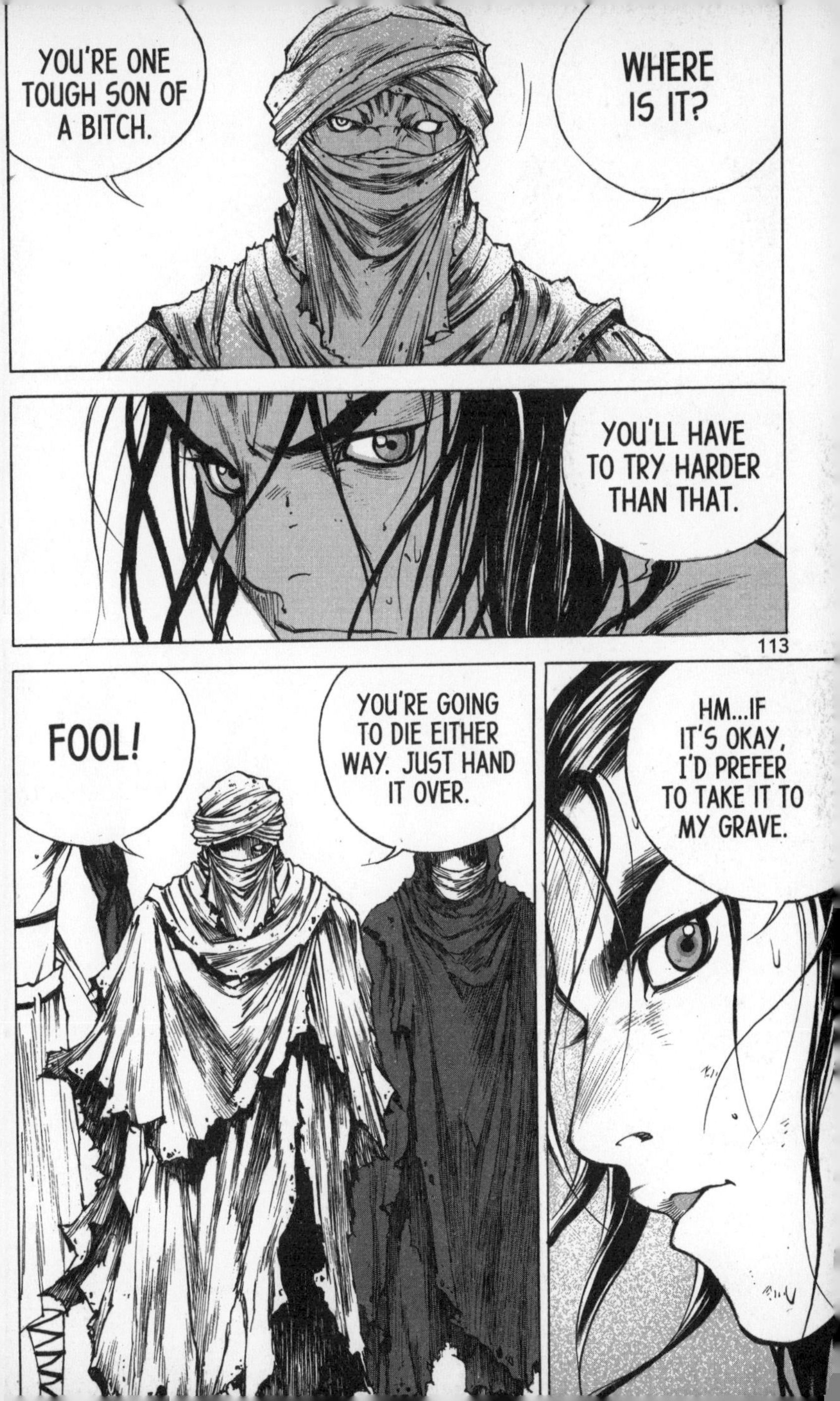
YOU'RE ONE TOUGH SON OF A BITCH.
WHERE IS IT?
YOU'LL HAVE TO TRY HARDER THAN THAT.
FOOL!
YOU'RE GOING TO DIE EITHER WAY. JUST HAND IT OVER.
HM...IF IT'S OKAY, I'D PREFER TO TAKE IT TO MY GRAVE.

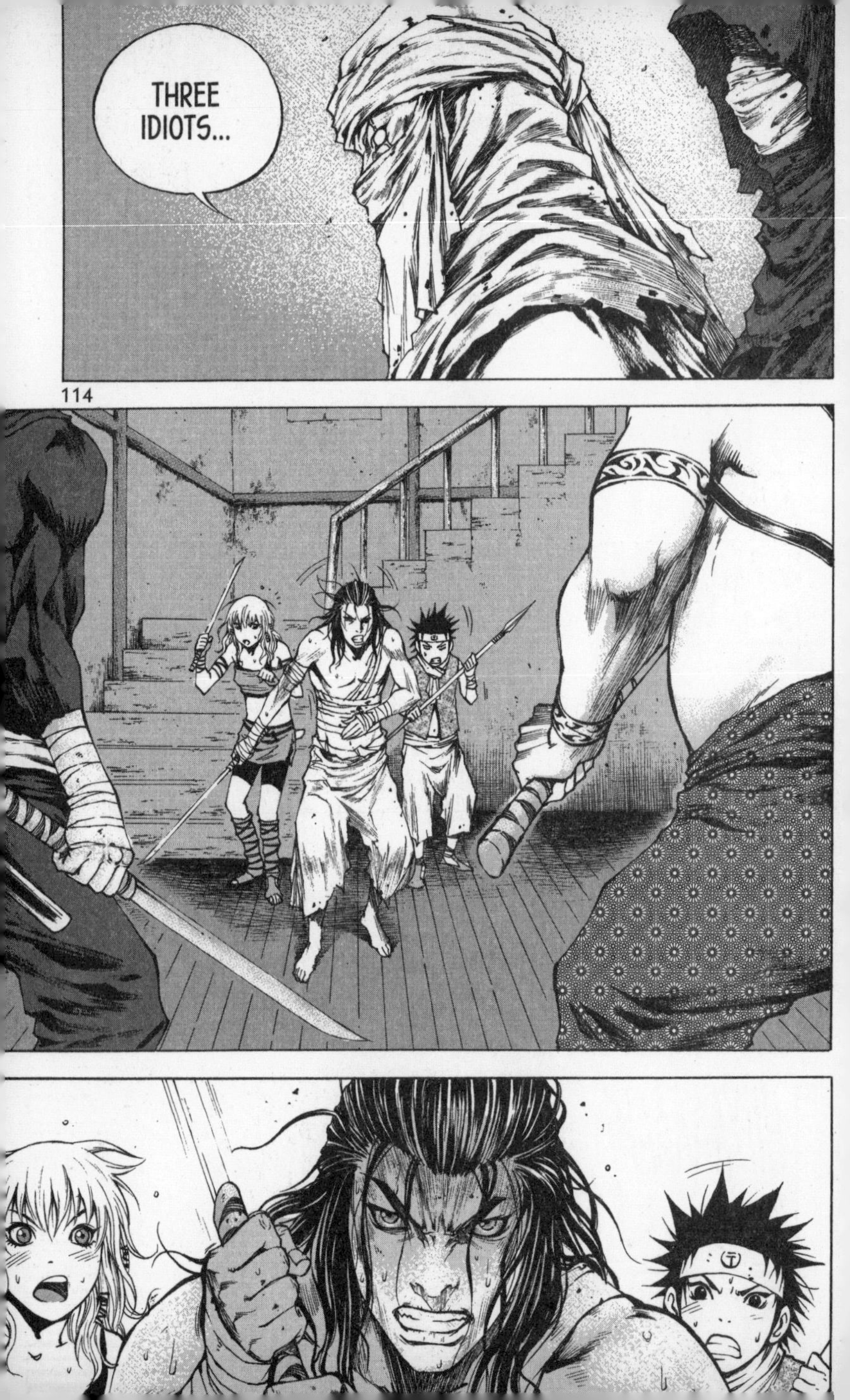
THREE IDIOTS...

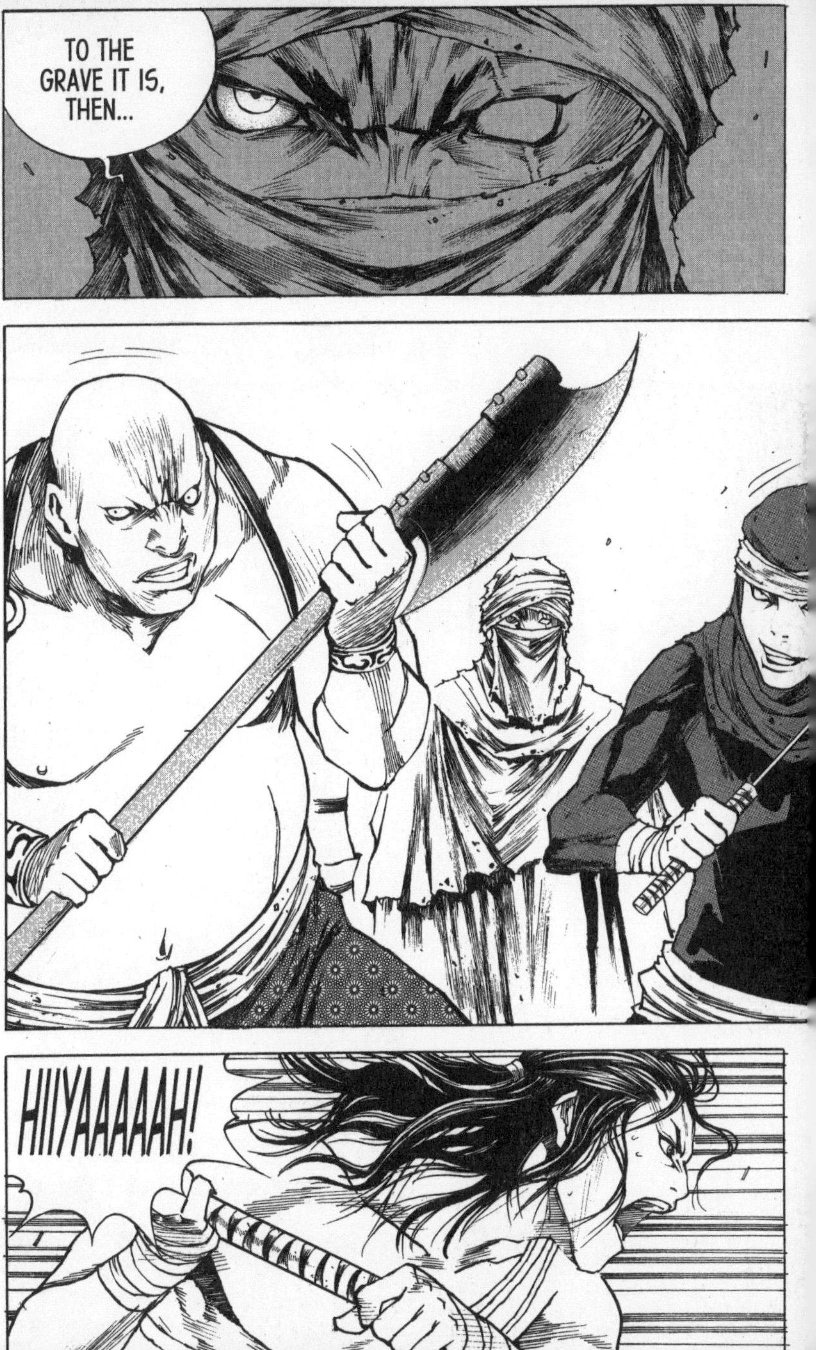
TO THE GRAVE IT IS, THEN...
HIIYAAAAAH!

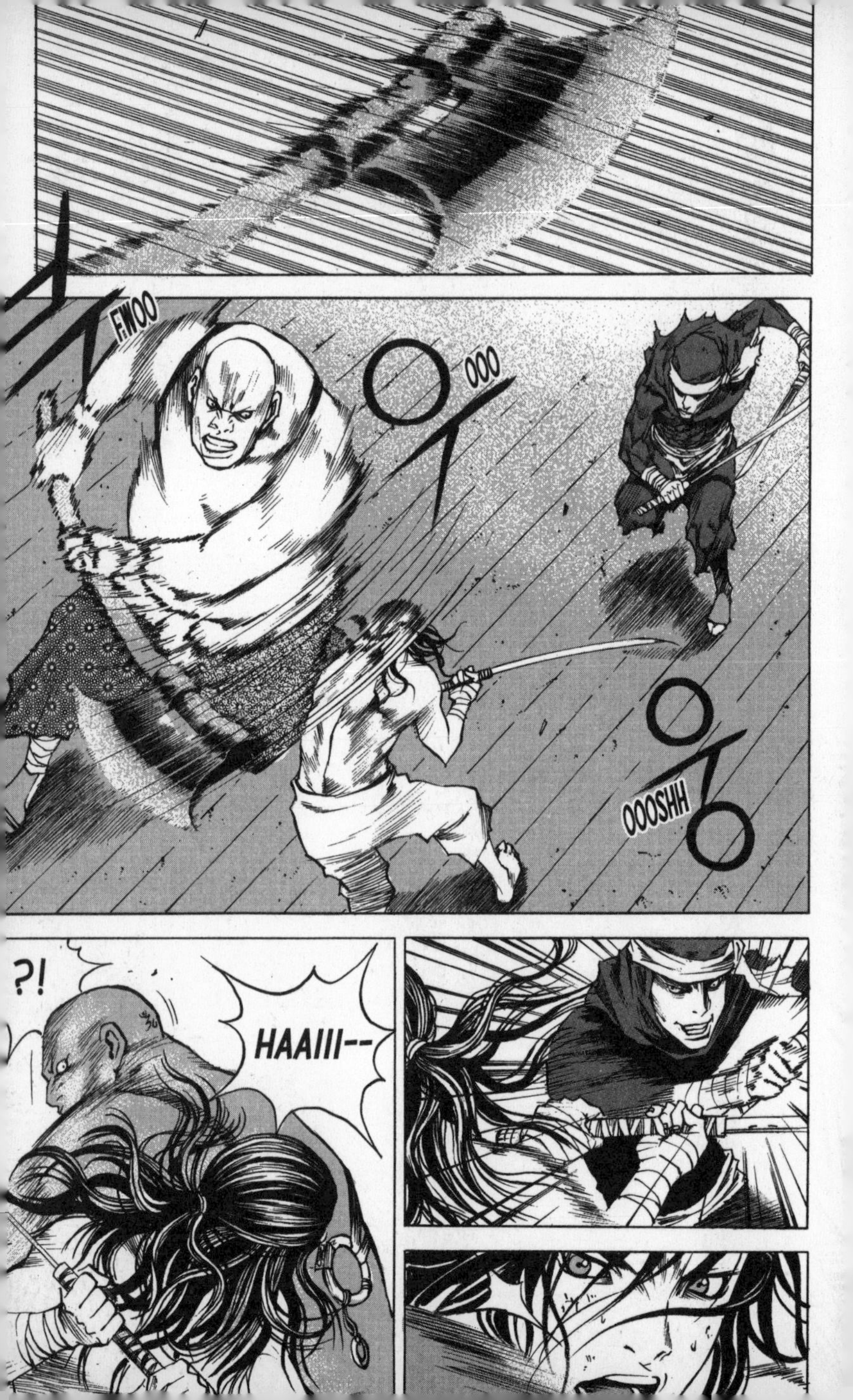
FWOO
OOO
OOOSHH
?!
HAAIII--

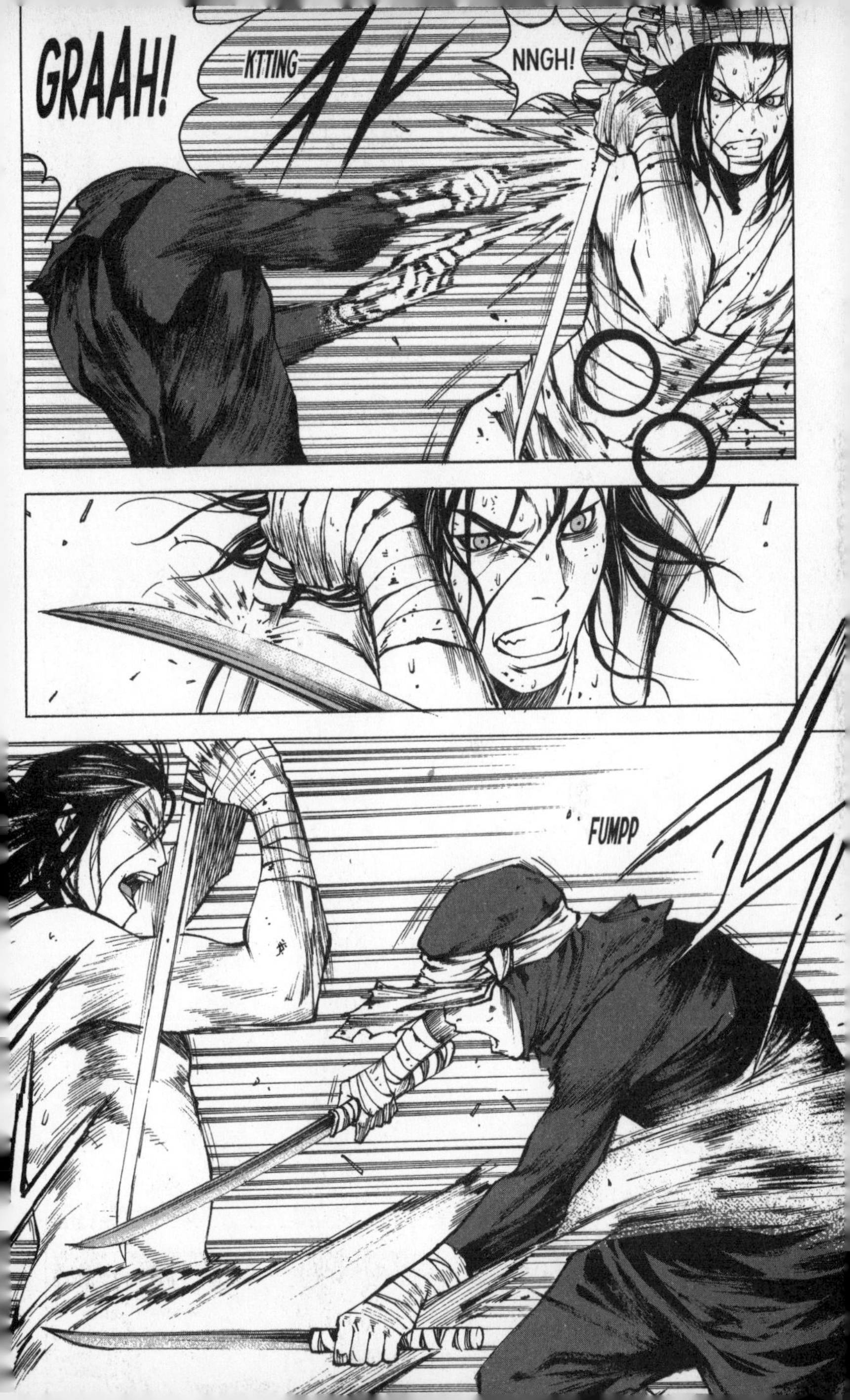
GRAAH!
KTTING
NNGH!
FUMPP

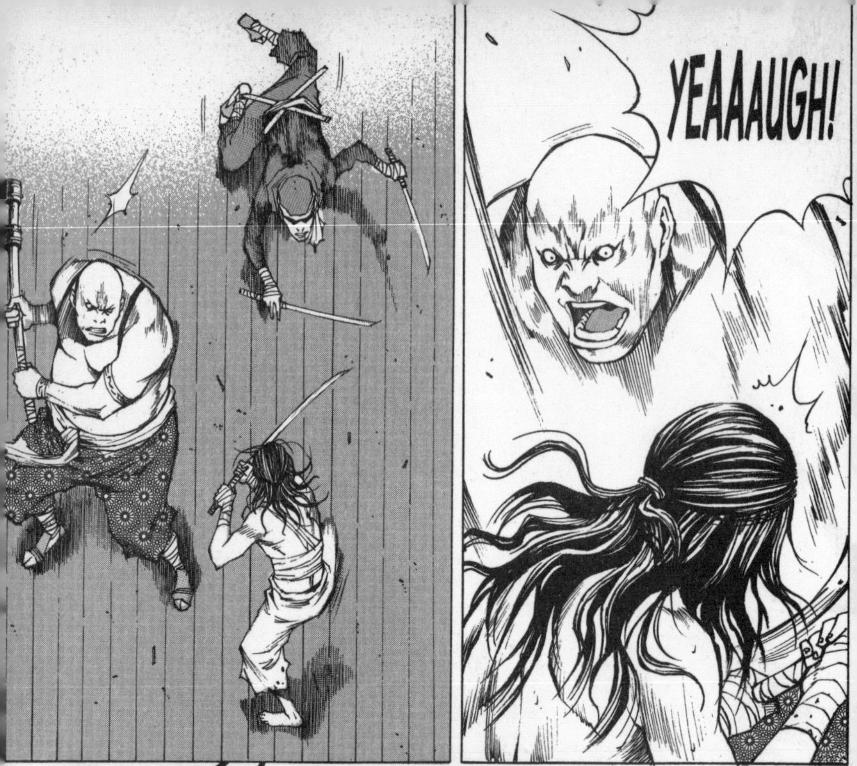
YEAAAUGH!

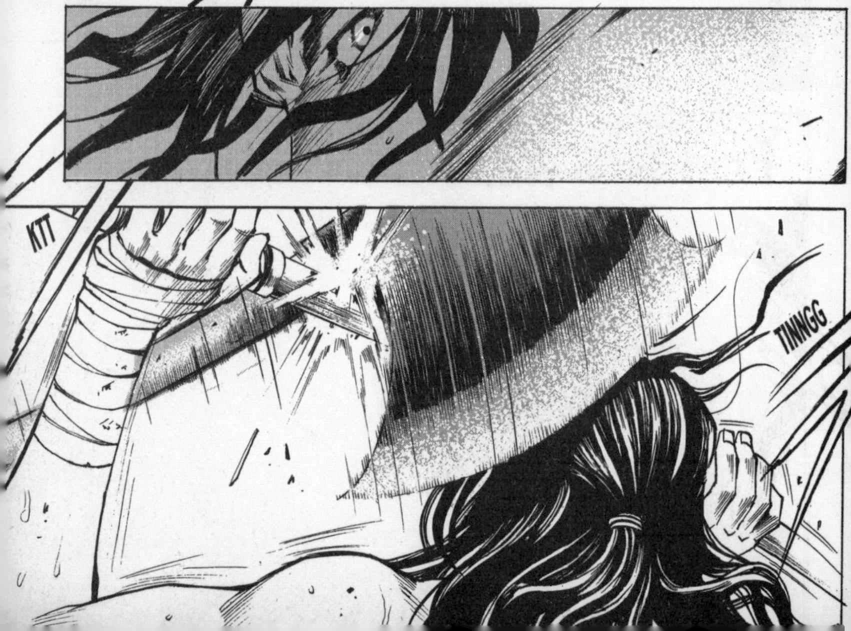
KTT
TINNGG

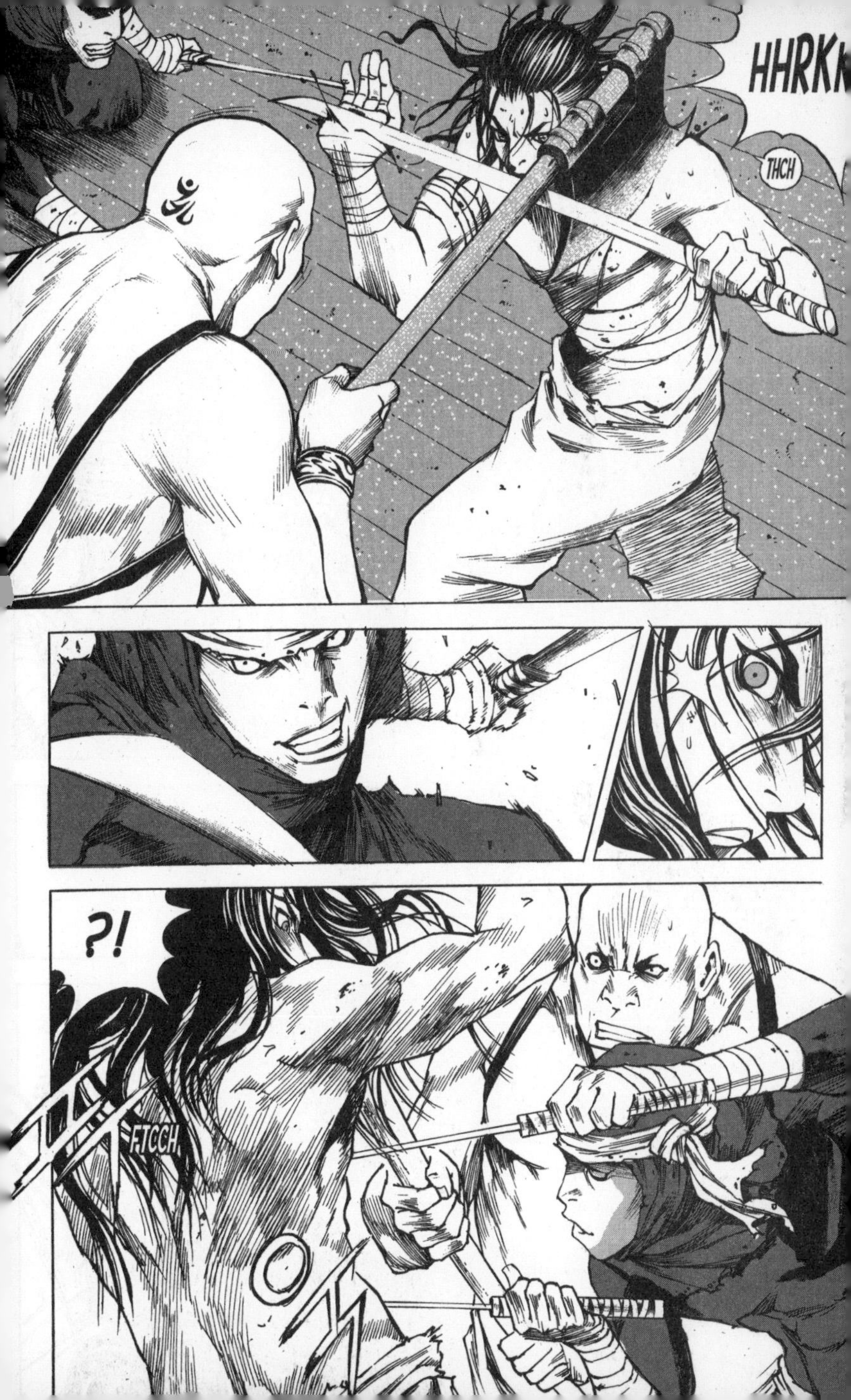
HHRKK
THCH
?!
FTCCH

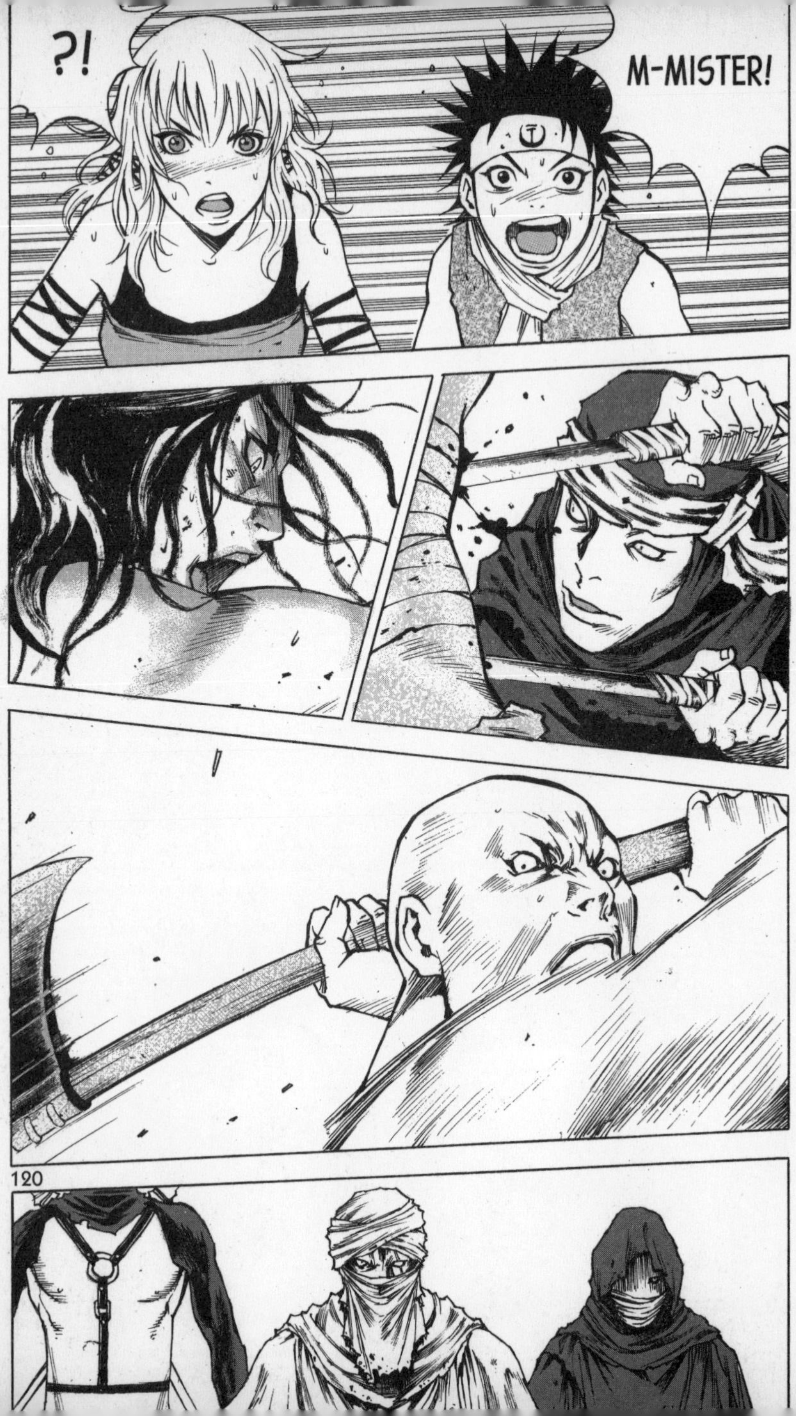
?!
M-MISTER!

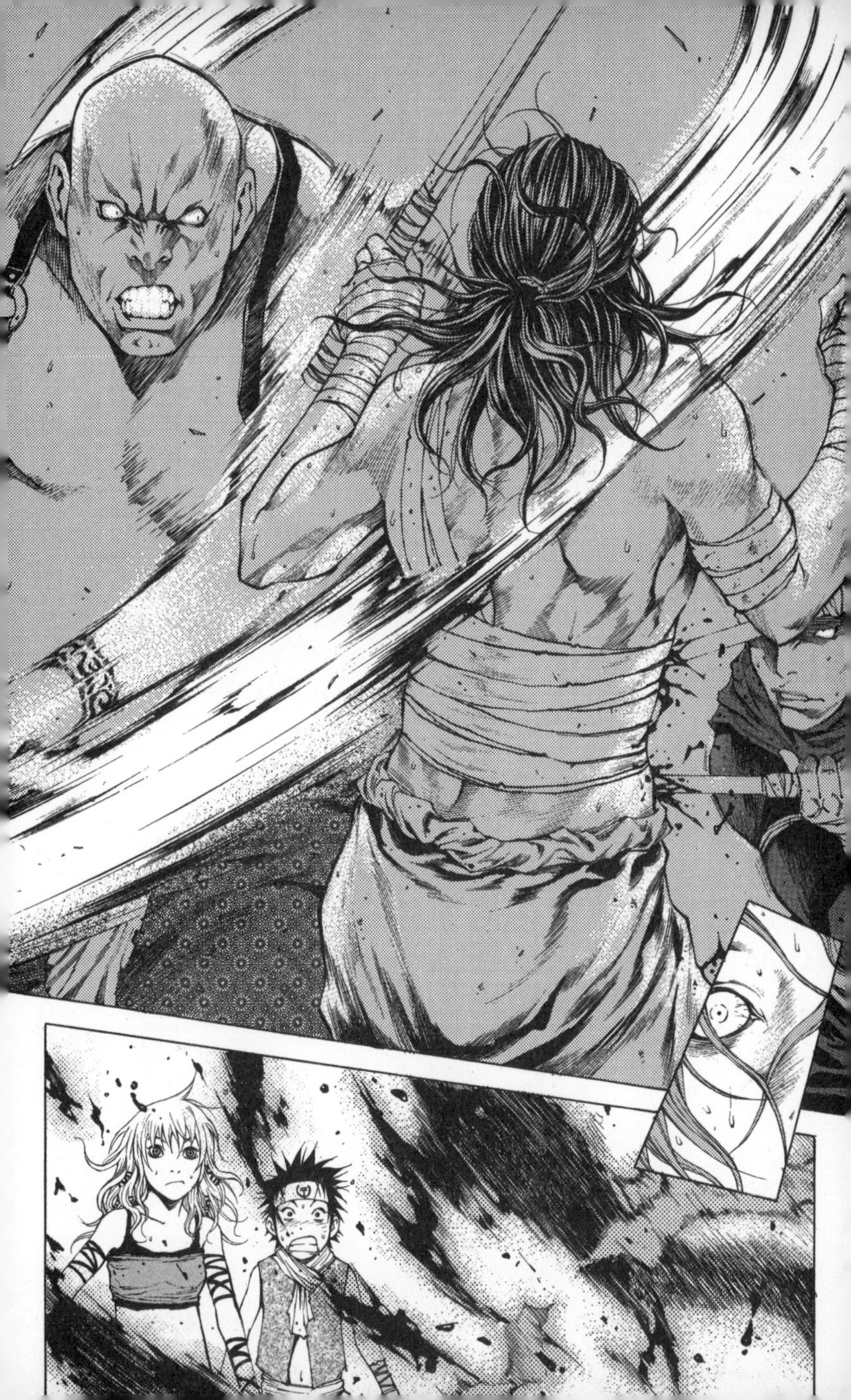

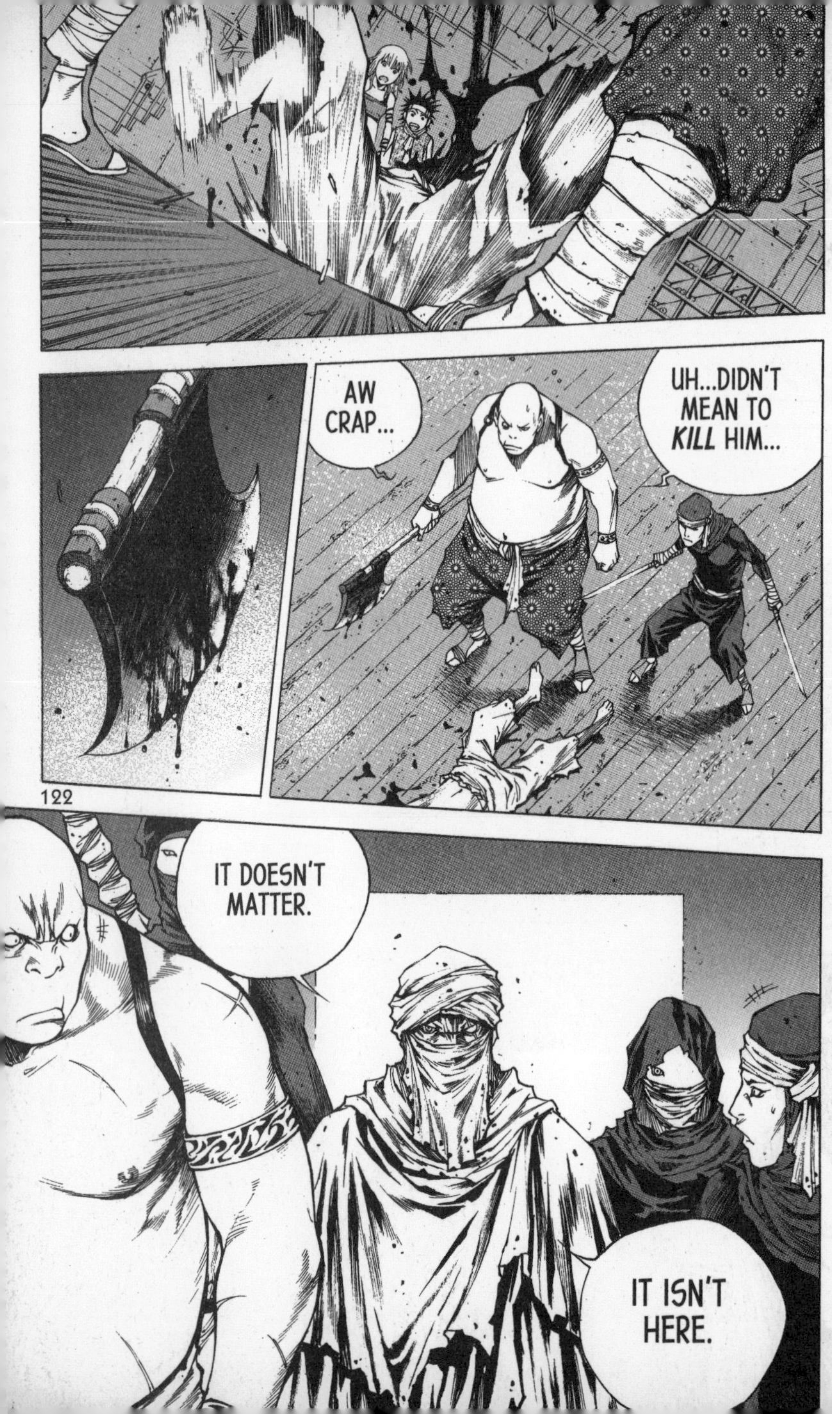
AW CRAP...
UH...DIDN'T MEAN TO *KILL* HIM...
IT DOESN'T MATTER.
IT ISN'T HERE.

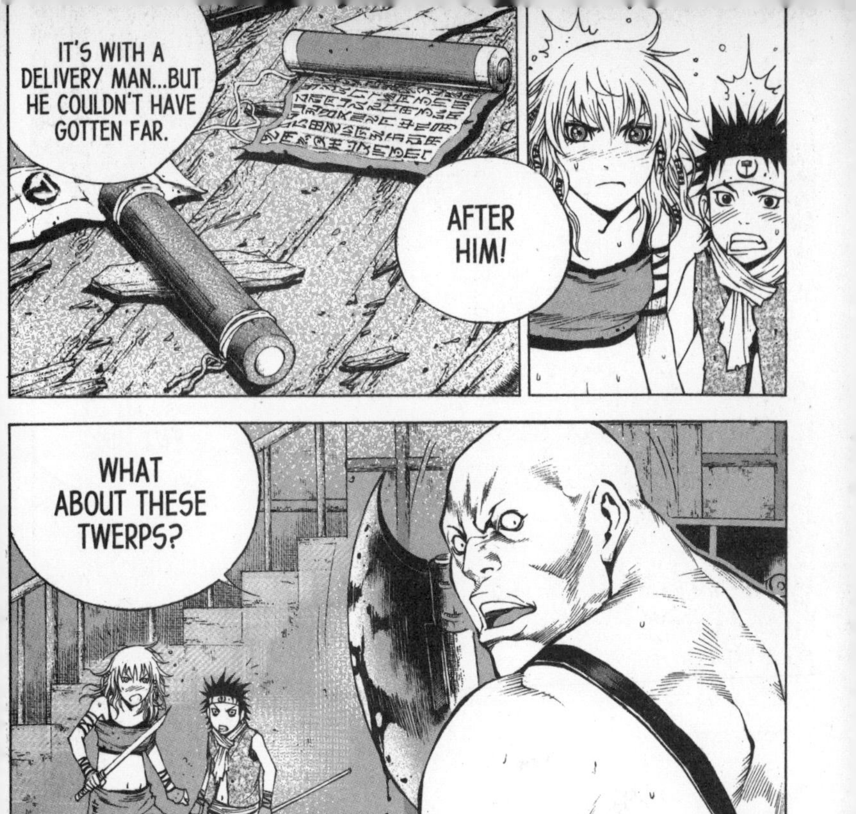
IT'S WITH A DELIVERY MAN...BUT HE COULDN'T HAVE GOTTEN FAR.
AFTER HIM!
WHAT ABOUT THESE TWERPS?

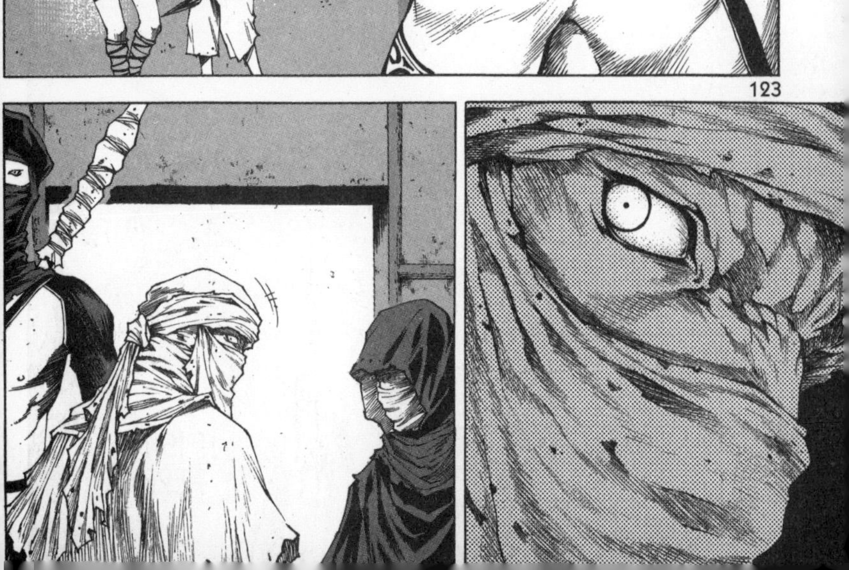

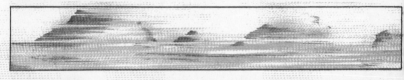

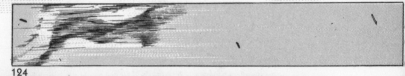

124

Chapter 5
SEPARATION

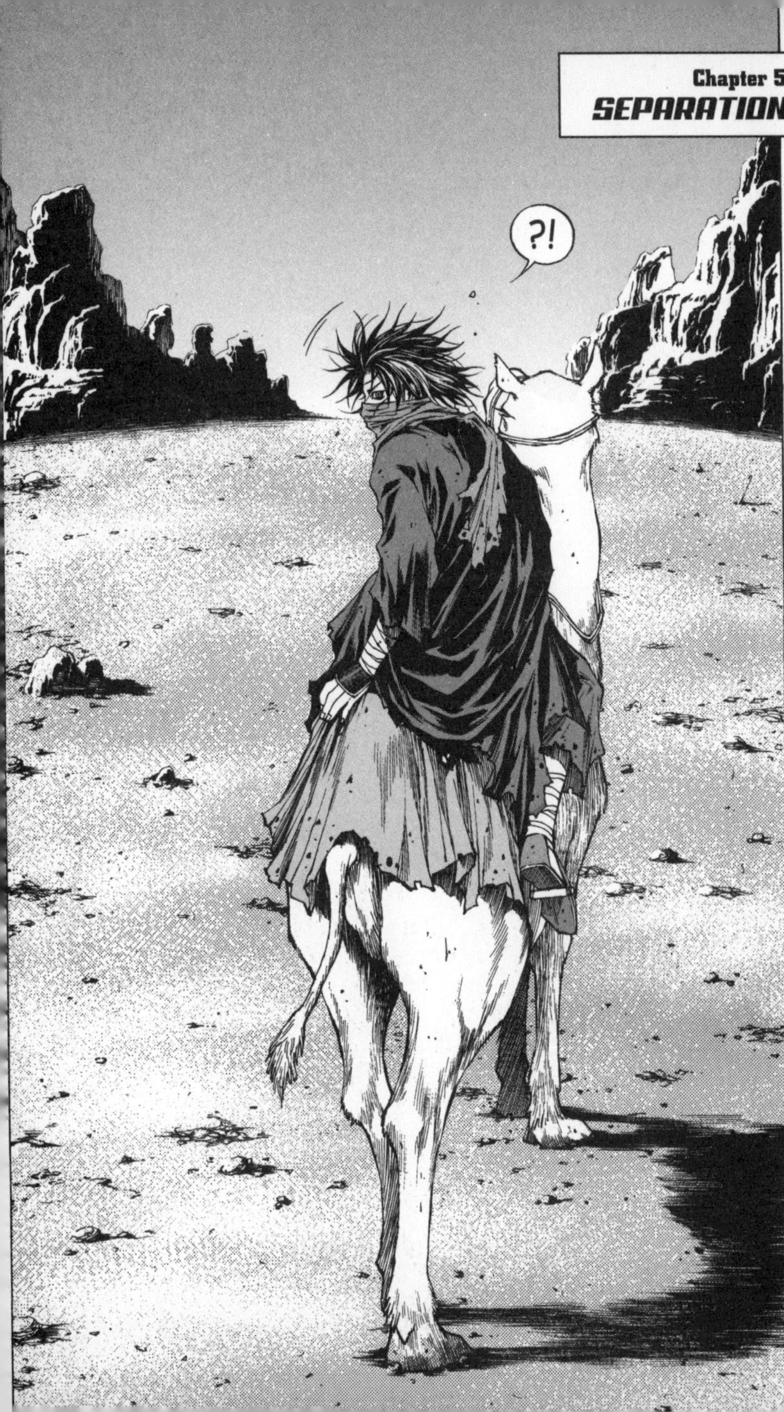
?!

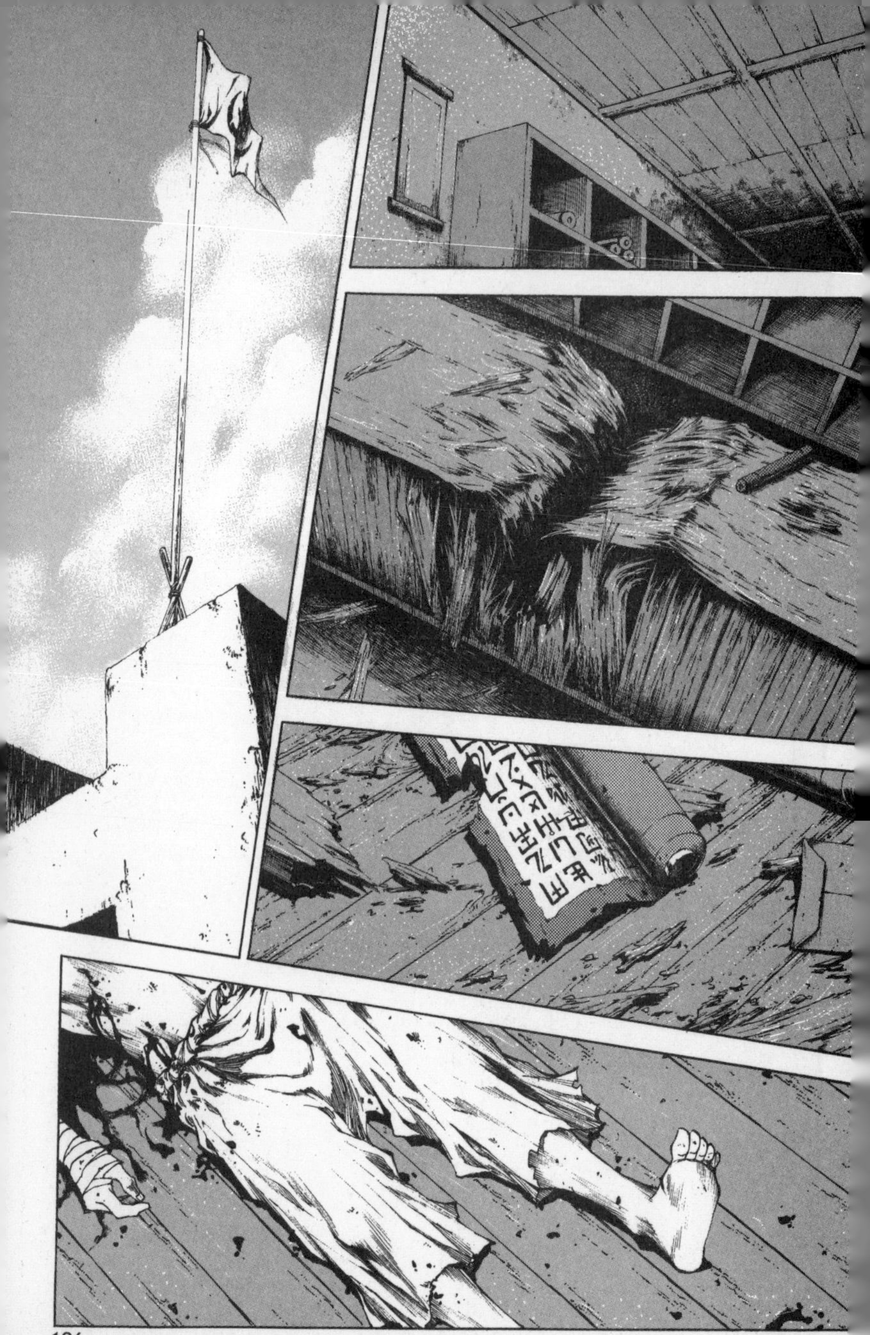

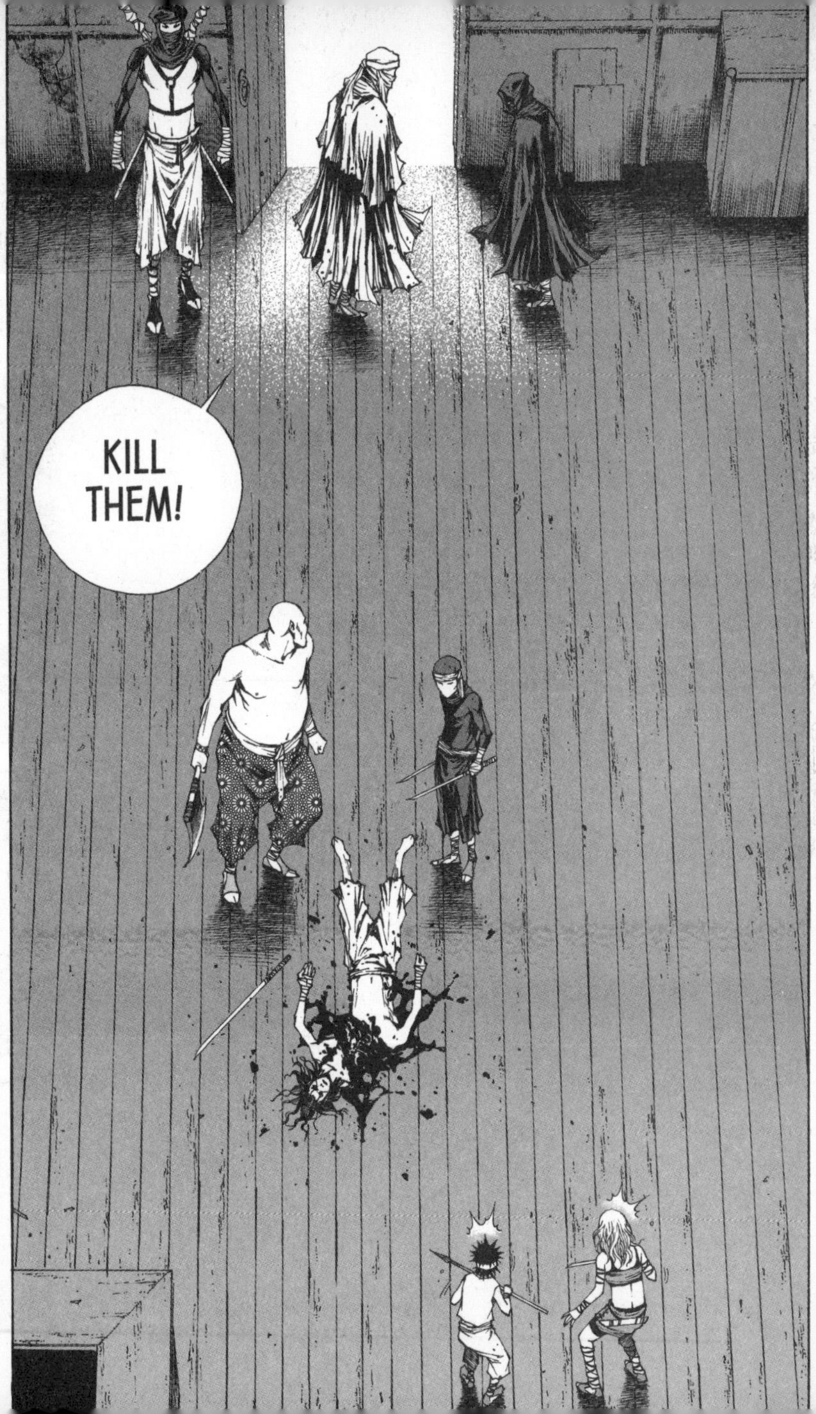
KILL THEM!

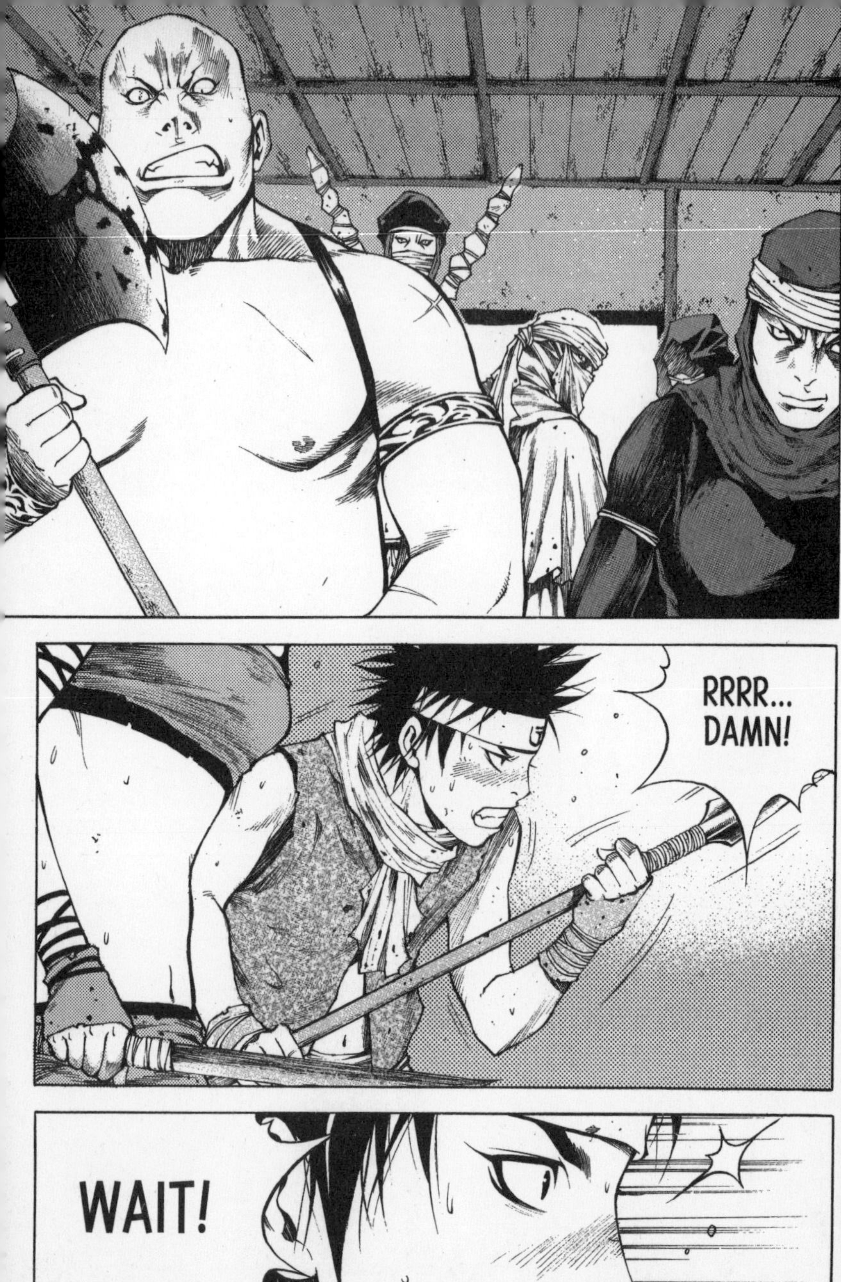
RRRR... DAMN!
WAIT!

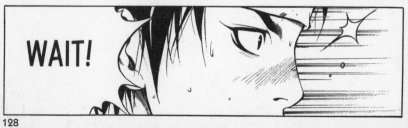

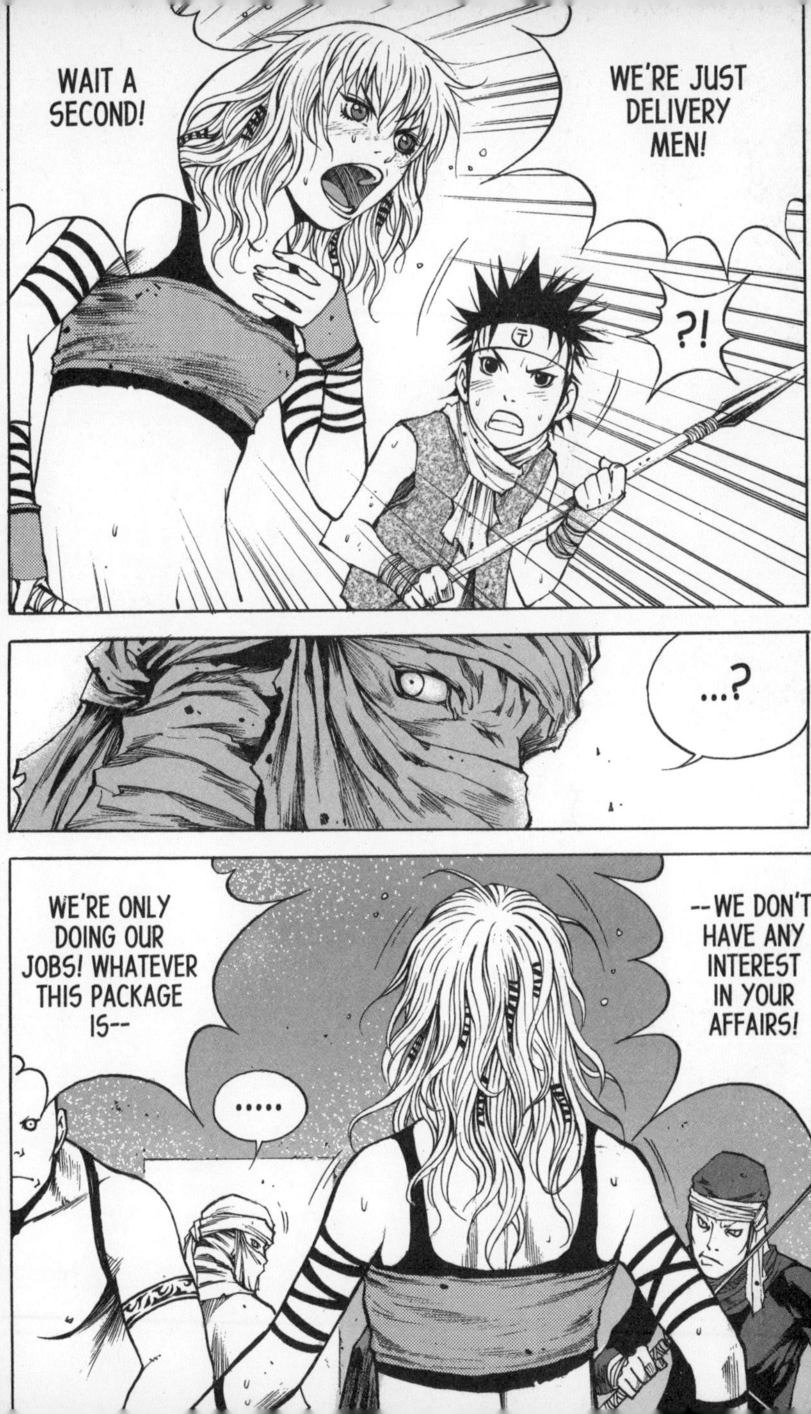
WAIT A SECOND!
WE'RE JUST DELIVERY MEN!
?!
...?
WE'RE ONLY DOING OUR JOBS! WHATEVER THIS PACKAGE IS--
--WE DON'T HAVE ANY INTEREST IN YOUR AFFAIRS!
.....

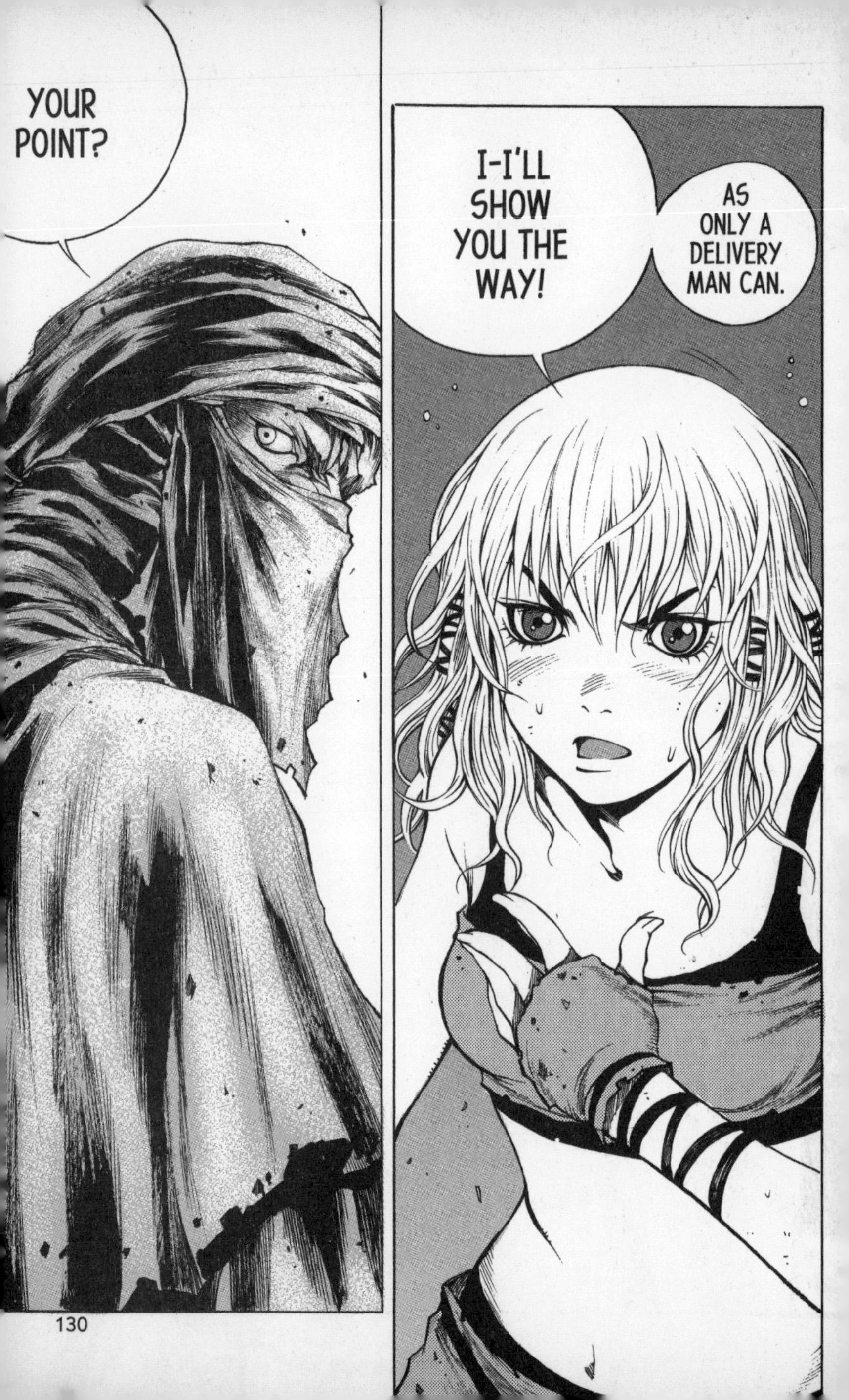
YOUR POINT?
I-I'LL SHOW YOU THE WAY!
AS ONLY A DELIVERY MAN CAN.

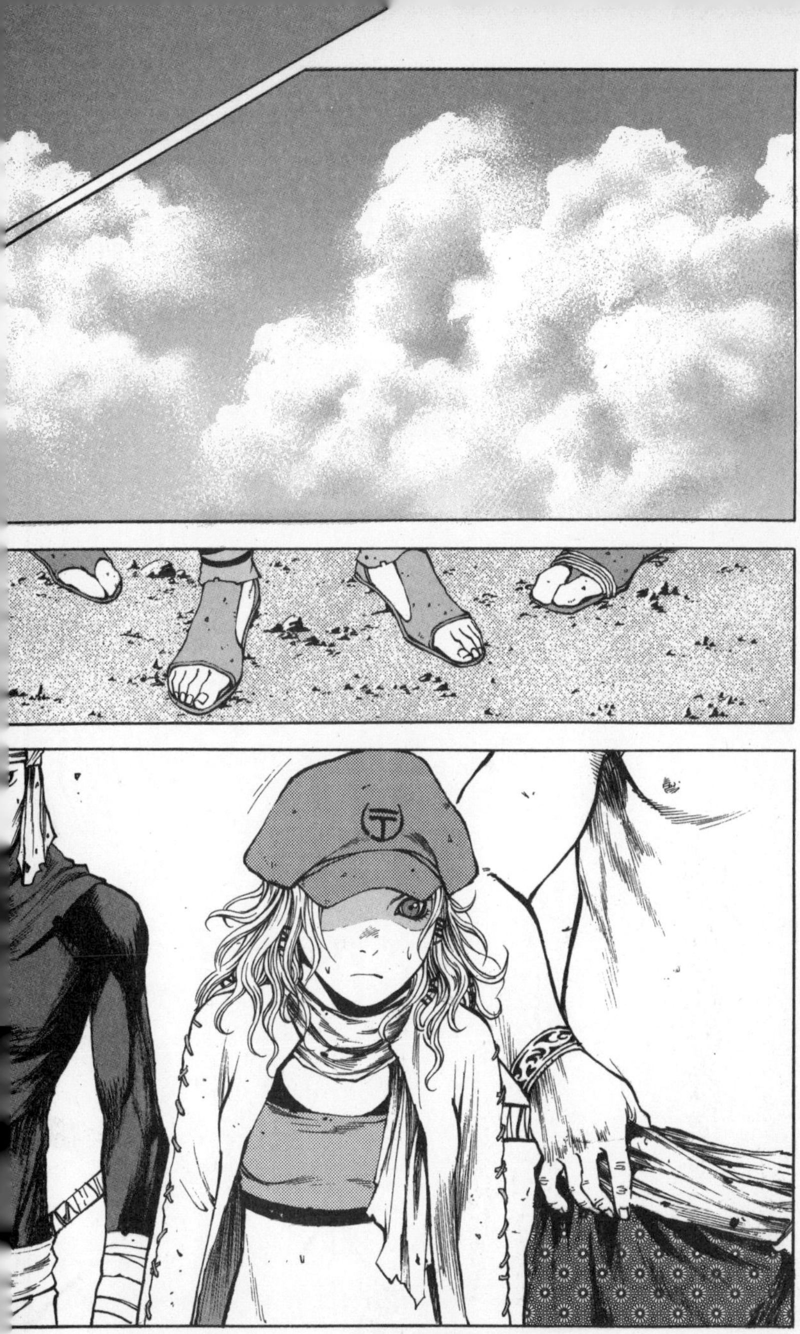

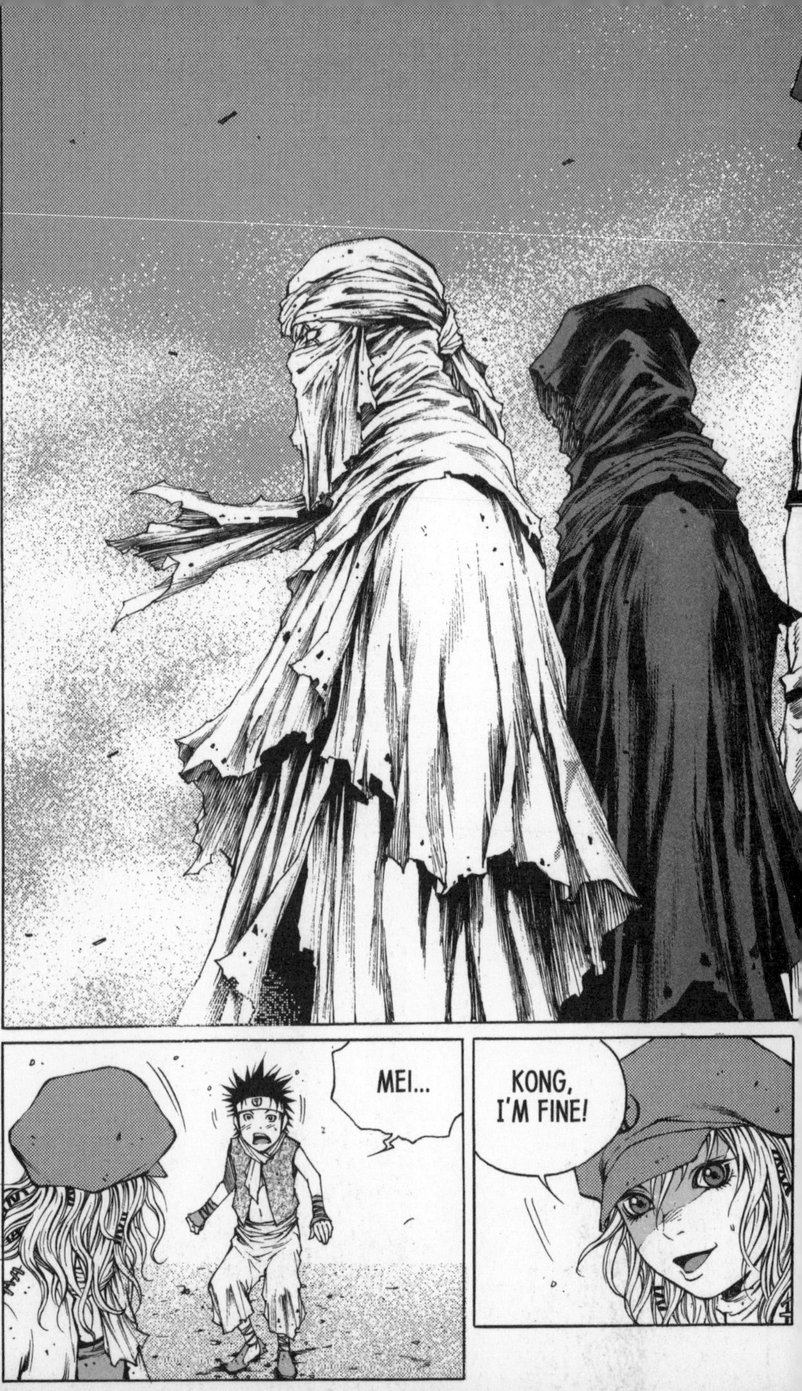
MEI...
KONG, I'M FINE!

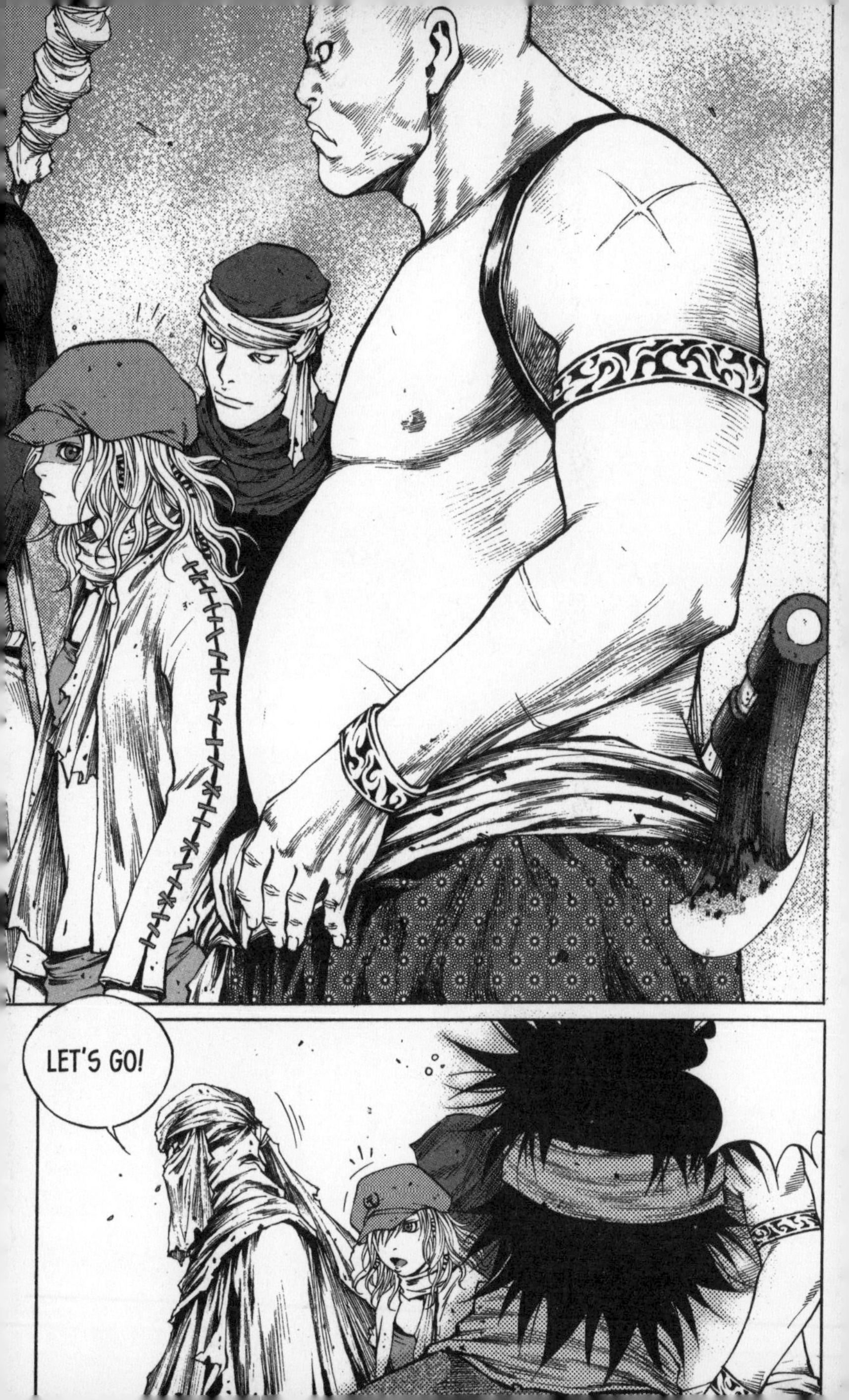
LET'S GO!

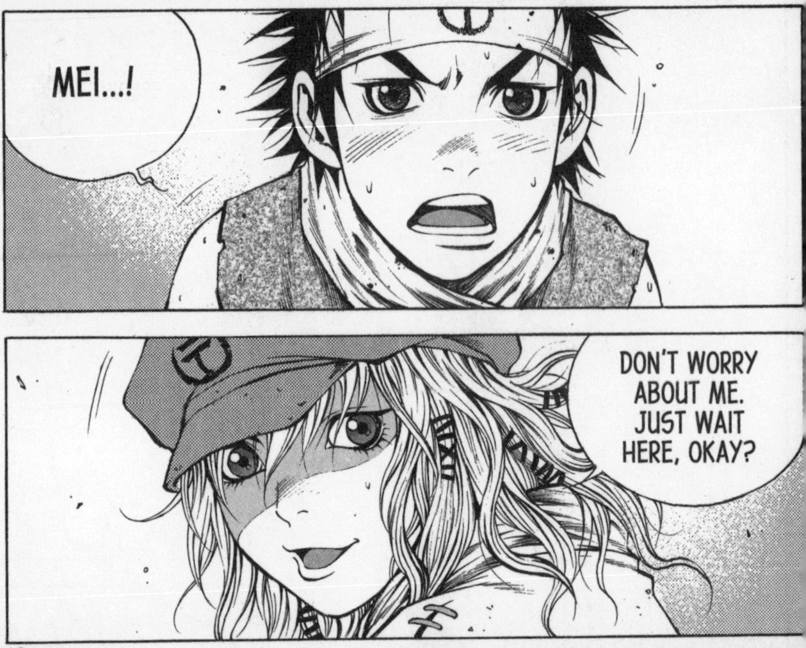
MEI...!
DON'T WORRY ABOUT ME. JUST WAIT HERE, OKAY?

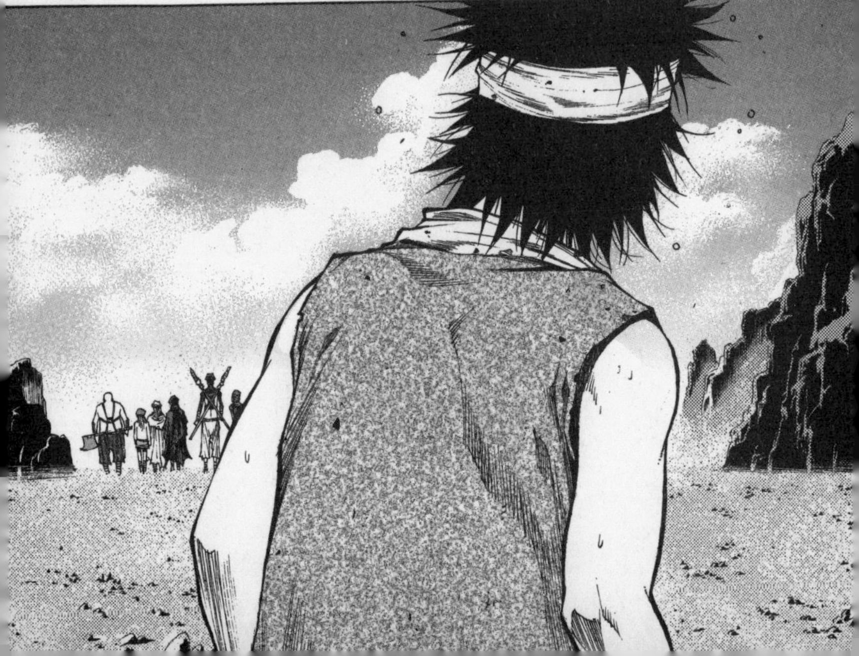

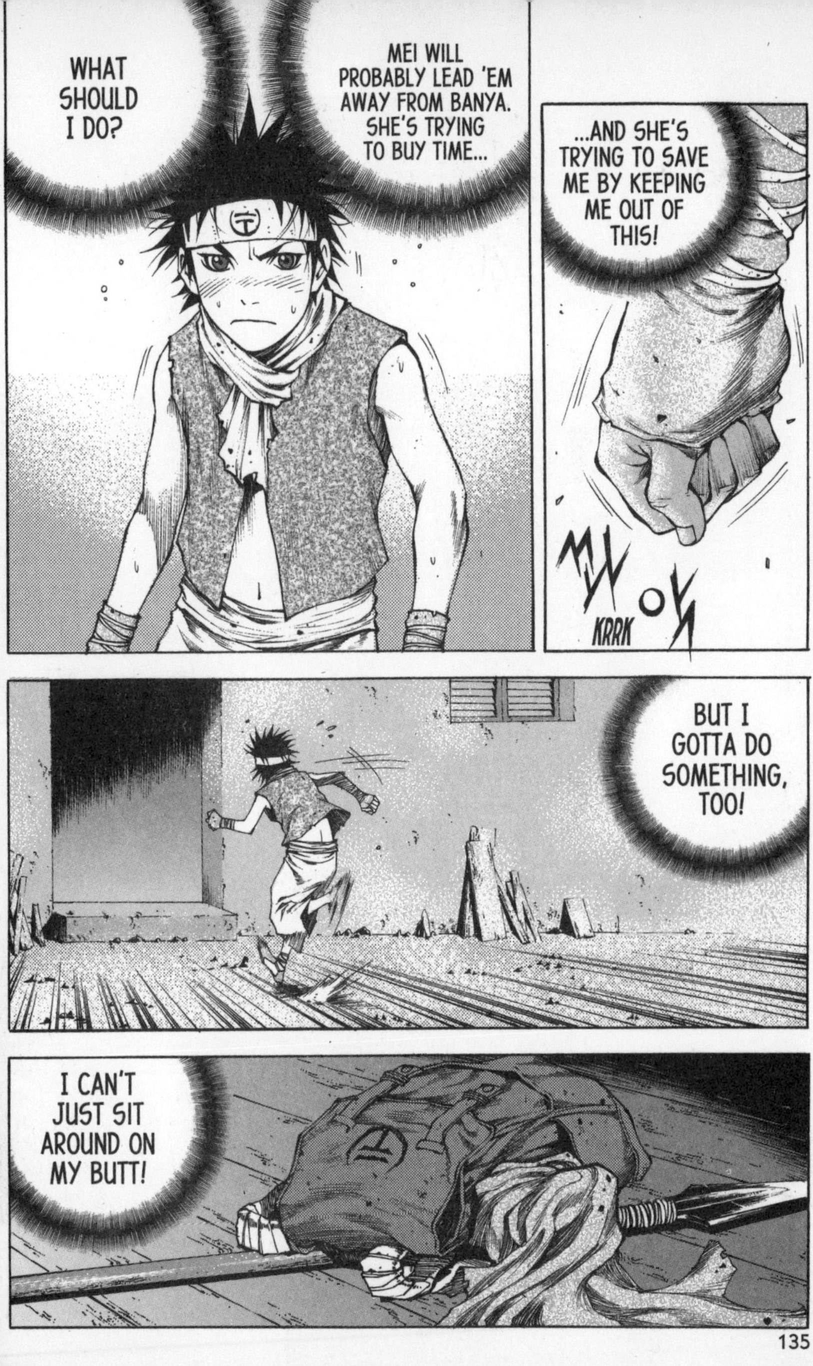
WHAT SHOULD I DO?
MEI WILL PROBABLY LEAD 'EM AWAY FROM BANYA. SHE'S TRYING TO BUY TIME...
...AND SHE'S TRYING TO SAVE ME BY KEEPING ME OUT OF THIS!
KRRK
BUT I GOTTA DO SOMETHING, TOO!
I CAN'T JUST SIT AROUND ON MY BUTT!

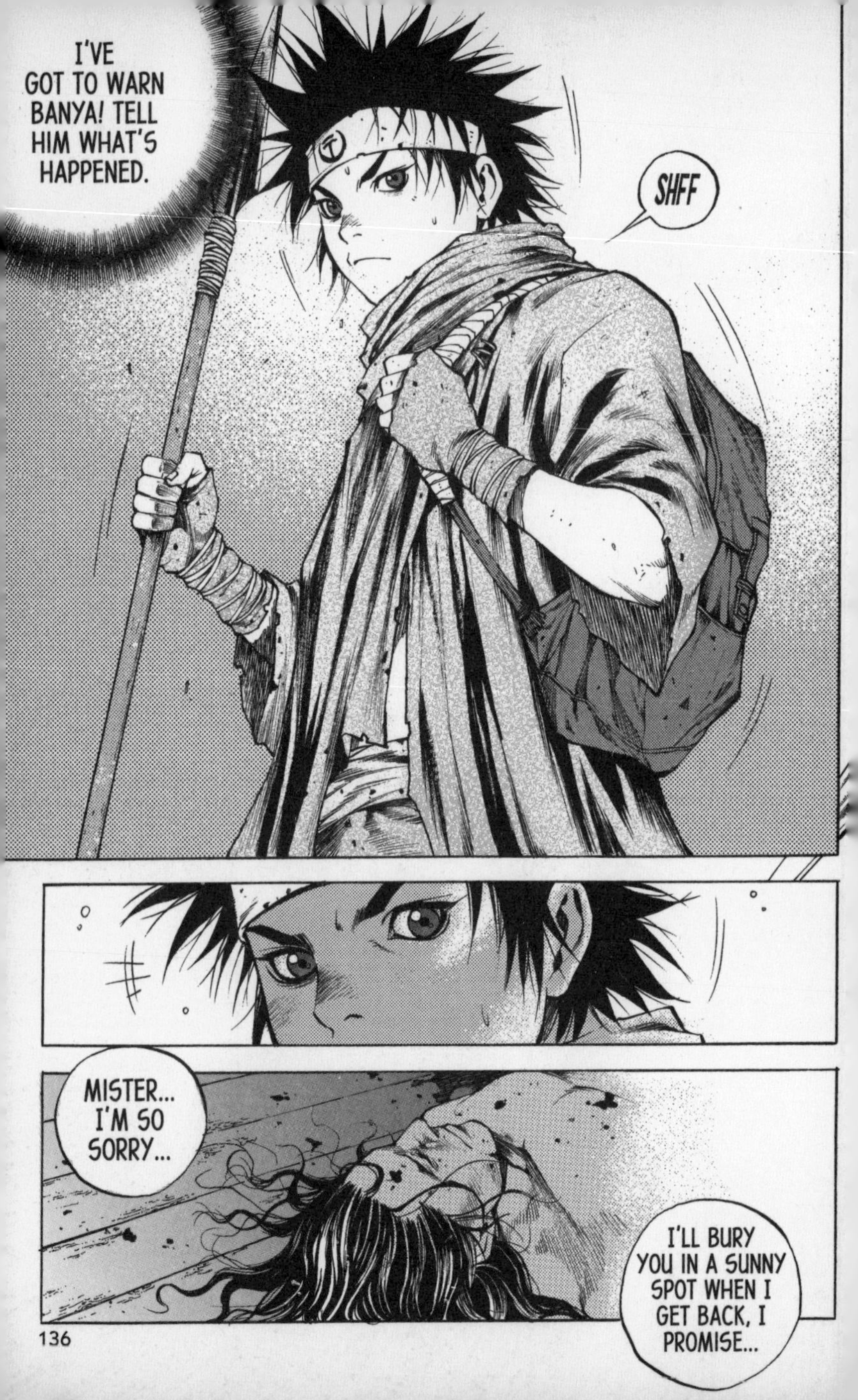
I'VE GOT TO WARN BANYA! TELL HIM WHAT'S HAPPENED.
SHFF
MISTER... I'M SO SORRY...
I'LL BURY YOU IN A SUNNY SPOT WHEN I GET BACK, I PROMISE...

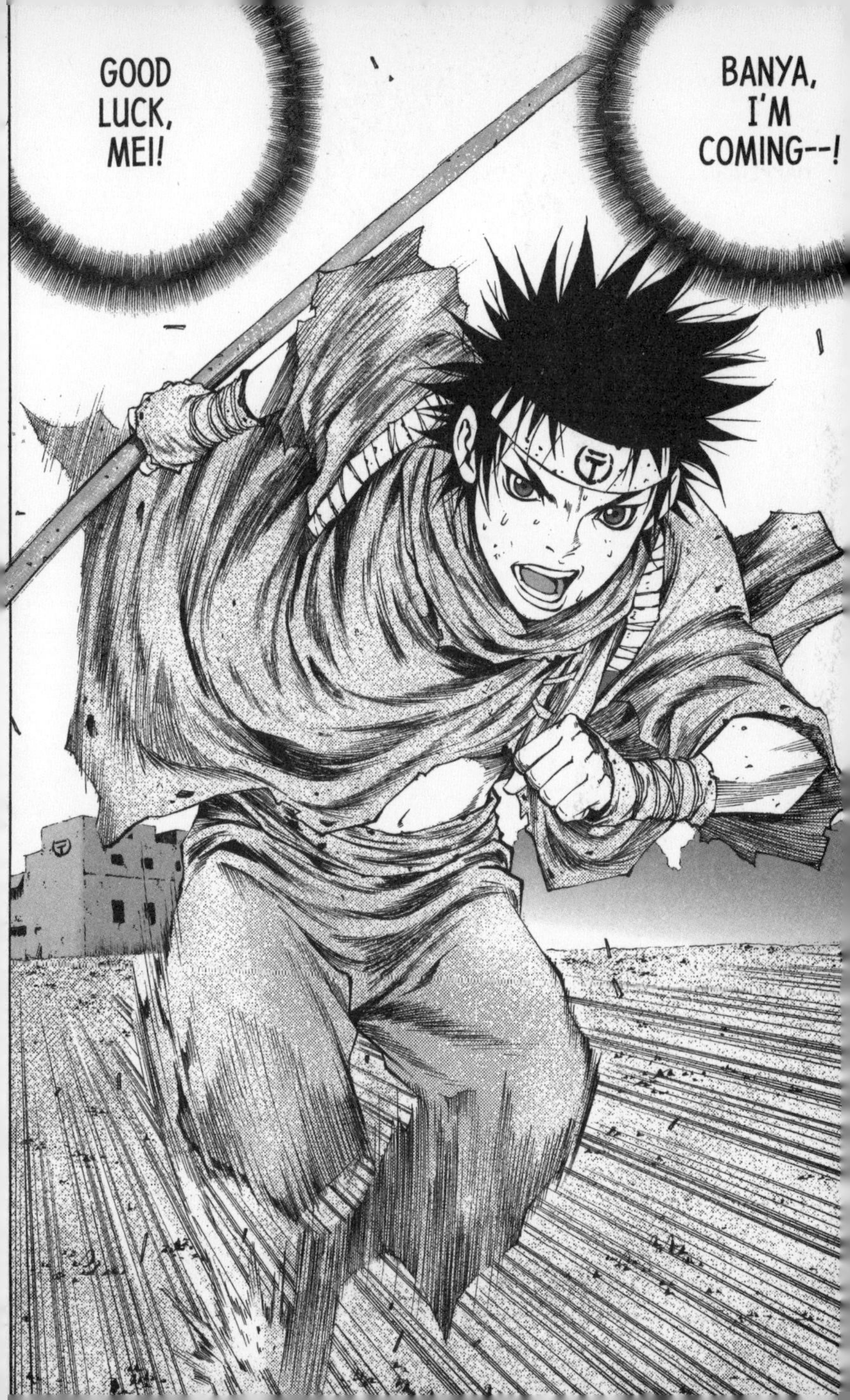
GOOD LUCK, MEI!
BANYA, I'M COMING--!

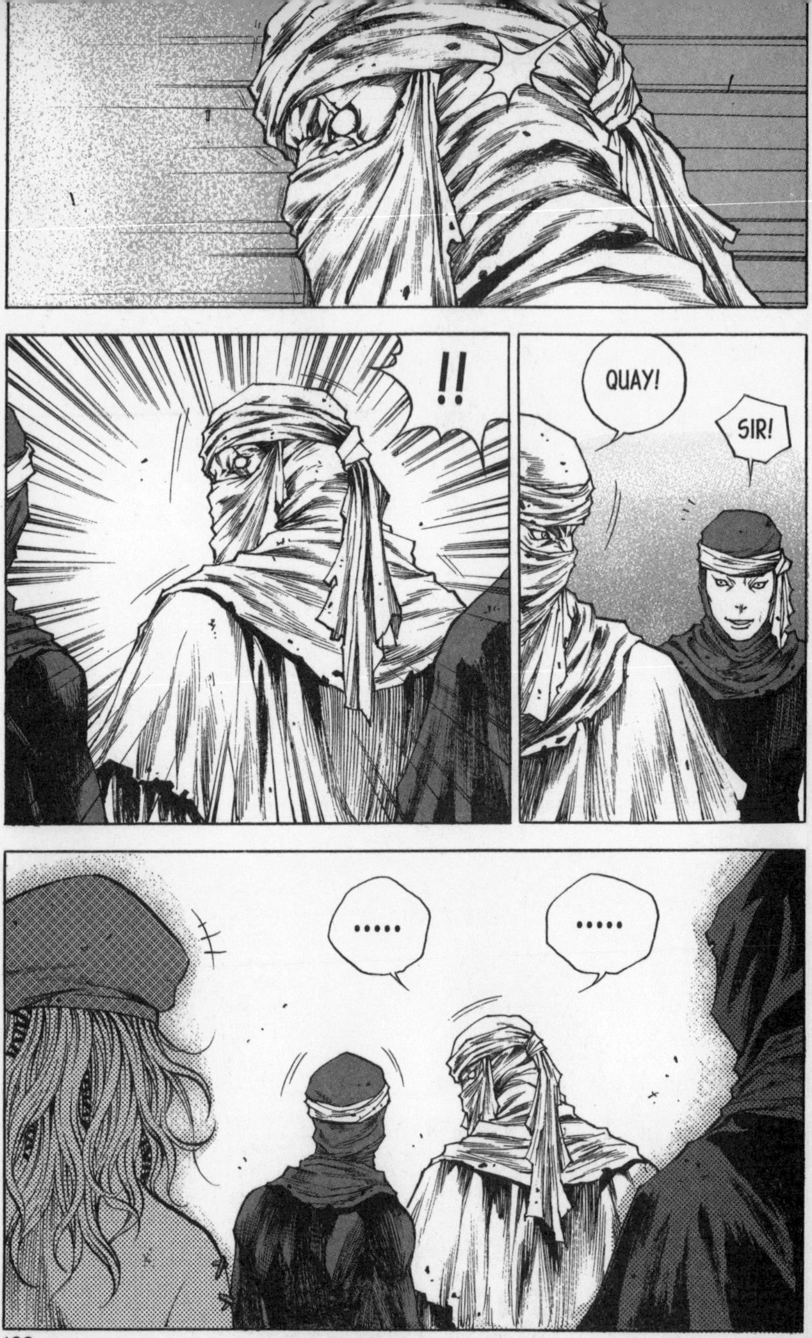
!!
QUAY!
SIR!
.....
.....

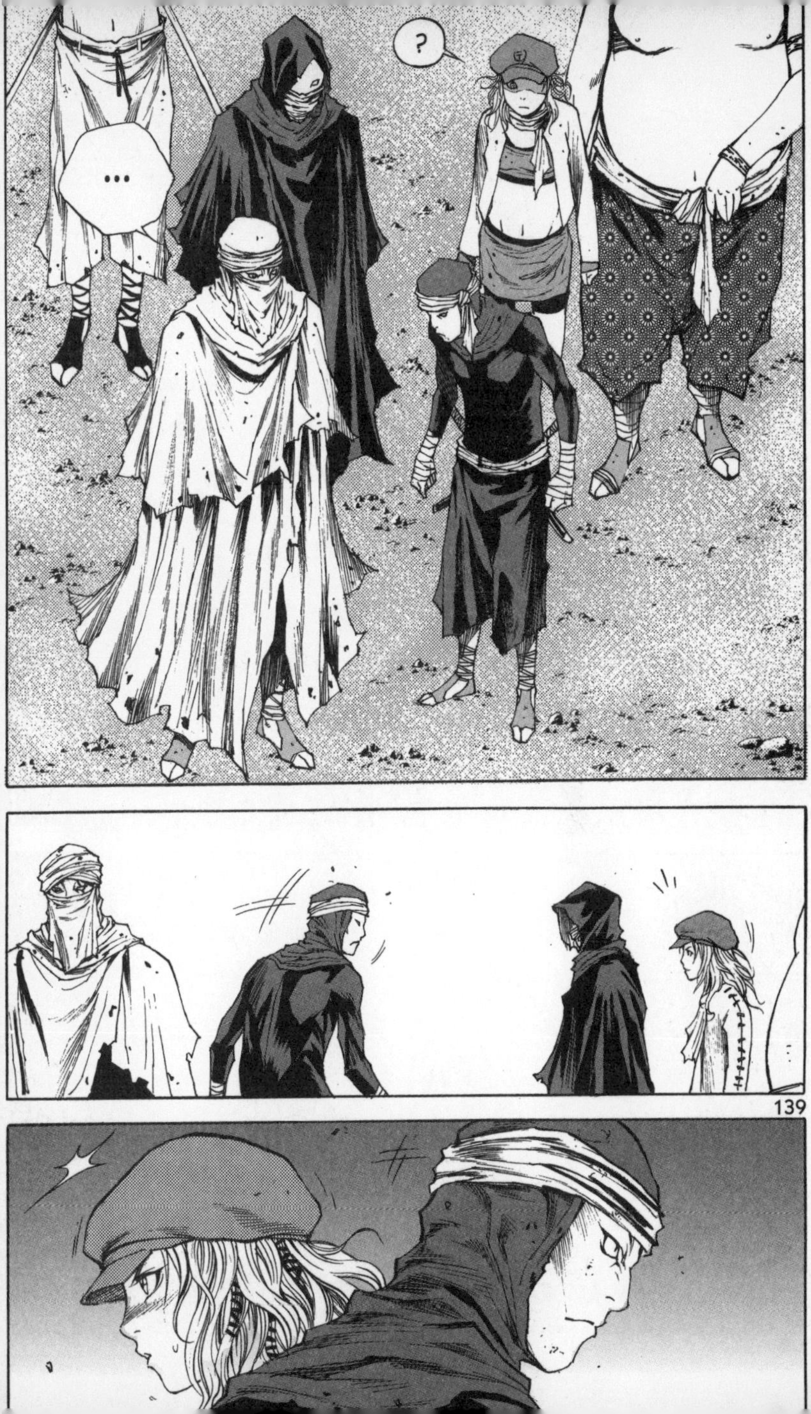
...
?

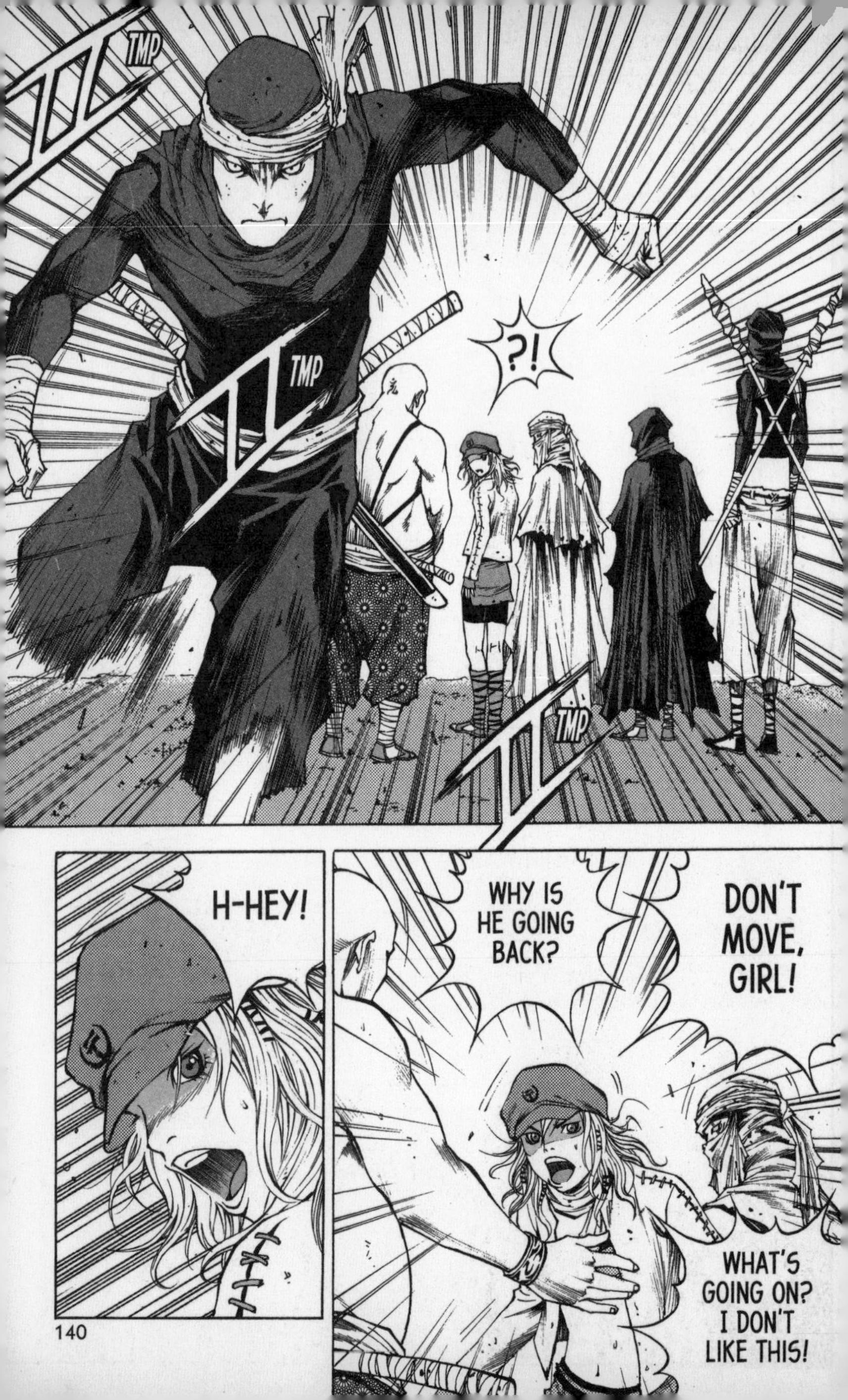
TMP
TMP
?!
TMP
H-HEY!
WHY IS HE GOING BACK?
DON'T MOVE, GIRL!
WHAT'S GOING ON? I DON'T LIKE THIS!

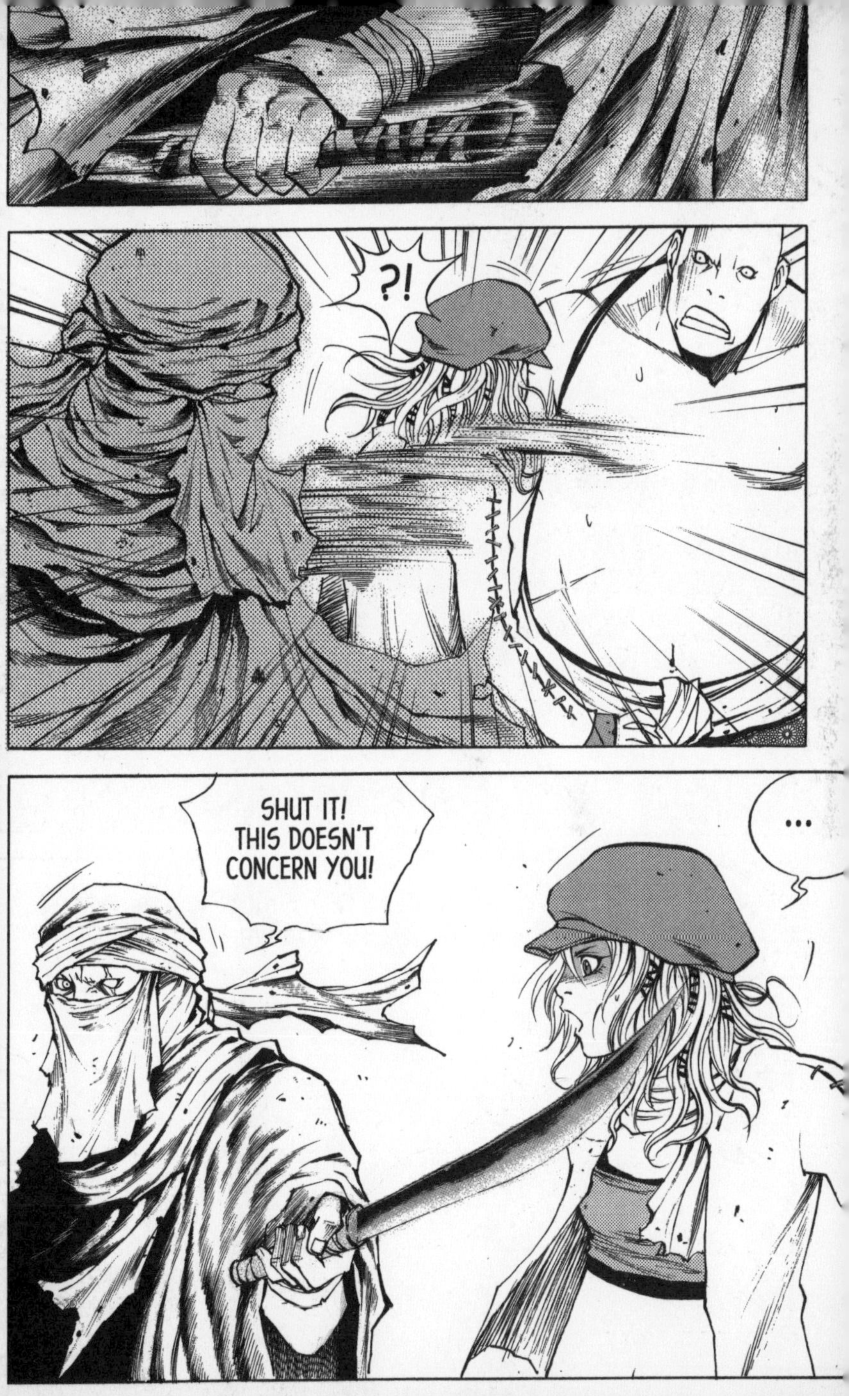
?!
SHUT IT! THIS DOESN'T CONCERN YOU!
...

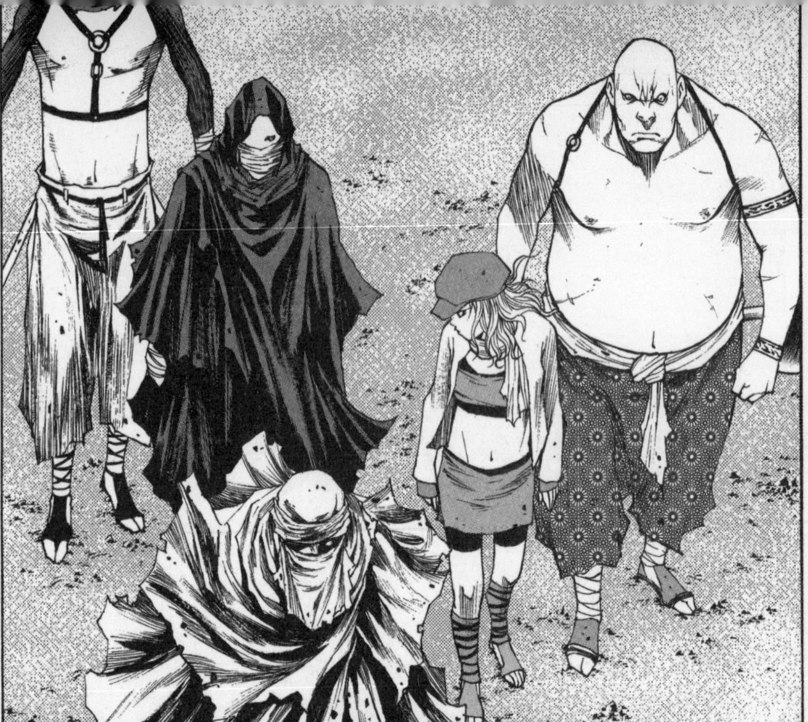
STOP WASTING TIME!

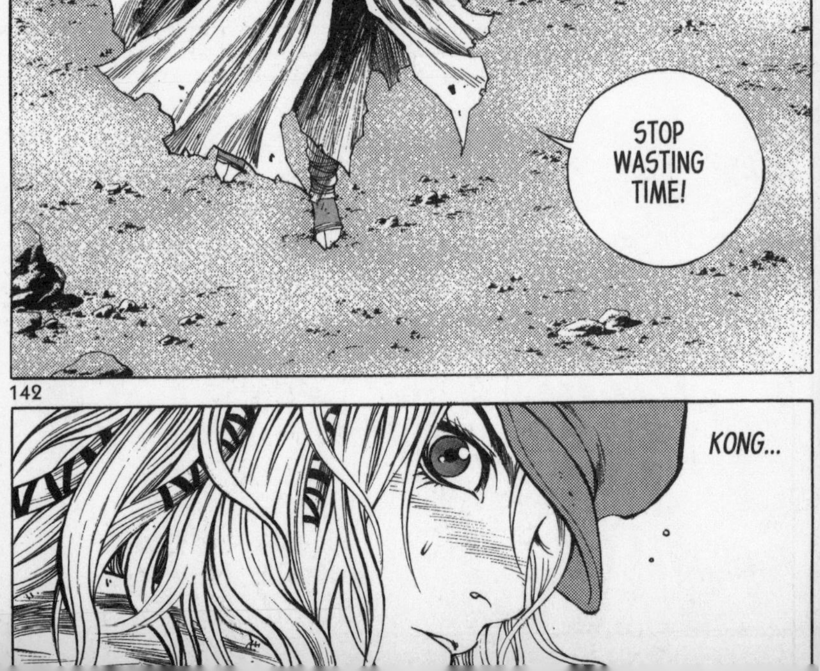
KONG...

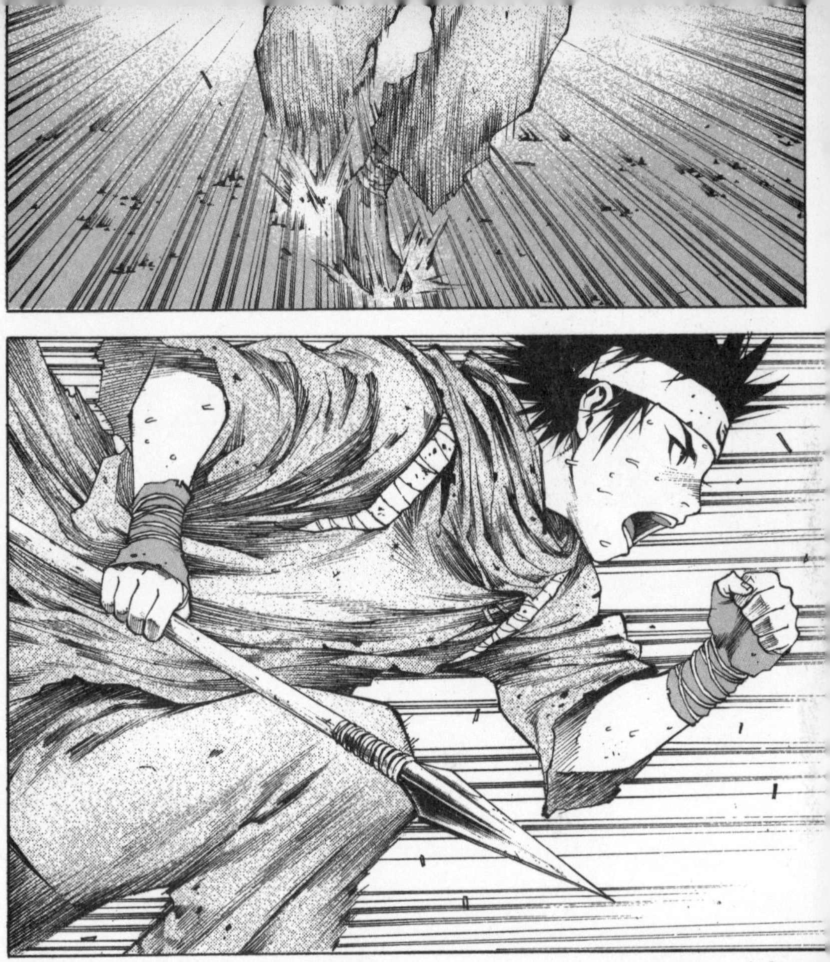

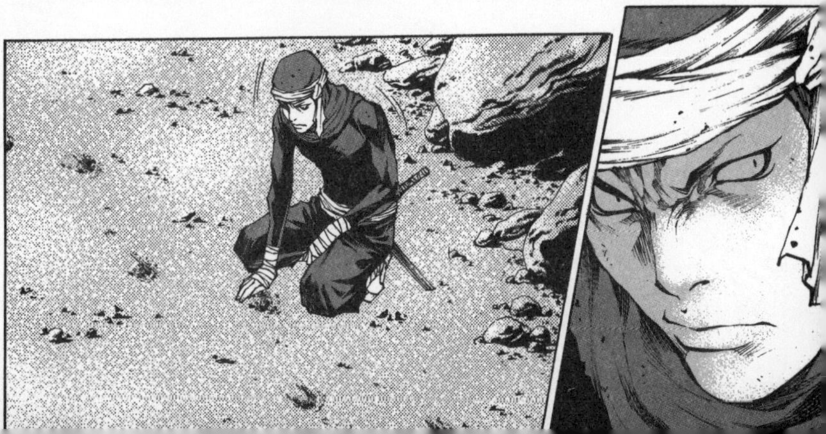

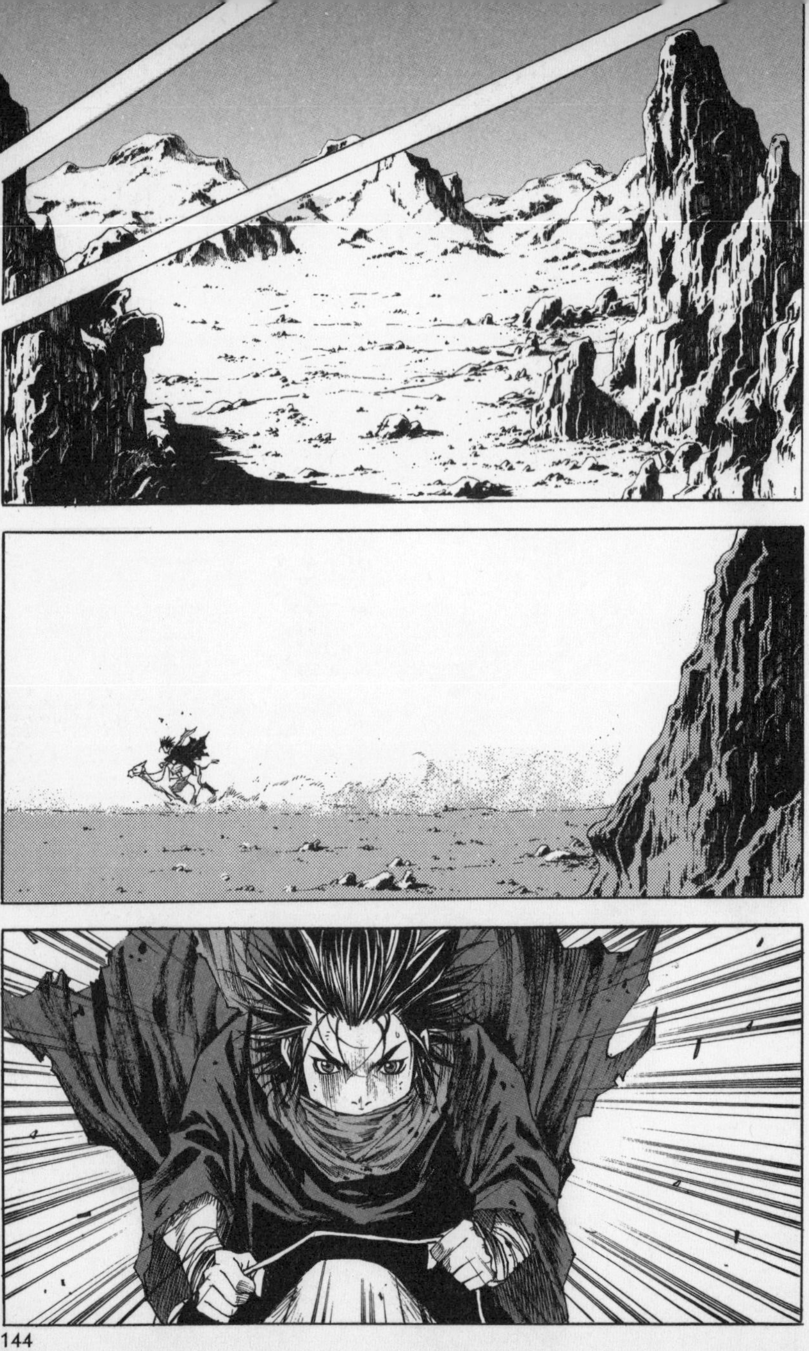

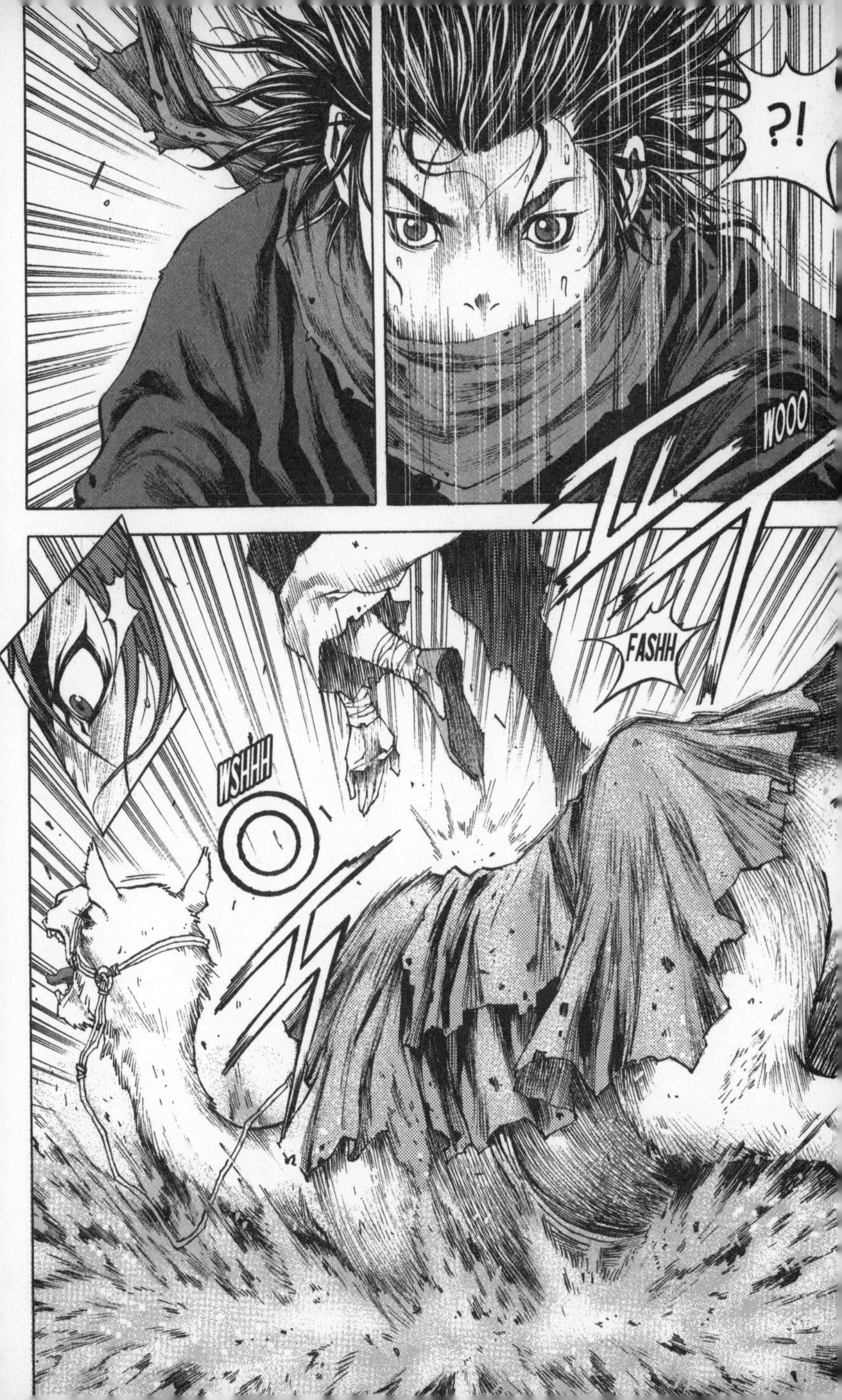

?!
WOOO
FASHH
WSHHH

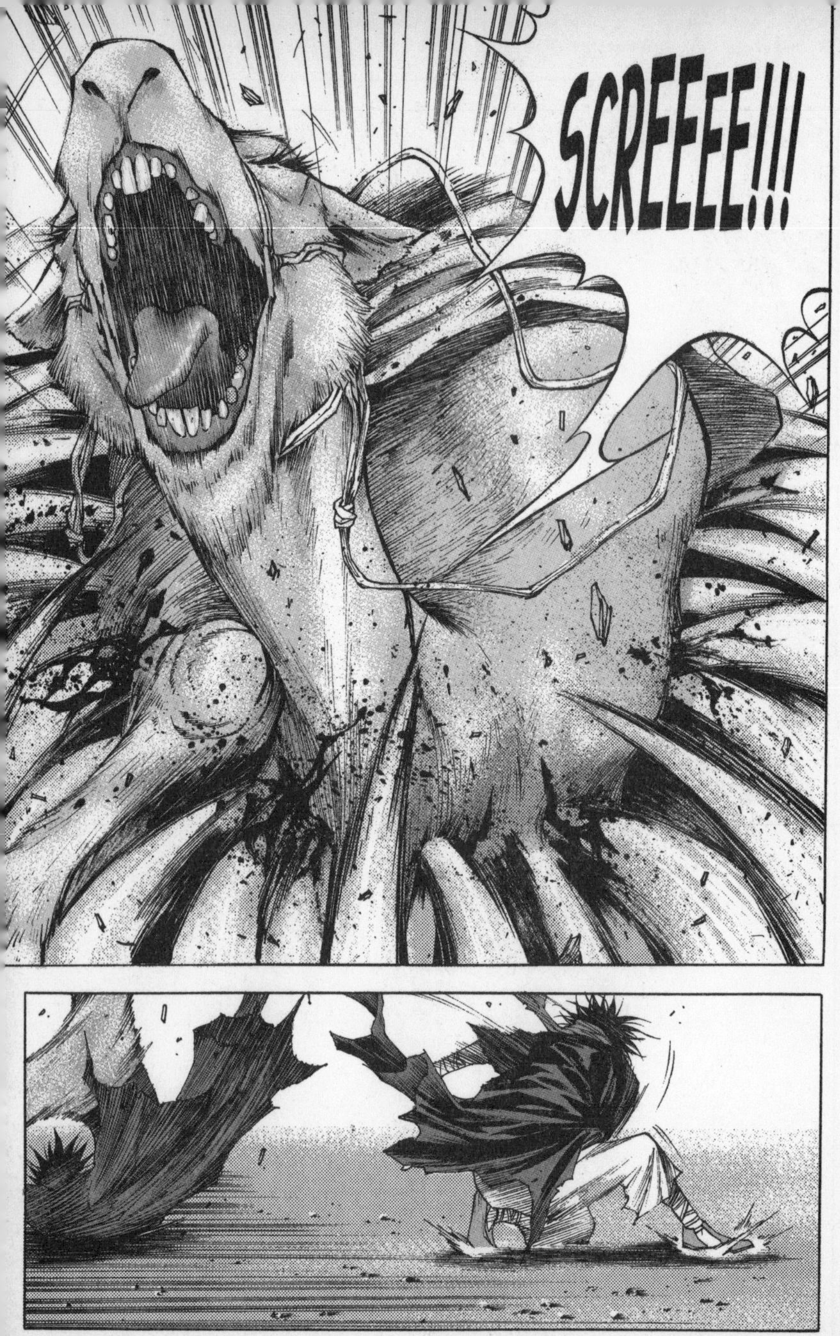
SCREEEE!!!

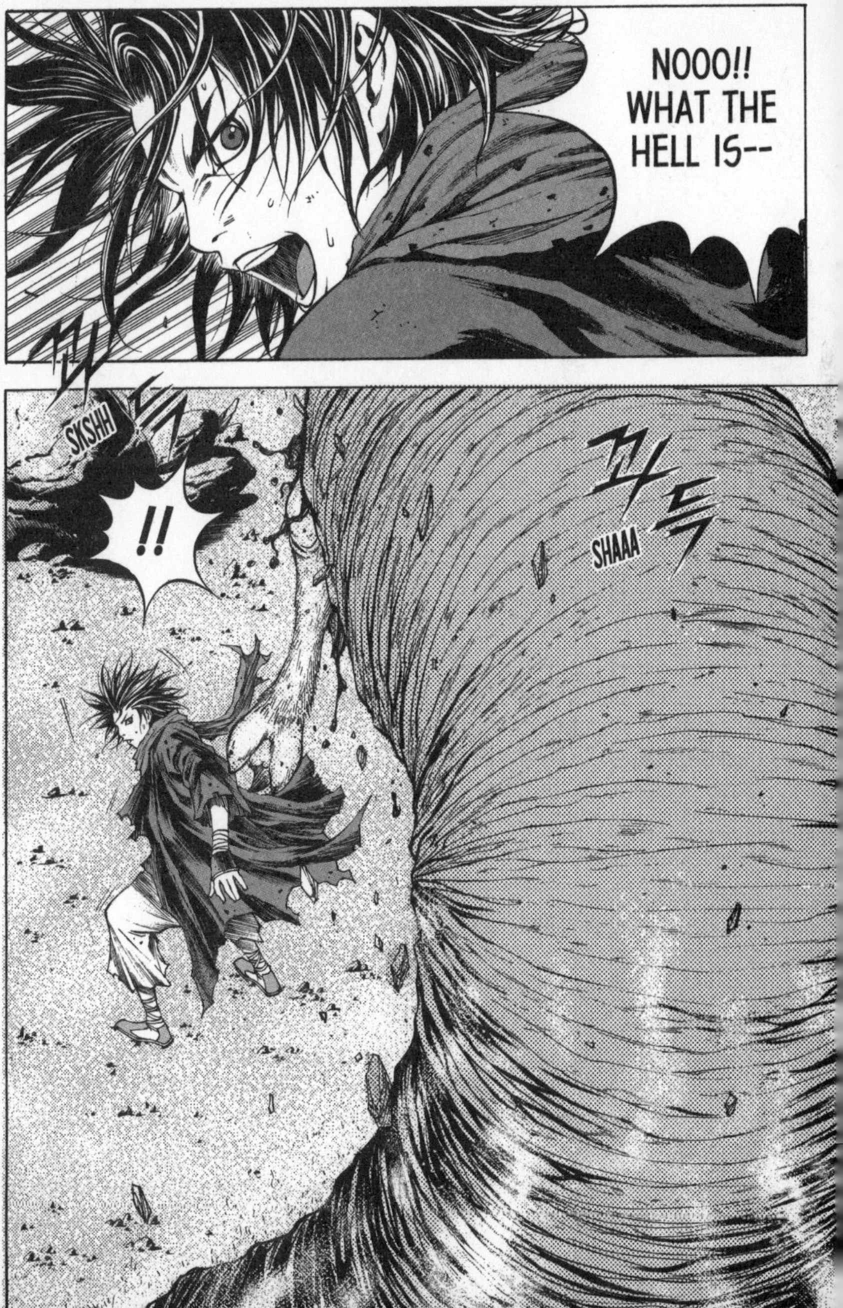
NOOO!!
WHAT THE
HELL IS--
SKSHH
!!
SHAAA

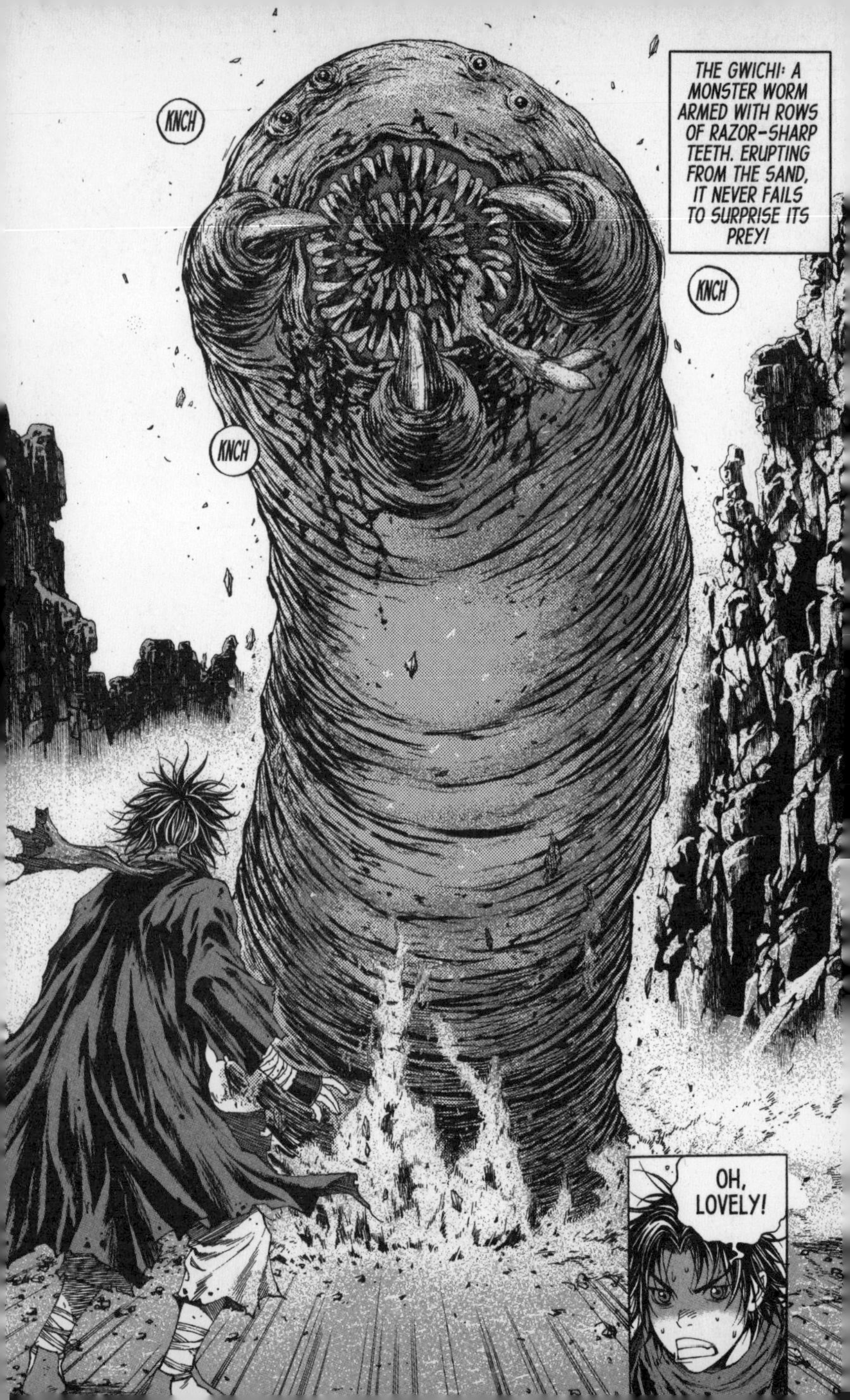
KNCH
THE GWICHI: A MONSTER WORM ARMED WITH ROWS OF RAZOR-SHARP TEETH. ERUPTING FROM THE SAND, IT NEVER FAILS TO SURPRISE ITS PREY!
KNCH
KNCH
OH, LOVELY!

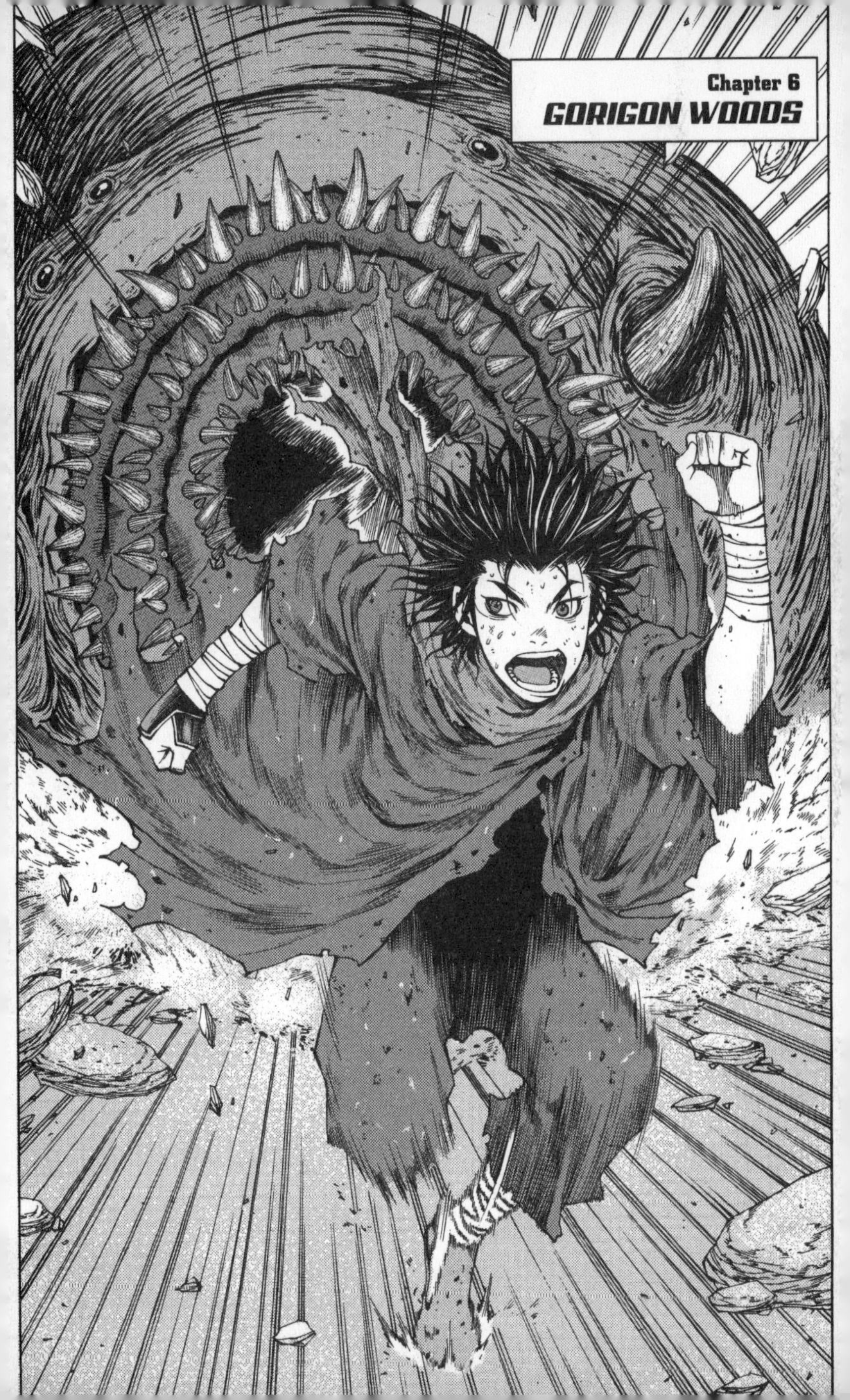
Chapter 6
GORIGON WOODS

BRRMM

RMM

RMM

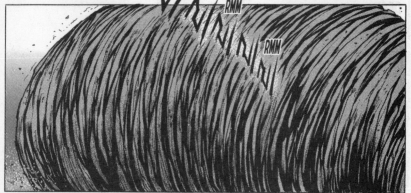

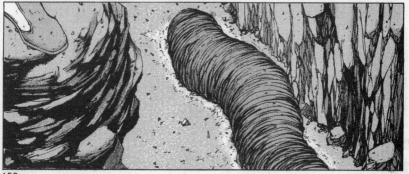

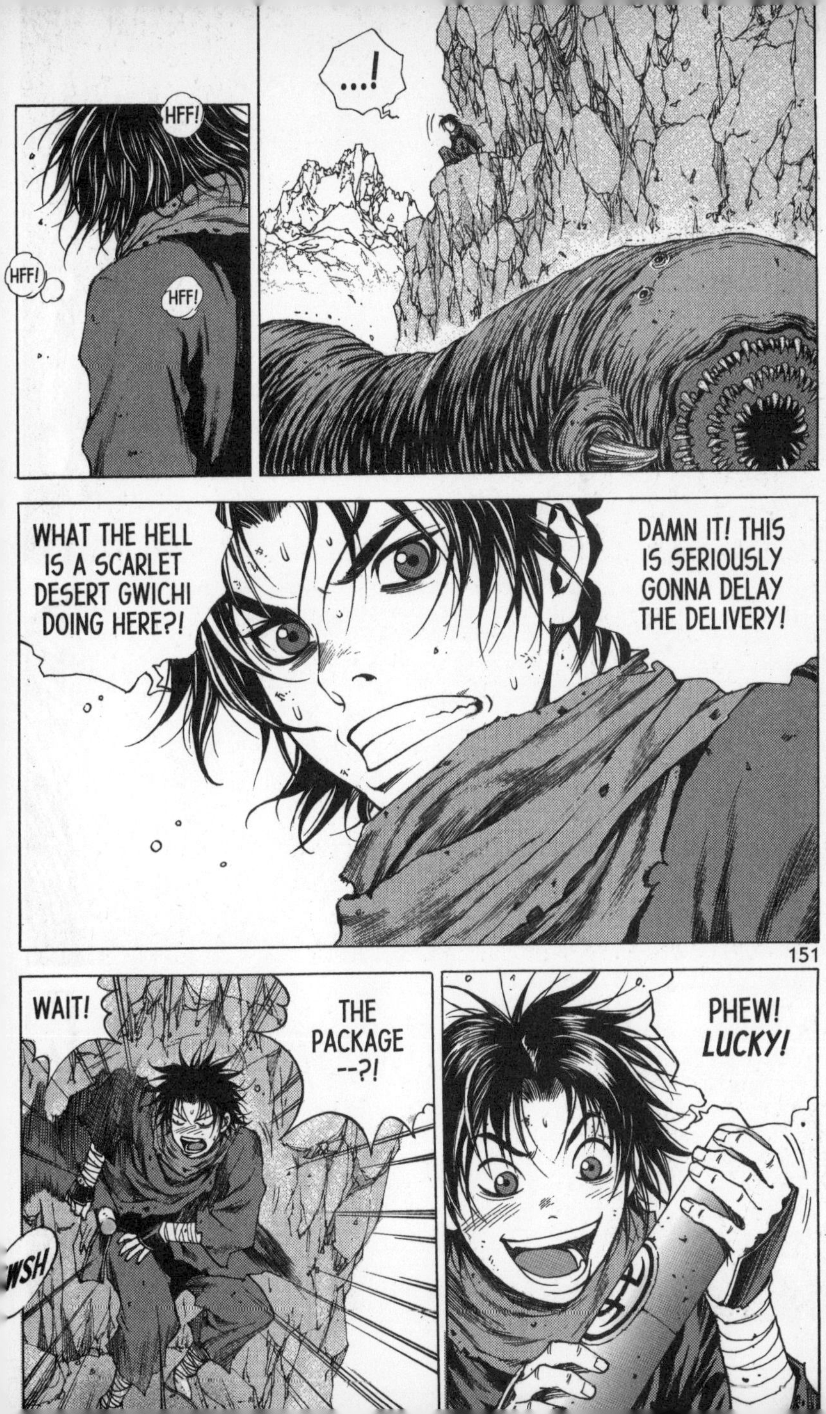
HFF!
HFF!
HFF!
...!
WHAT THE HELL IS A SCARLET DESERT GWICHI DOING HERE?!
DAMN IT! THIS IS SERIOUSLY GONNA DELAY THE DELIVERY!
WAIT!
THE PACKAGE --?!
WSH
PHEW! LUCKY!

STILL, I'M REALLY IN IT THIS TIME...

NOT ONLY AM I GONNA BE LATE...

...MEI'S GONNA BEAT ME SENSELESS WHEN SHE HEARS ABOUT THE CAMEL!

.....

BAH! FOCUS! FIRST-- FINISH THE DELIVERY!

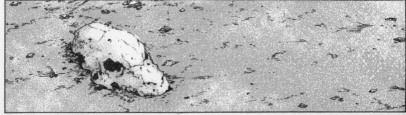

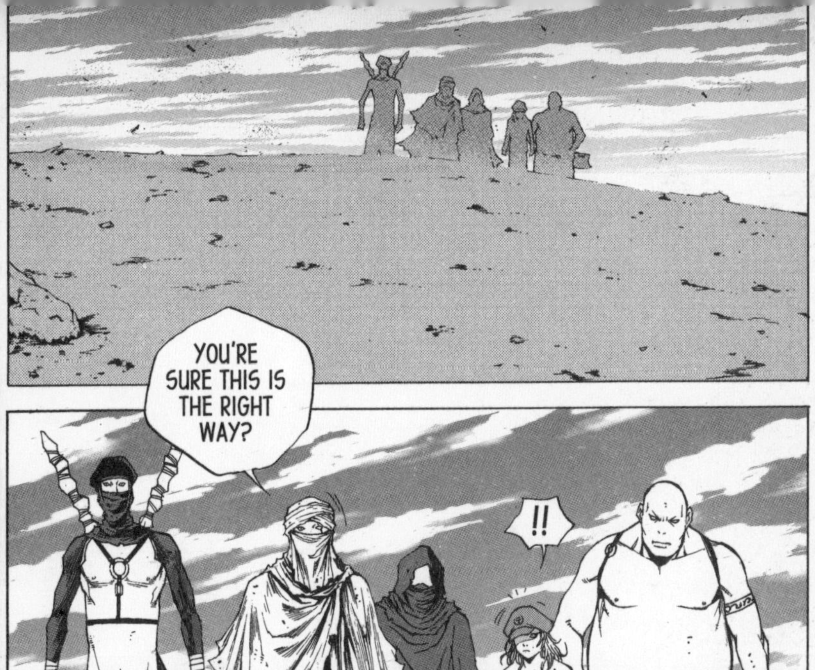
YOU'RE SURE THIS IS THE RIGHT WAY?
!!

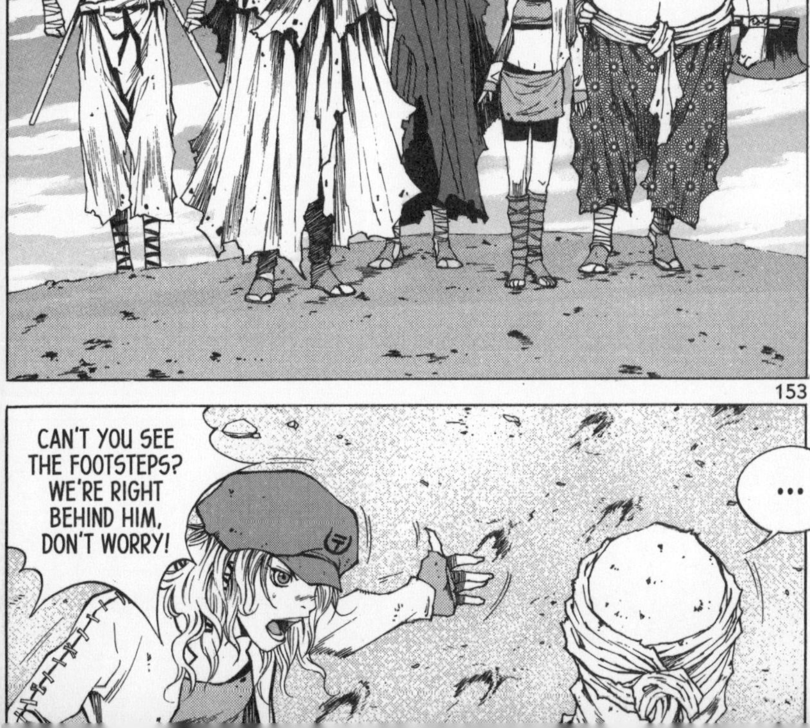
CAN'T YOU SEE THE FOOTSTEPS? WE'RE RIGHT BEHIND HIM, DON'T WORRY!
...

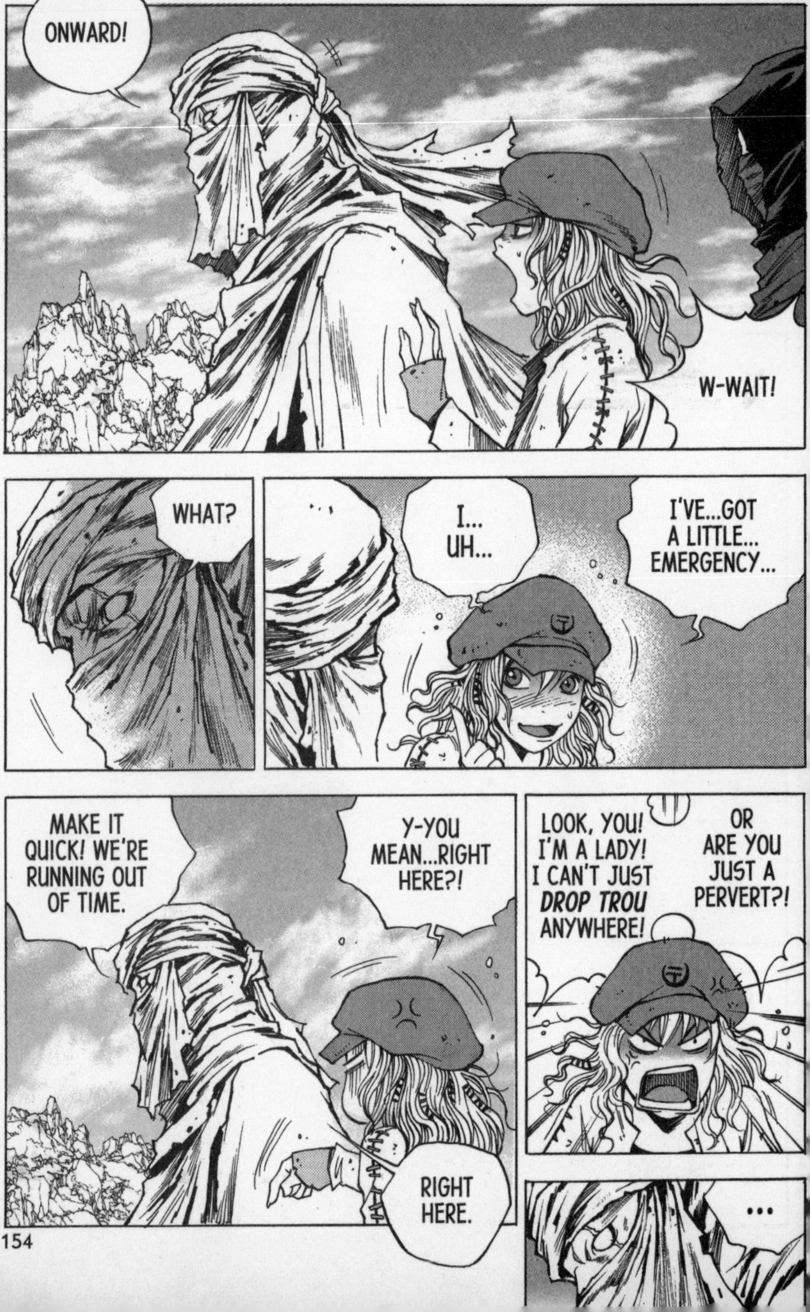
ONWARD!
W-WAIT!
WHAT?
...
I... UH...
I'VE...GOT A LITTLE... EMERGENCY...
MAKE IT QUICK! WE'RE RUNNING OUT OF TIME.
Y-YOU MEAN...RIGHT HERE?!
RIGHT HERE.
LOOK, YOU! I'M A LADY! I CAN'T JUST *DROP TROU* ANYWHERE!
OR ARE YOU JUST A PERVERT?!
...

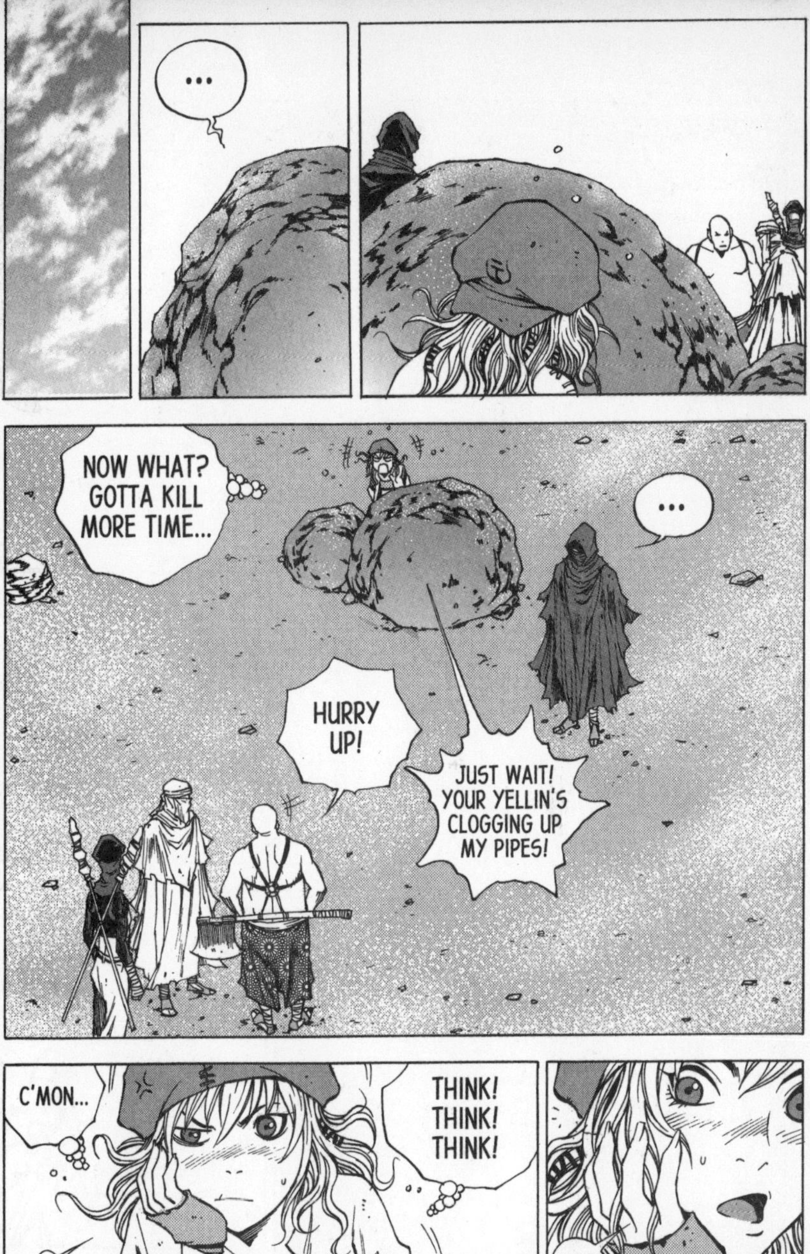
...
NOW WHAT? GOTTA KILL MORE TIME...
...
HURRY UP!
JUST WAIT! YOUR YELLIN'S CLOGGING UP MY PIPES!
C'MON...
THINK! THINK! THINK!
HUH?

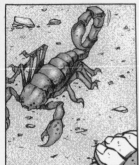

THAT'S IT!

THE BLUEBACK SCORPION: FOUND ONLY IN THE GAYA DESERT.

YAIEEE!!

WHAT? WHAT HAPPENED?

UUUGH...

OWW!

THROB

THROB

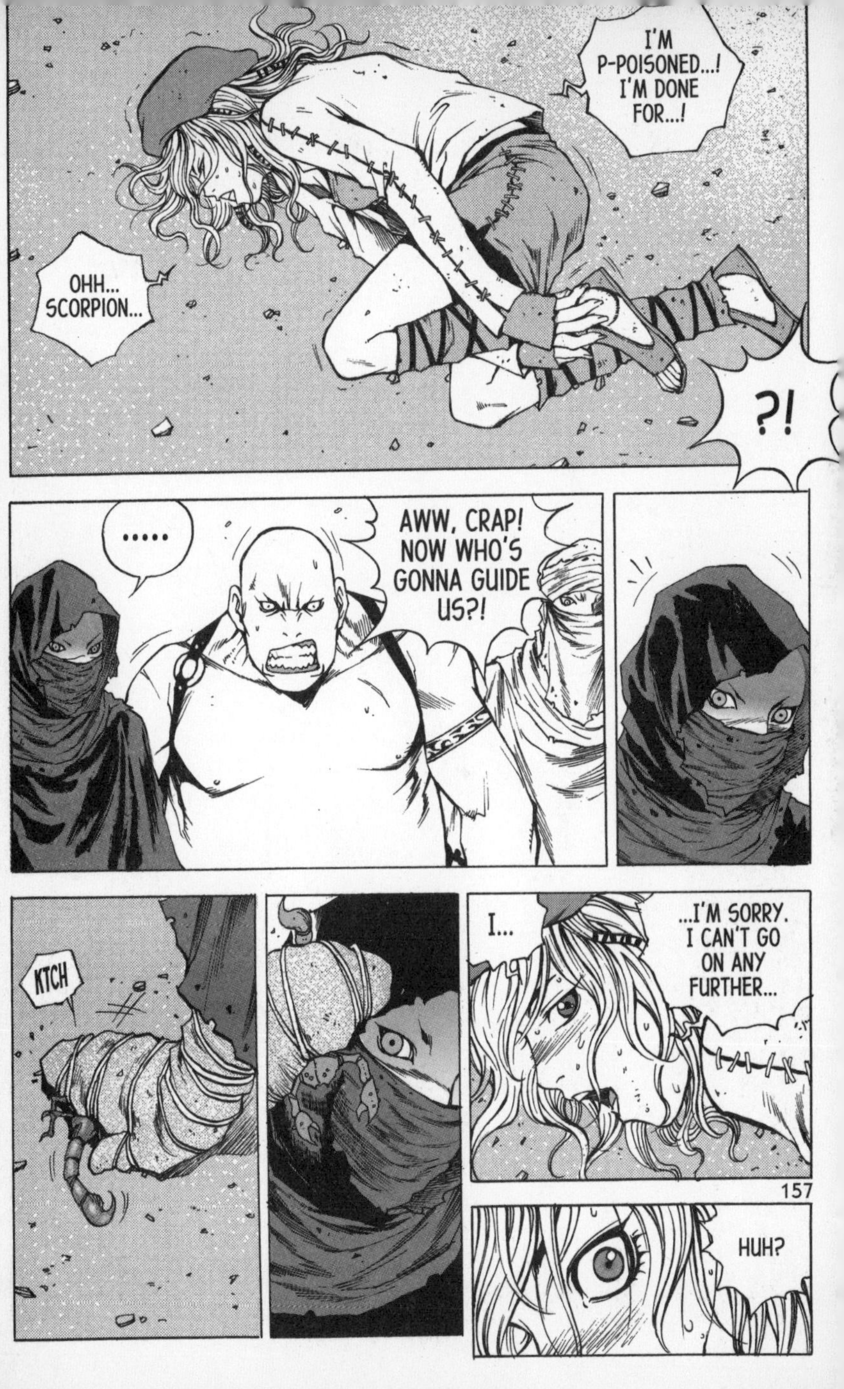
I'M P-POISONED...! I'M DONE FOR...!
OHH... SCORPION...
?!
.....
AWW, CRAP! NOW WHO'S GONNA GUIDE US?!
KTCH
I...
...I'M SORRY. I CAN'T GO ON ANY FURTHER...
HUH?

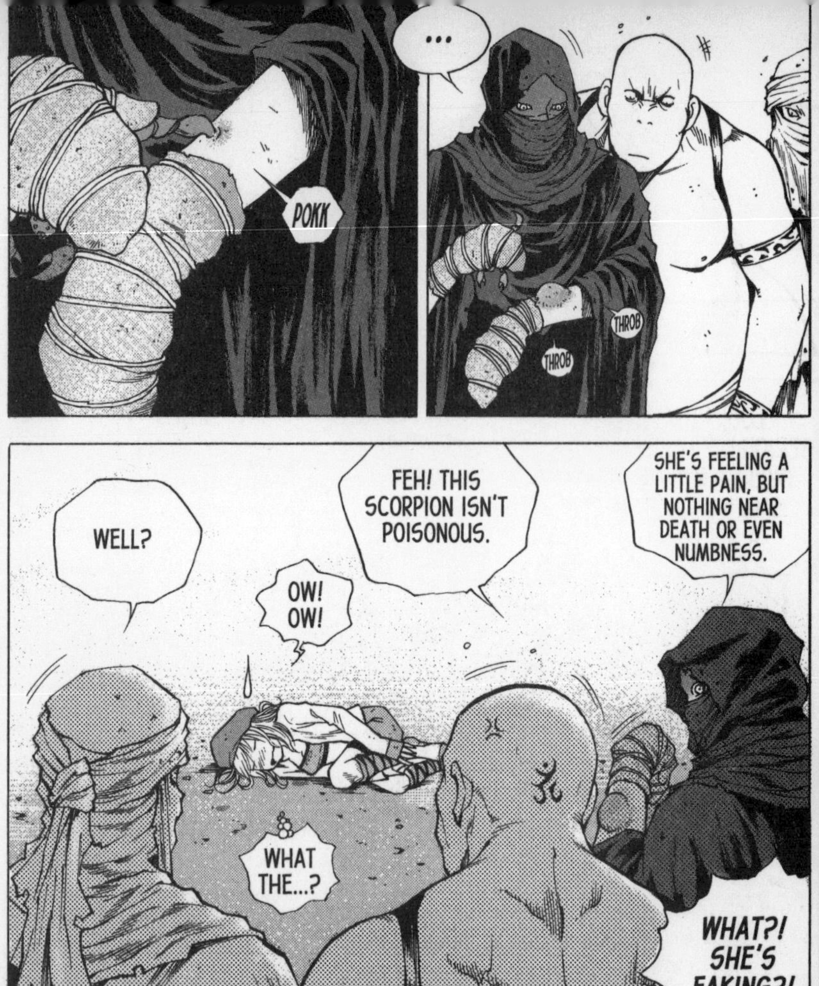
POKK
...
THROB
THROB
WELL?
OW! OW!
FEH! THIS SCORPION ISN'T POISONOUS.
SHE'S FEELING A LITTLE PAIN, BUT NOTHING NEAR DEATH OR EVEN NUMBNESS.
WHAT THE...?
WHAT?! SHE'S FAKING?!

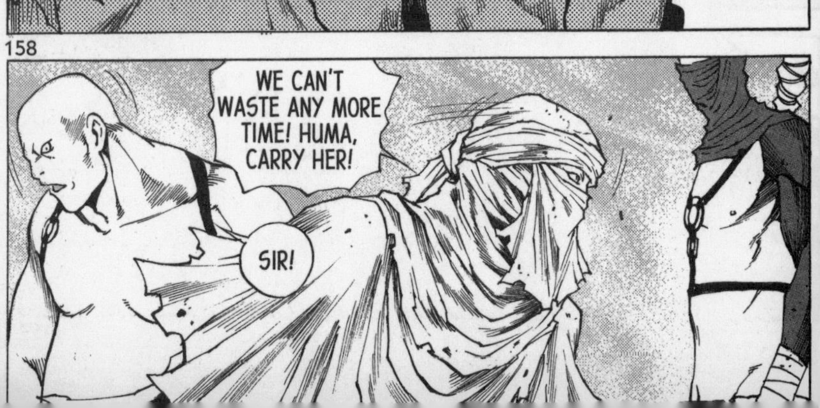
WE CAN'T WASTE ANY MORE TIME! HUMA, CARRY HER!
SIR!

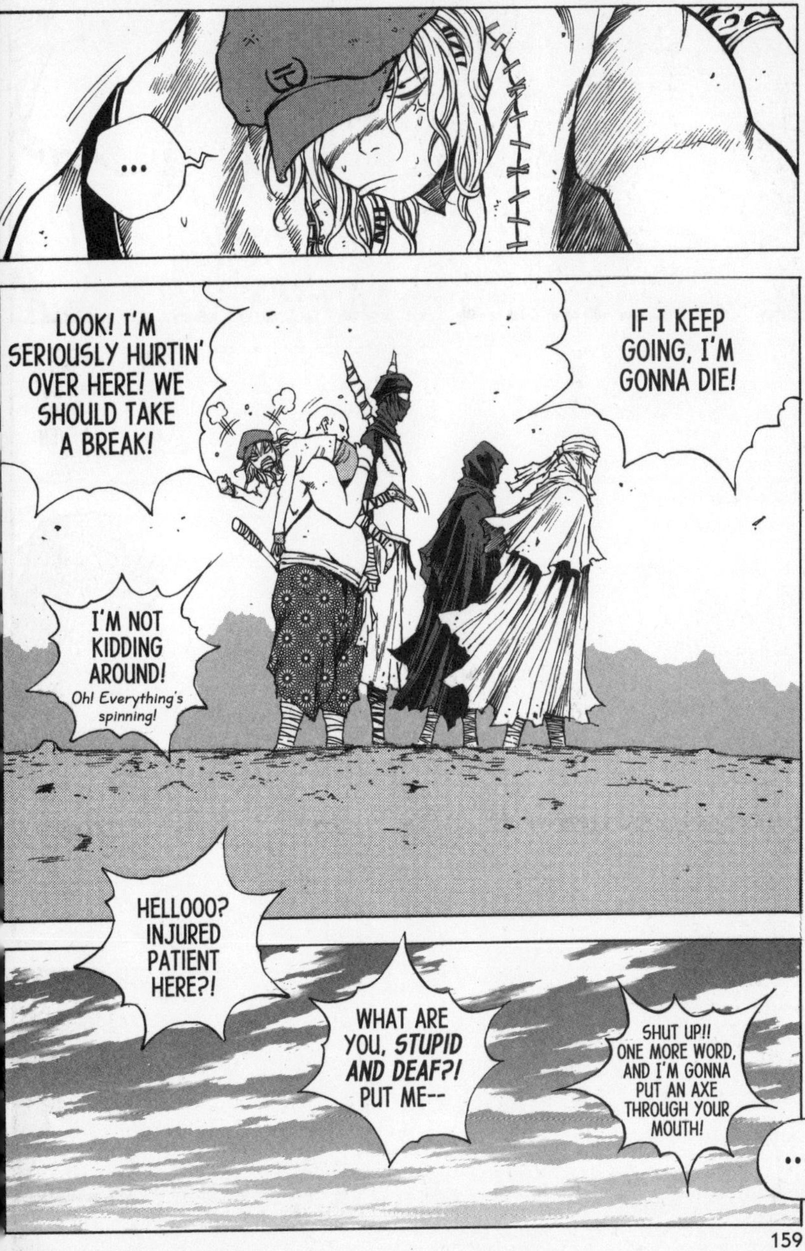
...
LOOK! I'M SERIOUSLY HURTIN' OVER HERE! WE SHOULD TAKE A BREAK!
IF I KEEP GOING, I'M GONNA DIE!
I'M NOT KIDDING AROUND!
Oh! Everything's spinning!
HELLOOO? INJURED PATIENT HERE?!
WHAT ARE YOU, *STUPID AND DEAF?!* PUT ME--
SHUT UP!! ONE MORE WORD, AND I'M GONNA PUT AN AXE THROUGH YOUR MOUTH!
...

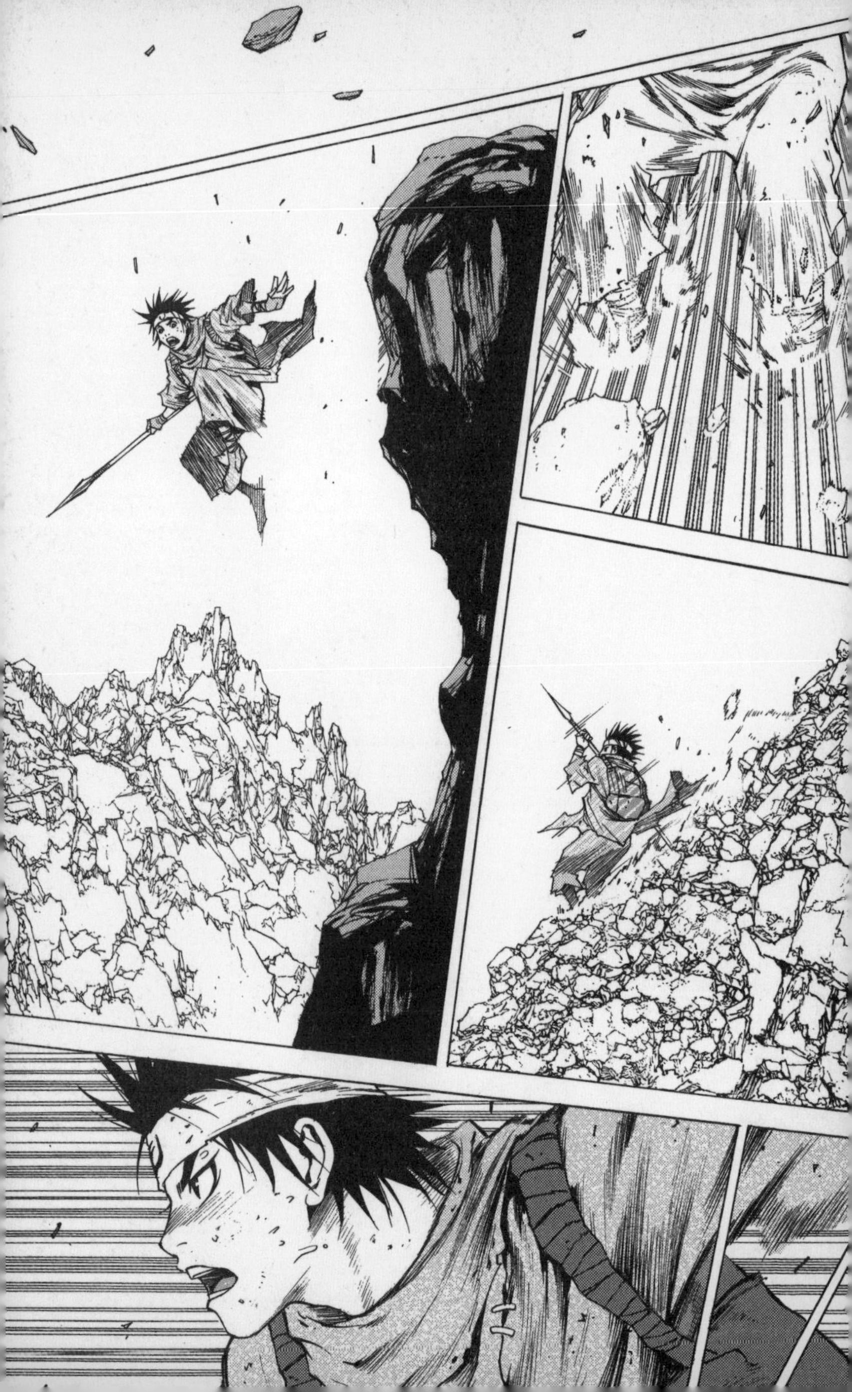

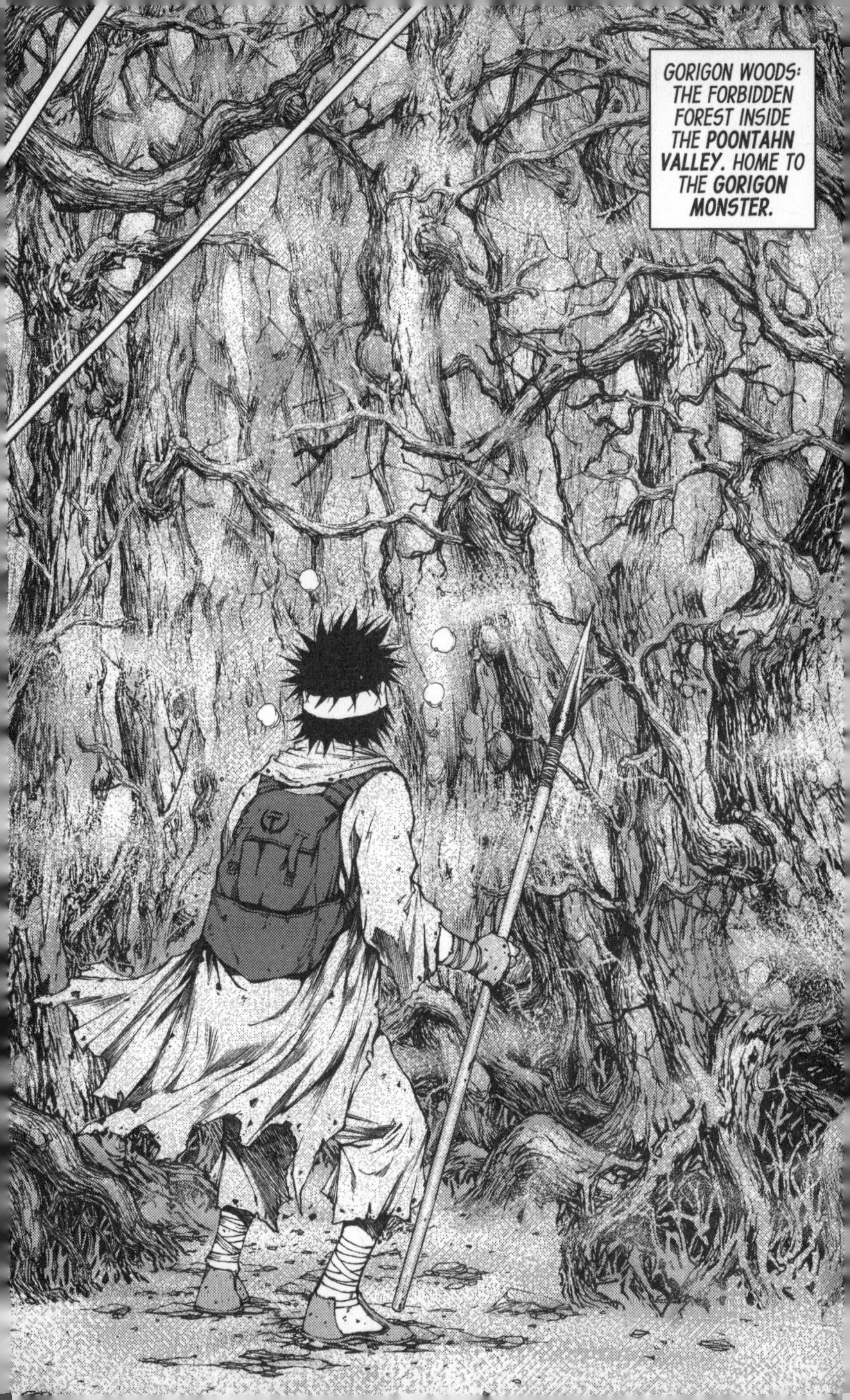
GORIGON WOODS: THE FORBIDDEN FOREST INSIDE THE **POONTAHN VALLEY**. HOME TO THE **GORIGON MONSTER**.

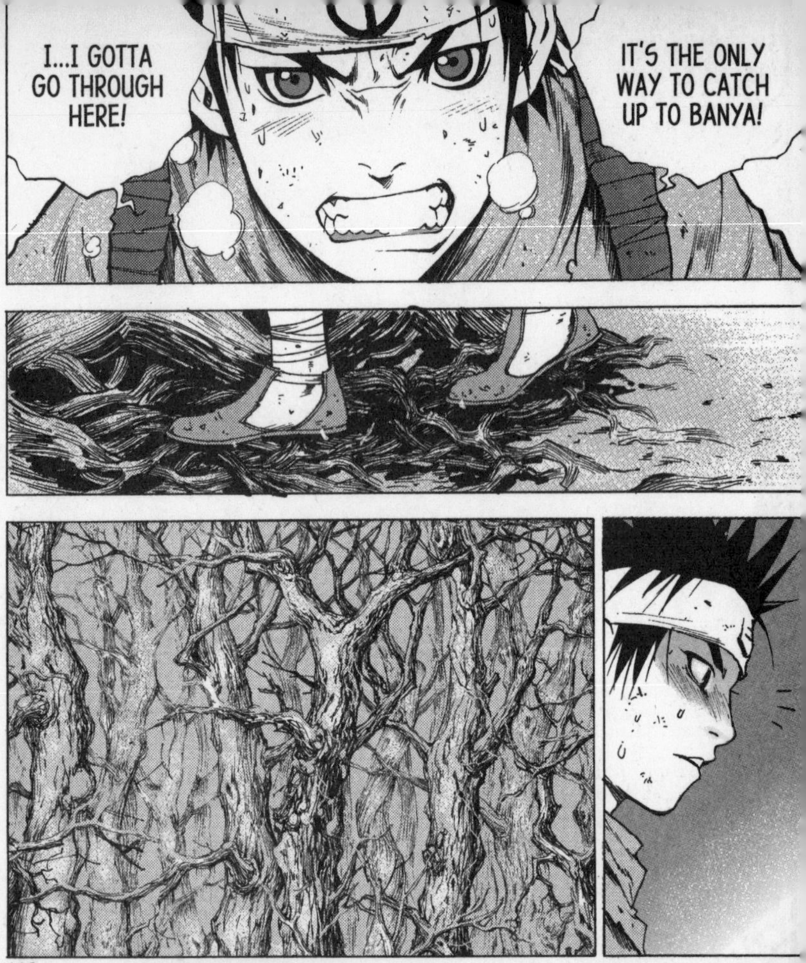
I...I GOTTA GO THROUGH HERE!
IT'S THE ONLY WAY TO CATCH UP TO BANYA!

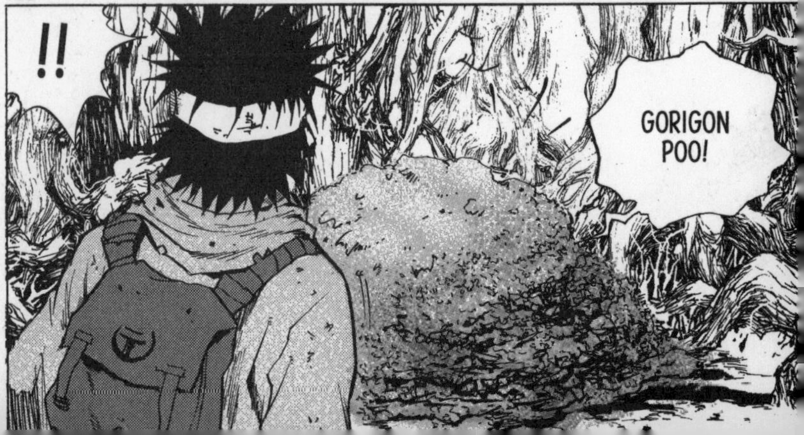
!!
GORIGON POO!

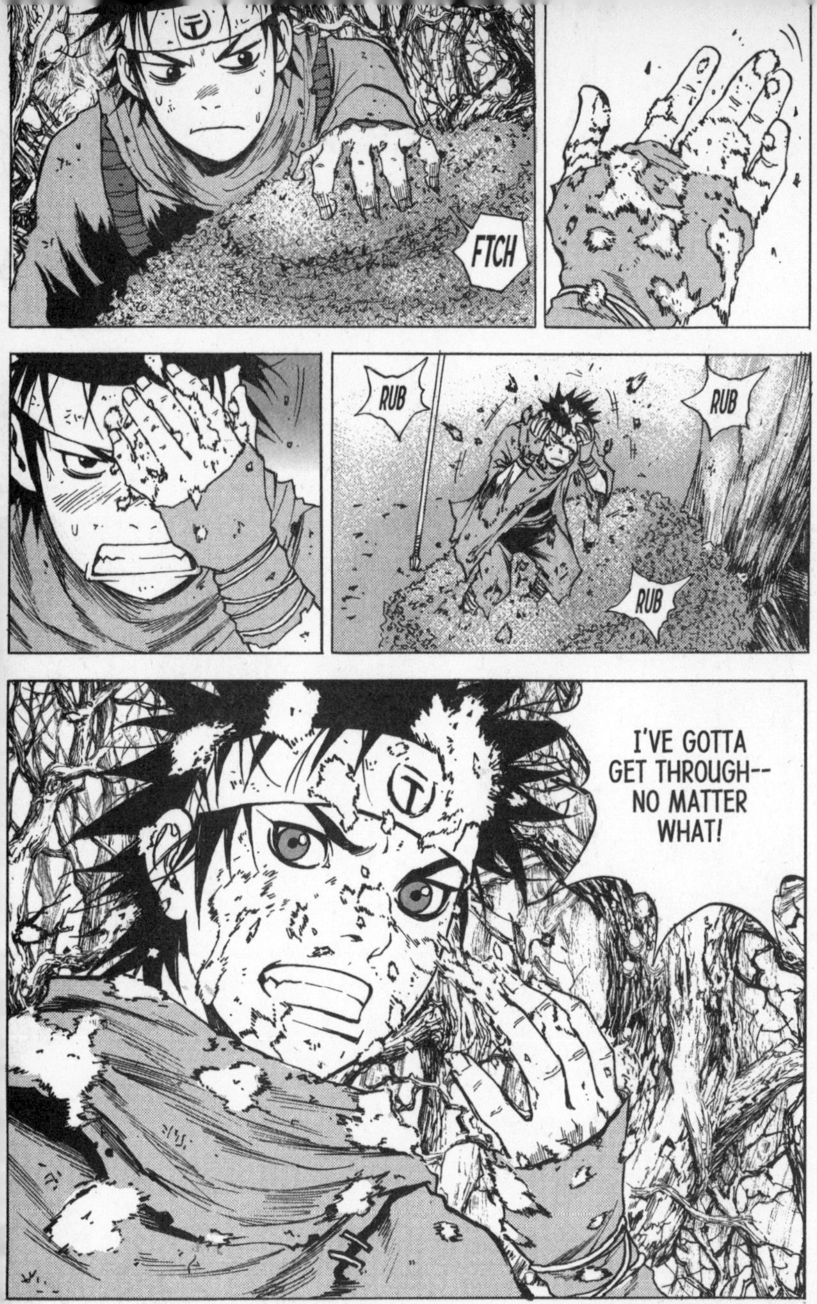
FTCH
RUB
RUB
RUB
I'VE GOTTA GET THROUGH-- NO MATTER WHAT!

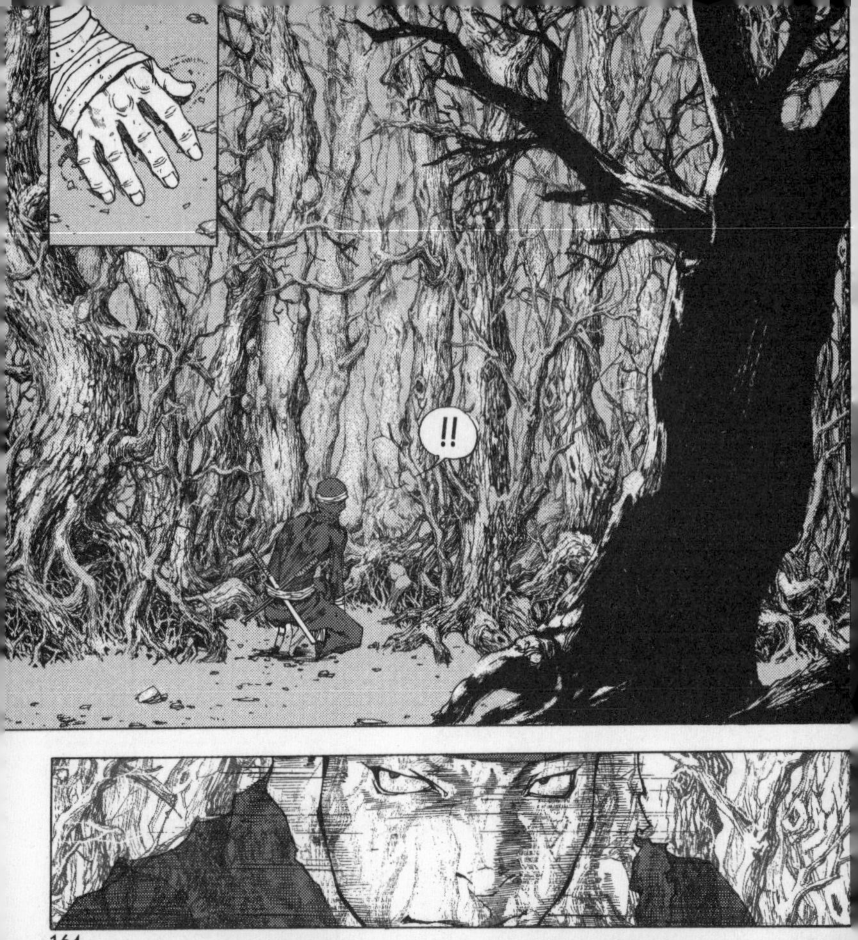
!!

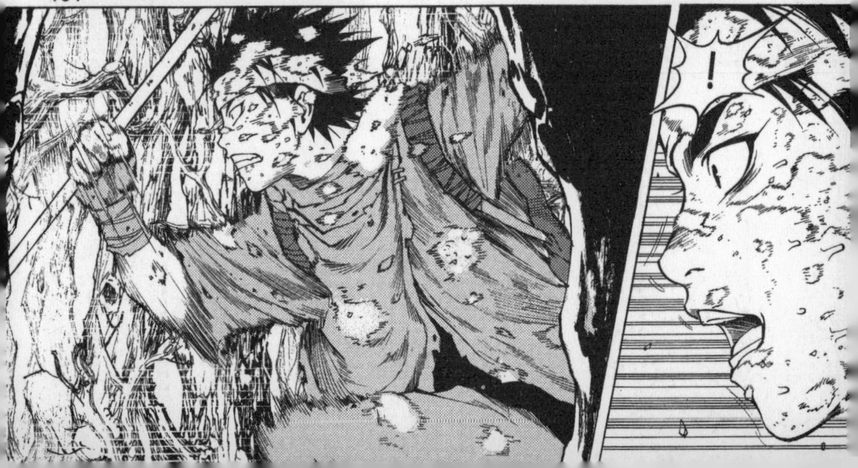
!

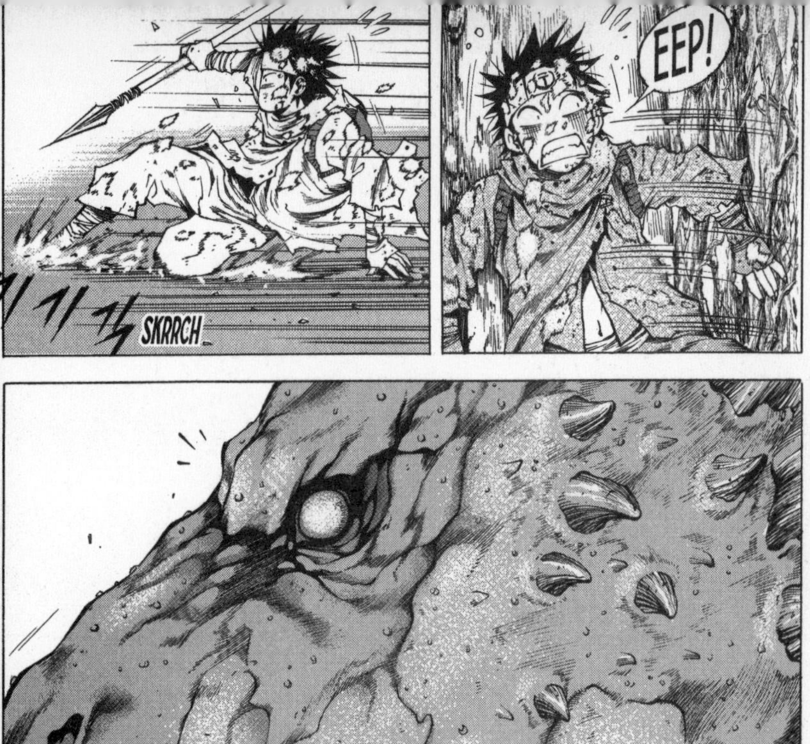
SKRRCH
EEP!

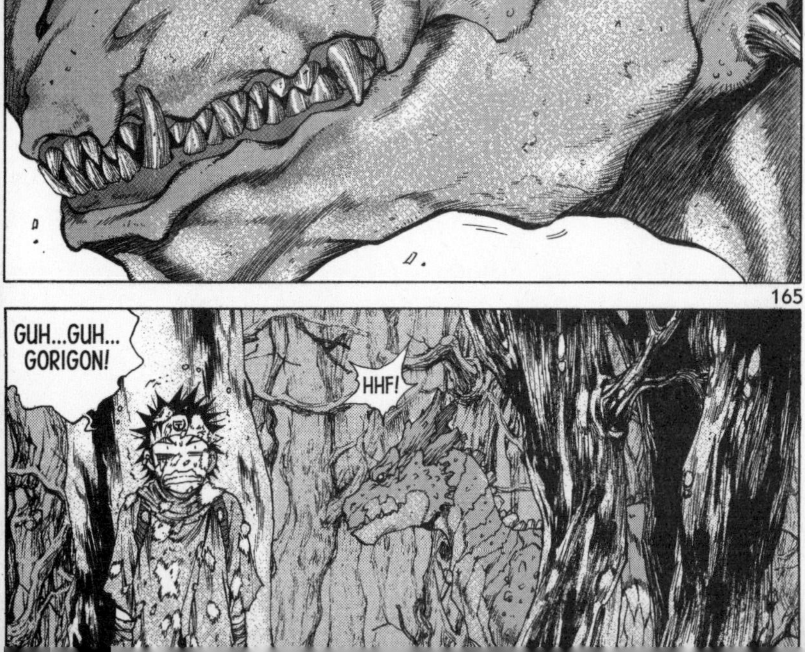
GUH...GUH... GORIGON!
HHF!

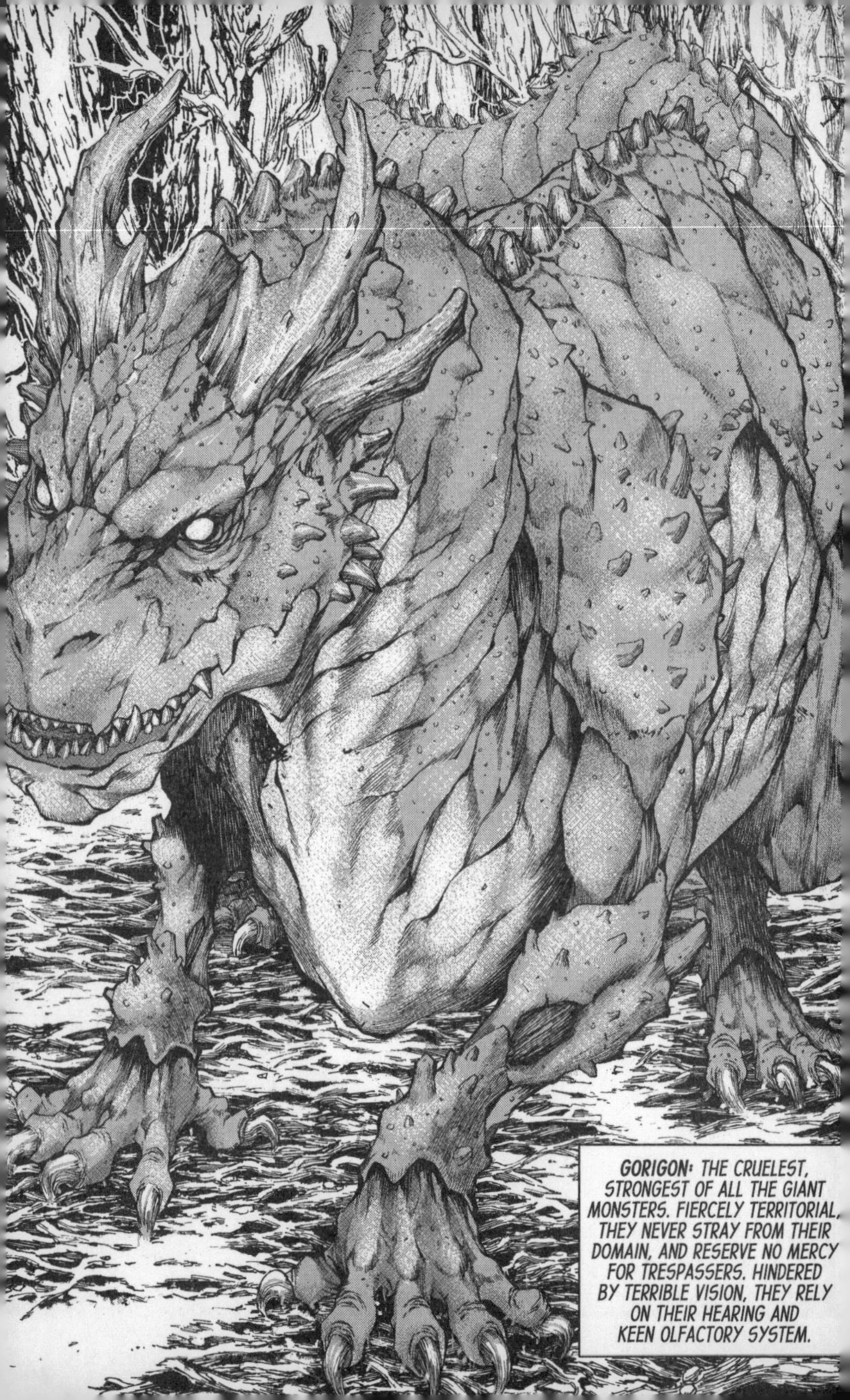
GORIGON: THE CRUELEST, STRONGEST OF ALL THE GIANT MONSTERS. FIERCELY TERRITORIAL, THEY NEVER STRAY FROM THEIR DOMAIN, AND RESERVE NO MERCY FOR TRESPASSERS. HINDERED BY TERRIBLE VISION, THEY RELY ON THEIR HEARING AND KEEN OLFACTORY SYSTEM.

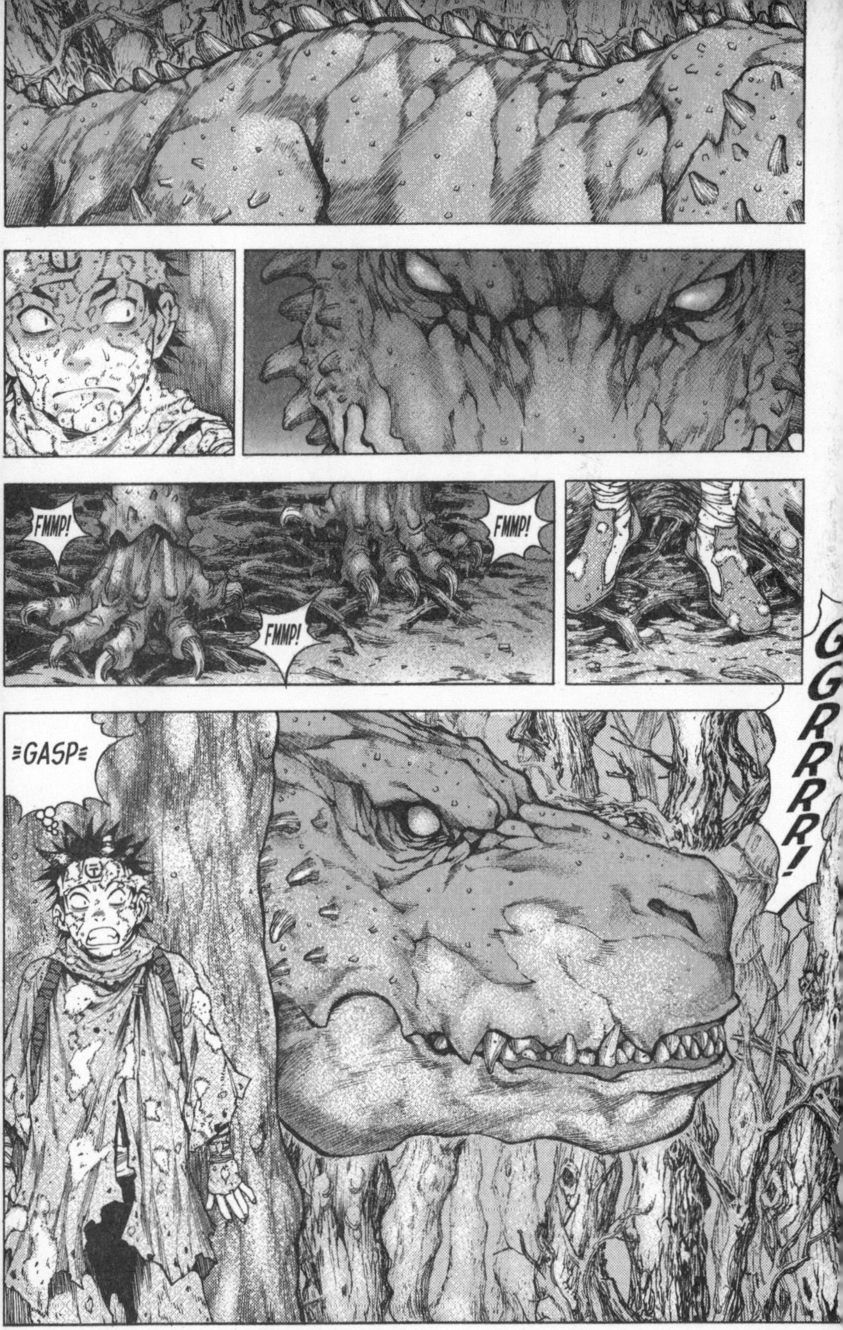
FMMP!
FMMP!
FMMP!
GGRRRRR!
GASP

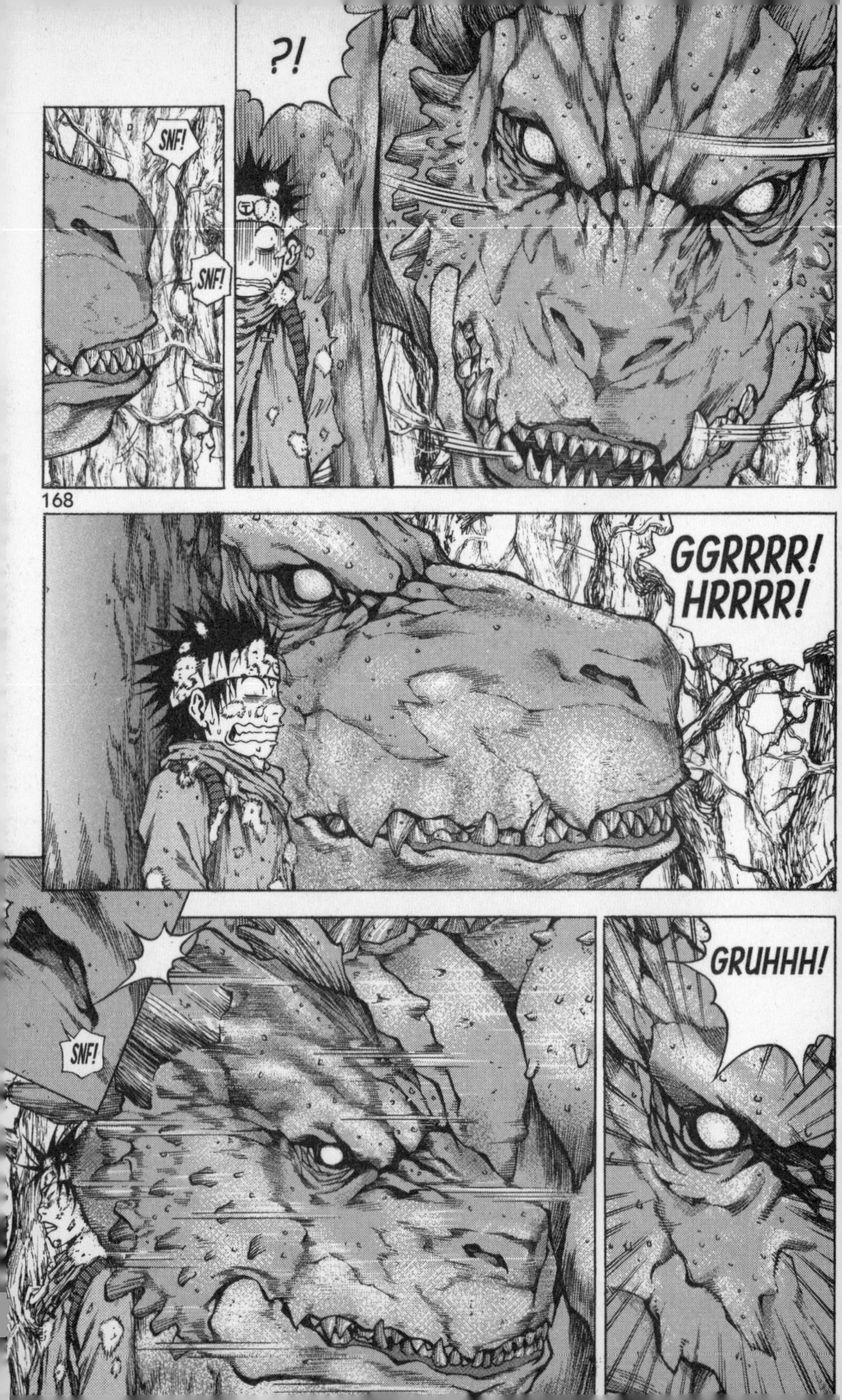
SNF!
SNF!
?!
GGRRRR! HRRRR!
SNF!
GRUHHH!

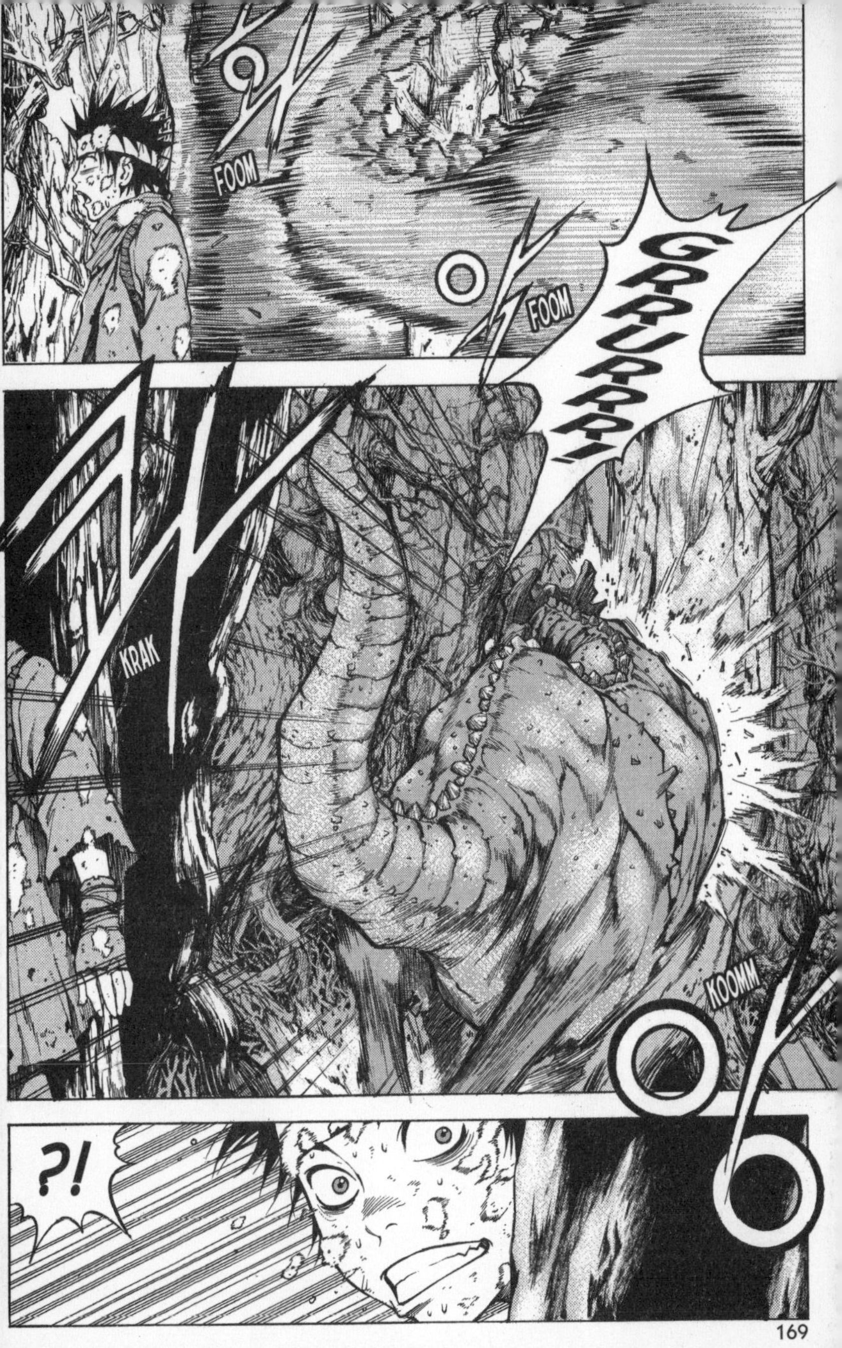
FOOM
FOOM
GRRURRR!
KRAK
KOOMM
?!

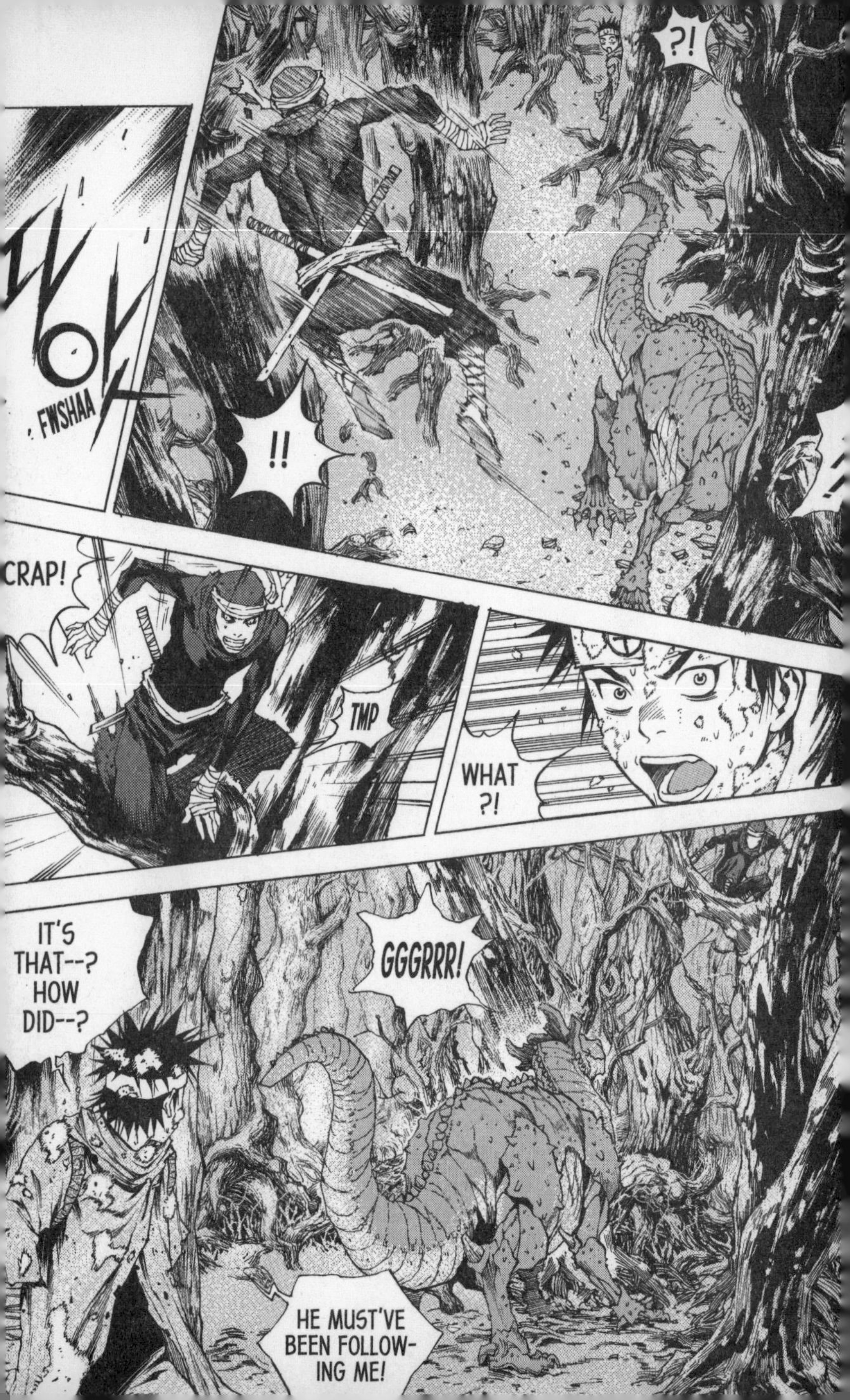
FWSHAA
!!
?!
CRAP!
TMP
WHAT ?!
IT'S THAT--? HOW DID--?
GGGRRR!
HE MUST'VE BEEN FOLLOW-ING ME!

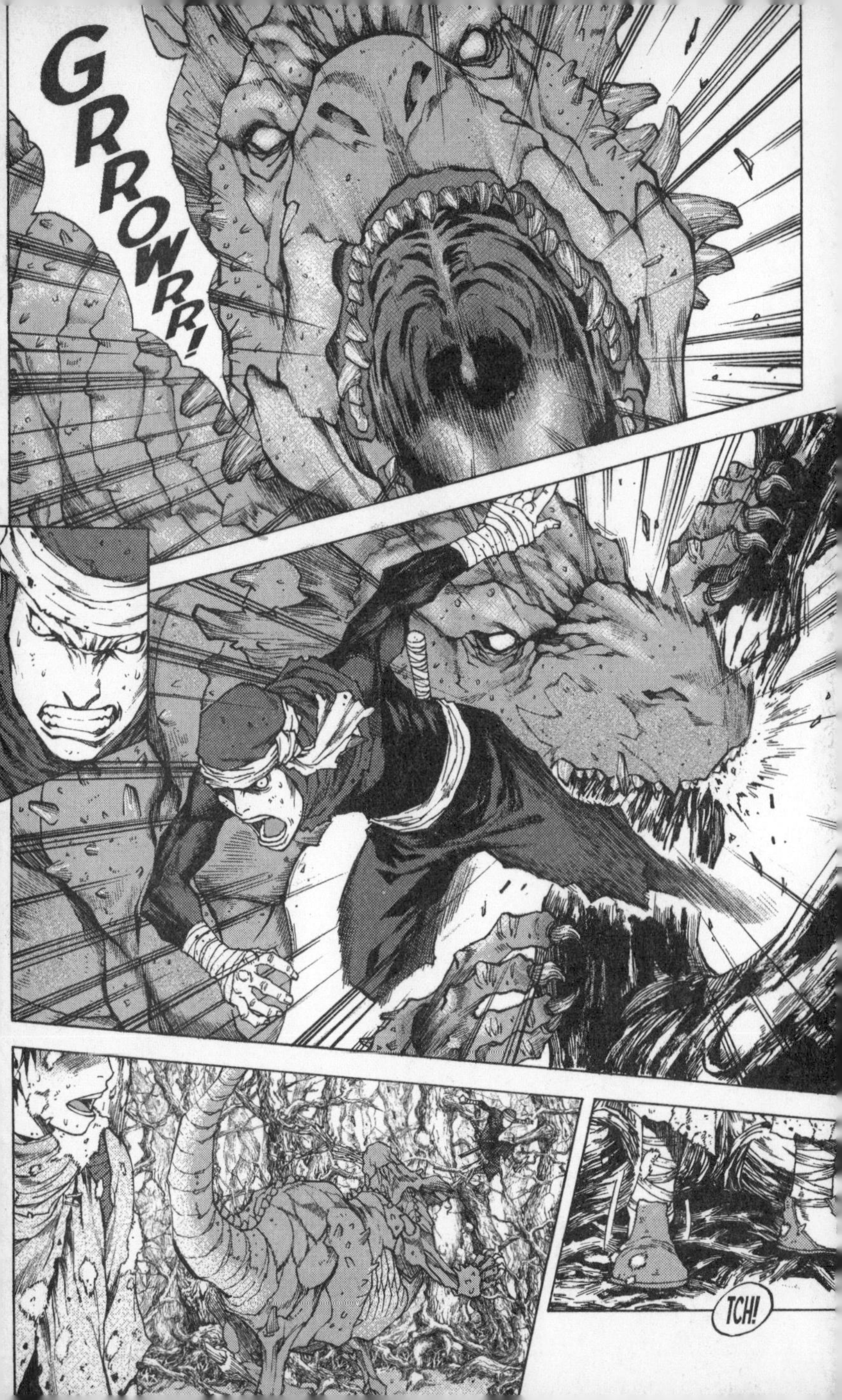
GRROWRR!
TCH!

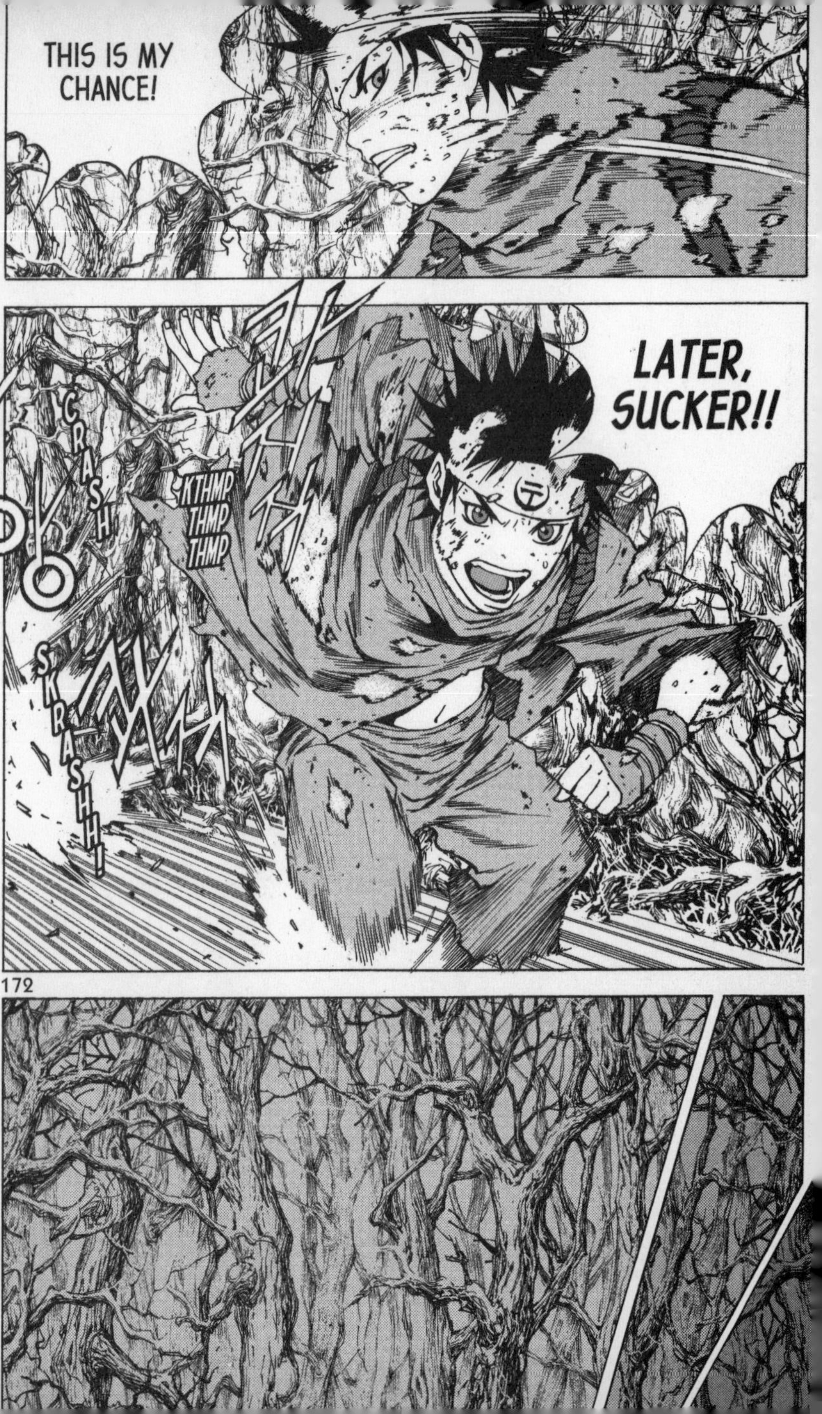
THIS IS MY CHANCE!
CRASH
KTHMP THMP THMP
SKRASHHH!
LATER, SUCKER!!

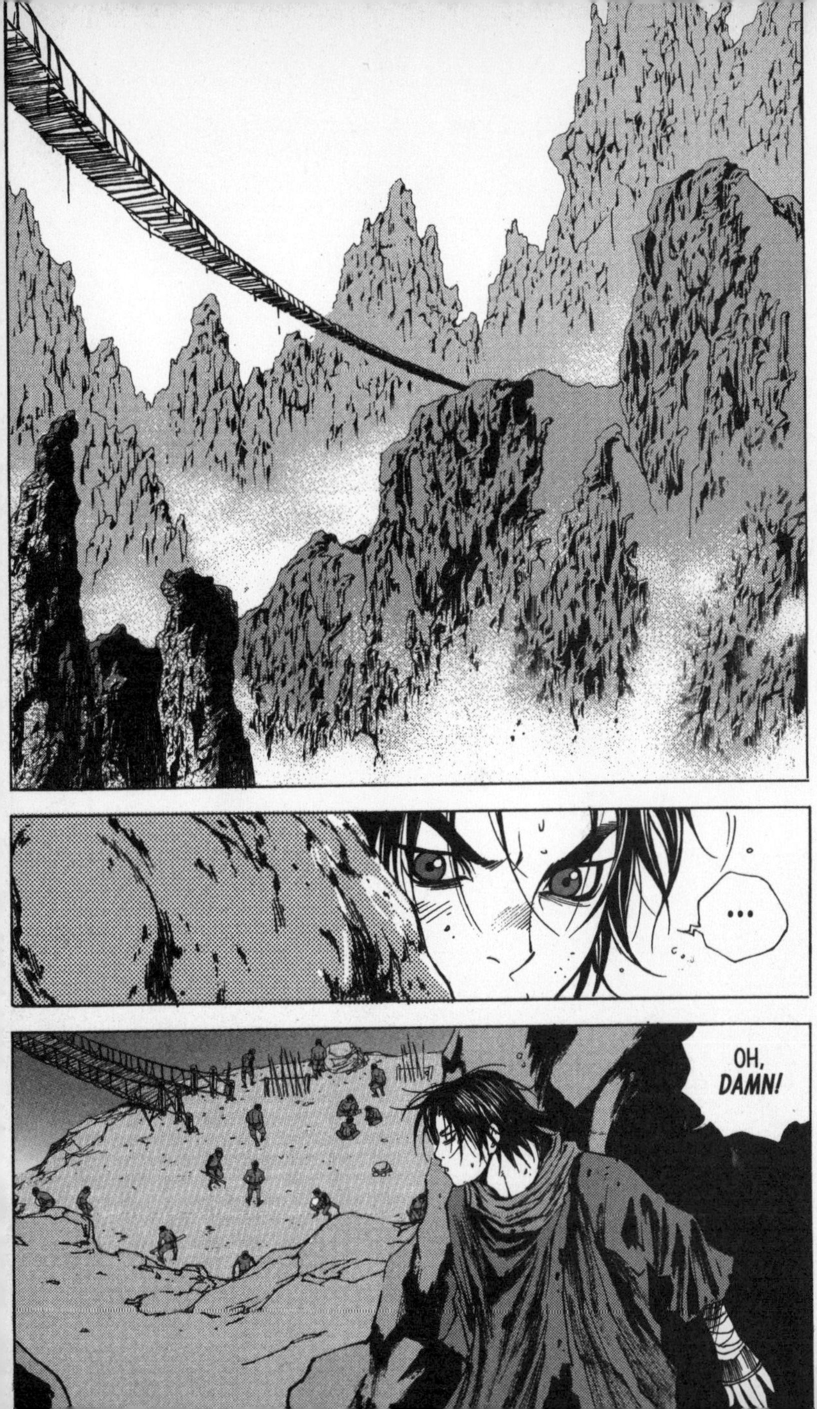
...
OH, DAMN!

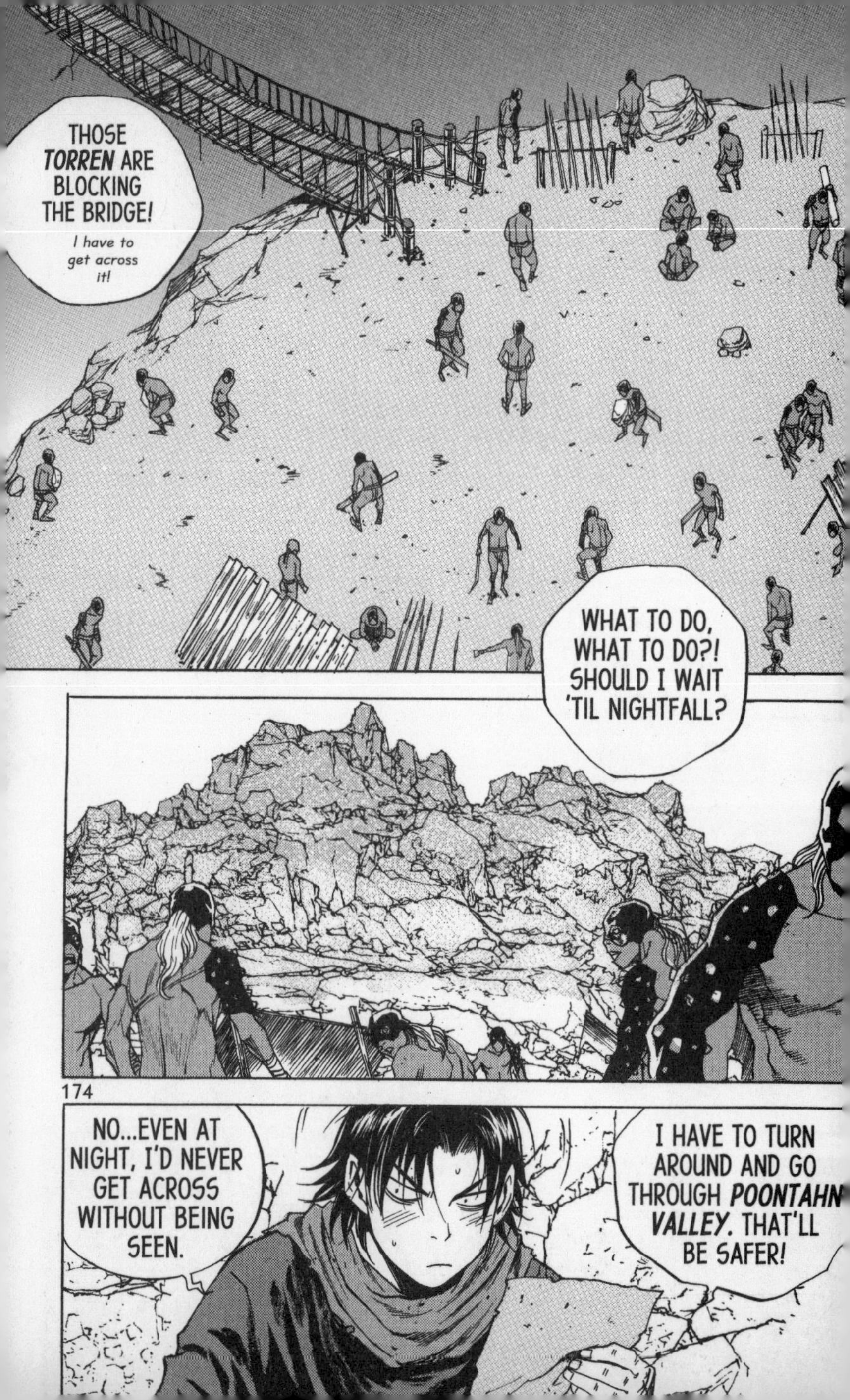
THOSE TORREN ARE BLOCKING THE BRIDGE!
I have to get across it!
WHAT TO DO, WHAT TO DO?! SHOULD I WAIT 'TIL NIGHTFALL?
NO...EVEN AT NIGHT, I'D NEVER GET ACROSS WITHOUT BEING SEEN.
I HAVE TO TURN AROUND AND GO THROUGH POONTAHN VALLEY. THAT'LL BE SAFER!

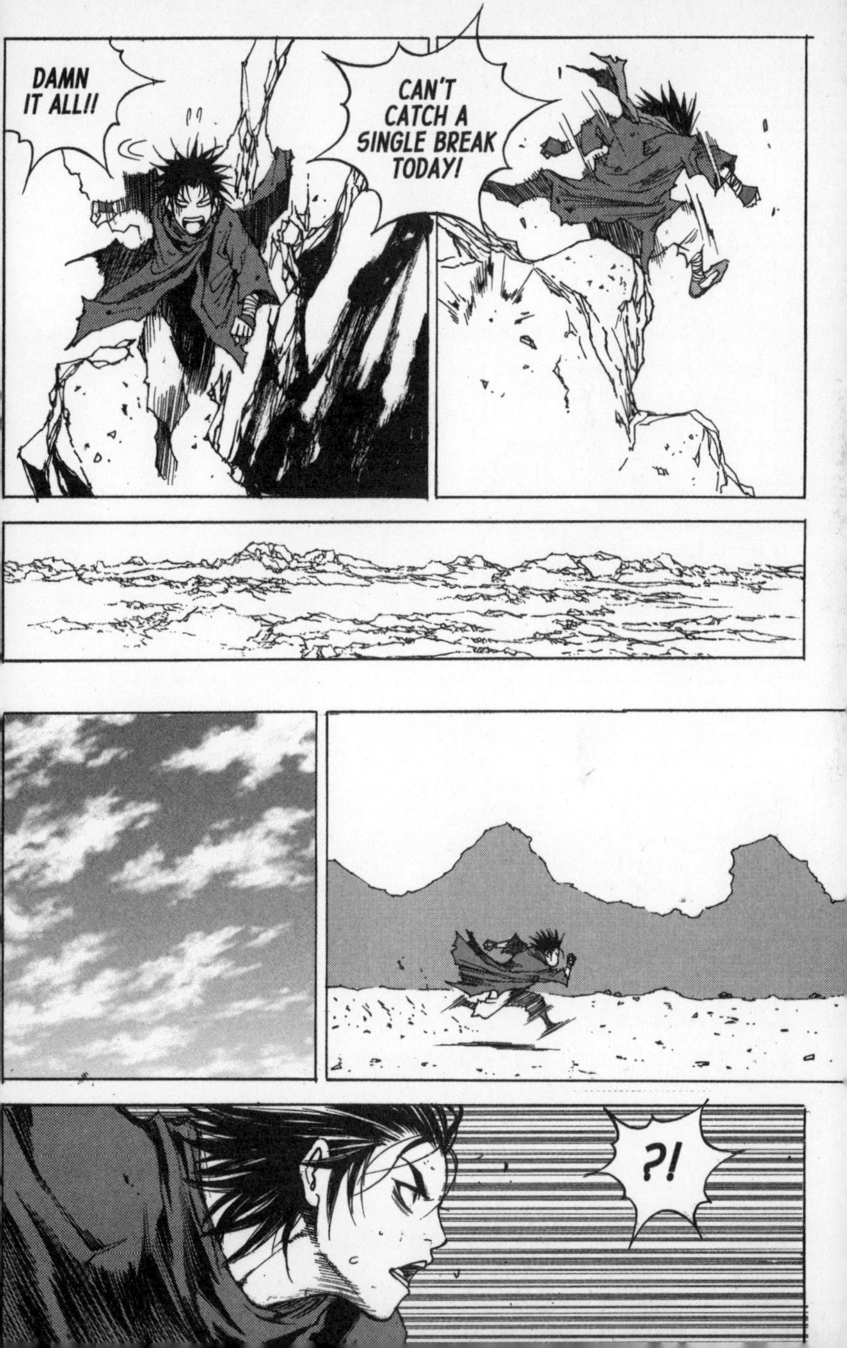
DAMN IT ALL!!
CAN'T CATCH A SINGLE BREAK TODAY!
?!

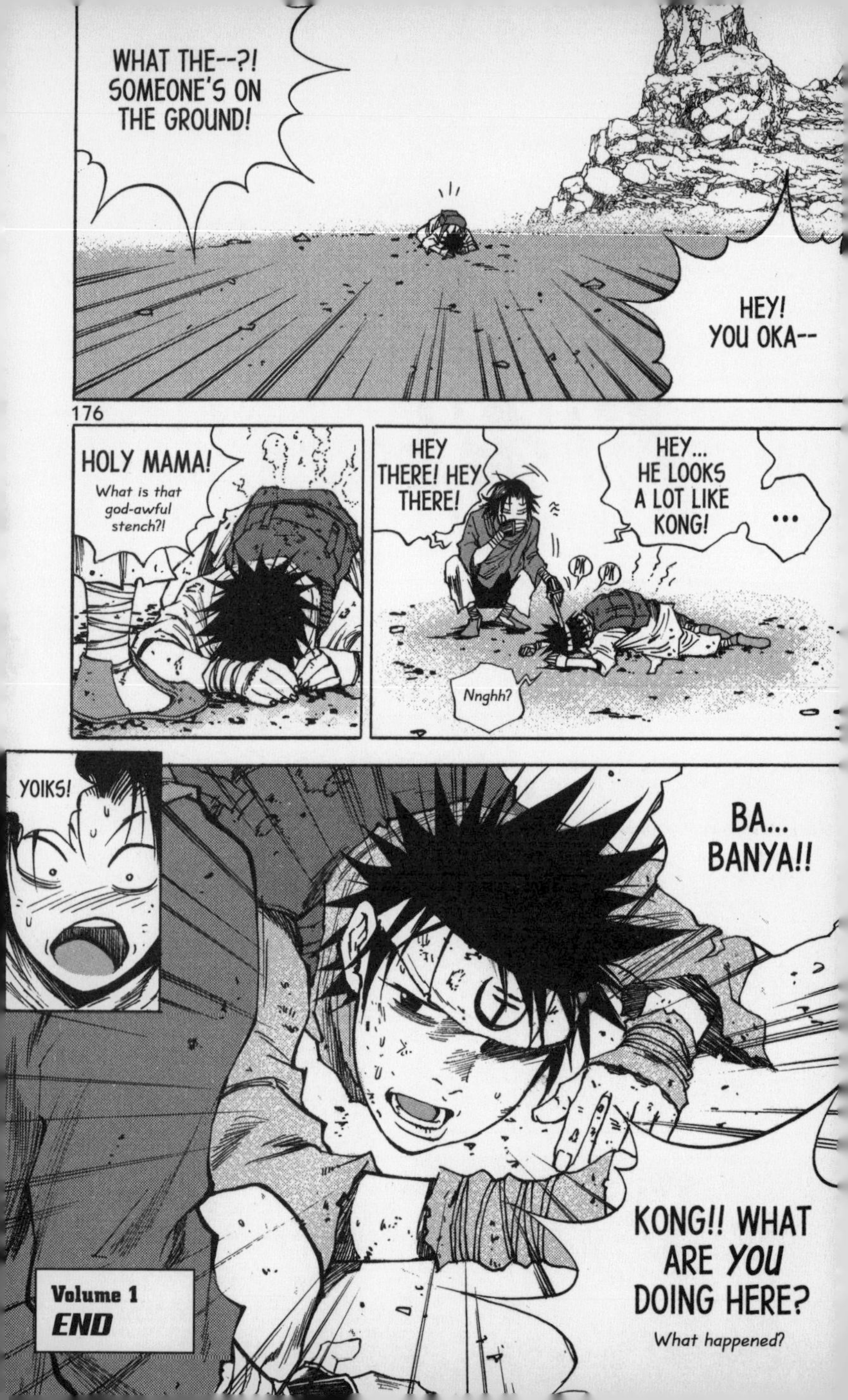

WHAT THE--?! SOMEONE'S ON THE GROUND!
HEY! YOU OKA--
HOLY MAMA!
What is that god-awful stench?!
HEY THERE! HEY THERE!
PK
PK
HEY... HE LOOKS A LOT LIKE KONG!
...
Nnghh?
YOIKS!
BA... BANYA!!
KONG!! WHAT ARE *YOU* DOING HERE?
What happened?

Volume 1
END

publisher
MIKE RICHARDSON

editor and English adaptation
PHILIP SIMON

editorial assistants
JEMIAH JEFFERSON and RYAN JORGENSEN

collection designer
M. JOSHUA ELLIOTT

art director
LIA RIBACCHI

Special thanks to Michael Gombos, Dr. Won Kyu Kim, J. Myung Kee Kim, and Julia Kwon.

English-language version produced by DARK HORSE COMICS.

BANYA: THE EXPLOSIVE DELIVERY MAN Volume 1

DARK HORSE MANHWA
A division of Dark Horse Comics, Inc.
10956 S.E. Main Street
Milwaukie OR 97222

darkhorse.com

To find a comics shop in your area, call the
Comic Shop Locator Service toll-free at 1-888-266-4226

First edition: September 2006
ISBN-10: 1-59307-614-2
ISBN-13: 978-1-59307-614-6

10 9 8 7 6 5 4 3 2 1
Printed in Canada

AUTHOR'S NOTE

It was an utterly hot day, as I recall. Riding a beat-up motorcycle and covered in sweat, he delivered the mail. There was not a moment to relax before going on to the next stop, and I can still see that delivery man working, in my mind.

Come rain, come snow . . . they finish their exhausting duty with dignity. And though it is hard work, this pride in their work makes them beautiful . . .

And so to all of our country's mailmen, I give thanks. This manhwa book is dedicated to them.

By Kim Young-Oh
with help from Noh Min-Yong

(Author's Note translated by Dr. Won Kyu Kim and J. Myungkee Kim)

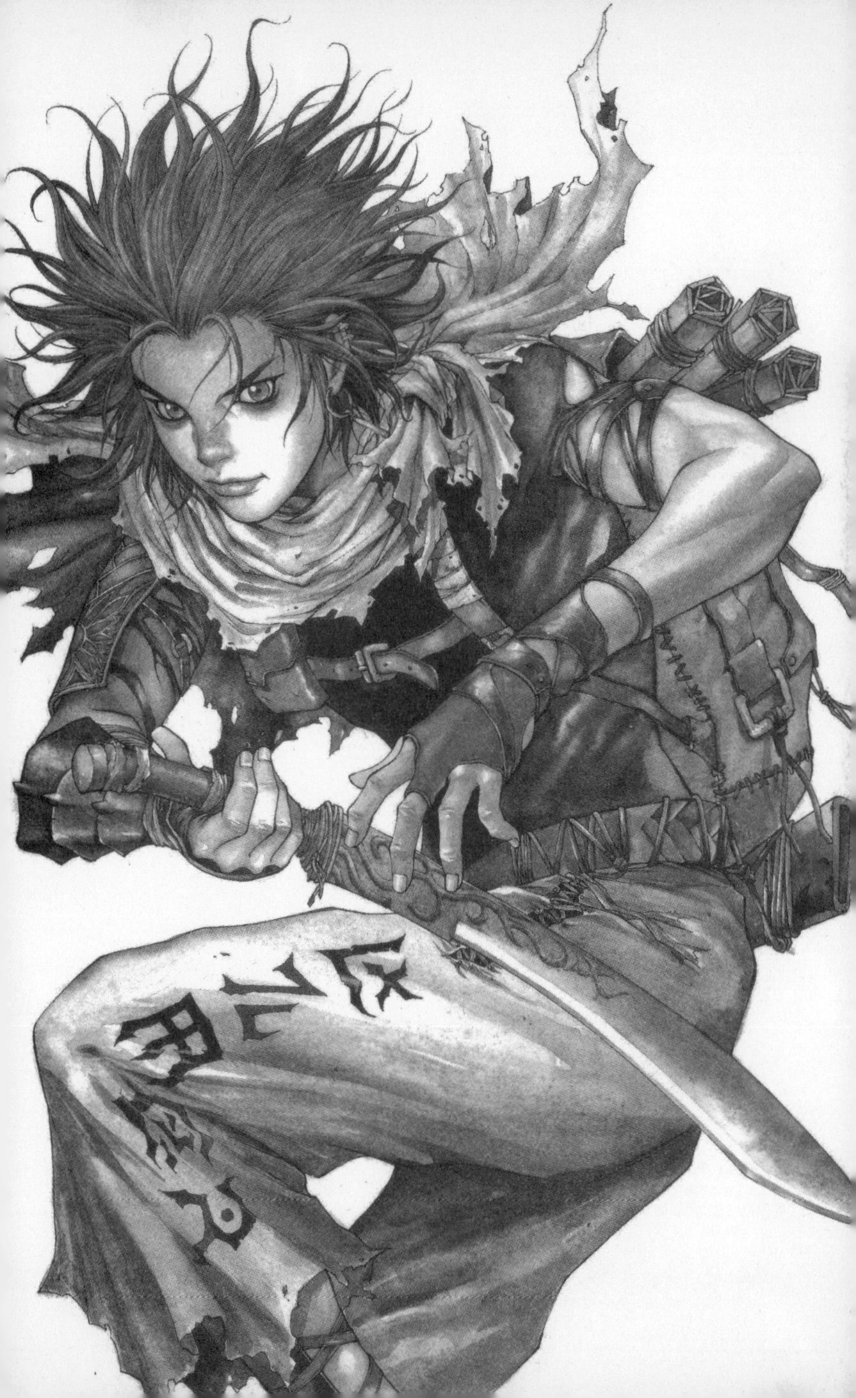

Banya

the explosive delivery man

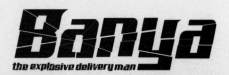

BANYA: THE EXPLOSIVE DELIVERY MAN Volume 2!

Banya schemes to free Mei from her captors, and instead of fighting fire with fire, he fights monsters with monsters! The delivery men of the Gaya Desert Post Office have only one motto: "Fast. Precise. Secure." Banya, the craziest and craftiest of the bunch, will stop at nothing to get a job done. Whether it's transporting a rare artifact or reuniting a mother with her long-lost son, Banya will speed through war-torn deserts and mysterious forests, relying on flexibility, daring, and wits to complete his missions – no matter what the odds! Coming soon from Dark Horse Manhwa!

DARK HORSE MANHWA

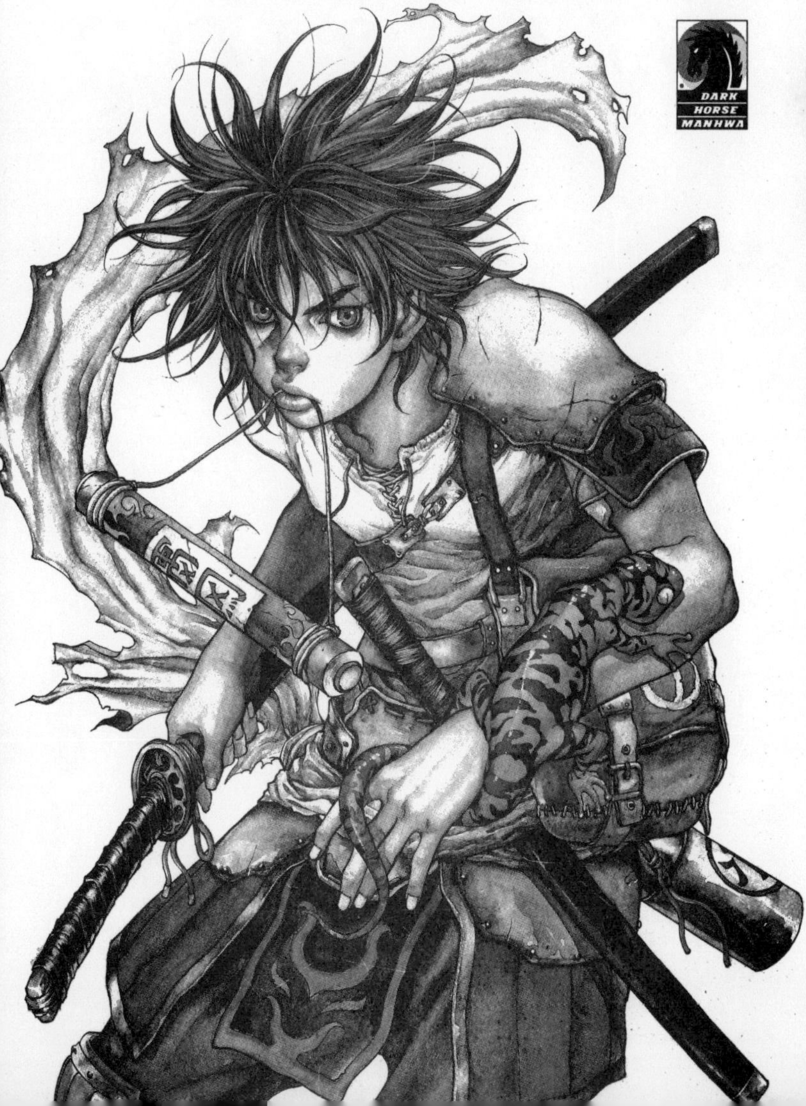

S · H · A · M · A · N
WARRIOR

박 중 기

PARK JOONG-KI

SHAMAN WARRIOR
by Park Joong-Ki

One of Korea's best-selling manhwa titles joins the Dark Horse Manhwa lineup! *Shaman Warrior* is a dramatic fantasy series with a kinetic style that will appeal to fans of *Banya: The Explosive Delivery Man*, *Blade of the Immortal*, and *Lone Wolf and Cub*! From the desert wastelands emerge two mysterious warriors, master wizard Yarong and his faithful servant Batu. On a grave mission from their king, they have yet to realize the whirlwind of political movements and secret plots which will soon engulf them and change their lives forever. When Yarong is injured in battle, Batu must fulfill a secret promise to leave Yarong's side and protect his master's child. As Batu seeks to find and hide the infant, Yarong reveals another secret to those who have tracked him down to finish him off—the deadly, hidden power of a Shaman Warrior!

Previews for *SHAMAN WARRIOR* and other DARK HORSE MANHWA titles can be found at darkhorse.com!

Shaman Warrior Volume 1 © 2003 by Park Joong-Ki. All rights reserved. Originally published as Dan Goo in Korea in 2003 by Haksan Publishing Co., Ltd. English Translation rights arranged with Haksan Publishing Co., Ltd. through Shinwon Agency Co., in Korea. English edition copyright volume 1 © 2006 by Dark Horse Comics, Inc. All other material © 2006 by Dark Horse Comics, Inc. All rights reserved. Dark Horse Manhwa™ is a trademark of Dark Horse Comics, Inc. (BL 7002)

STOP

THIS IS THE BACK OF THE BOOK!

This manhwa collection is translated into English and oriented in the authentic Korean left-to-right reading format. If you've been reading comic books and graphic novels in English, you already know how to read this book and should flip over right now and get started. Prepare to be blown away by Kim Young-Oh's unique, exciting epic chronicling the adventures of the Gaya Desert Delivery Men! Our next volume is coming soon! If you've never read manhwa before, we welcome you to a world of rich characterization and lush, detailed artwork. Enjoy!

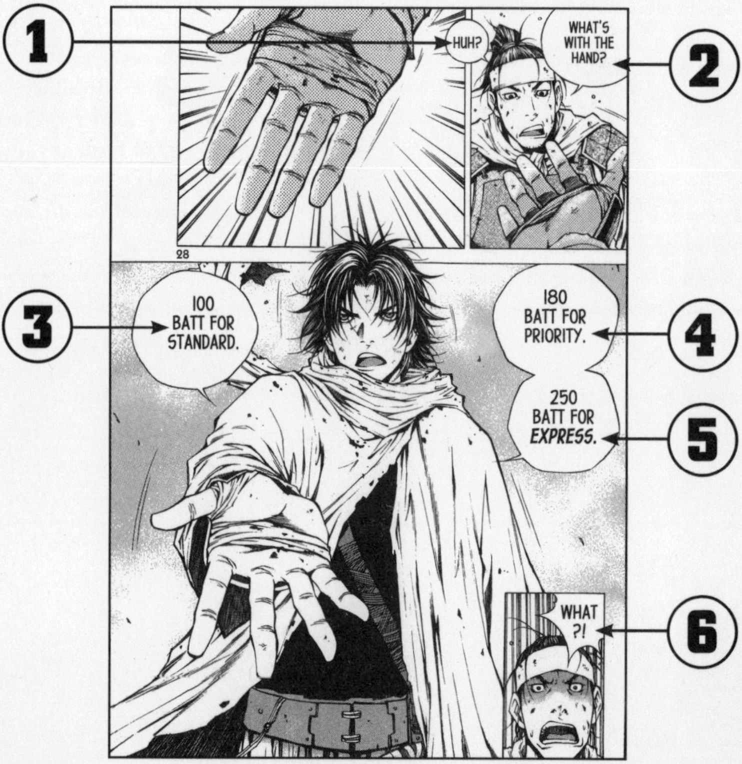
1
HUH?
2
WHAT'S WITH THE HAND?
28
3
100 BATT FOR STANDARD.
4
180 BATT FOR PRIORITY.
5
250 BATT FOR *EXPRESS.*
6
WHAT ?!